also by Louis Charbonneau

No Place on Earth
Night of Violence
Nor All Your Tears
Corpus Earthling
The Sentinel Stars
Psychedelic-40
Way Out
Down to Earth
The Sensitives
Down from the Mountain
And Hope to Die
Barrier World
From a Dark Place
Intruder
The Lair
The Brea File

Trail

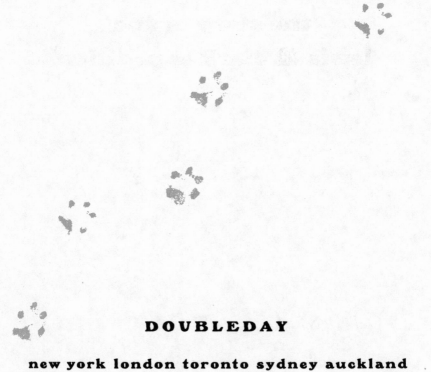

DOUBLEDAY

new york london toronto sydney auckland

Trail

the story of the
lewis & clark expedition

Louis Charbonneau

Published by Doubleday,
a division of Bantam Doubleday Dell Publishing Group, Inc.
666 Fifth Avenue, New York, New York 10103

Doubleday and the portrayal of an anchor with a dolphin
are trademarks of Doubleday,
a division of Bantam Doubleday Dell Publishing Group, Inc.

This is a work of fiction. Names, characters, places, and
incidents either are the product of the author's imagination or
are used fictitiously.

Library of Congress Cataloging-in-Publication Data
Charbonneau, Louis, 1924–
Trail : the story of the Lewis & Clark expedition / Louis
Charbonneau.—1st ed.
p.   cm.
ISBN 0-385-24211-5
1. Lewis and Clark Expedition (1804–1806)—Fiction. 2. Lewis,
Meriwether, 1774–1809—Fiction. 3. Clark, William, 1770–1838—
Fiction. 4. West (U.S.)—History—To 1848—Fiction. 5. Dogs—
Fiction. I. Title.
PS3575.O7T74   1989
813'.54—dc20   89-32153
                                                                CIP

For Diane
who made this possible,
with love, always

acknowledgements

*I*n writing Trail, *I have been indebted to a great many writ-
ers, editors, and historians who have followed this route before
me.*

*Without trying to give a complete bibliography, I can iden-
tify my principal sources as my own copy of the eight-volume
edition of the* Original Journals of the Lewis and Clark Expedition, *edited by Reuben Gold Thwaites, which includes the
journals of Charles Floyd and Joseph Whitehouse as well as those
of Lewis and Clark;* The Field Notes of Captain William Clark,
edited by Ernest Staples Osgood; The Journals of Lewis and
Clark, *edited by Bernard DeVoto;* The Journals of Captain Meriwether Lewis and Sergeant John Ordway, *edited by Milo Quaife;
and* A Journal of the Voyages and Travels of a Corps of Discovery *by Patrick Gass. Much of my work on the novel was
completed before the first volumes of the new ten-volume edition
of* The Journals of the Lewis and Clark Expedition, *edited by
Gary Moulton, became available. I can only regret that I did
not have more of this superbly annotated edition available to
me sooner.*

The journal of George Shannon, from which I quote liberally in the novel, is fictional, although the times, places, details, and incidents narrated are all factual. It has been speculated that Shannon actually wrote his own journal; if so, it has never been found.

Other sources of special value to me included The Men of the Lewis and Clark Expedition, by Charles G. Clarke; The Letters of the Lewis and Clark Expedition with Related Documents, by Donald Jackson; Meriwether Lewis, by Richard Dillon; Lewis and Clark: Partners in Discovery, by John Bakeless; The Course of Empire by Bernard DeVoto; among many Indian books, The Mystic Warriors of the Plains, by Thomas E. Mails; Firearms, Traps, & Tools of the Mountain Men, by Carl P. Russell, and a whole raft of articles in We Proceeded On, the official publication of the Lewis and Clark Trail Heritage Foundation, Inc.—among which I would be remiss in failing to mention Ernest Staples Osgood's "Our Dog Scannon—Partner in Discovery," and Donald Jackson's "Call Him a Good Old Dog, But Don't Call Him Scannon." Fielding's Lewis & Clark Trail, by Gerald Olmsted, is especially useful and enjoyable to anyone seriously following the trail, as it was to me. On Thomas Jefferson, I relied principally on Dumas Malone's Jefferson and His Time, especially volume 4, Jefferson the President. On the Newfoundland, I would mention particularly The New Complete Newfoundland, by Margaret Booth Chern, and This Is The Newfoundland, the Official Breed Book of The Newfoundland Club of America, edited by Mrs. Maynard K. Drury.

I would also like to express my appreciation to the librarians at the San Pedro Branch of the Los Angeles Public Library, who, in the aftermath of the fire that destroyed Los Angeles' Main Library, were able to obtain from various other sources the books and materials I sought; Harold Kuebler, for his editorial support in the beginning; Jennifer Brehl of Doubleday for her perceptive editing of the long manuscript; and my wife Diane, whose involvement and encouragement from the start kept me going through the long journey.

a note about seaman

his is a work of fiction—I am a novelist, not a historian. Nevertheless, with few exceptions, the people, incidents,
and circumstances portrayed are as close to the historical record
as I could make them, relying principally on the field notes,
journals, and letters of those who were actually there on the
Voyage of Discovery.

A principal focus of the novel is Meriwether Lewis's dog
Seaman. Historical purists may object that too much is attributed
to the Newfoundland in these pages. I can only say that I have
used the novelist's license only where the journals are silent, and
then only within the context of the historical record. Otherwise,
Seaman's encounters, whether with antelope, beaver, bear or
buffalo, wolves, Indians, or the Missouri River, are based upon
the sparse details given in the various journals, merely fleshed
out by the novelist.

The first mention of Seaman occurs during Lewis's Ohio
River journey. Thus, in the early scenes I was forced to rely largely
on imagination to suggest scenarios, consistent with the known
facts, for Lewis's acquisition of the dog in Philadelphia, their

overland trip from Harpers Ferry to Pittsburgh, and incidents
during the long, exasperating delay while Lewis's hard-drinking
boatbuilder finished his work.

I confess that, where the journals do not say otherwise, it
suited the dramatic purposes of a novel to have Seaman present
at critical moments of the expedition, such as Lewis's first crossing
of the Continental Divide or his later clash with Blackfoot Indians. With regard to the latter, it has been suggested that Seaman couldn't have been with Lewis's party because he wouldn't
have been able to keep up (or catch up) when the men were
forced to flee on horseback. Since we here enter the area of pure
speculation, the writer of fiction can only ask eagerly, "But since
we don't know, what if he were there? What would have happened?"

Aside from such disclaimers, I have attempted, in filling out
Seaman's remarkable story, to keep always within the context
of known facts and historical probability. Seaman's achievements and character, like those of his companions of the Corps
of Discovery, need no embellishment.

There are many theories regarding the origin of the Newfoundland. One frequently put forth holds that it was a Basque dog
brought to the New World on fishing ships. As with most other
suggestions—that the Newfoundland was originally a Viking
dog, a descendant of the Greenland wolf, or related to Tibetan
Mastiffs—there is no evidence, only conjecture.

I am indebted to the late Margaret Booth Chern, author of
The New Complete Newfoundland and one of the outstanding
Newfoundland breeders, exhibitors, and historians of this century, for evidence that the breed was indigenous to the North
American continent. Based on osteometrical analysis, ethnol-
ogical records, anthropological and biological findings, as well
as the observations of early dog authorities, Mrs. Chern reached
an unequivocal conclusion: "One fact is undeniable: The Newfoundland is the American Indian's dog, a truly basic breed."

A Note About Seaman

For the writer, the attractiveness of this argument in relation to Seaman's journey is obvious.

Meriwether Lewis's dog was long known as Scannon, a textual misreading of the journals corrected by the late historian Donald Jackson, who convincingly demonstrated, in an article published in March 1986, in We Proceeded On, that the dog's name was Seaman.

Seaman is usually pictured in the guise of a modern Newfoundland. Although the breed has a history in this country that is centuries old, today's familiar Newfoundland type has emerged in the United States within the last fifty years. Lewis's dog, based on early sketches, paintings, and descriptions of the breed, was rangier and had a somewhat longer muzzle. Newfoundland owners may be surprised to read of Seaman pricking his ears, since today's Newfoundland has pendant ears. In the eighteenth and early nineteenth centuries semi-pendant ears were common in the breed, and even prick ears were not unknown.

Finally, I would like to thank the members of the Southern California Newfoundland Club for the pleasure of observing their Newfoundlands, both puppies and mature dogs, at work and play.

Louis Charbonneau
Lomita, California
January 10, 1989

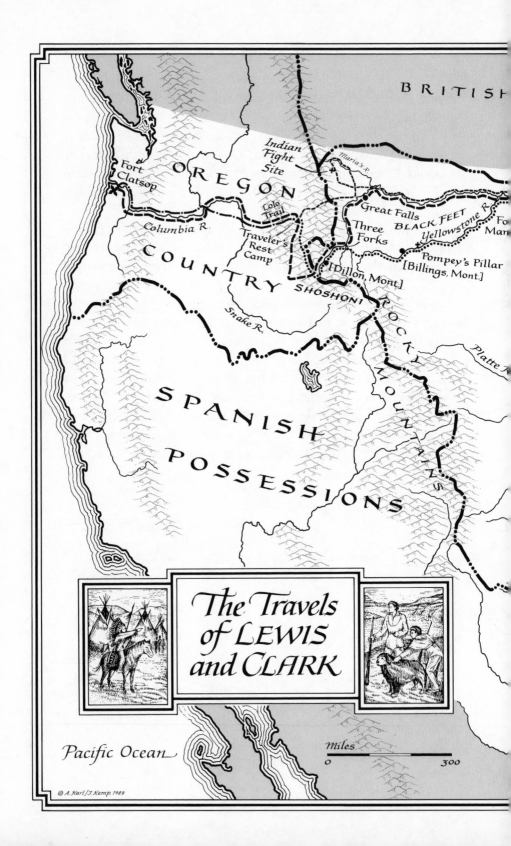

BRITISH

OREGON

Fort
Clatsop

Indian
Fight
Site

Maria's R.

Great Falls

BLACK FEET

Yellowstone R.

Fo
Man

Lolo
Trail

Columbia R.

Three
Forks

COUNTRY

Traveler's
Rest
Camp

Pompey's Pillar
[Billings, Mont.]

[Dillon, Mont.]

SHOSHONI

ROCKY

Snake R.

Platte

SPANISH

MOUNTAINS

POSSESSIONS

The Travels
of LEWIS
and CLARK

Pacific Ocean

Miles

0   300

© A. Karl / J. Kemp, 1989

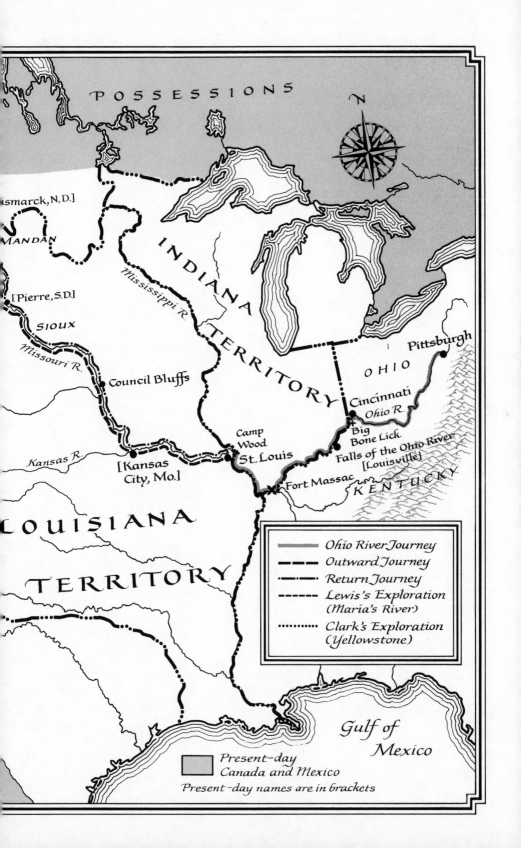

POSSESSIONS

N

[Bismarck, N.D.]

MANDAN

INDIANA

Mississippi R.

[Pierre, S.D.]

SIOUX

TERRITORY

Missouri R.

Council Bluffs

OHIO

Pittsburgh

Cincinnati

Ohio R.

Camp
Wood

St. Louis

Big
Bone Lick

Kansas R.

[Kansas
City, Mo.]

Falls of the Ohio River
[Louisville]

Fort Massac

KENTUCKY

LOUISIANA

TERRITORY

	Ohio River Journey
	Outward Journey
	Return Journey
	Lewis's Exploration (Maria's River)
	Clark's Exploration (Yellowstone)

Gulf of
Mexico

Present-day
Canada and Mexico
Present-day names are in brackets

Part one

down
the
ohio

1 I am now able to inform you, tho' I must do it confidentially, that we are at length likely to get the Missouri explored, & whatever river heading with that, leads into the Western ocean. Congress by a secret act has authorized me to do it. I propose to send immediately a party of about ten men with Capt. Lewis, my secretary, at their head . . .

—THOMAS JEFFERSON, March 2, 1803

*W*hen Captain Meriwether Lewis, private secretary to the President of the United States, arrived in Philadelphia on the first of May, 1803, a glittering sheath of ice coated the branches of the trees along the Schuylkill River. That very day the unseasonable cold changed, as if the young officer had brought a breath of warmth with him. The ice began to crack and drip as spring made its belated arrival.

A balmy Sunday afternoon a few days later found the young officer at loose ends. Thomas Jefferson's prominent friends of the city, who had both befriended and instructed Lewis, were otherwise occupied. The Schuylkill Arsenal, where Lewis was selecting huge quantities of supplies and equipment for a still secret mission, was closed on Sunday; so were most of the city's merchants. It was this combination of circumstances that brought the young officer, early in the afternoon, to the vicinity of the docks. And it was there he saw the dog.

He was a black Newfoundland, about eight months old, large and big-boned and at a gawky stage of growth. He was sitting at the end of a rope held by a young sailor—off a British ship, Lewis thought. In the confused turmoil along Dock

3

Street, the young dog sat quietly, watching every passerby with friendly interest.

On impulse Lewis picked his way across the muddy street to the sailor's side. He nodded at the Newfoundland with a smile. "He's young for a ship's dog, isn't he?"

"Aye, sir, he's that. But he's no ship's dog—not that he couldn't be," the sailor added quickly. "His breed has a fine reputation for it, sir."

"He's your dog, then."

"Aye, sir." The sailor, whose accent was a strong Scottish burr, hesitated, appraising the officer. He was obviously a gentleman, wearing a perfectly tailored uniform of a captain in the 1st Infantry Regiment, the blue coat short-waisted and with a high collar, white buttons, and gold braid, the vest and breeches white, the resplendent whole accented by a black cocked hat with a white plume. The young seaman's hopes rose. "Would you be interested in him, sir? That is . . . well, he's for sale, you see."

4   "Ah," murmured Lewis, who had guessed as much. He studied the dog more closely. The pup reacted to his interest by rising to his feet, his tail wagging tentatively. A calm, amiable temperament for a youngster, Lewis thought. And he would be a large, powerful animal even for his breed, if the enormous feet were an indication. "My name is Meriwether Lewis. And you, my lad, are . . . ?"

"Ian Campbell, sir."

"Off one of the ships anchored here?"

"Aye, sir, you can see it there." He pointed proudly toward a three-masted merchant ship at anchor near the foot of Dock Street. "We've been in port a week, but will be sailin' day after tomorrow."

He did not add that he had been hoping for a sale of his Newfoundland pup since the day of his arrival. He had purchased the dog during a layover at St. John's in Newfoundland, when his ship was kept at anchor for nearly a fortnight by storms and heavy seas along the Atlantic seaboard. One of the lads who had sailed with him from Portsmouth had pointed out the large dogs that were everywhere in evidence on the island, used for pulling and hauling chores, and even for carrying lines out to ships in the harbor, swimming through the choppy waves. "They pay a fancy price for 'em in the States," the lad said. "Ye should think on't, Ian, my boy."

A sailor, Ian Campbell's friend had said, would never make his fortune on his ship's wages. What a wise sailor learned was how to buy for little in one port what might be sold high in the next.

"You've thought of a price, I suppose?" the American officer asked.

Ian Campbell hesitated. He had, reluctantly, after haggling with a canny islander who had several puppies available from a litter, paid a guinea for the Newfoundland. He hoped to more than double his investment. "Well, yes, sir . . . that is, he be twenty dollars, sir. In gold!"

"Twenty dollars?" The officer's tone was dubious.

"It's a fair bargain," Campbell insisted, though his quick response was more an estimate of the potential buyer than of the dog's value. "You wouldn't be disappointed in him. He has good strong bones and easy ways."

5

Thoughtfully Meriwether Lewis stroked the dog's broad head. The pup looked up at him, jaws open and tongue lolling out in what appeared for all the world to be a huge grin.

"I'd need to spend a little time with him. I must be certain of his disposition."

"You'll find him docile, sir, like all of his breed, and agreeable to your wishes."

"But you've no objection to my having him for a short time, I take it, Mr. Campbell?"

"Well . . . no, sir, none at all," Campbell said, though in his heart he felt objection forming. Still, the captain was his first prospective buyer in nearly a week, albeit a cautious one, and the young dog was wolfing down six or seven pounds of a food a day. On board ship Campbell had been able to feed him scraps from the ship's mess; ashore he had had to scrounge on his own for garbage.

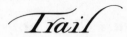

"Good." Meriwether Lewis called out suddenly, in the firm tone of one accustomed to giving commands. "Here, boy!"

The Newfoundland pup's head came up alertly. He felt a friendly curiosity, for in his short span of life he had yet to know harsh treatment or the meaning of fear. He took a tentative step toward the man who called him . . .

An hour later, above the steep bank of the Schuylkill River, the pup hurled himself at the captain, who laughed as he was nearly bowled off his feet. Lewis picked up the stick that had become the centerpiece of their play and threw it out over the slope. The dog bounded after it enthusiastically, mouth open, tongue hanging out from his exertions. Spotting the stick in the grass, he pounced upon it. He picked the stick up in his jaws, turned, and trotted eagerly back toward Lewis.

They had been at this for nearly an hour. At first, setting off beside the stranger on his black horse, the dog had been uncertain. On the small Newfoundland farm where he had been born, strangers had rarely appeared. On four occasions he had watched one of his brothers or sisters being led or carried away, not to be seen again. And one day the young sailor had come to take him away. So there was in his mind an element of mystery about strangers, a vague concern that was short of fear.

The city was quiet on this Sunday afternoon. When they reached the banks of the Schuylkill River, Meriwether Lewis dismounted. He squatted before the dog and talked to him quietly. Although he did not understand the words, the dog recognized the gentleness of the man's tone and manner. He accepted the firm strength of the fingers that prodded and poked, testing muscle strength and bone size, examining the huge feet and the strong white teeth. "We have a long way to go, you and I," the officer murmured after a while. "I would judge you more fit for the journey than most."

They walked together through the new grass above the riverbank, and the dog began to feel a growing affinity with this stranger, an eagerness to please him that was made more acute by his lingering uncertainty about what lay ahead. When the man picked up a stick and threw it out, urging the dog to "Fetch it!" he needed no more encouragement. The longer the game went on, the more his joy increased. He felt a new sense of belonging, along with a rising confidence.

At last Lewis paused. After a moment's thoughtfulness— with the late arrival of spring the river would be bitterly cold —he said, "Let's try it on the water. With those webbed feet of yours, boy, you should be a born swimmer."

The stick arched out over the river. The young dog charged down the slope, hit the bank on the run, and leaped fearlessly into the river. The current was strong with the spring runoff from the surrounding hills, but the dog struck out powerfully, though he had never been in the river before, never felt its icy chill or the pull of a swiftly flowing current. He saw the stick bobbing on the water, paddled quickly toward it, and took it in his mouth. Before he managed to return to the bank, he had been carried well downstream, but he bounded happily up the slope a moment later to deposit his prize at the soldier's feet.

Meriwether Lewis squatted beside him, oblivious as the dog suddenly shook his wet coat and rained a fine spray of water over the impeccable uniform. The dog then returned to the river's edge and, to Lewis's astonishment, buried his whole head in the water, drinking from the bottom. When he lifted his head at last and looked up, jaws dripping, Lewis laughed aloud. "You're a true seaman," he exclaimed. "And since I'm told you don't have a name, and you came to me off a ship, perhaps that would serve you well. What do you say to that, Seaman?"

The Newfoundland gazed at him happily.

"Seaman you are," the captain said, "and Seaman, you shall be."

By the time they turned back through the quiet city toward the docks, the sun was low against the blue-clad hills above the Schuylkill. After a short distance Lewis noticed that the young dog was limping. Without hesitation he reined in his horse, dismounted, picked up the tired, footsore pup, and lifted

7

him over the saddle. There Seaman lay, boneless with fatigue and complete trust.

When the afternoon had drawn late with no sign of the American captain, Ian Campbell had become more worried by the minute. The officer had seemed a proper gentleman, someone you could trust, but even gentlemen had been known to cheat an honest sailor. An admonition of his father's popped into Ian's head unbidden. "If iver thee gi' aught for naught, gi' it to tha se'n." Well, he'd given up his dog and received nothing for him in return. What if the fancy-dressed captain were not what he appeared? What if . . .

Campbell's anxiety gave way. There! Coming down the road . . . but why was the captain walking? And where was the dog?

Then Campbell saw the Newfoundland draped over the saddle, wet and limp. He rushed forward in alarm. "Oh my God, sir! What has happened? Surely he hasn't drowned?"

"Never fear," the captain said quickly. "He takes to water like a duck. I'm afraid he is weary from unaccustomed adventure, that's all."

The sailor sighed in relief. He watched as the soldier lifted the pup down from the saddle and placed him on his feet. The dog sat instantly, gazing up at Lewis, whose smile already revealed a growing fondness. He had grown up with dogs, hunted with them in the woods of his beloved Albemarle County, Virginia, and often felt closer to them than he did to many men.

"Twenty dollars, you said." Half a month's pay for a captain of the 1st Infantry. "It's a dear price, but I believe he's worth it. I must have him."

"You won't be sorry, sir." The seller's hazel eyes glinted as if reflecting the color of the gold coins that clinked into his hand. "He'll be traveling far with you, sir?"

The young captain gazed over the sailor's shoulder with that far-off look in his blue eyes that Ian Campbell had seen in sailors long at sea, gazing toward the horizon in search of their first glimpse of land.

"A very long journey, lad," said Meriwether Lewis. "A very long journey indeed."

On the same Sunday afternoon that saw Meriwether Lewis tossing a stick for a gangling puppy on the banks of the Schuylkill, Thomas Jefferson, third president of the United States, was entertaining three U.S. senators at the President's House in Washington. Prior to sitting down with his guests to a sumptuous dinner, the President strolled through the garden he was attempting to create to relieve the sterility of the lawns. The President's House had been first occupied by John Adams in 1800, the second President's last year in office, and by Jefferson for two years. Like the capital itself, the building that was the President's office and residence was in a raw state, surrounded much of the time, especially this spring, by a sea of mud. An ardent gardener at Monticello, Jefferson had personally brought a number of plants and cuttings to Washington to create the small garden he was now proudly determined to display.

9

"I envisage a formal garden here one day," Jefferson mused, "where some future President may mull over affairs of state. A garden, you know, offers the tranquillity conducive to quiet reflection."

The senators, accustomed to Jefferson's habit of envisaging future wonders, merely nodded.

The white-haired President walked with his head thrust forward, eyes intent as he pointed out the flowers already in bud or bloom. "That purple hyacinth bloomed early this year, in late March. We'll be losing it soon. Like the puckoon there, its flowers already blown, and the narcissus. But nature always compensates," he added with a smile. "That purple flag is ready to bloom."

The senators nodded again, looking down at their muddy shoes, thinking not of flowers but of pheasant and veal, fruits and nuts, puddings and wines, soon to be consumed at Jefferson's long table. Affairs of state seemed far away.

So, too, were Thomas Jefferson's thoughts, even as he kept up a congenial intercourse with his guests. Across the ocean in Paris, the U.S. minister to the French government, Robert Livingston, had been carrying out Jefferson's instructions to negotiate with Napoleon Bonaparte's foreign minister, Talleyrand, for the purchase of the port of New Orleans.

Those discussions had been stalled for months, but Jefferson, sensing that the time was now propitious, had sent James Monroe to France as "minister extraordinary" to lend his subtle, judicious mind to the delicate negotiations. Even now, Jefferson thought, Monroe must be approaching the coast of France, if he was not already in Paris; and the President, who had a well-earned reputation for far-ranging vision, could not help speculating about the outcome.

Napoleon was in trouble. After forcing Spain to recede the Louisiana Territory to France in the Treaty of San Ildefonso in 1800, Bonaparte had hoped to establish a French empire in North America. His plan had been to send two armies to the Western Hemisphere, one to crush the slave rebellion on Santo Domingo led by Toussaint L'Ouverture, the second to link up with that force and occupy Louisiana. The success of the plan would have placed France in a position of strength in the New World, ready for the clash with Great Britain that Napoleon envisioned as a war to be fought on two continents.

Napoleon's grand scheme had foundered in the West Indies.

In the Caribbean the mighty Bonaparte had been defeated by an enemy he could not even see. Although the French army under General Charles Leclerc had eventually defeated Toussaint and taken him prisoner, the price of victory had proved catastrophic. The French forces had been decimated by yellow fever. The regiments of the Second Expeditionary Army, intended for Louisiana, had had to be diverted to Santo Domingo to support the depleted forces already there—and the new regiments quickly fell victim to the same attrition from disease.

Louis Charbonneau

By the end of the year 1802 the magnitude of Napoleon's losses had become clear to the American President in Washington. Jefferson realized that the threat he had most feared —a powerful French presence in Louisiana to replace the weak Spanish occupation—was over. Napoleon had no choice but to turn his attention entirely to Europe, where that inevitable conflict with Great Britain awaited him.

Jefferson believed that Bonaparte desperately needed money to carry out his campaign against Britain. The President was prepared to help him—by purchasing New Orleans. To gain that prize, which would mean control of the mouth of the Mississippi for U.S. cargo ships, Jefferson was prepared to stretch his authority to dip into the U.S. Treasury.

That purchase was only the first step in what Thomas Jefferson saw as an opening up of the trans-Mississippi West to American commerce. The second step was an exploration of the upper Missouri River by a small American party, with a view to finding passage to the Pacific Ocean.

The two goals were closely linked in Jefferson's mind. As far back as November, 1802, he had broached the subject to the Spanish Minister to the United States, wondering if the Spanish government would "take it badly" if the United States were to send a small expedition "to explore the course of the Missouri River" through the territory known as Louisiana. Even though those lands had officially been ceded to France, they were still governed by Spanish authorities, backed by Spanish troops.

Then, within a single week in January, Jefferson had made two decisive moves. The first, on January 13, was the appointment of James Monroe for his mission to France. Five days later, in a secret session of Congress, the President delivered a confidential message asking for a special appropriation of $2,500 to finance a small expedition for the specific purpose "of exploring the Missouri and whatever river, heading with that, leads into the Western Ocean." Disingenuously, Jefferson called this a merely "literary pursuit," an enlargement of present knowledge of the territory. Its unstated purposes were no less than winning the fur trade of the Rockies for American merchants, gaining access by a convenient transcontinental route to the China trade of the Pacific, and reinforcing the United States' tenuous claim to the Columbia River basin.

Jefferson was more farsighted than anyone guessed. Opening the West to American commerce, he thought, would not be the end of it. It would only be the beginning . . .

"I have an excellent French Bordeaux I thought we might try today," Jefferson said to his hungry and thirsty guests, whose interest immediately quickened, "one that I've been saving for a special occasion. The French really have achieved remarkable things with their wines, though I'm not convinced that many of their grapes couldn't be grown as well in this country . . ."

His focus shifted, from subtle negotiations with the Emperor of France to the problems of growing fine grapes in soil foreign to them. His vision was as keen as ever.

"I'll warrant you gentlemen are hungry . . . and so am I. Shall we go in, then? What's that, Senator? I have your vote? By George, that's a first!"

Unknown to Jefferson, events in France had taken an extraordinary turn.

When James Monroe reached Paris at the end of April, 1803, he found the normally reserved U.S. minister to France, Robert Livingston, in a state of unnatural excitement, hardly able to contain his agitation until the two men were alone in Monroe's hotel room.

Talleyrand, Livingston said in a voice that rose a notch as he spoke, had done a complete about-face in negotiations. No longer "too busy" to consider an American offer seriously, he was now haggling with Livingston over the price—not just for the port of New Orleans, Livingston announced triumphantly, but for *all of Louisiana!*

Monroe was stunned by the revelation. "How much is he asking?" he finally whispered.

"More than I've been authorized to offer by a third. But that was for New Orleans alone. Now the Emperor is ready to separate France from all of Louisiana."

"Why in heaven . . ." Monroe's agile mind seized upon the answer to his own incredulous question. "But of course! If Bonaparte can't keep it for himself . . ."

Livingston nodded. "He wants to deny it to the British. And what better way than by selling it to us?"

Monroe stared at him for a long moment. Then, to Livingston's astonishment, the minister extraordinary to France performed an impromptu jig on the elegant Persian rug on the floor of his hotel room. "And so he shall!" cried Monroe. "And so he shall!"

2

The object of your mission is to explore the Missouri River and such principal streams of it, as, by its course and communication with the waters of the Pacific Ocean, whether the Columbia, Oregon, Colorado, or any other river, may offer the most direct and practicable water communication across this continent for the purposes of commerce . . .

—THOMAS JEFFERSON, June 20, 1803

*I*n the inns and taverns and meeting halls of Boston, New York, Philadelphia, and especially Washington, D.C., the rumors had been whispered from ear to ear for days. Was it possible? Had Long Tom Jefferson put one over on Napoleon? Had Livingston and Monroe bested Talleyrand? My God, was it possible? All of Louisiana for less than fifteen million dollars?

Confirmation of the news reached the President late on the third day of July, 1803. By the following morning it was all over the city, in the rooms of the consuls and their aides, in the homes of congressmen and cabinet members, in the hotels and boarding houses, and in the streets. The Federalist boarding houses, where Jefferson's name sparked explosions of hate, were places of gloom that morning. Not for them the strings of firecrackers dancing in the streets, the boom of cannon from the Potomac shore, the glasses raised in toast to the triumph of the scheming old man in the White House.

On the evening of July 4, Meriwether Lewis joined the third President of the United States in his downstairs office, a large room dominated by bookshelves and a long table bearing piles of papers and stacks of rolled maps. Jefferson released his pet mockingbird from its cage and watched it flit about the room, from the top of a bookcase to the arm of a wing chair to the old globe on its stand to a familiar perch on Jefferson's shoulder.

The President poured glasses of brandy for himself and his secretary. He seemed pensive after the day's turmoil, rolling the fat glass thoughtfully between the curved bowls of his fingers. "You'll be off early in the morning, I presume. I will see you before you go."

"There's no need for you to rise so early. I should like to catch the first light."

"I will not be asleep," the President said with a small smile. He did not need to add that he had slept little these last few days of urgent preparations, tired eyes poring over maps, a bony finger tracing each detail of Lewis's lists of supplies and expenditures, his mind restlessly reviewing all the problems that lay ahead and the contingencies that had been provided for . . . or possibly forgotten.

This was the moment the two had waited and planned for, Jefferson for more than two decades, since his imagination first fed on stories of the unknown lands beyond the Mississippi. Twenty years ago Jefferson had broached the idea of an exploration of the Missouri's headwaters to George Rogers Clark, but Congress had failed to authorize the project. Ten years later, in 1893, Jefferson, then Secretary of State, became acquainted with André Michaux, a French botanist who had traveled through parts of Canada and the South. Michaux expressed interest in exploring the Missouri to its source, and Jefferson eagerly took up his cause, soliciting funds from his friends in the American Philosophical Society in Philadelphia—George Washington was among those who responded, personally contributing twenty-five dollars. It was at that time that Meriwether Lewis first made a strong impression upon Jefferson when he brashly volunteered to join Michaux in his venture. Jefferson knew the eighteen-year-old Lewis and his family, Albermarle County neighbors in the shadow of the

15

Blue Ridge, but he turned Lewis down as being too young and inexperienced.

In the event, Michaux had turned out to be an agent of Citizen Edmond Charles Genêt, then the French minister to the United States, in a scheme to encourage a French-supported insurrection in the West designed to drive the Spanish from their outposts on the Mississippi. When George Washington learned of the plot, he acted swiftly, expelling Genêt from the country. Michaux's venture was aborted.

But Thomas Jefferson had not forgotten the eager young man in whose eyes he had caught a reflection of the light he sometimes saw in his own mirror. He had followed Lewis's army career at a distance, and shortly after his inauguration as President he had written to Lewis, asking him to come to Washington to be his private secretary.

I wasn't wrong about him, thought Jefferson.

Jefferson's deep-set eyes regarded his protégé with affection as Lewis brushed imaginary lint from his sleeve. During his time in the capital Lewis had become something of a dandy, as meticulous about his dress as he was in all things, perhaps in an effort to overcome his natural reticence. Mature and self-possessed in private, cool and confident in danger, firm and decisive in commanding men, he remained a soldier more at home in the wilderness than in capital society. Nevertheless, Jefferson reflected with a trace of amusement, Lewis was very popular with the ladies of the city, who seemed to find the tall, lean, fair-haired young officer uncommonly handsome. Even his awkwardness appealed to them.

In the past two years the relationship of the President and his secretary had become almost that of a father and son. Jefferson, now sixty-two, was not unmindful of the fact that the twenty-eight-year-old Lewis had lost his father in boyhood. He credited the circumstance, in fact, for Lewis's early maturity and resourcefulness.

Jefferson knew Lewis's family background well. Lewis's father had given his son an early baptism of patriotism. Meriwether was a child of two when, in 1776, his father became the third signer of Albemarle County's own declaration of independence from the British crown. William Lewis joined the Revolutionary Army as a lieutenant, voluntarily serving without pay and bearing his own expenses. In the early winter of 1779, returning to his family on leave, Lieutenant Lewis was caught in a flood, took a chill from the icy water, and came down with pneumonia. He died shortly thereafter. Meriwether Lewis was five years old.

Jefferson recalled Lewis's mother as a pretty, lively, genteel Virginia lady, from whom he had sometimes purchased exceptionally tasty Virginia hams for his own table at Monticello. She had introduced her eldest son to a respect for good manners, a love of books and learning, and—as a herbalist widely respected in Albermarle County—had given Lewis a familiarity with natural medicines that should serve him well in the wilderness journey ahead.

The widowed Lucy Lewis had soon remarried, but her second husband, John Marks, had also left her a widow. At the age of seventeen Meriwether had become the true head of his family, a devoted son who might well have lived out the comfortable life of a successful Virginia plantation owner—his energy, diligence, and attention to detail would have assured that success, Jefferson thought—but for the chance intervention of a government tax on whiskey.

When George Washington called for a volunteer militia to put down the Whiskey Rebellion in 1794, Lewis, like his father before him, was quick to respond. With the militia he pursued the fleeing rebels through western Pennsylvania and across the Alleghenies to Pittsburgh. The angry tax protest died, its leaders scattered. But by then Meriwether Lewis had had a good taste of army life. He had found what he wanted to do, and he promptly enlisted in the regular army.

At the time Jefferson called him to Washington, Lewis had risen to the rank of captain as the paymaster of the 1st U.S. Infantry. There was no shortage of ambitious young men in Washington competent to be the President's secretary, men with perhaps more formal education, more polish in drawing

17

room debate, more ease in the ballroom. But none had young Meriwether Lewis's knowledge of the West, his acquaintance with Indians, his experience in the wilderness, his bent of mind and spirit, qualities that had little to do with the routine duties of a private secretary. For Meriwether Lewis, Jefferson had something else in mind.

When Jefferson assumed the Presidency, the idea had taken firm root in his mind and heart: the dream of finding a continuous water passage across the continent, linking the source of the Missouri River to the Columbia, with at most a short, easy portage across the intervening mountain range. And he had decided that Meriwether Lewis would be the instrument he would use to trace that journey.

In the two years Lewis had been with Jefferson, they had spent countless hours here in the President's office, talking and planning, Jefferson guiding the younger man toward books and studies that would prepare him for this day. Lewis had a speculative intelligence. He shared Jefferson's curiosity about science and nature. He had a lively interest in how things worked and, like Jefferson, a talent for invention and design. If he lacked formal scientific training—the reason Jefferson had sent him to his friends in Philadelphia to study—he made up for it with his many other admirable qualities. And if he was sometimes prey to darker moods, Jefferson judged that the challenges of the expedition would leave little time for melancholy.

Jefferson sipped his brandy. His belly must be awash with the day's surfeit of punches and ales and other spirits, he thought, for it had been a holiday of joyous celebration such as the young nation had not known since the year of its birth twenty-seven years ago today. Thoughts of his constitution, no longer as hardy as it once had been, reminded him of Benjamin Rush's prescriptions for the good health of Lewis and those under his command. "Dr. Rush recommends a little spirit to wash your feet when you have had them much chilled." He spoke without smiling, but there was enough light from the lamp on the desk for Lewis to catch the humor in his eyes.

Louis Charbonneau

"I warrant that we will find better use for it." Then, as if constrained to soften any criticism, Lewis added, "The doctor was most obliging while I was in Philadelphia, and I'm sure that many of his questions about the Indians, particularly concerning diseases and customs we may discover among them, will be most useful."

"You consulted him, of course, in the selection of drugs and other medical supplies for your requirements?"

"Yes, he was very helpful in preparing my list. I've included a large supply of his bilious pills, which are said to be efficacious."

"Mm . . ."

These were matters the two men had been over before during the two weeks since Lewis's return from Lancaster and Philadelphia, where he had tried to cram into nine weeks all of the knowledge of botany and zoology available to the best scientific minds of the day, as well as methods of celestial navigation, including the uses of sextant and chronometer and artificial horizon.

The silence between Thomas Jefferson and Meriwether Lewis, so comfortable most times from long association, was momentarily awkward. At length the President turned toward his desk and opened a drawer. "I have no doubt you will reach the Pacific successfully. But it may well be that the difficulties you will overcome to reach it will not encourage you to return by the same route. I think it might prove best for some or all of your party to return from that shore by sea, as I've explained in my instructions. You will need provisions, money, clothes, and other necessities. This"—he handed an envelope to Lewis, unsealed—"is a letter of credit, with the full backing of the United States, to use as you shall find necessary."

Meriwether Lewis nodded, understanding the older man's retreat into formality for what it was, sensing the deep emotion Jefferson brought to this eve of the culmination of all their plans.

"Is there anything you haven't told me? Anything I may yet do to further the success of our venture?"

19

"I can think of nothing." Suddenly Lewis smiled. "I go by way of Harpers Ferry, where my wagons from Philadelphia should precede me. There I'll also pick up my first recruit, the dog I spoke of. He'll be old enough to travel now, I believe."

"Oh, yes . . ." Jefferson saw no harm in Lewis's decision to take a dog along on the arduous journey ahead, though he was quite certain the principal reason was the fact that the Scotsman, Alexander Mackenzie, had had a dog with him on his successful expedition across Canada a decade earlier.

"He's a Newfoundland," added Lewis. "I believe Mr. Washington owned one of the breed, and Benjamin Franklin as well."

Jefferson smiled. "Samuel Adams, too," he said, referring to the Revolutionary patriot and signer of the Declaration of Independence. "I was told his dog Que-que hated the sight of redcoats almost as much as you do."

"An intelligent dog." Lewis did not bother to try to deny his well-known antipathy toward the British.

20 "There are different theories as to your dog's origins," Jefferson observed, pursuing naturally his scientific habit of inquiry. "I recall Mr. Franklin insisting his Newfoundland was an Indian dog. The Algonquians are said to have placed great stock in such large black dogs. They were called Bear Dogs— as I believe Newfoundlanders still name the breed."

Meriwether Lewis laughed. "You seem to know more of them than I do."

"It would be fitting," Jefferson mused, "if your dog's ancestors were once at home on the American plains. I'm sending you into territory entirely new to us, but this recruit of yours . . . well, he might be visiting the lands of his forebears!"

Jefferson placed a hand on Lewis's shoulder. He had drained the last of his brandy and for a moment stared into the empty glass as if at a loss for words. "Our heart will go with you."

What Meriwether Lewis felt in that moment for the older man blended a son's love for his father with a soldier's admiration for a commander he would follow to the death. They were powerful emotions, but this was an age of formality, one in which strong feeling sought expression not in passionate demonstration but in a graceful turn of phrase. With that sudden gravity that was a part of him, sometimes disconcerting, Lewis said, "It is a burden I most gladly carry."

The President of the United States smiled. "I believe it is in good hands, as are all our hopes and those of your countrymen. And now . . . get some sleep."

He went up the stairs from his office slowly. His pet mockingbird followed him, hopping up one step at a time.

On that Fourth of July at Harpers Ferry in Virginia, cannon bellowed the news of a young nation's independence, and the rolling crackle of rifle shots racketed off the hills above the banks of the Shenandoah. A young black dog came to his feet at the booming of the guns, adding his deep bark to the sounds of celebration.

Before departing from Philadelphia for Washington, Meriwether Lewis had left his newly purchased dog in the care of William Linnard, the military agent attached to the Schuylkill Arsenal. He instructed Linnard to send the Newfoundland along as far as Harpers Ferry with the wagonload of Lewis's supplies that were destined for delivery to him at Pittsburgh.

When Lewis left him, Seaman felt a strange emptiness. He did not understand the intense longing that took over his spirit, and the sense of loss. In a few short hours by the Schuylkill riverbank a pact had been sealed between the young dog and the soldier, a commitment that Seaman accepted without question.

Seaman rode out of Philadelphia on the seat of a lumbering wagon beside a taciturn drover who felt himself sufficiently burdened with his cargo without a dog to look after as well. It was a long, dusty ride along rough roads that wound through green-clad hills. At the end of it, Seaman, who was prepared to give affection even to the cranky wagoneer, was once more abandoned, this time at the Harpers Ferry Arsenal.

21

The soldiers on duty there, young, rough-natured frontier soldiers, had been friendly enough with the dog, but also wary of interfering with an animal said to belong to the demanding Captain Lewis of the 1st Infantry, the President's own secretary. As a result Seaman was largely left alone.

During the two months since he had seen Meriwether Lewis, while spring brimmed into the heat of summer, Seaman had grown several inches taller. He now stood twenty-six inches at the shoulders, and a deeper cushion of muscle covered his big-boned frame. The muzzle had lengthened slightly, though his was still a blocky head, the skull triangular, the jaws deep and powerful. His coat, a glossy black with a distinctive star of white hairs on the chest, had thickened; it was much thinner on the legs, where there was little feathering, revealing the well-muscled drive of his hindquarters. He was not yet full-grown, but he was no longer the awkward, gangling pup who had floundered after the stick the soldier had thrown over and over again so patiently.

That evening, when the guns were silent, Seaman returned to his vigil beside the road that led to Harpers Ferry from the east. The shadows gathered slowly in the long twilight of a midsummer evening. He waited until the end of the road was no longer visible.

The soldier on the black horse had not come.

Yet something whispered to the dog. The man would return. The bond forged between them during that afternoon by the riverbank was invisible, but it was not like the mist that drifted above ground in the mornings here in Virginia, vanishing with the first rays of the sun.

In the afternoon following the booming of guns at Harpers Ferry that heralded Independence Day, Seaman, resting in the shade of a big oak that bordered the main yard, was idly watching the road leading toward the Arsenal. He saw the plume of a rider's hat bobbing in the distance above a line of brush. A black horse came into view. Seaman felt a surge of joy as he leaped up.

There he was—the cocked hat, the military coat, the polished boots, the man!

Seaman ran toward him, a growl of pleasure rising from deep in his chest.

3 I shall set out myself in the course of an hour, taking the route of Charlestown, Frankfort, Uniontown and Redstone old fort to Pittsburgh . . .

—MERIWETHER LEWIS, J u l y 8, 1 8 0 3

Meriwether Lewis set off from the armory at Harpers Ferry early in the afternoon of July 8, 1803. Trotting down the road after him, Seaman did not look back. His allegiance to the soldier on horseback had been confirmed.

Rarely now did the Newfoundland remember the bearded islander who, in the fall of the previous year, had bred a litter of black dogs on a small farm just outside of St. John's. The memory of the sailor who had taken the dog off to sea had also begun to fade. Seaman was capable of offering great loyalty and affection. Neither the breeder nor Ian Campbell had claimed that devotion. The Newfoundland farmer was a man as sparing of affection as he was of words or coin. He had bred his dogs not out of a particular love of animals but as a practical source of income, much as another farmer might breed hogs or horses. Ian Campbell, for his part, had simply exercised a common sailor's practice of buying something in one port that might be sold at a profit in another.

Now ten months of age, Seaman, like most young dogs of large breeds, was still leggy and clumsy in his actions. His personality was friendly and exuberant. He threw himself into each new adventure with heedless enthusiasm. In his excitement the dog frequently veered away from the road whenever he spotted something moving in the woods, a squirrel or a bird or an opossum. Each time, after a wild chase, he would come back empty-jawed but happy, hurrying to catch up to the rider on horseback.

Meriwether Lewis made no attempt to reprimand his young dog or to curb his enthusiasm. Some lessons, after all, could only be learned by experience. Conserving energy when traveling long distances was one of them.

Lewis himself was glad enough to be under way. On his arrival at Harpers Ferry from Washington on the evening of July 5, he had discovered that the wagoneer hired by the military agent in Philadelphia had already driven past the armory. After dropping off Lewis's dog, he had refused to take on additional cargo, insisting that his five-horse team was already overburdened. Lewis rode at once to nearby Fredericktown, where he engaged the owner of a light two-horse wagon after exacting his promise to be at Harpers Ferry on the morning of the eighth.

That morning the wagoneer had not appeared. In disgust Lewis had to seek out another drover in Fredericktown. Lewis pressed the man, a cheerful, red-faced Irishman named Tumulty, about keeping his commitment to be at the armory that evening to pick up his load. "Sure, an' you'll no have to gi' it another thought more," Tumulty said. "I've a brother in Pittsburgh I've been after wantin' to visit."

Trusting his hunch about the man, Lewis did not wait. Left behind as he set off in the early afternoon was the precious cargo Tumulty would carry to Pittsburgh. It included blunderbusses and three light swivel cannons, rifles, tomahawks and knives from the Harpers Ferry arsenal. There were musket locks and ballscrews and molds, powder horns and bullet pouches, repair tools and other supplies. Among the rifles were fifteen of Lewis's own design, adapted from the .54 calibre long rifle famed among Kentuckians. Lewis's design featured a shorter, sturdier stock, reducing the overall length of the rifle

25

to forty-seven inches. As his own tests of his armory the previous afternoon had demonstrated, this Harpers Ferry rifle was as accurate as the long Kentucky rifle and less fragile—no small concern for the arduous journey ahead.

Tumulty's wagon would also carry other examples of the young officer's ingenuity. There were 52 waterproof lead canisters carrying 176 pounds of gunpowder. The canisters in turn could be melted down to make new rifle balls. And there was the iron frame of a collapsible canoe of Lewis's design, appropriately named *Experiment*. Although the forty-foot frame weighed only ninety-nine pounds for easy portage, wrapped in bark or skins it would carry a load equal to that of a conventional canoe many times its weight.

The day was hot and sultry. Locusts sang in the fields, and dust rose in the wake of the rider and his dog. Seaman's excitement kept him on the run, for he had never before been free to run like this through fields and woods. Everything along the road was new, every floating shadow among the trees, the tang of leaves on the forest floor, the spoor of nameless wild creatures.

By midafternoon of that first day on the road Seaman was dragging along in the wake of the two horses. Eventually missing his young dog, Meriwether Lewis dismounted and walked back along the road, his boots kicking up little clouds of dust. He found Seaman lying in the shade of a small grove of alder by the side of the road. The dog lay on his side, the whites of his eyes showing as he looked up at Lewis, his long tongue lolling out of the side of his mouth. He panted steadily, his rib cage rising and falling visibly like a bellows.

"You're a sight for a traveler," said Lewis. "You'll soon learn what any soldier learns on the march, to save a bit of yourself for the next mile. I don't suppose you caught any of those squirrels? No, I thought not." The words were tempered with a thin smile. The gentle patience in his tone would have surprised those soldiers who had served on the western frontier under the demanding young captain of the 1st Infantry. He patted the broad-skulled head. "I'll wager you will learn as

fast as many a soldier. We'll rest now, but tomorrow"—the
faint smile returned—"you'll walk farther."

That evening, watered, fed, and rested, Seaman was showing
signs of complete recovery from his first day on the road when
Lewis's familiar figure emerged from the inn where they had
stopped for the night. Seaman came toward him with an eager
wag. He followed Lewis to a nearby clearing, where he watched
curiously as Lewis took sightings of the moon and stars, using
one of the two sextants he had purchased in Philadelphia. The
rest of the precious instruments he had acquired in Philadelphia and Lancaster were packed in the wagon that had gone
ahead to Pittsburgh before Lewis reached Harpers Ferry. He
would have to wait to put to full use the lessons he had received
from Jefferson's Pennsylvania friends, Robert Patterson and
Andrew Ellicott, who had tried in a few short weeks to give
him an education in making celestial observations. Although
Lewis had a curious mind and was quick to learn, he recognized his shortcomings in this area. His measured altitudes
were invariably either too high or too low. He would need all
the practice he could get if he was to meet the President's high
expectations.

27

The night sky was partly cloudy, and, soon after Lewis
began his sightings, a cloud mass moved across the face of the
moon. Lewis gave up his efforts for that night, frustrated more
by his struggle to master the new science than by the passing
clouds. He thought ruefully of Patterson's reference to "simple
lunar observations" for computing longitude. Simple for him.
There was so much to learn, so little time! Lewis was as impatient with his own shortcomings as with laggardly performance in others.

The candles burning in the windows beckoned. Seaman
watched Lewis until he disappeared through the heavy oak
door at the front of the inn. Then the dog curled up in a corner
of the stables, reassured, in spite of the strangeness of his
surroundings, by the familiar smells of barn and horses. The

stable boy spoke to him briefly, and Seaman thumped his tail in response to the friendly tone. The boy found his own corner, curled up like the dog, and both were soon asleep.

Seaman and Lewis were a week on the road, climbing up through the mountain forests to the pass and beginning the descent toward the Monongahela. Along the way they learned something of each other's ways and temper. Lewis was pleased to see that his dog's stamina increased, his muscles toughened, his tender footpads became hardened. He adapted well to the trail while remaining always alert, as avidly curious as Lewis himself. Some days, while resting during the heat of the day or in the early evening, Lewis also began to teach Seaman some simple tricks, such as lying down on command or sitting up on his haunches. Lewis was not interested in having a performing bear; he was testing Seaman's quick intelligence, and he knew that the more a dog learned, the more confident and responsive he became.

28

The days remained hot and thick with dust along the road. Each day, passing through such settlements as Charles Town, Frankfort, Uniontown, and Redstone Old Fort, Lewis felt the pull of the Ohio becoming stronger.

One persistent worry occupied his thoughts. Would William Clark respond as he hoped?

Lewis's choice as a partner in command of the expedition, a necessity urged upon him by the President, had been made almost impetuously, after little reflection. The fact that Clark's name had come immediately to mind was a mark of the warm admiration he still felt for the fellow Albemarlean whose command he had joined some eight years ago.

When Lewis, then a young ensign, had been transferred in 1795 to Lieutenant Clark's Chosen Rifle Company, a band of experienced regular army sharpshooters, he had not known what to expect. William Clark had welcomed him warmly and quickly won his friendship. Lewis had soon learned that Clark was a fair but strong-willed officer, a skilled frontiersman, at home in the wilderness, knowledgeable of Indians, and respected by all who knew him. Lewis had served with no officer he held in higher esteem.

He remembered the sharp regret he had felt when, only a few months after he had joined Clark's company, he learned that his new friend was resigning his commission, compelled by family affairs to return to civilian life.

Would Clark now be free to respond favorably to Lewis's invitation to join him in sharing the trials and honors of the expedition? How could any man refuse such an opportunity? Would Clark's reply be waiting for him in Pittsburgh? There was so little time to lose, so much still to be done. Midsummer already, and Lewis hoped to be well up the Missouri before winter made river travel impossible.

The gloom of the endless forest stole out of the trees to envelope the road. It was dusk, and Lewis saw that his young dog was trotting wearily at the side of the road, favoring one foot. They would have to stop soon, he decided reluctantly. They had too far to go together to risk any serious injury.

29

That night Meriwether Lewis took his dog up to the room he had taken at yet another country inn. He bathed Seaman's foot and treated a cut on the pad with a herbal ointment.

When full darkness came, Seaman lay contentedly on a rag rug and watched the young officer. Their room was small, but it contained a writing desk. A flickering candle on the desk threw shadows across the room and etched Lewis's grave expression as he wrote. Seaman listened to the scratching of the pen across the page, a quiet, oddly soothing sound. From below, somewhere in the inn, came an occasional guffaw, a roar of derision as an argument heated up, heavy footsteps on the stairs that caused Seaman's ears to prick alertly. The steps plodded along the narrow hallway, and a door closed.

Lewis smiled approvingly at his dog's reaction. Then he bent his head once more to the page, the quill pen scratching like a paw at a door.

 Trail

When Meriwether Lewis at last fell into bed and went immediately to sleep, Seaman remained awake. He listened to the gradually receding sounds of life inside the inn—a door closing, a woman's subdued laughter, stairs creaking under a footstep—and the other whispers from the darkness outside, the voices of the wilderness. Seaman quickened with wonder as an owl hooted near the window and a dog barked somewhere down the road.

The pad of his right front foot was sore, and he licked it quietly.

He felt a deepening bond between himself and the man who now slept on the straw mattress that rustled each time he moved. But there was something else that kept the dog awake until the inn was dark and still and even the night animals had withdrawn into the depths of the surrounding forest.

Seaman's life had permanently changed. The companions of his youth were behind him. What lay ahead was beyond the darkness, beyond anything he had known. Yet, whatever his future held, he seemed to move toward it as naturally as a turtle toward the sea.

4
This is an undertaking fraited with many difeculties, but my friend I do assure you that no man lives whith whome I would perfur to undertake such a trip &c as yourself ...
—WILLIAM CLARK, J u l y 1 8, 1 8 o 3

The log cabin was set high on a promontory overlooking the Falls of the Ohio, on the north side of the river in Indiana Territory, opposite Louisville. George Rogers Clark had selected the site long ago, but only recently—the poplar logs were still shiny and yellow—had the cabin been completed. The view, George proclaimed, was the best to be had of the falls from any point on the north shore.

William Clark had taken the ferry across the river that morning to talk with his brother. He glanced at the letter that lay open on the scarred oak table beside George's chair, next to the cold stone fireplace. The room held a smell of stale ashes and whiskey. The smell of sickness, too, and despair.

William Clark's first thought, upon receiving the remarkable communication from Meriwether Lewis, had been of George. Twenty years ago the same Thomas Jefferson who was now President of the United States had asked George Rogers Clark to lead an expedition westward to search out the source of the Missouri River and a connecting route to the western ocean. The timing had not been right, and the proposal had died. Thirteen years later, in 1796, William had been compelled to resign his commission in the army and return to Louisville to try to straighten out his family's affairs—in George's financial circumstances, a near hopeless task in which William was still engaged.

When William had handed George the letter, the older man had fumbled for a pair of reading glasses, blinking red-rimmed eyes that had once scanned the farthest horizon with a keenness few Kentucky sharpshooters could match. He had read the letter in silence. For a long time he had sat holding it in a big, gnarly hand, now misshapen with its enlarged knuckles. Without a word he had left the room. William heard his footsteps dragging through the kitchen at back of the cabin. Then a door banged shut.

George frequently had to visit the privy out behind the cabin, but William knew that he had also wanted to be alone.

Now he heard George's voice raised in the yard, and he went to the window. His brother was talking to their sister Fanny. Beyond them, in the sloping meadow, Fanny's two older sons, Johnny and Ben O'Fallon, were playing with a stick and a ball. They were energetic, lively youngsters. Fanny's youngest, Charles Thruston, named for her late second husband, was quieter, more withdrawn, but the five-year-old was a favorite of George's. Thank God for Fanny! William thought. She and her children had breathed new vigor into George's life. The arrangement had also given Fanny, twice widowed before she was thirty, a home and a purpose.

Listening to them, William Clark found himself peering through a mist, though the afternoon was warm and bright. Like the man himself, George's voice was only a husk of what it once had been. Although he was only in his early fifties, he was crippled in both body and soul, an old man before his time. Frail and almost helpless, he found his only solace in the bottle.

Standing at the window and staring out across the meadow toward the tumbling rapids of the Ohio, William

Louis Charbonneau

Clark, eighteen years younger than his brother the general, was a figure in startling contrast. His erect bearing was that of a soldier, though he had been without his old command for seven years this month. At the age of thirty-three he had a reputation on the western frontier almost as illustrious as that of his famous brother. Generous and warmhearted, he was also a respected Indian fighter, a frontier soldier equally at home on the river or in the woods. His posture—back straight and head high—exaggerated his six-foot height, enabling him to stand out in any company. His stride was long rather than brisk, the walk of a tall man and also a steady, even-tempered one. The sunlight slanting through the window flashed off his head of flaming red hair, supplying it with orange glints, a banner worn by most of the Clarks.

Across the way a man in a small boat was rowing toward a landing on the Kentucky side of the river, where William lived in the family home on Mulberry Hill, above Louisville. The lone oarsman pulled slowly, the sun beating upon his back. In the wake of the small boat the current moved sluggishly. Low water this year, Clark thought, and it would continue to sink. Here, close to the falls, the river was deep enough, but farther upstream Meriwether Lewis would certainly encounter treacherous bars and shoals on his way downriver from Pittsburgh, especially in a heavily laden boat.

Extraordinary!

Turning back into the room, William Clark picked up the letter from the low table where George had dropped it. Absently, he smoothed out the pages, already creased from his frequent foldings and unfoldings. William lowered his tall frame into a sturdy wooden chair. His gaze returned to the careful script and its remarkable proposal.

The letter was dated June 19, 1803, posted from Washington, D.C. Written on cream-colored stationery in a tight, precise hand, it confirmed the news—already rumored as far west as the inns and drawing rooms of Louisville—of Jefferson's astounding success in obtaining for the United States, by negotiation with the French Emperor, Napoleon, the entire territory west of the Mississippi known as Louisiana. Meriwether Lewis asked Clark to keep this news secret, as well as the plans Lewis outlined in detail for an exploration of the newly acquired territory by way of the Missouri River, with a view of finding passage to the western ocean. Reading between the lines, Clark guessed that the President was afraid his political enemies might seek to obstruct his plans if they became known too soon. And he probably also wished to keep the suspicious Spanish authorities from becoming alarmed about American intentions in the Southwest.

The adventurer in William Clark felt a quickening in his blood. His heart beat a little faster. His eye leaped to the news confirmed in Lewis's words. ". . . very sanguine expectations are at this time formed by our Government that the whole of that immense country wartered [sic] by the Mississippi and its tributary streams, Missourie inclusive, will be the property of the U. States in less than 12 months . . ."

Small wonder that Jefferson was so eager! If all that vast, uncharted territory was to become part of the United States, then it must be mapped and defined. Only the stubborn steps of men could solidify what was claimed on paper.

Clark paused in his reading. Setting the letter aside, he fished a large, blackened briar pipe from his jacket pocket along with a leather tobacco pouch. At once he realized that he had forgotten his flints. He looked around the room, finding none, and glanced at George's cold fire. Then he sat quietly, holding the unlit pipe, staring across the room at the window, where the slanting rays of the sun created bars of light and shadow across the pine boards of the floor. A trace of movement drew his keen eye even before he heard the honking of a flight of geese passing overhead, momentarily visible out of the upper corner of the window.

The Clark family had once lived in Albemarle County in Virginia, home of both the Meriwether and Lewis families, as well as Thomas Jefferson. The Clark cabin, in fact, had been

34

on land adjoining Jefferson's. But the Clarks had moved away to Caroline County, where William had grown up. Though he and Meriwether Lewis had had similiar boyhoods, their paths had not crossed.

Clark's first meeting with Lewis was one that he recalled quite vividly, occurring when both men were in the army, Lewis a young ensign, Clark a lieutenant in command of his own rifle company. Assigned to Clark's company, Lewis had reported to his new commander with a stiff, truculent formality, his thin mouth a tight line above his stubborn jaw, as if he anticipated some rebuke over recent difficulties he had experienced involving a dispute with another officer.

With a broad grin Clark had extended his hand. "Always glad to welcome an Albemarlean!" he had said with unfeigned enthusiasm. "We need men here who can fight and shoot like true Virginians!"

They had become immediate friends, in spite of the fact that two men of more different temperament would have been hard to find. A big man physically, William Clark was amiable, steady, even-tempered, and naturally sociable, his open nature accounting for his popularity among all who knew him. Meriwether Lewis, slender, bowlegged, and of average height, was a less imposing figure, although he was regarded as something of a dandy. He was more reserved than Clark in company, more impetuous in action, so stubbornly determined that he could be careless of danger. His moods could be mercurial, ranging from the euphoric to the deeply melancholic. And although Lewis had had more formal schooling, at the time they met, Clark had a broader range of experience as a fighting soldier on the frontier.

But with all their differences, the two officers had shared much more than their common origins in Virginia. Both were intelligent, serious-minded patriots raised in family traditions of service to their country. Both were dedicated men of high honor and considerable ambition. Both were natural leaders, comfortable with command and fond of wilderness army life.

35

Both relished the challenges of battle, of breaking new trails, of pursuing new adventures, and in such pursuits they were fearless and resourceful.

What's more, they *liked* each other, a mutual regard that had been strengthened during their army service together and reinforced in Lewis's later visits to Mulberry Hill when he traveled the Ohio between posts in Detroit and Pittsburgh.

Thoughtfully, and with undeniable pride, Clark's gaze returned to Lewis's letter. "If therefore there is anything under those circumstances, in this enterprise, which would induce you to participate with me in it's fatiegues, it's dangers and it's honors, believe me there is no man on earth with whom I should find equal pleasure in sharing them as with yourself . . ."

"Extraordinary!" Clark thought again, unaware that he had spoken aloud.

"Yes, quite extraordinary," said George Rogers Clark.

William glanced up quickly, surprised to find his brother standing in the doorway.

George labored across the room, leaning heavily on a walking stick cunningly carved into the shape of a rattlesnake. He dropped into his favorite chair, his breathing harsh, his features briefly contorting in pain. His once ruddy face was now pasty, a pudding laced with fine threads of red.

"Well, now, what d'ye think of it all?" William finally asked, when George made no effort to speak.

"It matters little what I think, surely."

"Ye know it matters, George. It always has." After a moment's silence William added, "Ye should have been the one. Jefferson wanted ye to undertake this venture."

"Yes, I should have been," George Rogers Clark retorted with a flare of his old vigor. "The time wasn't right for me. Besides, he had ideas then, him and his Philadelphia friends, but little money. It's different now. It's the right time for you."

"I'm not sure. It would mean leaving so many things up in the air . . ."

"Rubbish," George said brusquely. "We'll manage." He did not say how, nor could he. But it was true that, although there were still heavy debts to be satisfied, there had been improvements in his situation. Debtors who were being satisfied, however slowly, tended to be more patient. And there was little that William could do personally for his brother now that others could not accomplish as well.

How long would the journey take? Lewis had written of his hope of progressing well up the Missouri by late fall. According to the plans outlined in his letter, he hoped to reach the western ocean by the following autumn and then to return as quickly as possible. Even if all went well, more than a year seemed certain, two years possible.

"Ye're thinking of going," said George Rogers Clark.

"It will be a long, difficult, and hazardous undertaking," William said. "And there's no minimizing the Indian danger. There are hostile Nations beyond the Mississippi who will not welcome our intrusion."

George grinned, for a moment his old commanding presence overriding the mask of illness. "Hell, yes, it will be long, difficult, and dangerous! That's what makes it so goddamned exciting. It will also be a great opportunity to win high honors and to serve your country in a manner few men can ever know. And, as for our own miserable affairs, by which I mean mine, such meritorious service to our nation as this may prove to be would no doubt be well-rewarded."

"Your services were not so well-rewarded."

George's grin faded away. "I asked for no reward," he said sullenly. But the bitterness was unmistakable.

For some time the two brothers were silent, George rocking back and forth in his chair as if he could not sit still, William occupied with the rush of thoughts. In his heart, he thought, his decision had been made even before he put down Meriwether Lewis's long letter, with a shaking hand, after his first reading.

37

 Trail

The sun was behind the two-story cabin, lengthening its shadow across the clearing surrounding it. A small vegetable garden, carefully tended now that Fanny was living here, defined one edge of the clearing. Beyond it the woods were a mysterious play of light and shadow. To penetrate the darkness of that vast country beyond the Mississippi, thought William Clark, to be the first . . .

George Rogers Clark seemed to read his thoughts. "Go for the glory, Billy," he said huskily. "Go for the glory!"

5

It was not until the 31st of August that I was enabled to take my departure from that place owing to the unpardonable negligence and inattention of the boat-builders who, unfortunately for me, were a set of most incorrigible drunkards . . .

—MERIWETHER LEWIS, S e p t . 2 8 t h 1 8 0 3

Bewildered by the chaotic scene all about him, Seaman trotted nervously beside Meriwether Lewis—changed into full uniform after his arrival at Fort Pitt—as Lewis made his way down the steeply sloping road from the massive earthenworks of the fort toward the crowded docks along the Monongahela.

It was the afternoon of July 15, 1803, another hot day in a long, dry summer. Lewis and his dog had arrived in Pittsburgh in the early afternoon. Already Lewis had dashed off a letter to Thomas Jefferson to announce his arrival at the Ohio, hastily completing the brief message in time to catch the late afternoon post. Now he was on his way down to the boatyard to see about the status of his keelboat, the primary means of transportation for the men and the tons of cargo he meant to take down the Ohio and up the Missouri. The boat had been promised for July 20, just five days away. Hurrying beside him, the dog sensed his master's impatience, the urgency in his stride.

Pittsburgh burst upon the young dog as an astonishing

scene of noisy, dusty, smoky, crowded confusion. Even his brief stay in Philadelphia had not prepared his senses for the assault of so many sounds, so many strange and pungent smells. There were people everywhere in overwhelming numbers—men with the smell of fish about them, uniformed soldiers, men wearing leather garments blackened with age and grease, finely dressed men and women, powdered and beribboned, passing by in fancy carriages and coaches. Scattered among the crowds, a few Indians shuffled, their faded blankets and ill-assorted discards of clothing drawing little notice. Most of the people who saw the young officer noticed his big black dog; the Indians stared at him with undisguised wonder. One old Algonquian, who had felt the searching winds of seventy winters, stopped to stare at Seaman as if he had seen a ghost from his childhood. The white-haired man stood rooted in the path of a heavy freight wagon. Only at the last instant did he stumble clear of the pounding hoofs and grinding wheels.

Seaman steered a course along the road among the mounds of horse droppings, but their smell paled beside the odors of human waste, of fish cuttings and garbage heaps steaming in the sun, of drifting sawdust and the pall of smoke that lay over the sprawling city.

And dogs! Dogs were everywhere—small dogs, big dogs, spotted and solid, long-jawed and short-muzzled, hounds and hunters. They foraged in every alley between the stone and log buildings; they dug into the garbage dumps and refuse piles. They barked and ran and chased and bred. And when a small, foxlike dog set up a nonstop yapping at sight of Seaman, running behind him and darting away when the Bear Dog turned, other dogs joined in. Soon there was a pack strung out behind Seaman, excited and curious, reacting to the newcomer's size. One or two showed hostility, in particular an ugly, undershot mongrel with a disfiguring scar that split the left side of his face from eye to jowls, causing part of his lower lip to hang permanently down. Named Two-Face with the cruel humor of the riverfront, this large, ill-tempered dog prowled aggressively among the pack. The other dogs ducked cautiously out of his way, and his aggressive stalking compelled Seaman to wheel about several times.

Seaman was not used to such pandemonium or strange dogs in such numbers. Not even the week on the road with Meriwether Lewis, crossing the mountains and passing through much smaller settlements, had prepared him for this crowded city. Here he felt out of his element, uncertain and insecure, beset on all sides and not knowing what to expect. By nature he was friendly and playful. Some of these city dogs bared their teeth at him as they growled and barked. They didn't seem to be playing.

Exasperated by the bedlam, Lewis turned at last on the parade of dogs, shouting and waving his arms. The pack broke. Most of them scattered and ran—in truth, much of their excitement had begun to wane even before Lewis's intervention, for the giant black dog seemed amiable and not disposed to cause trouble.

The brown, scar-faced mongrel skulked behind Lewis and Seaman as they went on their way past the market square with its colorful stalls and down toward the riverfront. Two-Face watched from a distance, suspicious and hostile. His was an attitude Seaman had never before encountered. It made the Bear Dog wary, alert, stiff-legged.

As luck would have it, the brown mongrel was a boatyard dog. He was one who had been trained by abuse and neglect, and this experience was reflected in his outlook. He was mean and a natural bully. His reaction to the strange new dog, one his match in size and weight, had a single dimension: enmity.

In the days that followed, Seaman observed the surly dog on numerous occasions at a distance. Always he seemed to be watching the newcomer, his glare revealing open hostility. Kept by one of the Monongahela boatyards as a guard dog, perhaps he sensed a rival in the big black dog who came frequently to one of the busy yards along the riverfront.

Two-Face watched and waited, but kept his distance.

The boat was not ready as promised. For Meriwether Lewis, anxious to be under way after months of planning and preparations, the days dragged into frustrating weeks.

Pittsburgh was familiar to him, for he had been here often. Long ago he had come to public notice in the town, arriving from the northwest with the Wyandot warrior Captain Enos Coon in tow. That was back in 1796, shortly after Lewis had been transferred to the 1st U. S. Infantry Regiment. In later years, shuttling between Colonel John Hamtramck's Detroit headquarters and Fort Pitt in his role as regimental paymaster, the young officer had come to know Pittsburgh well, and to be as well known among its society—including its eligible young unmarried women.

But if Pittsburgh society had known him before, it fawned over him now. He was the secretary of the President of the United States, about to embark on a special mission. On July 14, the President had received the treaty from Paris ceding Louisiana to the United States, and by August in Pittsburgh the goal of Lewis's expedition—to explore the upper Missouri, not the Mississippi—was no longer secret. There were countless questions about the affairs and gossip of Washington and speculations about the Spanish intentions in the West. Meriwether Lewis was at the center of it all.

There were parties and dinners in his honor, more invitations than he could accept. There were old friends to drink with among the soldiers at Fort Pitt, including many who had served with Captain Lewis before his appointment as Thomas Jefferson's secretary. And there was one at the post who waited anxiously for Meriwether Lewis to receive any word from William Clark in response to the invitation to join Lewis on his western expedition. If Clark declined, Lewis had already made his alternate choice, and Lieutenant Moses Hooke was eager to take up the challenge of becoming Lewis's second-in-command. Would not such an expedition, undertaken in partnership with the President's chosen leader, be a feather in any young officer's cap?

As the days dragged by, even the company of old friends and engaging young women could not soothe Lewis's growing impatience. Progress on the fifty-five-foot keelboat was appallingly slow. Lewis soon discovered that not only the boatwright but also many of his workmen were heavy drinkers. "Incorrigible drunkards," Lewis declared in an outburst of exasperation to Lieutenant Murray, newly arrived from Carlisle, Pennsylvania, with a detachment of soldiers under orders to accompany the captain down the Ohio. The builder and his workmen thought little of abandoning their work in the middle of the day while they hurried off to a favorite wharfside tavern. For the impatient, dedicated, and disciplined officer, accustomed to giving orders and having them obeyed, the indifference and unreliability of the boatmen was intolerable. They provoked him to outbursts of anger.

"You're a blackguard and a scoundrel!" Lewis shouted on one occasion, losing all patience. "Do your promises mean nothing? Nothing at all? We're already a fortnight past the date we were to sail. By the Lord, man, you've taken that long to shape the oars and poles!"

"Now, Cap'n Lewis, sir, there be no cause to speak so ill. It's true the first part goes slow, an' we was short of timber like I told you. But it's the hasty ship that sinks the quickest, sir."

"Then the *Discovery* should damned well be unsinkable!"

"I've not been well, Cap'n, and that's a fact—"

"You have been drunk, sir! That's the sum of your illness. And where are those louts who should be working now? Asleep with their jugs cradled in their arms, I suppose."

"Now, Cap'n Lewis, sir, it do no good to be so hard on 'em—"

"I want this boat finished," Lewis interrupted. "If you can't do the job, I'll find someone who can."

Thus threatened, the boatbuilder turned surly. "Ye'll find no one on this river will serve you better," he muttered.

Unfortunately, Meriwether Lewis knew that at this late date he would not locate a more dependable boatwright in the area. For one thing, most would hesitate to take the commission already given to another with whom they would have to deal long after the demanding captain had sailed away downriver. Lewis considered abandoning the larger keelboat entirely and buying several smaller pirogues. He was dissuaded from this course by the advice of experienced rivermen and, in cooler-headed moments, by his unwillingness to depart so drastically from his own carefully laid plans.

He tried cajolery, threats, anger, pleading, all to little avail. The builder hired additional workmen, and his crew worked fitfully. Sometimes the boatwright disappeared for entire days on pleas of sickness; at other times he appeared at the boatyard in a drunken state, making Lewis fearful of the quality of the boat's construction when he saw its builder stumble around the framework, red-eyed and unsteady of hand and foot.

44 Only one event relieved the nagging frustration of those days. On July 29, the letter arrived from William Clark. Yes! He would be delighted to go!

The work on the boat crawled along into August. Each day Lewis would come down from the fort to prowl worriedly along the banks of the Ohio, testing the river's depth, convinced that it was sinking even as he watched and waited. The news he pried from rivermen and soldiers coming up to Pittsburgh from points west confirmed Lewis's fears. The Ohio had rarely been so low. The summer had seen little relief from heat and drought. Soon, he was told, the river would be unnavigable for a boat the size of the keelboat Lewis was having built.

One evening in mid-August Lewis's patience wore out once more. His martial temper erupted at the boatbuilder's expense. "Damn you, sir, for a wastrel and a whining liar! If you were a soldier, I'd have you whipped! I'm tempted to do it myself, but you aren't worth the sweat it would cost."

Louis Charbonneau

The boatwright, half in a stupor, chose one of his habitual responses, which varied from cringing supplication to sullen anger—in this instance, a whining plea for more time. "It's not my fault, Cap'n Lewis, an' I'll swear to that. It's these men of mine, sir, they's good for nought but whittlin' and not for buildin' a fine boat such as you want. It'll all be done in a fortnight, and that's my promise on the good book, Cap'n, sir, and on my poor mother's grave."

"That was your promise a month ago!" Lewis raged. "I'm on the President's errand, can't you understand that? I must be down the Ohio as soon as this craft can float, or by the Lord, I *will* take the whip to you!"

"You'll have it before month's end, sir, you have my word on it. It's keepin' these whittlers sober is my biggest problem, sir, an' that's a fact."

Meriwether Lewis turned to stalk off, muttering to himself. When Seaman started to follow, Lewis ordered him back to the boatyard, speaking sharply. "See to it one of those drunken whittlers doesn't do damage to this boat," Lewis told the dog, who cocked his broad head attentively, though the words were intended more for the boatbuilder and his workers than for the dog. "Stay and watch!" commanded Lewis. He pointed toward the unfinished boat, raised on its supporting framework, long and bulky in the gathering gloom of evening.

Although he did not fully comprehend Lewis's words, Seaman had learned the basic command to stay. He also sensed the anger in his master's tone and that the boatbuilder was the object of it.

When Lewis had disappeared in the direction of William Morrow's inn, where he spent many of his evenings in Pittsburgh, one of the builder's maligned workmen crept out of the shadows. His name was Scoggins. When sober, he was a surprisingly skilled carpenter—a condition, the boatbuilder reckoned, that came about as often as Christmas. "Officious bastard," Scoggins muttered after Meriwether Lewis's back. "Thinks he can order you about like some witless private in his army."

The boatwright bristled anew at this fresh affront to his dignity. Lewis's words and tone still rankled. "I've half a mind to see his precious boat in splinters when he comes back in the mornin'."

"Aye, that would take the starch out of that fancy uniform. Serve him right, it would."

"Take the whip to me, he said. Did ye hear him?"

"Errand of the President," Scoggins scoffed. "He talks as fancy as the clothes he wears." Himself clad in dirty, scruffy, liberally patched hand-me-downs originally made for his older brother, who was three inches taller and twenty pounds heavier, Scoggins felt a generalized resentment toward the army officer in the colorful uniform that fit him like moss on a tree and was always, no matter the heat and dust of the day, as neat and clean and freshly brushed as if it had come straight from the tailor's hands.

"Off to charm the ladies," the boatbuilder sneered. A bachelor whose rough manners and fondness for heavy drinking had won him little favor from the ladies, not even from the wenches of dubious reputation along the riverfront, he envied Captain Lewis's evident success with the pretty young women of Pittsburgh who were often seen in his company.

As if on signal, both men turned slowly. Their gazes came to rest on the unfinished keelboat, even now not fully planked, although the ten-foot deck had lately taken shape astern. It was true, as the builder had insisted to Lewis in self-defense, that he had had trouble earlier that summer procuring timber for the boat. But fancy-dress officers wouldn't listen to such talk if they didn't like what they heard.

Staring at the keelboat, the men paid little attention to the big, friendly, black dog who lay quietly near the scaffolding, his eyes intent on the street along which Meriwether Lewis had disappeared. The dog was familiar to them, being always in Lewis's company, and he had unvaryingly shown a friendly disposition.

Scoggins picked up a curving length of flat iron, about two inches wide, scrap from a wagon wheel. He stepped toward

46

the keelboat, smacking the length of iron across the palm of his calloused hand with a loud slap.

"Hold on, let's not be hasty," the boatbuilder cautioned him. After all, the boat represented weeks of his labor, in which he felt a certain pride in sober moments. "The Cap'n does have a commission from the army . . ."

"If somethin' was to happen," suggested Scoggins slyly, "who's to say who done it?" When he leaned close, his breath was strong enough to give one a hangover. It made the builder thirsty.

Grinning, Scoggins turned toward the boat and raised his piece of scrap iron threateningly.

Seaman rose before him, blocking his way.

"Huh? Here, now, what's this? Out of my way, you—"

He broke off. A low rumble emerged from Seaman's deep chest. It reminded Scoggins of a gravel slide.

Seaman did not understand the actions of the workman with the strong smell on his breath and on his clothes, but he recognized the man's gesture as a threat to the charge he had been given. The boat was his to defend.

47

The rumble grew louder.

"Back off, Scoggins," the boatbuilder said quickly. "I don't know what's got into him."

"I'll show 'im this iron!" snarled Scoggins.

"Don't be a fool! The Cap'n would have your hide."

The two men, more startled than frightened, retreated a few steps. The Newfoundland had always been so friendly that they were uncertain how seriously to take his unexpected new stance. They did not, however, dismiss the big dog's reaction as a formidable barrier to their vague intentions. What had been only a halfhearted purpose hardened in the face of opposition. No mere dog would stop them. A way had to be found to divert the dog's attention or . . .

"I know," said Scoggins.

"No harm can come to him."

"Not from us," the workman said with a malicious grin. "You know ol' Two-Face, that mangy spawn of the devil his-

self? He's been givin' this black dog the evil eye ever since he
come here. Two-Face don't like nothin' else on four legs, won't
tolerate 'em. If'n he was to tangle with the captain's pride and
joy . . .''

"I don't know . . .'' Misgivings swam out of the shadows
of the yard, making the boatbuilder's head spin. But he had
drunk enough to lose the edge of common sense and to yield
all too easily to a reckless impulse.

"Ye don't have to lift ary a finger,'' Scoggins assured him.
"I be back in a jiffy with ol' Two-Face.''

As he waited, the builder paced his covered shed with
nervous, unsteady steps. His gaze flicked again and again to
the captain's young black dog. Seaman now lay calmly before
the shell of the keelboat, appearing as puppy-friendly as indeed
he had been since his arrival in Pittsburgh. The boatwright
wondered why Captain Lewis had brought a dog along if it
was true that he planned to journey far to the west, as it was
said. It must be that he took great pride in his dog.

All at once the boatbuilder wished that he had not let
Scoggins entangle him in this escapade. It was Scoggins' idea!
He wished himself safely out of it, and with the desire came
a craving for the soothing contents of his jug of Monongahela
whiskey. This latter wish, at least, was readily gratified. The
jug was stashed near at hand.

The builder's other wish had skittered out of his control.
Scoggins was back all too soon, dragging the surly, scar-faced
boatyard dog on a heavy length of chain. Scoggins hauled Two-
Face into the long, roofed shed that covered the keelboat.

Even before the hostile brown dog was dragged around
the corner of a pile of lumber into view, Seaman sensed danger.
The Bear Dog was on his feet.

Scoggins gave a gleeful cackle. "Have at 'im, y' black-
hearted devil!'' he cried. And he slipped the chain from around
the snarling dog's neck.

With the brothers and sisters of his litter, Seaman had
been in countless mock fights, some of which had got out of
hand when one or another combatant was angered by a bite

48

in play that nipped too painfully. And once there had been a brief, snarling skirmish with an older dog on his breeder's farm. But none of these battles, real or feigned, had been truly vicious. None of them, even when tempers flared, had prepared the young Newfoundland for the sight of the raging boatyard dog as it leaped toward him, fangs bared, a killing light burning in its red eyes.

Instinct took over. Fighting for survival may have been no part of the Bear Dog's immediate experience, but the knowledge whispered in his blood. The hairs rose on the back of his neck. His tail stood out. His lips drew back over huge white teeth in an unconscious snarl. A jolt of excitement brought every sense alive, every muscle taut and ready.

Two-Face was a veteran alley fighter with a score of additional scars to give witness to his prowess. He attacked the moment he was turned loose. In many of his fights he had learned the trick of surprise, of the quick, hard strike before the victim was ready to meet it, a maneuver that often determined the outcome of a clash right at the start.

Although Seaman was still a young dog, not yet fully developed and sometimes clumsy afoot, he also had a youthful quickness. And his muscles were supple and hard, toughened by the long journey from Harpers Ferry in Virginia across the Allegheny mountains to Pittsburgh. When the other dog charged, Seaman reacted instantly. He leaped to the side, turning his body as he moved. The brown dog's clashing jaws closed on hair alone.

Seaman heard those big jaws crunch. He felt the pluck at his coat just behind his left shoulder. A genuine fury shot through him, a feeling he had never known.

With a sound that was more like a roar than a snarl, he pivoted as he landed. As Two-Face broke off his charge and wheeled about, he confronted a very large, angry dog every inch his equal in size and strength.

Two-Face had anticipated that the younger dog would bolt in panic and try to escape, as most dogs did. Certainly he expected the black dog to be tentative and uncertain. Instead,

49

as Two-Face skidded about and confidently prepared to launch another attack, he found a concentrated ball of bone and muscle and hair and anger hurtling toward him.

Seaman used his weight as he had learned to use it in playful battle as a pup. Now he did not hold back or blunt his attack. He caught Two-Face before the brown dog could either brace himself or dodge clear. Seaman's weight bowled the other dog off his feet. Two-Face crashed into a wooden crate behind him. He slid away from Seaman's slashing teeth the instant before they could clamp down on the big muscle of his shoulder.

In that moment Two-Face felt something alien and chilling: fear.

He struck back. Again the younger dog was too quick for him. Black hair clogged Two-Face's teeth. It dripped from his mouth like sawdust from the teeth of one of the boatyard saws.

Two-Face raged aloud. His fury was intensified by frustration. Again and again he threw himself at the Bear Dog, who began to evade the clumsy charges with increasing ease. The shed was filled with blood-chilling snarls as the two big dogs fought.

Seaman felt the brown dog's teeth rake his hind leg, striking for his stifle in a blow that would have crippled if it had found its target. Once again Seaman was just agile enough. There was only a surface cut, a coolness and a brief sting of pain.

Seaman was learning as he fought. Two-Face was a vicious bully, but he had never had to do much more than throw himself upon his smaller, weaker victims. He had needed little skill or cunning. The dog he fought now adjusted with startling adaptability. He anticipated the timing and direction of Two-Face's reckless charges. He saw how the brown dog favored his left side, how he dipped his head in the instant before his jaws struck, as if he favored the wounded half of his face. And Seaman had quickly learned that he could not win or even survive this battle simply by relying on his superior weight and strength, as he had with his littermates.

Learning, Seaman began to watch for Two-Face's next

50

attack, the left side turned away. He watched for the dipping of that ugly head. Two-Face lunged. His jaws snapped shut. Seaman felt the dog's hot breath and the bruising weight of his charge but stepped safely clear. As the brown dog bolted past him, Seaman's teeth slashed through coat and skin and muscle like a skinner's knife. The taste of blood was in his mouth. For the first time in his life, he knew the killing urge.

The boatbuilder and his sly workman had watched the fight at first with gleeful anticipation mingled with dread, then with sobering astonishment. Along this riverfront, no dog had ever stood up to Two-Face. The scarred brown dog had ruled the yards and wharf unchallenged. How could Captain Lewis's black dog be a match for him?

But he was—no, by God, more than a match!

The boatbuilder's hands shook as he drank from his jug and wiped his mouth with the back of his hand. He wished he had never allowed this fight to start in his shed. He cursed Scoggins for dragging old Two-Face here. Why had he listened to such scheming? Disaster faced him. He would surely lose his contract—or the skin off his back.

Suddenly Two-Face slipped. The ground was wet with his blood, and his front legs went out from under him. While he scrambled frantically to catch his balance, Seaman leaped on top of him and drove him flat to the ground. The Bear Dog's huge jaws opened above his rival's vulnerable throat.

And as suddenly as it had begun, the fight was over. The killing instinct was an ancient song in Seaman's brain, but part of the refrain was in the voice of the pack. Among your own kind, you fought to win, not to kill.

The brown dog squirmed free. For a moment it appeared that he might hurl himself once more at the black dog. Then he backed away, growling impotently. Blood flowed from two deep cuts where Seaman's teeth had slashed across flesh and bone. And Two-Face's legs were quivering, no longer coiled springs of muscle. By contrast, Seaman was fresh and eager and surefooted.

Two-Face's snarls became fitful, almost a whine. When Seaman took a step toward him, the brown dog retreated. He was beaten.

"By the devil's boots, I never thought t' see such a thing!" said Scoggins as the ugly boatyard dog disappeared into the shadows along the wharf.

"Be thankful ye saw what ye did!" The boatbuilder turned on his carpenter to vent his own anxiety. "If Cap'n Lewis's dog was the one stood bleedin', it would be y'er hide would feel the cut of the whip!"

"It weren't my doin' only!" Scoggins protested. He was now quite sober, and with clarity of mind came belated panic.

"Ye brought that ugly scarfaced devil into my yard on a chain and turned him loose. I should be done with ye myself for what ye might have brought upon me."

Excitement still made Seaman's blood race. Panting noisily, he paced back and forth before the shell of the keelboat for several minutes. He listened to the two men's whining voices with only half his attention, his eyes still alert for the possible return of his enemy.

Gradually his sides stopped heaving. The song in his head became quiet. At last the big dog lay on the ground in front of the keelboat he had been ordered to guard.

Seaman's gaze moved past the boatmen toward the dark road where Meriwether Lewis had disappeared.

The boatwright and his workman stumbled out of the shed and went off muttering into the night. The boatyard was quiet. High overhead a flight of mallards streamed across the face of the moon.

Seaman watched and waited. After a while he licked steadily at two small cuts, one on his stifle and the other on a front leg. By morning, clean and dry, they would be so little noticeable that Meriwether Lewis, distracted by his own concerns and the boatbuilder's unaccustomed eagerness to please, would not see them.

Louis Charbonneau

Progress on the boat in the last two weeks of August picked up speed. The builder had fired one of his workmen without explanation and hired two new carpenters, both sober men who worked hard and late. The boat's framework was complete. The finish details went quickly.

Early on the morning of August 31, 1803, when Meriwether Lewis came down the steep road to the boatyard, accompanied by another officer and with his black dog trotting at his side, the boatwright stood at the river's edge. The fifty-five-foot keelboat rocked gently beside the dock. It had been tested two days before in the water, but now the flurry of last-minute activity had ceased. The builder wore the perplexed expression of someone who has entered a room and can't remember why. Although there clung to him a stale aroma of whiskey, he was sober.

"What is it?" Lewis demanded, wondering what else could have come up to delay his departure.

"Why . . . why, nothin', Cap'n Lewis . . . nothin' at all. That is, the truth of it is, sir, ye'll be glad to know that y'er boat is as shipshape as ye could ask. A fine boat she is, sir, I don't mind sayin'."

Meriwether Lewis stared first at the man and then at the keelboat, for the first time aware of the absence of the familiar sounds of hammering and sawing. The workmen were all standing around the yard watching him or admiringly examining the craft in the water.

"Good! I've waited long enough." Lewis turned toward the young, dark-haired officer who had accompanied him down the hill. "Lieutenant Murray, assemble your men. We leave on the hour!"

It took longer. Half of Lewis's cargo had already been sent ahead to Wheeling by wagon. A pirogue, which Lewis had purchased as a second craft to carry additional stores, was already loaded with as much as it could carry. The rest of the

cargo stood waiting on the dock in bales and barrels and kegs. The crew pitched in, aided by the dockyard workers, and by ten o'clock that morning Meriwether Lewis had the last of his stores on board.

At eleven o'clock, low in the shallow water, the *Discovery* edged away from the dock. Its journey had begun.

6

The water is low, this may retard, but shall not totally obstruct my progress being determined to proceed though I should not be able to make greater speed than a boat's length pr. day.
—MERIWETHER LEWIS, August 3, 1803

*S*luggishly the heavy keelboat pulled away from the Monongahela landings, with the smaller pirogue worrying about it like a child trailing its mother. Some ragged cheers drifted out over the water as the boats felt the pull of the wide Ohio, heeled away from the steep bluffs across the way and swung downriver.

Mouth open in excitement, Seaman stood on the flat deck of the forward hold, scrambling for balance. The crew—seven soldiers from Pennsylvania and three local civilian volunteers who claimed some knowledge of the Ohio—dug in their oars. The recruits, destined for service in the West, were all, Meriwether Lewis observed, green, towheaded youngsters for whom a trip down the Ohio was an adventure.

Shortly after getting under way, Lewis had the river pilot steer the boat ashore at the tip of Brunot's Island in the middle of the Ohio River. Here, in a picnic atmosphere, more of Lewis's friends and well-wishers of Pittsburgh society had gathered to cheer him on and toast the success of his western expedition.

The brief interlude brushed close to tragedy. When Lewis was asked to demonstrate his remarkable air rifle, which few had seen, an over-enthusiastic spectator seized the weapon and fired it accidentally. The errant bullet grazed the temple of a young woman in the crowd. After the shaken Lewis assured himself that she was more frightened than harmed, he hurried his men back into the keelboat. He had had enough of ceremony and delay.

An hour later, standing knee deep in the Ohio, its current running between his bowed legs, Meriwether Lewis felt this day that had begun in such bright promise darken with new frustration. The keelboat had run aground on a shoal at McKee's Rock. Lewis's moods were capable of wide swings at the best of times, and his reaction to the shooting incident with the air rifle on Brunot's Island had threatened to plunge him into black gloom. To have that fiasco compounded so soon by this was almost too much.

The crew jumped out of the boats with alacrity at Lewis's command, however, and he soon joined them in the river. Standing in shallow water, they put their backs and shoulders into lifting the heavily laden keelboat over the gravel bar. "Heave, lads, heave!" Lewis urged. He felt the craft lighten in the water, breaking free of the drag of the gravel. For thirty yards the men floundered in the water, lifting and tugging at the boat. And as it cleared the bar at last and slid out into the current, they all slapped each other's backs and grinned with their early success, and Lewis's spirits lifted with theirs.

The *Discovery* followed the Ohio River toward the falls below Louisville, where William Clark eagerly waited. The sun beat down upon the boats, quickly drying wet clothes, and something of the morning's early promise returned.

But before the afternoon waned, there were two more riffles to struggle over, the water at times barely a foot deep, whereas the keelboat with its cargo drew closer to four feet. Then everyone but the pilot had to leave the boat; even Lewis's big dog was ordered into the water, a circumstance he seemed to take as a lark. By this time Lewis's mood had altered. His thin-lipped mouth became a hard, determined line. He had expected obstacles. The river was not going to defeat him be-

56

fore he had started. He had boasted to Jefferson, and again in a letter to William Clark, that he would go down the Ohio even if he should not be able to make a greater speed than a boat's length per day. The words may have sounded cavalier, but they had not been an idle boast.

The long drought of that summer persisted into September. In the steamy heat, the men struggled with the barriers in the river.

The obstacles had names—Little Horse Riffle, Big Horse Riffle, Woolery's Trap, Logstown Riffle, Alfour's Run, Atkins's Riffle, Walker's Riffle, Georgetown Bar. There were sand and gravel bars, collapsing riverbanks, hidden logs, weirs of driftwood on which the keelboat or the pirogue would become ensnared. Sometimes Lewis's boastful words returned to haunt him with a nightmarish force, so closely did the boats' progress approximate his worst imagined possibility.

On September 5 the hot dry weather broke. While the weary men camped at Brown's Island that evening, a cooling rain fell. Meriwether Lewis stood at the river's edge, grinning, watching the raindrops bounce off the surface of the water like flung pebbles.

The drought was over. For the first time Lewis knew that the Ohio's level would no longer fall.

For Seaman the Ohio River was an unending delight. The thick fog that clumped over it at dawn, making travel impossible, was a mystery to be sniffed at and peered into as eagerly as he gazed into the shallow water from the bow of the keelboat. When the *Discovery* hung up on a riffle and the crew, grumbling and swearing, clambered out yet again to grope and stumble in the water, trying to haul the fifty-five foot boat over a bar or to free it from a tangled weir, the young dog stood barking on the deck or plunged into the river to splash around the men, moving them alternately to fits of laughter or brief flashes of anger.

Water was Seaman's newly discovered element. Off the

coast of Newfoundland, his ancestors had long been used for rescues at sea, or to carry lines through stormy seas to ships in peril or from ship to shore. The breed's prowess in water rescue and its companionability had made the Newfoundland the most popular "ship's dog" throughout the fishing fleets of the Atlantic and Mediterranean. Even in the China trade, many vessels carried a Newfoundland aboard. A Newfoundland's experience was bred into him, and Seaman had no fear of the river. With his strong body, webbed feet and water-resistant double coat, he was a powerful natural swimmer.

Riding in the keelboat was an exhilarating experience of which Seaman never tired. He reveled in standing with legs spread on the forward deck, his muzzle lifted to the breeze, his gaze scanning the water ahead or the forested shoreline on either side, inspecting drifting logs or peering into the green depths of one of the many islands.

When, as often happened in those first weeks on the Ohio, Meriwether Lewis had to leave the boats to prowl among the neighboring farms or villages along the river in search of teams of oxen or horses to drag the boat free of a shoal too wide for the men to conquer, Seaman trotted beside him, enjoying the brief sojourn on land. But he bounded back just as happily, ranging ahead of Lewis and the plodding teams of hired animals, eager to return to the boats and the tired, disgruntled band of soldiers who awaited their return, sometimes still standing in the river.

The farms and settlements overlooking the Ohio—the Indian name for Beautiful River—were a frequent sight, but even more often the river was a quiet solitude, contained by bluffs and steep, forested hills, a green wilderness as far as one could see. By day, bright-winged Kentucky parakeets flashed among the huge sycamores that stretched their long arms over the riverbanks. At night those same sycamores, their bark peeling with the coming of autumn, gleamed white in the darkness like pale sentinels.

That long awaited rain in the first week of September which had ended the summer's drought had brought a wel-

58

come change in the weather. The breezes on the river were sharper, carrying a whisper of chill. The nights began to feel cold. The long summer evenings were gone, imperceptibly giving way to autumn's rapidly falling curtain of darkness.

Below Wheeling, where Lewis bought a second pirogue to carry some of the cargo he had sent down from Pittsburgh by wagon, the river began to run deeper. Rarely now did Lewis have to go begging among the river settlements for help to drag his keelboat over a gravel bar—at fees that moved him to outbursts of indignation. At times it was still necessary for the men to dig a channel through one of the broader bars, but they had become expert at it—capable, Lewis wrote in his log, of cutting a channel for the *Discovery* fifty yards long in an hour's time. The current, stronger now, aided their digging. It would rush into the trough they carved with their shovels and quickly cut it wider and deeper.

Besides the cooler days and nights, there were other signs of seasonal change. Enormous wedges of ducks and geese frequently passed overhead, migrating south for the winter. Clouds of passenger pigeons sometimes filled the sky, blotting out the sun and goading Seaman into yelps of frustration. The white puffs of their dung fell over the river and the travelers in the boats like flakes of snow, and the busy whirring of countless wings awakened in the dog's memory the buzz and clang of saws in the boatyards along the Monongahela. At night, above the croaking of frogs in the marshes and the occasional hoot of a great owl from the surrounding woods, sometimes there would come a loud crash as a tree branch broke under the weight of the roosting flocks of pigeons.

Below the settlement of Marietta, the little fleet of boats entered the Long Reach, a welcome straight run of some eighteen miles. Halfway along this stretch, as the boats pulled around a narrow island, one of the soldiers pointed ahead and shouted. "Somethin' in the river, Captain Lewis!"

A black smear stretched across the Ohio. Alarmed, Lewis ran forward to the deck where Seaman stood. He saw at once that the obstacle was in motion, proceeding steadily across the

59

river rather than toward them. It was not a single mass but a swarm of animals. They were swimming from the northern to the southern shore—at this turn of the Ohio, more from west to east—as if mirroring the migration of the birds overhead.

"By the saints, sir, they's squirrels!"

There was something frantic in the astonishing migration, and Lewis soon concluded that many of the animals would drown before reaching the far bank. Yet they seemed excellent swimmers, their dark bodies swift and light in the water.

"They's good eatin', Cap'n," one of the Carlisle soldiers said.

Lewis needed no urging. Quickly he rejected the notion of shooting the squirrels in the water. Instead he came to the swift decision to give his young dog another test. If Seaman was to be of genuine value on the expedition to come, perhaps, like the men to be recruited, he would have to be hunter as well as a sailor, worker as well as companion.

"Seaman!" The dog looked up eagerly at the sound of his name, his long tail waving in expectation. Lewis pointed toward the swarm of squirrels, not thirty yards away, parting as the keelboat approached. Seaman had already been watching the sleek fat bodies with mounting interest as they skimmed across the river, as thick as autumn leaves on the forest floor. "Catch us a squirrel!" Lewis ordered. As the dog hesitated over the unfamiliar command, Lewis said, "Fetch!"

Instantly the dog launched himself into the river. The crew stopped rowing. All three boats drifted. The men who were not already on their feet rose to urge Seaman on. "You can do it, boy!" "Get 'em!"

Their shouts followed him over the water, but he needed no encouragement. The excitement of the chase possessed him now. The squirrels tried to veer away from him. They were agile swimmers, but there were too many of them for all to escape. Seaman was also surprisingly quick in the water. He dove at one fat squirrel and missed. The line of brown and black bodies slid away from him, heads above water, eyes round and bulging in panic.

There was a brief thrashing in the water, a sharp shake of the dog's head that obscured what was happening. A cheer rang over the river as the Bear Dog's head turned toward the boats, the huge jaws filled.

"Fried squirrel tonight, lads!" cried the Carlisle soldier who had first spotted them. "A feast fit for a king!"

Writing in his journal a few nights later, in the cool of the evening, a few yards from the campfire where the smell of fried squirrel still lingered along with the memory of fat sizzling and spattering on the coals, Lewis confirmed the soldier's favorable verdict, finding the fat squirrels, when fried, a pleasant food. He speculated over the reason for the strange exodus of the squirrels from the west side of the river to the east, effectively taking them toward the south. He discounted a search for food, noting that the walnuts and hickory nuts, the favorite food of the squirrel, were in abundance on either side of the river, and concluded that a warmer climate to the south was their object. "I made my dog take as many each day as I had occation for," he wrote. "Many of these squirrels were black. They swim very light in the water and make pretty good speed. My dog was of the newfoundland breed, very active, strong and docile, he would take the squirrel in the water, kill them and, swiming, bring them in his mouth to the boat . . ."

Nearby, Seaman lay contentedly on the ground, having shared in the feast of squirrel as a reward for his labors—he had caught and killed a half-dozen that day—watching Lewis at the now familiar scratchings with his pen, unaware of the modest praise being recorded.

High overhead a wave of geese blotted out the moon, making the night as dark as a cave. The dog lifted his head. His ears came up at the sound of the distant honking. The call stirred something in him, a dim memory, as if, like the great flock passing overhead on its annual autumn migration to the south, he had embarked on a journey that was new and at the same time ancient.

Trail

A low whine came from his throat, causing Lewis to interrupt his writing and glance at his dog. He saw Seaman's gaze turned toward the dark sky, and for a moment Meriwether Lewis also paused to listen to the muffled beat of a thousand wings, like distant drummers of a celestial army.

7

On the evening of the 1st inst. I again dispatched my boat with orders to meet me at Big Bone Lick, to which place I shall pass by land . . .
        —MERIWETHER LEWIS, October 3, 1803

n September 28, 1803, Meriwether Lewis brought his little flotilla in to the landing at Cincinnati. In four weeks on the river, which was as low as it had been in any riverman's memory, he had covered five hundred miles—as much of it walking on the river bottom, he observed wryly, as riding its current.

The young soldiers of the crew were fatigued, and Lewis decided to lay over for a few days to allow them to rest and recuperate. As for his civilian volunteers, their faces had changed several times en route; some he had fired, others had lost enthusiasm with each new sandbar encountered.

At Cincinnati Meriwether Lewis took on two new recruits, but these were not casual volunteers. One, John Colter, had come aboard a short distance upriver at Mayville, Kentucky, and ridden down to Cincinnati. Now Lewis agreed to accept him provisionally for the western expedition. Colter was a lean, blue-eyed Virginian like Lewis himself, an experienced woodsman and hunter who had once served in Simon Kenton's Rangers on the frontier—exactly the kind of man Lewis had hoped to find for his permanent crew.

Of the second newcomer, who volunteered the day the boats came to at Cincinnati, Lewis was less sanguine. George Shannon was an appealing youth, a smooth-cheeked eighteen years of age, intelligent and possessed of some education. While not one of those "gentlemen's sons" Lewis was quick to turn down—this was not an expedition for dilettantes—he was not a frontiersman either. Still, he was eager, strong, willing to work, and Lewis took him on trial. "As far as Louisville," he told the young recruit. "After that, we'll see." A few weeks on the river would tell the tale, he thought.

Since leaving Pittsburgh, Meriwether Lewis had had little news of events concerning Louisiana. On July 14, he knew, Thomas Jefferson had received the treaty from Paris—"ceding Louisiana according to the bounds to which France had a right," Jefferson had written. Now, nearly three months later, the U.S. Senate was still debating the treaty—which was probably why the President still wished Lewis to remain circumspect about the true goal of his expedition, Lewis thought, even though the truth was a poorly kept secret. The men recruited were still to be signed on for a vaguely defined exploration of the Upper Mississippi. They would learn the real destination later, though that destination was hardly unknown to the British and French, who had provided Lewis with "passports" from their governments, or to the Spanish, whom Jefferson had sounded out about such an expedition even before Congress had authorized it. No, the President's concern was his political opposition. The Federalists remained bitterly opposed not only to any of Jefferson's schemes for the West but also to the purchase of Louisiana. As for Lewis's venture, "they would rejoice in its failure." Give them no ammunition, then, with which to stir up the public. Organize the expedition, collect the supplies, recruit the men, move into position on the Mississippi, learn as much as possible about the western country —that must be Lewis's agenda.

Since it was now clear to Lewis that he would no longer be able to proceed any distance up the Missouri until spring, he no longer felt the same urgency to travel as far as possible on the Ohio each day. He could, in fact, spare the time for a diversion of his course that was close to the President's heart. Jefferson was fascinated by evidences of the great woolly mammoth that had once inhabited the North American continent. He was even intrigued by the possibility, suggested in some Indian tales, that the great beasts might still be found in that untracked wilderness that Lewis and his friend Clark would seek to penetrate. Having heard of new discoveries at a place called Big Bone Lick near Cincinnati, Jefferson had hoped that Lewis might find time to visit the site . . .

Dr. William Goforth was a handsome man, elegantly attired for the afternoon, whose somewhat protuberant eyes fixed Meriwether Lewis with a quizzical gaze. Lewis had come upon the doctor just as he was leaving his office and examination room, which was located in the neat brick house in which he also made his home.

Goforth leaned on a gold-headed cane and said, "You have the advantage of me, sir. Captain, is it not?" He nodded at the single epaulet on Lewis's right shoulder, a sign of his rank.

65

"Captain Meriwether Lewis, at your service. And you, sir, must be Dr. Goforth."

"No 'must be' about it," Goforth retorted. His eyes, if that were possible, widened. "But, of course . . . Captain Lewis! The town has been agog with talk of your expedition up the Mississippi."

Lewis smiled. "I have some doubt that's an appropriate description, Doctor. But I believe it would describe the excitement over your own fossil discoveries. As you must know, Mr. Jefferson has a great interest in scientific matters, and I couldn't visit your city without affording him a firsthand report of what you've found."

"Splendid! You must see my collection at once. You're just in time, Captain Lewis. I was on my way to my studio at this very moment. Come along, dear boy, come along!"

He strode off, coattails flapping. Lewis, whose care for the cut and fit of his uniform was well known, appreciated the doctor's black broadcloth coat, the white linen shirt and brocaded vest, and the sartorial punctuation of the gold-headed cane.

The doctor's studio was a converted barn at the rear of his property, accessible by a side road as well as by a winding path through a well-tended garden. A horse and buggy stood next to the barn, suggesting that the doctor had had some other immediate errand that, out of politeness, he was prepared to postpone. He had brought many of his best specimens to Cincinnati, he explained as they followed the garden path, but they had soon overflowed the space in his house. Still more recent finds remained where they had been unearthed at Big Bone Lick.

At the door of the barn Goforth turned abruptly. For the first time he appeared to notice Seaman, who had followed the two men from the house, pausing to sniff amidst a small hickory grove. "A handsome dog. But surely, Captain, you didn't intend to bring your dog into this house of bones!"

With a rattle of laughter Dr. Goforth threw open the door to his studio. Belatedly, Lewis realized that the doctor's sally had expressed mock horror rather than real dismay. Nevertheless, he told Seaman to stay outside. Lewis stepped into the barn at the moment Goforth threw open the shutters over the south window, flooding the large, open room with afternoon sunlight.

Meriwether Lewis stood transfixed, staring at rows and piles and stacks of giant bones and artifacts, heaped and scattered about the barn in apparent confusion.

In the spring of that year Goforth, an avid student and collector of fossils, had dug a large pit at Big Bone Lick, uncovering quantities of what were said to be mammoth and elephant bones, many in an excellent state of preservation. Although Lewis had seen Dr. Charles Willson Peale's nearly complete skeleton of a mammoth at his museum in Philadelphia, he was unprepared for the size and range of Goforth's collection. There were many huge teeth, from four pound fragments to whole teeth weighing up to twenty pounds. There was a large thigh bone, entire ribs, and one whole backbone of a mammoth. Proudly the doctor led his visitor to two prizes set against the south wall near the window, where the light played over the smooth, yellowish surfaces of two mammoth tusks. One, about five feet in length, was as big around at its base as a heavy man's thigh. The other was even larger, a curving, spiraling tusk at least seven feet in length.

"By the Lord, I must have one for the President! These are remarkable finds, Doctor! Are there more like them? Mr. Jefferson will be anxious to receive a representative collection if it's possible."

A frown disturbed Goforth's cheerful countenance. "I am forbidden to continue my digging by the owner of the property on which the mud lick is situated, Captain Lewis. And his agent informs me that I must not remove any more bones from the Lick. Perhaps your good offices might be used to intercede in my behalf. After all, if the President of the United States desires it . . ."

"I'll do what I can, Doctor. I take it there are enough bones like these remaining at the Lick to make up a shipment?"

Goforth laughed. "Enough! There are bones scattered about like pebbles. There's a tusk even larger. I haven't seen it myself, but I have a young assistant continuing my work at Big Bone Lick, looking after what has been unearthed these past five months, which I've been unable to bring here. I'm informed he has found a tusk that weighs one hundred and eighty pounds—nearly twice the size of these, Captain Lewis! Imagine it!"

"I must see it."

"Then you must go to Big Bone Lick," said Goforth. "You must see for yourself how a taste for salt brought the greatest beast ever to roam this continent to a tragic end!"

On the first day of October, Lewis sent the keelboat and the pirogues downriver. Theirs would be a longer journey of some fifty miles around the point below Cincinnati, a trip expected to take three or four days. Departing three days later, Lewis would travel overland across the neck of land, about a third of the distance the boats must navigate. They would meet at the river below Big Bone Lick.

Riding horseback as far as the Lick, in the company of one Captain Findley, a friend of Dr. Goforth's, Meriwether Lewis set off with his dog on the morning of October 4. Refreshed by three days of rest, Lewis enjoyed the crisp air of a bright October day. The breeze was fresh, and the scattered clouds tumbled swiftly across a sky so blue as to seem a painter's exaggeration. The terrain was flat, a rich benchland ideal for farming, Lewis thought, an enterprise in which he had once expected to spend his life, far from thoughts of wilderness expeditions. Stands of gum and sassafras spun autumn gold in the brightness of the morning.

Near their destination the land became more barren, devoid of trees, covered only by dead grasses and dry brush. They came upon a wide buffalo path, worn a foot deep into the earth and as broad as a highway. It led straight as a ramrod to Big Bone Lick.

The salty mud of the lick, an irresistible lure to many animals over countless centuries, covered about an acre. It was trampled flat all around, with no vegetation, studded with rocks and fragments of what Lewis took to be bones sticking out of the ground. While Lewis and Findley exchanged greetings with Dr. Goforth's young assistant, Seaman began to roam around the lick, sniffing curiously. Sometimes he would stop and give a low moan deep in his throat, a sound of perplexity and disturbance.

Meriwether Lewis paused at the edge of Goforth's main excavation. It was a pit about thirty feet square, its floor sunk eleven feet deep. Here the lick was spongy underfoot, the

ground moist, and Lewis thought of the doctor's vivid description of giant mammoths unwittingly venturing onto the
swampy ground to search for the muddy salt, sinking into the
mud before danger signaled, caught at last as if in quicksand.
Over the flat, barren terrain Lewis's imagination conjured up
the hoarse bellows as the huge animals struggled to free themselves from the morass, only to sink deeper and deeper . . .

"I must see this giant tusk of yours," Lewis said to the
young man, who was eager to oblige the doctor's friends.

"Come down into the pit, then, Captain Lewis."

Lewis hesitated, an echo of the lost mammoths' bellows
lingering in his mind. With a rueful shake of his head over
his imaginings, he clambered down into the hole, out of the
sunlight and into shadow, where white bones were arranged
in piles, where the bottom of the pit was as cool and damp
and silent as a grave.

He stayed at Big Bone Lick most of the afternoon, fascinated by the ancient story it told, exclaiming over the size of
the huge tusk the youthful assistant had found in a nearby dry
pit, marveling at a nearly complete upper portion of a mammoth's skull, examining and weighing and pondering the
many fragments of ribs and legs and teeth. As the afternoon
waned, with the help of Goforth's assistant and Captain Findley, he gathered together a representative selection of teeth
and bones, including the large tusk. The news of Thomas
Jefferson's interest having quieted the landowner's objections,
Lewis arranged with Findley for the collection to be shipped
down the Mississippi to New Orleans, from where it would
eventually be sent to Jefferson at Monticello. The President,
thought Lewis, would be delighted with such fine specimens.

At last, with the sun low above a line of trees to the west,
Lewis thanked Findley and the young man, conveyed through
them his respects and gratitude to Dr. Goforth, and reluctantly
took his leave.

He whistled for Seaman, who, after exploring the area on
his own in the first hour after arriving at the Lick, had been
unusually subdued. He had spent the rest of the day lying

quietly near the large fossil pit where Lewis was preoccupied. At Lewis's summons, the dog bounded over to him. The two moved off together, walking across the flat bench, heading west.

The land seemed unnaturally silent and empty, devoid even of birds singing, as if the earth itself stood mute, remembering those ancient, trumpeting cries of death.

Approaching the Ohio in gathering darkness along a trail that wound between forested hills, Lewis was relieved to see the glow of a campfire in a clearing above the south bank of the river. Moments later he glimpsed the dark bulk of the keelboat, flanked by the two dugouts, tied up at the river's edge.

Shadows crossed before the flickering light of the fire. As Lewis and Seaman drew near, a sentry challenged them. "It's Captain Lewis," another soldier said at the same moment Lewis called out cheerfully. He felt the pleasure of any soldier returning from a solitary mission to rejoin his detachment.

Over a cold but welcome supper, Lewis learned that the boats had come around the point and reached this landing without incident. "We hoisted sail most of the way today," said one soldier. "Beats rowin' any time, Cap'n, when the breeze is up."

Seaman had hung back near the edge of the clearing. Glancing toward him, struck by the dog's unaccustomed withdrawal, Lewis noticed for the first time an unnatural bulge on one side of the dog's muzzle. Frowning, he called Seaman to his side.

Seaman came reluctantly, head down. When he sat before his master, his tail thumped the ground, not wildly but with a slow, ingratiating sweep, as if he expected to be scolded.

Gently Meriwether Lewis pried open the powerful jaws.

One of the soldiers whistled. There was a general murmur as Lewis held up a large fragment of bone, which on closer examination proved to be a piece of a tooth, the tip broken off. The fragment, Lewis judged, weighed at least two pounds. Dr. Goforth had enthusiastically displayed much larger teeth, several of them whole, but Seaman's fragment was still an impressive reminder of the formidable size of the mammoth jaw from which it had come.

Seaman had carried the tooth overland, concealed in his mouth, for four miles.

Meriwether Lewis laughed abruptly. He hesitated, then said, "All right, Seaman, it's your souvenir. By the Lord, I think even the President would approve!"

GEORGE SHANNON'S JOURNAL

October 5th 1803

I have been temporarily engag'd by Capt. M. Lewis to join his Expedition up the Mississippi. This journey which promises much honor and rewards if I should be Chose to become a member of the Permanint Party, will commence in the Spring, and is to last approximately 18 mos.

I joined the Expedition at Cincinnati, where we set forth on Oct. 1st, and made our way down the river without Incidence for 3 Days, where we were joined by Capt. Lewis and his dog. They had been to visit Big Bone Lick.

The next morning very foggy, and we was delayed two hours before our Departure. River has been very low but it is deeper below this place and it is expected that we will make easy passage. Some showers this evening. A flock of geese passed overhead at Dusk and continued for an hour a beautiful sight to see.

Oct. 18th 1803

Capt. Lewis's dog is of the Newfoundland breed. He is the largest dog I have known, and very friendly. He is also a fine Swimmer & Hunter &tc. He rides in the keelboat, which is the Discovery, and likes to look in the water and barks at the fish.

Besides myself there is another volunteer for the Expedition who is John Coalter from Virginia. He has been living in Mayville Kentucky and joined

71

Capt. Lewis there. He is 28 yrs. so he is ten years my senior, and is said to be a very excellent hunter. He is well disposed to me. The other members of this Party at present is not Permanint Party.

October 24th 1803

Today was cold & rained but we traveled 15 Miles. Tomorrow we will reach Louisville and the Falls. John Coalter and myself are to enlist in the Army, and will receive $10. per month pay plus clothing and necessaries. When we return from our Journey each man is also to receive a grant of land from the Govt. which is equal to the portion given by the U. States to those who served in the Revolutionary War.

I feel this is a very good Bargain, to be so well paid for taking part in this Great Adventure.

8

The young men that I have engaged or rather promised to take on this experdition are (four &c.) the best woodsmen & Hunters, of young men in this part of the Countrey. . . . A judicious choice of our party is of the greatest importance to the success of this vast enterprise . . .
——WILLIAM CLARK, August 21, 1803

y the Lord!"

William Clark laughed aloud at Meriwether Lewis's familiar exclamation, but he was moved more deeply by the obvious warmth and pleasure in Lewis's face as the two men clasped hands, while around them swirled the noisy confusion of the dock at Louisville.

"It's been much too long, Clark!"

"Ye're a sight for sore eyes, my friend. Your letter about the expedition was a bolt from the blue, but I can't tell ye what a fire it built in this cold stove."

"I hardly believe the fire had gone out."

"Near enough. But such a venture . . . no man could fail to be excited by it." William Clark read an answering gleam in Lewis's eyes. The fire burned there, he thought, and no mistake. "We have so much to talk of. Ye'll stay with me tonight at Mulberry Hill. And we'll find room for your men as well."

Lewis demurred. "The crew had best stay with the boats to secure our provisions." He glanced back at the dock, where the keelboat and the two pirogues had been tied up. "We'll have to unload to run the falls."

"Aye, your boats must needs ride high in the water."

The Falls of the Ohio were a formidable barrier to river passage, made more difficult by the fact that, during the two-mile stretch of rapids, the river dropped some twenty-four feet through a series of broad limestone steps. The whole way boiled over projecting rocks, and venturesome boats had to steer precariously along one of three narrow channels, called chutes by the rivermen, to get through without being smashed to kindling.

"The falls can't be worse than what we've been through," said Lewis. "The river is so low, it has been the very devil much of the way."

"I feared as much. I can't tell ye how many nights I've been awake these past three months, wondering how ye were getting on. And, I confess, thinking what a grand experiment this expedition will be." Clark felt an awkward embarrassment over his rush of enthusiasm. "But ye're here now, thank heaven."

74 "It was my first goal, to join you here without losing half of my provisions along the way." Lewis paused a moment. "Now this grand experiment can really begin."

The two men grinned at each other, the last few years when Lewis had been in the East sloughed off like an unwanted skin, their easy friendship revived in the instant of reunion. It was like that with a true friend, Clark thought. A year of absence, two years, even more meant nothing when you came together again. But Lewis looked drawn, he thought, more tired than he would admit. That was always his way, to push on regardless.

But that eager brightness in his eyes—ah, what a story that told! It was all that William Clark had hoped to see.

They rode up to Mulberry Hill at dusk, turning along a private road between two rows of tall locust trees. Then came a gate, and at the top of a rise the three-story log house with its wide porches and two huge stone chimneys that contained the house like giant bookends. Lewis glanced over his shoulder across the river valley, where the Ohio shone like old pewter in the fading light, toward the shadowed bluffs on the far side. Mulberry Hill had been built strong enough to defend against Indian attacks; it was also a setting of tranquil beauty.

The locust trees that flanked the drive, mature now, had been much smaller when Lewis saw them for the first time, accompanying Clark home on leave the first Christmas they had served together in the army. He remembered vividly the love and happiness that had filled the Clark house, the sense of solidity and warmth and permanence. But Clark's parents had both died within a few years, his mother on Christmas Eve in 1798, his father a short time later—of a broken heart, it was said.

Meriwether Lewis had kept in touch with William Clark after Clark's resignation from the army, through occasional letters and those rare but special visits when Lewis was able to stop at Louisville while traveling the river on his military duties, especially when, as regimental paymaster, he had traveled frequently from Fort Pitt to the far western posts. He had always found a warm welcome at Mulberry Hill.

William Clark had moved with his family from Virginia to the Ohio River valley when he was fourteen, joining George Rogers Clark, who had already settled there. As traffic on the river became a flood and the settlement grew, the new Clark home on Mulberry Hill soon became a center of Louisville society. But at the age of nineteen William had left home, following in the patriotic footsteps of his brothers—all five of whom had fought in the Revolutionary War—by volunteering for the Indian-fighting army on the western frontier. During the 1780s more than a thousand settlers had been killed by Indians in Kentucky alone. Having been too young for the Revolutionary Army, William was eager to do his duty by joining in the battle to defend the western frontier settlements against Indian raids.

The tall, serious-minded young soldier had learned back-country woodcraft, shooting, and riding as a boy in Virginia,

Indian lore and a love of adventure from his older brother
George. Courage, he had always had. In the army he honed
his survival skills. He became a self-taught mapmaker and
engineer. Comfortable with the discipline of soldiering, he
became an experienced Indian fighter and a natural leader.
He fought the Wabash under General Charles Scott in 1791.
He experienced the bitter taste of defeat when General Arthur
St. Clair's command was routed by the Shawnees under Te-
cumseh. And at the age of twenty-two, by then a lieutenant in
the 4th Sub-Legion serving under General Anthony Wayne,
he fought at the battle of Fallen Timbers that finally brought
victory in the long Indian campaigns of the Old Northwest
Territory. By 1796, when Clark retired from army service, relative peace had come to the frontier settlements.

William Clark had been a fine officer, Meriwether Lewis
thought. But it was not simply his soldierly qualities that had
led Lewis to choose him as a partner in command for the
expedition. Something else had always drawn him to Clark
. . . something in the man.

Ease. He was comfortable with William Clark to a degree
he enjoyed with few men. There was in Clark a core of stead-
iness and a total absence of malice. Venturing into battle with
him or into the wilderness, you knew that you would never
have to wonder where he was in a crisis. Nor would you lose
precious moments to petty wrangling or the need to dance past
an obtrusive egoism. He and Clark might disagree on some
matters—how could it be otherwise? But they could differ
without bitterness, reason without acrimony.

Eighteen months, Lewis thought. He allowed at least that
much for the journey to the Pacific. Time enough for countless
differences among even the most judicious of friends. Too long
to share command with a man of sharp edges and prickly
temper.

Over dinner that night, served by Clark's beaming manservant, York, who appeared as joyful of Lewis's arrival as his
master, the two old friends filled each other in on the intervening years. Clark's account ranged from his attention to his

family's affairs to the sadness that had come to Mulberry Hill with two deaths so close together. He also chronicled his occasional contacts with the army after his resignation.

"I heard that Henry Dearborn asked you to help with a fort on the Mississippi. When was that? Just last year, wasn't it?"

"Aye, I gave him my recommendations on the choice of a site and the design of a fortification to defend it." The request from the Secretary of War had gratified Clark at the time, acknowledging as it did the respect with which his experience as soldier and engineer was still regarded, even though he had been officially out of the army for the past seven years.

Lewis spoke of his time in Washington as the President's secretary, of the long evenings in Jefferson's study, of the President's wide-ranging scientific curiosity and remarkable intellect. And, inevitably, he responded to Clark's curiosity—not scientific, he pointedly observed—about the young women of Washington society and their predilection for parties and fancy dress balls.

"I'll warrant ye've become the very devil on the dance floor, Lewis!"

"You know better. I have barely learned not to inflict severe pain. And what of you? Are you going to become a fierce old Kentucky bachelor like George? I would've thought you would have been well and truly broken to tandem harness by now."

"Give me time, give me time. In fact, I've met a young beauty I have my eye on . . ." He had, in fact, though Clark thought Judith Hancock was still hardly more than a child, albeit a bewitching one. When he returned from the western expedition, however—the errant thought brought a quickening to Clark's heartbeat—perhaps then . . .

"I trust she'll wait till you return. If she has a good head on those white shoulders that you no doubt fancy, she will. A dandy catch, you'll be."

"Ye're a fine one to talk! I'd give anything to have seen ye with your ballroom belles!"

Their banter was ritual, a signature of friendship that found no risk in good-natured ragging. They retired to Clark's study where York brought brandy, and the talk went on by candlelight while the big house grew quiet around them.

"These men you've engaged," said Lewis. "I'm anxious to hear more of them."

"Ye'll meet them tomorrow. There are seven of them, all Kentuckians, all but one of them unmarried. For the most part, they're young and hardy, and they know the back country. I've had many other volunteers, as ye can imagine, all manner of gentlemen's sons who would savor the adventure, but I've turned them down as unsuited to our purpose."

"We need stout young fellows used to hard work."

"Aye. And I think ye'll like these Kentuckians. They're staying across the river now at my brother George's place, below the Falls in Indiana Territory."

"I'm sure we agree on the kind of men we need. I've taken on two recruits only—that youngster you saw on the docks, name of Shannon, and John Colter, who is a good hunter—another Kentuckian, though he came across the mountains from Virginia as a boy. They'll do, I think." For a moment Lewis paused. The fatigue he had been denying all evening seemed to fall like a great weight across his shoulders. "The soldiers watching the boats go only as far as Massac."

Clark rose as York appeared quietly in the doorway, as if on signal. When Clark picked up the lamp from the corner of his desk and held it higher, his red hair caught the glow of the candle and appeared to burst into flames. "Your room is ready, Lewis. I know ye're tired."

"I'm not sure I'll be able to sleep," Lewis protested.

"Come to bed," said Clark with a smile. "Before ye fall down on your face."

Meriwether Lewis looked at him. Though he had never seriously doubted his choice, still . . . the confirmation of his judgment during this day's reunion brought him intense relief. William Clark was the best kind of soldier and friend with

whom to share the burden of the expedition's command ...
and the honor.

Good for the long haul.

Five days later the Corps of Discovery prepared to leave Clarksville, west of the Falls on the Indiana side. Down on the quay
below George Rogers Clark's cabin, the three boats of the
expedition were drawn up. Members of the Clark family of
Louisville—who made up a crowd all by themselves—had
been joined by friends and well-wishers. There was even a
small group of local musicians, ready to blend fife and drum
in a salute to the parting adventurers.

During these few days at the Falls, Seaman had discovered something new to him, the joys of playing with children.
The three young boys of the Clark brothers' twice-widowed
younger sister had brought a lively turmoil into George's sometimes gloomy bachelor loneliness, and their noisy, scampering
play had excited in the Newfoundland a joyful, puppyish enthusiasm. All three of Fanny's boys cavorted now with Seaman
on the sloping meadow that overlooked a spectacular view of
the Ohio River's rapids.

"Come on, Seaman—fetch!"

"It's my turn," Benjamin O'Fallon protested as the Newfoundland bounded across the meadow to retrieve a stick his
older brother Johnny had thrown. In this as in other games
with the children, Seaman was tireless, retrieving the thrown
stick or a ball over and over again. And the boys neither noticed
nor cared if in his excitement he drooled a little over the prize
he brought back each time.

Meriwether Lewis had shown the boys the few tricks he
had taught Seaman during relaxed moments on their travels
and while they waited in Pittsburgh for the *Discovery* to be
completed. The dog would perform his tricks for the boys with
patient amiability—sitting up, retrieving, or rolling over on
command. The latter was such a comic turn, given Seaman's

79

ungainly size, that it never failed to send Charles Thruston—Fanny's youngest boy, from her second marriage—into spasms of uncontrollable laughter, so that he too ended up rolling on the ground.

"Sit!" Ben O'Fallon ordered sternly. "Seaman, sit!" One clear command, Captain Lewis had told the boys, was better for both dogs and men than a multitude of different urgings.

The Newfoundland sat on his haunches, front paws dangling before him, jaws open and long tongue lolling, looking like a large black bear.

It was a bright, warm, October day, and the boys and the dog paused a moment as they heard the trilling of a fife from the quayside below them. The cheerful sound was oddly sobering, in spite of its lilt, as if it were a signal that these innocent, playful moments would soon be over.

Meriwether Lewis and William Clark lingered on the long front porch of George Clark's log house as if reluctant to take their leave. For several moments no one had spoken. It was like the quiet time before a battle, Lewis thought, when men spoke in low voices if at all, wrote letters, or lay on their blankets staring up at the sky and picturing the faces of loved ones. The battle to conquer the vast uncharted continent was not imminent—it was still many months away—but the approaching moment of departure from Clarksville awakened such feelings.

From the porch Lewis could see most of his new recruits standing around the quayside or in the boats, their preparations complete, doing what soldiers had always done—waiting. "You've done well with those Kentuckians, Clark," said Lewis.

Most of the men Clark had recruited were not, in fact, Kentucky-born, though they called themselves Kentuckians now. Sergeant Charles Floyd was a "true Kentuckian," in his own words. But his cousin, Nathaniel Pryor, had moved west from Virginia, as had Lewis's recruit, John Colter. The Fields brothers, Reuben and Joseph, had fought for Kentucky but they came from Culpeper County, Virginia.

One of the lucky finds among the men was a cousin to Daniel Boone, John Shields, who had moved from Virginia to Tennessee. At thirty-five, the oldest of the recruits signed up so far, he might prove to be one of the most valuable, the leaders felt. He had run a blacksmith shop and was a skilled gunsmith. He could also shoot as well as any of the recruits. The corps would be well qualified in gun repair and black-smithing, for the tall Irishman, William Bratton, shared those skills with Shields.

Among the Kentucky woodsmen who had signed on, there was also one Pennsylvanian, George Gibson, whose value was enhanced by his experience as an Indian interpreter. He had another talent that would be appreciated on a long wilderness journey: he would bring his fiddle along.

All were rugged backwoodsmen, not afraid of hard work or in awe of the wilderness. They would form the nucleus of the detachment, capable of meeting any exigency. The seven soldiers from Pennsylvania who had dug a path in the Ohio for the keelboat would leave the expedition for reassignment at Fort Massac, a hundred miles downriver.

"Aye, Billy knows his men," said George Rogers Clark. "And the two ye had on board, Captain Lewis, should also do well, though the one is a mite green, I'm thinkin'. What age is young Shannon, anyway, seventeen?"

William laughed. "Eighteen, or so he claims. And how old were ye when ye first came down the river, George? Not much older, I reckon. And alone, to boot."

"Save for Indians and the Good Lord," George admitted with a smile. "But I was old for my age."

William did not deny it. His brother had been an officer in the frontier militia when he was barely twenty, the commander of the fort at Harrod's Town at the beginning of the War of Independence when he was only twenty-four. Lewis's youngest recruit might not be another George Rogers Clark, but he was an eager, hardy youth. Some were man enough at such an age; others would never be.

George disappeared into the cabin, emerging a moment later with a jug in his hand. Ceremoniously he popped the cork. "I have some of Kentucky's finest blackberry brandy here, Captain Lewis, if ye'll join me in a toast to you and Billy and your expedition."

Concealing a smile at the careful phrasing, Lewis said, "I'd be delighted, General."

"It's a jug I've saved for such a special occasion. As ye may have heard, I'm not one to keep good drinkin' whiskey long on the shelf."

"I put no stock in gossip, General."

George poured the brandy into cut glass snifters. William did not remember them. A gift, he supposed, from one of the men who had served under George and now lived back in these Indiana woods, men who still idolized their former leader. George was stone cold sober, William noted gratefully, as he had been since Lewis's arrival. He had welcomed the much younger officer cordially and treated him with an almost deferential respect. He wants it to go well with me, William thought. He felt a sting of emotion, a welling-up of love for the older brother he too had idolized.

"All going well," said George Clark, "the Senate will approve the French treaty ceding all of Louisiana to the United States, and the Spanish will be gone from their posts on the Mississippi by Christmas. I'll drink to that."

"You would've hurried them on their way a bit sooner, I recall," said Lewis. "I've heard little news since I left Pittsburgh. But there is no doubt of the circumstances already published here. Louisiana is ours by purchase as soon as the Senate approves."

"By God, Jefferson gambled!" George said admiringly, gazing toward the west, where the ribbon of the Ohio pointed like a shining arrow. "But he knows what it will mean. He's long had his eye on the lands west of the Mississippi."

Lewis nodded, sipping his brandy, which was heavy with

fruit but smooth to the taste. "The President is more concerned now with the British than the Spanish or French. The Spanish are weak in Louisiana, and Napoleon has his hands full in Europe. But the British . . ." He shook his head. "Did you read the journal Alexander Mackenzie published of his expedition across Canada?"

"Aye, I've read it," said George.

William Clark glanced at him in surprise. "The Scotsman who reached the western ocean? Ye never spoke of reading his account, George." I shouldn't be surprised, William thought. George read everything of exploration he could get his hands on.

"There's little that Mr. Jefferson also hasn't read that could be of moment to our purpose," said Lewis. "Mackenzie claimed to have discovered the headwaters of the Columbia, but I'm doubtful of it. The river he found forbade passage, and that doesn't correspond with other accounts. An American ship, under Captain Gray, sailed up the Columbia a hundred miles from its mouth about the same time Mackenzie was claiming to have found the river impassable. There's little doubt the Scot was too far north and found another river entirely."

"But in his book he set forth a plan for British posts at the Columbia and other western ports," George said thoughtfully. "If they could succeed, they would control much of the fur trade as well as trade with the Orient. Captain Gray, of course, has given us a prior claim."

Lewis agreed. "And if we can get there by way of the Missouri as we propose, there will be no denying our claim. The French treaty cedes to us all of the lands west of the Mississippi drained by that river, the Missouri, and its tributaries, as far as the Continental Divide. But if we succeed in reaching the Pacific, America will have not only Louisiana; the Columbia basin will also be ours."

"Aye." George's eyes were bright. "From the Mississippi to the western ocean, gentlemen, Americans will come and plant their corn and build their churches. There will be no

83

stopping them." He raised his glass. "I envy the two of you. If I were a younger man . . ."

Meriwether Lewis and William Clark drank with him in silence. Like Thomas Jefferson, Lewis thought, George Rogers Clark had peered beyond most men's horizons. The strength and passion and vision which had made him one of the dominant leaders on the western frontier still throbbed in his voice.

A clamorous shouting broke the momentary silence. Two of Fanny's boys hurtled up the steps to the porch. Behind them Seaman paused, tongue lolling out from the joy of his romp with the children in the meadow. The dog swung his gaze toward the river, as if to reassure himself that the boats and his companions were still there.

"We've been playing with Seaman!" Johnny O'Fallon cried.

"Can we have a dog like him, Uncle George?" his brother Ben pleaded. "Can we?"

The general laughed. "Ye'll not so easily find another dog will ride the Falls in a boat."

"But can't we have one like him?"

"We'll see. Ye'll have to ask your mother about that."

The boys exchanged eager glances. "Let's ask!" cried Ben.

"No, let's get Charles to ask."

They shared small boy cunning over the knowledge of their mother's weakness for her youngest child. The two boys tumbled off the porch to race down the slope toward the gathering below, where Fanny had gone to watch the preparations for departure. Two other Clark brothers, Edmund and Jonathan, were also there, along with their sister Lucy and each of their families, all of them having come across the river by ferry that morning for the occasion. Seaman bounded after the two boys, his exuberance matching theirs.

"He's a fine lookin' dog," said George.

Meriwether Lewis smiled. "But you're wondering why I chose to bring a dog along on such a venture."

Louis Charbonneau

William, who had entertained the same question, said, "If I know ye at all, Lewis, ye had a good reason."

"Yes." For a moment Lewis hesitated. "Mackenzie took a dog along."

George Clark chuckled. "I wouldn't have thought ye a superstitious man, Captain Lewis."

"Call it what you will, but there's no denying what the Scotsman accomplished, even if he didn't find a successful trade route across the continent, going too much overland. We can learn from him, as we must learn from everyone who has made the attempt. Besides," he added, "I believe you'll like my dog well enough when you know him. And he'll make a fine guard dog."

"Ye'll be glad of that," George said diplomatically.

"He looks big enough to tangle with a bear," said William Clark. "And if I know Indians, they'll like as not fear him more than they will fear us."

Meriwether Lewis regarded his old friend with pleasure. It was the kind of calm, reasoned judgment he had anticipated when he made his choice of a partner in command of the expedition.

George broke a momentary silence. "Ye'll want to catch what light is left of the day," he said. "The night comes early by the Saints' Day."

William chuckled. "George knows what it's like to set off from the falls when the dark comes early."

"Eh? What's that ye say?"

"Don't pretend ye've forgotten, George. D'ye know that story, Lewis? Back in '78, when George organized the campaign in the West that took Kaskaskia and Cahokia and forced General Hamilton to surrender at Vincennes, they set off from Corn Island, just there above the falls—ye'll have seen it coming by. It was midday, the sun high overhead, and just when those benighted soldiers pushed their boats into the river, preparin' to ride the falls and prayin' they wouldn't take a dunking, just then the sky turned dark and the sun

85

blacked out. It was an eclipse, of course, but I believe at least half those men thought George had done it himself, and the other half were certain that it was a sign of what was in store for them."

"Aye." George's rumble was reminiscent, a half-smile on his lips. "I had to talk faster'n a preacher on a foundering ship to make it look a favorable sign."

Meriwether Lewis smiled. "I've heard that story in every army barracks in the west, General. And I've heard it said that George Rogers Clark could enlist the heavens above if that's what it took to whip the British."

The three men on the porch laughed over the old story. And by the time their amusement faltered, each knew that the awkward moment of departure had come. William cleared his throat noisily and said, "Come along, George, and see us off."

"I'll not be comin' down."

William and Meriwether Lewis both protested. Lewis said, "The men will be disappointed, General. As will I."

"I can see ye off from the bluff. My bones don't take kindly to the climb."

William knew it was more than that. George would watch from the palisades overlooking the river, where his gaze could follow them long after they would be lost to the view of those down by the quay. It was a bittersweet time for George, William understood, a moment mingling old hopes with new pride in seeing one of his own blood continue the American journey he had once taken so far.

That promontory was the reason George had acquired this particular point of land for his own, long before he was able to build the cabin. From this high lookout, he could gaze down the river toward the west, his far vision seeing beyond the reach of ordinary eyes, into the realm of dreams.

"George . . ."

George Rogers Clark gripped his younger brother's hand in both of his. "Remember what I said, Billy . . . go for the glory."

Louis Charbonneau

Down by the river road, the Kentuckians watched Captain Lewis's dog cavort on the grassy slope with the children. They commented among themselves in the skeptical manner of soldiers, causing the youngest recruit, George Shannon, to rise to Seaman's defense. "He be a fine, friendly dog," Shannon insisted. "He traveled the river like he was born to it."

Shannon was in awe of the leathery Kentuckians who had enlisted in the expedition here at the Falls. They were a taciturn lot, at least on first acquaintance, and he had a feeling that he would have to prove he belonged in their company before he would be accepted as one of them.

It was an approval he was determined to merit.

"Ain't no place for a dog, goin' upriver," one man said.

William Bratton, a tall Irishman with a stern, dour outlook more like a Scot than a son of Erin, suggested that the black dog looked strong enough to pull a plow. "By the looks o' that keelboat, maybe the Cap'n oughta brung a team of them big dogs."

"He's big," said Reuben Fields, "but he ain't tall enough to pull in the river without drownin'."

"Well, hell, you ain't much taller," said his brother Joseph with a chuckle. "We best keep you outa the water."

Reuben rested a cool gaze on Joseph's lean, elongated features and said, "It ain't how far you is off'n the ground what counts, it's how long you can stay upright."

The bantering ceased for a moment when the imposing figure of York, William Clark's black manservant, came into view down the steep path toward the quay, with Clark's campaign chest carried nonchalantly on one shoulder. A tall, very dark-skinned man with an impressive paunch that threatened to burst the front of his white shirt, York had a jovial personality that had already earned grudging acceptance among the hard-eyed Kentuckians. If any of them were surprised that Captain Clark was bringing his servant along on the expedition, it was not their place to question that decision. And York—as John

Shields, the thick-armed blacksmith, muttered—was obviously able to carry his weight. "Or d'ye think that chest is empty?" he inquired incredulously.

York arrived with his own entourage—hordes of Clark family children who adored him and, weeping in contrast to the youngsters' excitement, Cupid and Venus, George Clark's two ancient black servants. Whereas York, along with the family home across the river on Mulberry Hill, had been left to William in his father's will, the two old female slaves had been George's only inheritance, under the practical realization by old John Clark that anything of greater value would have been claimed by George's many creditors.

Enjoying the attention he was receiving, York consoled the two old women cheerfully. "I'll be fine now, I'll be jes' fine. You jes' got to look after your own selves now, an' you look after Gen'l Clark. He'll be needin' you more than ever now, with me an' Cap'n Clark gone away up the Miss'ippi." The attempt at consolation produced an anguished wailing. York merely grinned and patted Venus gently on one of her sticklike arms. "Stop fussin', Venus, I'll be back before you knows it. You jes' be here waitin'."

"I done lived my time," Venus sobbed. "It be time f' me to go."

"Well, now, you got a good reason to stay awhile, so's you can see me an' Cap'n Clark come back up the river one day. You promise me you'll hang on an' not let the Good Lord take you till you see me comin' home?"

The old woman sniffed tearfully. "You gives me a reason to hang on," she said, " 'til I sees you home safe."

"You promise?"

"Ah promises."

"Cupid? You promise, too?"

"Ah promises."

The two old slaves, white-haired and bent—shrunken, George said, to half the size they had been when they were John Clark's servants—clung to each other as York, still carrying the campaign chest, stepped easily onto the keelboat.

Louis Charbonneau

Moments later the Kentuckians and the other soldiers dropped their casual air and came alert as Meriwether Lewis and William Clark descended the path that wound down to the quay, Clark in his new captain's uniform, Lewis with his bicorn hat perched jauntily atop his fair hair, his clear blue eyes sharp and eager. While Clark accepted handshakes and hugs and well-wishes from his horde of relatives, Lewis cast a critical eye over the cargo portioned out among the three boats, noting with a frown that the keelboat was low in the water. He stepped aboard as William tried to escape the earnest affection of his family. A veritable river of red hair, thought Lewis, gazing over the crowd. He spotted William's sister Lucy among the throng, and her name alone was enough to make him think of his mother, Lucy Marks. He had written her from Washington on the eve of his departure. Was she thinking of him now, back home in Virginia, wondering where her oldest son was and how he was faring, with a mother's habitual worry? He felt a surge of nostalgia for the early years of family love and warmth he had left so far behind—and now proposed to place an entire continent away.

Then Clark was standing beside him on the plank deck of the *Discovery*, and Lewis called out the order briskly, "Cast off!"

The crew jumped to it, casting off the ropes with the unsolicited help of one of William's red-haired nephews. Seaman happily took his station on the forward deck, and when cheers rose from the crowd and a drum rolled, the dog's deep bark joined in. Amidst the chorus the boats pushed out into the current. The rowers' oars dug deep, and the boats swung downriver.

Glancing up at the familiar bluff, William Clark felt his excitement lanced away and his eyes smarted. The tall, stoop-shouldered figure of George Rogers Clark stood on the rim, outlined against the sky in lonely isolation.

Go for the glory, Billy. A fleeting thing, glory, when it could so easily be snatched away. Still, it was a tribute to George that even now he found words in his heart to encourage

his younger brother, so long after the cheers for his own towering achievements had died.

For God and country. William Clark heard the words in his mind as if George had spoken them.

"And for you, George," he said aloud. The gusting river breeze plucked the words from his lips and blew them away.

Long after the boats had vanished around a bend in the river, the tall figure stood alone on the high bluff, peering toward the haze that shrouded the far western hills.

9

I inclose you also copies of the Treaties for Louisiana. . . . The act for taking possession passes [the Senate] with only some small verbal variations from that inclosed, of no consequence. Orders went from hence, signed by the King of Spain & the first Consul of France, so as to arrive at Natchez yesterday evening, and we expect delivery of the province at New Orleans will take place about the close of the ensuing week . . .
—THOMAS JEFFERSON TO MERIWETHER LEWIS,
November 16, 1803

he black dog crouched in the tall grass at the edge of the clearing, a rumble in his chest like distant thunder. Then he hurled himself at the figure on all fours before him.

George Shannon rolled clear. As he tried to scramble to his feet, his scuffed black boots skidded on the wet turf. While a few of the watching soldiers called out encouragement— "Get 'im, Seaman!" "Chew his leg off!"—the dog threw his weight at the young recruit, catching him off balance, and the two tumbled along the ground, Seaman growling ferociously, Shannon laughing as he covered his head with his arms.

So, in the cool of autumn, Seaman was initiated into the rough humor and horseplay of the corps of volunteers. His first birthday had passed in September. By now he had grown to his full height, about twenty-eight inches at the shoulder; in the coming months his bones would continue to thicken, and he would gain more weight and power. His glossy coat, marked by the single white star on the chest, was dense and full with the approach of winter. And though he still brought a puppy exuberance to mock fighting and wrestling with one of the soldiers to enliven idle moments in camp, he had gained ma-

turity during the first river months, like a boy on the edge of manhood.

For Seaman the journey down the Ohio had become an accepted pattern of life, one to which he adapted even more readily than the men manning the oars and poles. He took his place each day in the *Discovery* as if by natural right. He enjoyed the company of the Pennsylvania soldiers and the Kentuckians, and even more those forays on shore with Meriwether Lewis, the dog sniffing out stray scents along the river bottom while Lewis tried to make use of Benjamin Smith Barton's botany lessons, cataloging specimens of early winter growth.

At night the big dog explored the area around the campsite, satisfying himself that the woods and brush were innocent. Then, as the men rolled into their blankets, the fire burned low and the camp grew quiet, Seaman would take his self-appointed place near the entrance to the officers' tent where Lewis and Clark, Sergeant Floyd, and York slept.

He was aware, always, of the casual stirrings of tired sentries, any unexplained rustling in the woods nearby, or the scent of a strange animal in the vicinity. Then his nose would lift and his ears prick, until he was satisfied that no danger threatened.

Seaman shared the men's food, receiving scraps of meat or fish or bread. Game was plentiful along the river, but there was little time for hunting. Although the mass exodus of squirrels from the north side of the river had diminished, Seaman was still occasionally sent on an eager plunge into the river to catch one of those sleek, plump animals, a stray from that season's mysterious migration.

With the coming of November, cold air masses moved down from the north, tightening an icy grip over the Ohio River valleys. On some mornings frost crusted the ground; on others chill, damp fogs settled over the river, turning the surrounding wilderness into forests of mystery where cold smoke curled among the blackened trunks.

A week after leaving Clarksville, the three boats sailed past Shawneetown, just beyond the Wabash. On November

10, the detachment encamped below the mouth of the Cumberland, which here ended its long tumbling run from high in the Allegheny Mountains near the Virginia border. At noon the following day, a smudge of smoke defined a bluff overlooking the north shore; shortly thereafter the blunt shapes of the blockhouse and barracks of Fort Massac took shape. There were murmurs among the seven soldiers from Carlisle; this was the end of their journey.

George Drouillard was a tall, lean man. His weathered face was the color of his buckskin leggings and jacket. His hair, tied into a single queue that hung down the back of his neck, was long and very black. His cheekbones were high and prominent, his nose a narrow beak, his dark eyes steady, revealing little of the thoughts behind them. Everything he did was quiet, thought Meriwether Lewis, even his silent walk, toes turned in and steps close together in the Indian manner, his feet clad in a pair of blackened moccasins that passed over the ground without a whisper. He spoke little, and Lewis could not decide if it was simply his nature or the fact that both his English and his French were often somewhat fractured.

Drouillard was, in the French jargon, a *métis*; his mother had been a Shawnee, his father a French trapper. Pierre Drouillard had also been a scout and interpreter for George Rogers Clark, at whose urging the two captains had sought out his son, then stationed with the U. S. Army at Fort Massac.

The three boats of the western expedition had arrived at Massac on November 11, breaking the monotony of daily routine for the soldiers stationed there. Drouillard shared the interest of all the soldiers at the fort in the two captains and their mission. He was by nature an adventurer, born on the frontier and as native to the woods as a deer. But he was also, Meriwether Lewis thought, a cautious man.

Rumors of the western expedition had arrived well ahead of the boats, and a number of volunteers, including seasoned regulars from Captain Daniel Bissell's company like Virginia-

93

born Joseph Whitehouse and John Newman of Pennsylvania, had promptly signed on. But the man Lewis and Clark coveted more than any other, Drouillard, seemed in no hurry to commit himself, though he had agreed to travel on assignment to South West Point, Tennessee, to lead a group of potential recruits from that military post to the expedition's winter camp.

Everything Meriwether Lewis had heard about Drouillard was favorable. The officers at Fort Massac had offered high praise both for Drouillard's prowess as a hunter and his skill in the use of Indian sign language. Moreover, he did not appear to be an indecisive man; the opposite was true. Drouillard was as self-contained as anyone Lewis had met. Yet the western expedition, with its goal of exploring the upper Missouri and whatever river, heading with that, might offer passage to the Pacific Ocean, ought to have intrigued him more than he had shown. How could it fail to do so?

Or was he, Lewis wondered with sudden intuition, weighing the commanders he would serve under during such a hazardous adventure, much as Lewis himself judged his volunteers?

A grudging smile touching his lips, Lewis accepted this possibility.

In the late afternoon the two men paced slowly along the edge of the bluff, glancing down occasionally at the activity around the boats tied to the wharf below. The expedition had been delayed several days at Massac, partly because Lewis had taken ill with ague and a fever, from which he had now recovered. Behind them the muffled beat of a drum rolled over the parade ground at retreat. Now and again Drouillard's thoughtful gaze wandered toward the captain's black dog, who, after accompanying the men for a while, had now decided to lie quietly on a patch of turf, watching them with an alert, intelligent gaze, as if he understood what they were saying.

"General Clark could speak no ill of your father."

"*Mon père* . . . he alway speak very high of de general."

"And Captain Clark and myself would be happy to have

you join us. There are excellent hunters among the men who have enlisted, but you would be first hunter and interpreter."

"They be good men."

"If it's a matter of pay, we can offer you twenty-five dollars per month for the duration of the expedition, the pay of a second lieutenant. Plus a warrant for land to be awarded on your return, the same as each man will receive."

"Pay's fair," said Drouillard laconically.

He watched Lewis's big dog rise and stretch languidly. Seaman strolled closer, as if he found Drouillard as interesting as the man found the dog. He sniffed at Drouillard's buckskin pants and worn moccasins. Observing them without comment, Lewis found himself reluctant to appear more eager to have Drouillard sign on than he had already shown himself.

There was a long silence, marked by the muted call of retreat from within the fort behind them, before the hunter said, "You will make de winter camp soon, I think."

Lewis nodded. "It'll be spring before we can move at all up the Missouri. In any event, there are matters still to be addressed with the Spanish at St. Louis, and we'll also be hiring more men, as you know, at Kaskaskia, besides those you'll be bringing from Tennessee. The time will be well spent."

"This expedition . . . she be very big, I think." Drouillard's tone suggested an unspoken skepticism about so large an enterprise. Perhaps, like many trappers and traders—even an adventurer like George Clark—Drouillard had misgivings about the unwieldy size of the expedition Lewis planned, believing that it might more successfully be accomplished by a smaller group, unencumbered by big boats carrying tons of provisions, a few men able to travel swiftly and lightly and offering no visible threat that might alarm potentially hostile Indian tribes.

"Captain Clark and myself are determined to reach the Columbia. I'll feel even more confident of our success if you choose to join us." Lewis concealed his impatience with dif-

95

ficulty, an effort he would not have made for a lesser man.
Lewis and Clark had privately agreed that Drouillard would
be invaluable to the corps, which would call upon all of his
skills as an Indian interpreter, hunter, and woodsman. Lewis
could be stiff-backed, but for this half-breed frontiersman, he
would bend a little. "When might we have your word?"

"Fore ye leave, I reckon."

Lewis checked a reply. After a moment he said, "We'll
make our camp on the east side of the river, close to the Missouri's mouth. No point in antagonizing the Spanish authorities
at this stage. Our flag will fly over St. Louis soon enough. But
you'll come with us to the Mississippi? I'm anxious to visit that
Indian camp you spoke of."

"*Oui.*"

"Good. You can leave from there for South West Point."
Getting Drouillard to make the recruiting trip to Tennessee,
even without his own enlistment, was the first real commitment of any kind from him. Let a man take one step, Lewis
knew, and the next was always easier.

Drouillard merely nodded. Like others of his kind on
the frontier, he was not one to waste words when a nod would
do.

Lewis gazed down at the wharf, where his three boats
were tied up, loaded, and ready for departure. "We'll go
down to the Mississippi on the morrow," he said. The quiet
words gave no hint of the excitement they brought him.

After Lewis had gone down the steep steps toward the riverfront, followed by his black dog, Drouillard continued to watch
them from the top of the bluff. In the soft light of dusk the
river had a silver sheen, like a polished mirror. Clark, the
hunter noted approvingly, had been busy with the boats, su-
pervising details of checking and redistributing cargo. Lewis
joined him at the dock. Seaman, tail waving jovially, greeted
members of the corps.

Drouillard had said nothing to Lewis of his interest in

the captain's dog. The fact that he was a large, handsome, and imposing animal was not enough in itself to kindle so much curiosity. Seaman had awakened memories of tales and legends that took Drouillard back to his childhood.

Drouillard's father had given him his name, a lean tough constitution, a Frenchman's pragmatism, and an early training that had made him at home in the wilderness and an excellent rifle shot. But his Shawnee mother had raised him during his earliest and most impressionable years. From her, he had learned a different way of looking at nature, at life and death, at dreams and mysteries. In her stories, told in a soft voice that still whispered in his mind like a gentle breeze stirring the tall grass of the prairie, he had been transported to the time and place of her people before the coming of the white man, before the Spanish gold hunters and the French trappers and the English fur traders and soldiers. They were stories in which the spirits of the forest, of the wind and the earth, of wolf and bear and buffalo were more real than the harder edged reality of growing up.

Once, across the river from Detroit in Canada, George Drouillard had studied some centuries-old cave drawings, too ancient for anyone to know who had made them. Crude, simple drawings of stick figures, with colors as natural to the rock on which they were drawn as a berry among leaves, they were nevertheless vivid fragments of history. In one of them, a panorama of scenes from many seasons and many hunts, there had been a drawing of a magnificent black dog, as large and full-coated as a bear. In the pictograph he was not shown as a camp dog, a creature of no importance, the property of women, like most camp dogs; rather he was one with the hunters and warriors. He was there, a creature of legend, because he had earned the homage of those unknown ancient hunters and warriors. He was like the Great Dog to whom it was important to pay tribute when a deer was slain ...

Such a dog, thought Drouillard, was an omen of good fortune. He thought of the large encampment of Shawnees and Delawares on the west bank of the Mississippi, almost

opposite the mouth of the Ohio. What would they make of Captain Lewis's dog? And what of the tribes of the Missouri and the Great Plains, the Osages and Arikaras, the Sioux and Blackfeet and Shoshonis? Was the Bear Dog also part of their histories?

Drouillard, weighing Meriwether Lewis's offer to join the western expedition, knew that the Bear Dog was a part of his decision.

10 I believe that his mission has no other object than to discover the Pacific Ocean, following the Missouri, and to make intelligent observations . . .

—GOVERNOR CARLOS DEHAULT DELASSUS
St. Louis, December 9, 1803

The Corps of Discovery left Fort Massac on November 13, a cold, rainy evening. Three days and thirty-five miles later they passed the point where the Ohio River flowed into the Mississippi.

The men in the boats felt the Mississippi before they saw it. The Ohio had widened visibly, now more than a mile from shore to shore, its waters dark and swift under a leaden sky. What the men felt was a strong pull, as if a giant hand beneath the surface of the river had seized the boats and thrust them forward. There was no need for oar or pole or sail, except for the keel oar to steer. The boats surged forward on the swift tug of the current.

Coming around the point, they were suddenly hurled outward into the Mississippi, and in moments they were carried downstream. The men dug in their oars, pulling against the powerful drag of the river as they fought to turn upstream. The lighter pirogues had easier going, but now, for the first time, the crew felt the full, frightening weight of the keelboat fighting against a relentless current. While they had only a short distance to travel up the Mississippi, in the spring they would try to push and drag and tow this heavily laden barge more than sixteen hundred miles up the Missouri.

They kept close to the east bank, portions of which had crumbled, and slowly edged past the mouth of the Ohio and the debris it spilled into the larger river. The men strained and sweated in spite of the biting cold, feeling the astonishing power of the river.

Lewis pointed toward a cove, whose shelter was made more favorable by a huge tree that had fallen full length into the river and buried itself, becoming a reef against which mud and branches and river detritus of all kinds had piled up. The boats struggled into the calm water of the inlet, out of the cold wind and free of the pull of the Mississippi's current.

They made camp. Soon after the tents were thrown up and fires built, Drouillard approached Lewis and Clark, who were standing beside their tent, and pointed across the river. A smudge of smoke spread over a large area, drifting out over the river on the westerly wind. Sketched in charcoal against this horizon were the domes of some huts and wigwams. The shelters appeared to stretch for some distance along the riverfront, marking the dimensions of a sizable Indian camp.

The two captains exchanged glances. "That's the village you spoke of?" Lewis asked Drouillard. "Would you know any of those Indians?"

Drouillard grinned. "If I look hard enough, might be I even find some kin."

Anxious to cross the river to meet the first large body of Indians to be encountered on the expedition, Meriwether Lewis was prevailed upon by the sudden coming of darkness to wait until morning. At dawn Drouillard went across. He returned about two hours later. The encampment, he explained, was home for a band of Shawnees and Delawares who had moved south from Cape Girardeau.

A prominent Indian trader, Louis Lorimier, had origi-

Louis Charbonneau

nally suggested to the Spanish governor the idea of a Shawnee and Delaware Indian settlement at Ste. Genevieve, above St. Louis, as a peaceful buffer against the forays of the more war-like Osages. The Spanish had readily acceded to the proposal. And if they had been pleased by the resulting peace along the river and at St. Louis, Lorimier had also profited, for he was in a strategic and officially sanctioned position for trading goods with other Indian tribes as well as with Missouri River trappers. Eventually the main settlement had been moved south to Cape Girardeau, with Lorimier as the commandant. The encampment near the mouth of the Ohio had been formed by members of that village.

Both the Shawnees and Delawares were Algonquian in origin, Drouillard explained as the small party crossed the river later that morning in a pirogue. The Delawares had been es-tablished on the Atlantic seaboard, but conflict first with the savage Iroquois and later with the equally ferocious English settlers had driven them from their ancestral lands over the mountains to the Ohio River valley. Some of those had drifted farther west to the Mississippi, where the Shawnees had long been established. Louis Lorimier's contract with the Spanish had enabled the Indians to settle in Spanish territory on the west side of the Mississippi. Both tribes were corn growers, friendly to Americans, weary of conflict.

A group of leaders of the settlement were on hand as Lewis and Clark, Drouillard, and three soldiers disembarked on the west bank. Among the first to jump from the bow of the pirogue was Seaman.

The village, which sprawled across a grassy meadowland above the river bottom, was even larger than it had appeared at a distance. It was organized into clusters of round wigwams interspersed with the rectangular longhouses familiar among many Eastern tribes. The structures were permanent, anchored by posts set in the ground and covered with woven saplings plastered over with mud. All of these houses, which sur-rounded several open central areas like plazas, were roofed

101

over with cypress bark. There was a smoke hole in each roof, and the pall of smoke from continuous fires in every dwelling hung over the entire village.

The area was crowded. Women worked by their houses or under thatched open shelters; children raucously played games in a large game field or among the dried brown stalks in the corn field; men smoked and talked and curiously watched the white men from the far side of the river. Many seemed impressed with the visitors' uniforms—Lewis had insisted on full dress for the occasion—and all were openly intrigued with the large black dog accompanying the white men, chased at a safe distance by a congregation of excited Indian camp dogs.

At a meeting with several leaders of the village in the largest of the central plazas, before a large round winter council house, Lewis tried out a speech he would refine in coming months. He told the Indians of his mission on behalf of the Great White Father in Washington, who was now to be the
Father of all the peoples on both sides of the Mississippi and Missouri rivers. If the Indians understood him, or were impressed, it was difficult to know, for their faces remained impassive. They responded politely, sharing their tobacco and hospitality with obvious intent to demonstrate their friendliness to the emissaries of the Father in Washington.

Among them were many striking figures. The Delawares were taller than most Indians, lean and fine-featured. One chief, whose hair had been plucked from his scalp except for a single central crown or cock's crest, wore a handsome coat of turkey feathers that fell from broad shoulders to his knees. His prominent cheekbones bore slashes of vermilion, a color favored among the Delawares and many other Algonquian tribes. The term "redskin" had first been given to the Indians on the Atlantic seaboard by early English settlers not because of the color of their skin but because of the bright red makeup they liked to wear.

The tall Delaware chief was joined by an equally impressive Shawnee, a man of middle age and dignified bearing whom Meriwether Lewis thought to be as handsome and respectable, he murmured in an aside to Clark, as any member of the United States Congress. They accompanied the visitors through the village, and after a while Lewis noted that the Shawnee leader shared the village's fascination with one particular member of the party—Seaman. They marveled at the amiable black dog's calm demeanor amidst the clamor of the village and his quick responses to Lewis's slightest command.

When the members of the expedition finally returned to the palisades overlooking the Mississippi, preparing to return to their camp across the way, the tall, dignified Shawnee reappeared. This time he carried in his hands a beaverskin pelt of obviously fine quality. He held it out toward Lewis, his gesture suggesting that he wished Lewis to take it.

Lewis turned to Drouillard. "What does he want? Is it supposed to be a gift?"

Drouillard spoke to the Shawnee, his knowledge of the language making the use of signs unnecessary. After a brief conversation, Drouillard's eyebrows lifted. He hesitated a moment before turning to Lewis. "He want you to inspect de quality of his beaverskin, *Capitaine*. But he offer you no gift. He want purchase your dog."

Lewis stared from him to the Shawnee, too startled to reply.

"He offer t'ree of his best skin for de dog," said Drouillard. He added quietly, "For him it be a very fine offer. He want you know he admire your dog . . . *beaucoup*."

"But . . . by the Lord! Why? Why would he make such an offer?"

"He say . . . de Bear Dog would bring honor and good fortune to his house."

The offer, Meriwether Lewis realized, was a serious one and must be treated with respect. Setting aside his wonder, Lewis sought an appropriate response. "Tell him . . . tell him I'm honored. But my dog has been especially chosen for this

journey I make on behalf of the Great White Father in Washington. It would be . . . bad medicine for me to sell him at any
price."

Drouillard nodded impassively. His explanation to the
Shawnee seemed to take much longer than Lewis's brief
speech warranted. When he paused at last, the Indian bowed
with a politeness that could not conceal his disappointment.
He replied at equally ponderous length.

"What does he say?" demanded Lewis.

Drouillard grinned. "You no can hurry an Indian when
he is be polite, *Capitaine*. He say he understand. He say he
have one fine white horse he have turn down many offer for.
Your dog be like dat white horse."

Lewis took leave of the village quickly, sending Seaman
down to the boat ahead of the party, for he was determined
not to engage in further haggling or to provoke an incident.

"You best get used to it, *Capitaine* Lewis," said Drouillard
as they boarded the pirogue. From the bluff above them, dozens of Indians watched—among them, Lewis saw, the disappointed Shawnee who had coveted his dog.

"What do you mean?"

"Did you no see de way dey all watch your dog? He be
something very special to them. You best know it, *Capitaine*
. . . there will be other Indian want him. It might be they won't
all be so polite."

Arrival at the Mississippi seemed to release something in Meriwether Lewis. Instead of pushing on immediately, he lingered.
Setting up a base camp a short distance above the mouth of
the Ohio, he went on exploratory excursions up and down the
Mississippi with Clark and a small group of the men. He practiced his celestial observations and made botanical and zoo-
logical notes to add to his journal.

The detachment left its mooring near the mouth of the
Ohio on November 20. When Clark came down with a chill,
Lewis left him with the boats while he was put ashore south

of Cape Girardeau, where he intended to call on the commandant. George Drouillard had set off for Tennessee, but Lewis carried a letter from him addressed to Louis Lorimier. Lewis had discovered that Drouillard was Lorimier's nephew, related through the French trader's Shawnee wife.

When Lewis came to Cape Girardeau, he found Lorimier at a horse race on the highland south of the settlement. The turbulent scene reminded Lewis of the boisterous, colorful horse races in backwoods Kentucky, with rough frontiersmen drinking and wagering, betting with reckless enthusiasm, and often brawling over the outcome.

Lewis arrived just after the main race and found Lorimier busy settling disputes, surrounded by a din of shouting men. The old trader greeted him warmly before turning his attention back to two bettors who were close to blows over the last race. One man had seized the other's horse—horses, cattle, and cotton were the principal medium of exchange in the wagering, Lorimier explained.

Amidst the turmoil Lewis studied Lorimier, who was something of a legend along the Mississippi frontier. During the Revolution he had been a fiercely loyal Tory. He was credited with having led an Indian war party that captured Daniel Boone, and he had fled to the safety of Spanish territory across the Mississippi when George Rogers Clark attacked his post in retaliation.

Now sixty, Lorimier remained a vigorous, dynamic man. His hair was still black, with scarcely a thread of gray in it, and reached in a long queue down his back to his knees.

When he had resolved the most serious of the quarrels, Lorimier turned to Lewis with a Gallic shrug. "*Eh bien*, my luck she is bad, *mon Capitaine.*"

"You lost, then?"

"*Oui, oui*, I have lost four good horse in this race . . . maybe two hundred dollar. Ah, what the hell, a fool who bet on a horse will never be rich—at least not for long, eh?"

Cheerful in his loss, Lorimier invited the young officer to his home for supper that night. Lewis was so taken with the

meal and with his cordial reception that evening that he even forgot Lorimier's Tory sympathies. Not only was the food the most decent he had had since departing Louisville, but, as Lewis reported enthusiastically to William Clark when he rejoined the boats late that evening where they had landed above Cape Girardeau, the company was even more memorable.

"Lorimier's squaw is Drouillard's aunt, I take it?"

"Yes, yes, and a handsome woman for her age. But the daughter! You should have met her, Clark!"

"Ah," said Clark, understanding dawning.

"No, really, she is a delight! Quite the most agreeable, affable girl. She dresses plainly, I admit, but that is even the fashion in the East these days. And she is remarkably handsome, as pretty as a painting, absolutely the most decent-looking female I've seen since leaving Louisville."

"Let's sit down, Lewis, and you can tell me about her. Sick as I am, I'm not sure I can take this standing up."

The boats made good progress up the Mississippi from Cape Girardeau, averaging better than ten miles a day against the hard current, and in just four days they arrived at Fort Kaskaskia. Here, where official notification of the western expedition had preceded them by several weeks, the captains found no shortage of men anxious to join them. The problem was weeding out the best from so many. They remained at the fort a week, interviewing dozens of eager volunteers and culling from them a few hardy young regulars with the right glint in their eyes or a particularly useful skill.

John Ordway, a twenty-eight-year-old Yankee from New Hampshire, an experienced Indian fighter and hunter, was signed on as a sergeant. A Pennsylvania Irishman, Patrick Gass, offered a valuable carpenter's skills, volunteering over his own commander's objections. Lewis had to intervene on his behalf before Gass could join up, relinquishing a sergeant's stripes to enlist as a private for the western expedition. Also from Captain Russell Bissell's company at Kaskaskia came hard-drinking Hugh Hall and John Collins, a couple of rough-and-ready regulars who could ride and hunt and shoot. Black-haired John Potts, born in Germany, was accepted. So were Silas Goodrich from Massachusetts, an expert fisherman; Peter Wiser, a twenty-two-year-old Pennsylvania Dutchman; and brawny Alexander Willard from New Hampshire, a skilled gunsmith. Soon the roster had surpassed twenty-five, the nominal figure Meriwether Lewis had chosen for the permanent party.

On November 30, 1803, while the two captains interviewed volunteers at Kaskaskia, it was a gray, chilly day far to the south. In the crowded plaza before the Cabildo at New Orleans, the Spanish governor, the Marquez de Casa Calvo, stood at attention as the Spanish flag slowly descended to the steady beat of a drum. Moments later, rescued from a gust of wind, the French tricolor rose on the staff.

The formal transfer of power over Louisiana from Spain to France was complete at last. There remained only the final ceremony, which would mark France's transfer of sovereignty over the territory to the United States in fulfillment of the new treaty signed by Napoleon.

That moment was still three weeks away.

On December 4, under the command of William Clark, the Corps of Discovery left Kaskaskia for Cahokia, a settlement on the eastern side of the Mississippi across from St. Louis.

Meriwether Lewis left a day later, riding overland on horseback and making much swifter time than the boats battling the Mississippi. He arrived at Cahokia in the afternoon of December 7. He had been given a name of a man to call on, and he quickly sought out John Hay, a former fur trader who was postmaster of the town and one of its leading citizens.

Lewis outlined his mission. He intended to cross the river and call on the Spanish governor at St. Louis.

"Don Carlos Dehault Delassus," Hay said.

"I mean to establish my bona fides and then request formal permission from the Spanish for my expedition up the Missouri."

"Hell, Captain Lewis, you don't need his almighty permission now!" Hay, who had no love for the Spanish, spoke emphatically.

"The President doesn't want to ruffle any feathers at this time. The transfer of authority takes place this month at New Orleans. It's only a matter of weeks before official word reaches His Excellency across the way. We can be patient. I'll press my case, but in any event I plan to make a winter camp on this side of the river."

Hay nodded approvingly. A cool head, this one, he thought. "Delassus speaks no English. He speaks French well enough, but you'll need an interpreter along."

"What about yourself, Mr. Hay? You speak French?"

"Mmm. Yes, but if we are to get into diplomatic niceties, perhaps Monsieur Jarrot will accompany us."

108

Nicholas Jarrot, an Indian trader residing in Cahokia, had also been recommended to Lewis. He readily agreed to act as interpreter. Everyone in Cahokia, it seemed, was excited about the prospect of American possession of the lands west of the Mississippi. "It cannot happen quick enough, Captain Lewis," said Jarrot. "It's been a long time coming."

Don Carlos Dehault Delassus, military and civil governor of Upper Louisiana, was a small, dapper man with a neatly trimmed black beard and mustache, a courtly manner, and an earnest desire to exchange the muddy streets of St. Louis for the cobblestoned boulevards of Madrid. The impending loss of Spanish sovereignty in Upper Louisiana—though he did not convey this to his visitor—did not leave him dismayed.

Captain Merry Weather Lewis—Delassus had difficulty with the name, which seemed to him somewhat comical—was an educated man of obvious talents, the Spaniard thought.

Moreover, he had a soldier's directness and honesty. Delassus was prepared to believe that his mission had no object sinister to His Majesty's government but was intended to do only that which Lewis professed—to find a passage to the Pacific Ocean by following the Missouri.

Still, though the lure of summer in Madrid was strong, Delassus suggested that his duty was clear. He wished Lewis success in his venture, but he was compelled to insist, in the absence of official communication from His Majesty's government, that he could not grant permission for such a journey through Spanish territory. He would, however, seek permission promptly from the Governor General in New Orleans. If Captain Merry would be patient . . .

The two men liked each other, and their meeting was cordial. The captain was full of questions, but he was also, Delassus thought, a sensible man. He agreed that he would make his winter camp on the American side of the Mississippi. The rest would come in due course.

The transfer of power, thought the military and civil governor of Upper Louisiana and commandant of St. Louis, would not be as painful an experience as he had feared.

On the day following his presentation of his credentials to the Spanish governor, Meriwether Lewis rejoined William Clark, who had arrived at Cahokia. The next evening the entire detachment proceeded four miles upriver and camped overnight on a point directly opposite St. Louis.

There the two captains separated. Lewis was to return to St. Louis, this time with a view, as he explained in a letter to Thomas Jefferson, "to obtain from the inhabitants such information as I might consider useful to the govt . . . or to me in my further prosecution of my voyage." Clark would lead the expedition up the Mississippi in search of a suitable winter campsite, as close as possible to the junction of that river with the Missouri.

On December 12, 1803, William Clark chose the site for

the winter camp, on the bank of a small creek the French called Riviere du Bois, or Wood River. Here a rich, well-timbered bottomland stretched inland three miles to an open, undulating prairie, rich in game and, as Clark put it in his field notes, "butifull beyond description." From the site on the south bank of the creek, he was able to gaze across the wide Mississippi into the very mouth of the Missouri. The sight made his spine tingle.

Clark immediately set the men to work clearing the land, cutting logs for huts, working hastily in an attempt to provide shelter before the onslaught of winter. The hard wind and flying clouds were warning enough of what was to come.

Two days later it snowed.

On December 20, 1803, a warm, sunshiny day on the eve of the first day of winter, the French flag that had flown over New Orleans since the beginning of the month was lowered. The Stars and Stripes of the United States climbed from the shadows of the plaza into the bright sunlight. A spectator's shout trembled in the morning air, provoking a volley of cheers. "Louisiana is ours!"

11 a Cold Clear morning, the river Covered with Ice from the Missoure, the Mississippi above frozed across, the Wind from the West, The Thermometer this morning at 19° below freesing, Continue Cold & Clear all day . . .
—WILLIAM CLARK, J a n u a r y 4, 1 8 0 4

*O*n Christmas morning, at the camp opposite the Missouri's mouth, William Clark listened to the boisterous sounds of celebration among the men. The morning had already been marked by at least one fight, an early discharge of rifle fire as a salute to the day, and evidence that more than a few of the recruits had got drunk.

A lot of culling still to be done, thought Clark. By this time the detachment had grown to more than fifty men, a total augmented a few days earlier by George Drouillard's arrival with eight recruits from Tennessee—a disappointing lot, Clark thought, few of whom would last the winter.

Still, the news he had for Meriwether Lewis was not all bad.

Clark bent his head once more over his field desk, dipped his quill into the fresh ink, and wrote with no little satisfaction, in a letter to be carried to Meriwether Lewis at St. Louis, "Drewyear says he will go with us, at the rate ofd and will go to Massac to Settle his matters."

On New Year's Day, 1804, some of the country people of the surrounding area came to Camp Wood to trade sugar and other goods. After some celebrating and good-natured boasting, a shooting contest was agreed upon, Captain Clark putting up a dollar as a prize. A target was affixed to a tree, and the relatively sober country men, expert hunters all, hit it time and again.

The men of the expedition, laughing and jeering, staggered out to take their turns. John Colter and John Ordway and Alexander Willard, Hugh Hall and John Collins and others—most of whom had been cited in William Clark's field notes for being drunk the night before—were so confident as to be almost disdainful of the contest. They took up their guns with a soldier's careless confidence. Rifle fire crackled in the thin cold air, and powder smoke hung thick.

An hour after the shooting began, the soldiers stared at each other in disbelief. One after another they had shot wide of the crudely drawn target, all except sober George Gibson, who had had the best shot of anyone. But according to the terms of the contest, the *two* best shots took the prize, and the country people won the dollar.

William Clark, who had tolerated the New Year's Eve celebrations, looked on with a feeling of satisfaction over the soldiers' humiliation. With Lewis spending most of his time in St. Louis, it was up to Clark to try to drill and bully their unruly lot of volunteers into a cohesive, disciplined military unit. These were young frontier soldiers or backwoodsmen, hardheaded and fiercely independent, with a reflex resistance to orders. They were nearly as fond of quarreling and brawling as they were of their daily whiskey ration. Even an extra gill a day for each man was not enough for many of them, who supplemented their needs from the whiskey peddlers who had set up shop near the camp.

Clark had encouraged the idea of a shooting contest, guessing the outcome. He had to find ways to instill pride in this collection of volunteers. Shooting contests—making their sharpshooting a matter of pride—were one way.

There would be other contests, he thought. No man liked losing, whether his money or his claim of prowess in some skill. In that respect, his men were no different.

When the country people had gone off with their dollar, chuckling and bragging among themselves, Clark went back to his newly finished hut. It was proving snug against the cold January wind that blew off the big river, which was now clogged with muddy sheets of ice that thundered out of the Missouri to blunder across the Mississippi and smash against the ice fixed to the eastern bank.

York had prepared tea. "Hot tea, Cap'n Clark, suh, you needs somethin' to warm your insides."

Clark smiled. York, who had always said "Master William" back home, was now firmly attached to "Cap'n Clark, suh." Clark thought idly of the fact that neither he nor Meriwether Lewis used rank when addressing each other in private. Lewis preferred his last name to Meriwether or the abominable "Merry," and Clark was equally comfortable with Lewis calling him simply "Clark." Their choice of address did not diminish the enduring respect and real affection the two men shared.

"I need something to warm my outside as well," Clark said. His nose and ears and cheeks were so cold they smarted in the sudden warmth of the hut.

He took his cup of tea and stood before the fire, baking first his front and then his backside. He gave a sudden grin. "York, you rascal, where have ye hidden that bottle of good Monongahela whiskey George sent along with us?"

"Got it right heah, Cap'n Clark, suh, right heah." York chuckled as he brought the bottle from its hiding place, safely tucked behind some books on a makeshift wooden shelf.

William Clark poured a generous dollop of whiskey into his tea, sniffed the aroma in pleasurable anticipation, and downed a hearty swallow. The hot tea scalded his throat and the whiskey burned all the way down. It continued to glow in his belly like a hot coal.

There was a scratching at the door. York opened it to

113

admit Seaman, Lewis's dog. He brought a gust of cold into the hut with him. Padding over to Clark, he pressed a moist cold nose into the palm of Clark's hand. Smiling, for it was hard not to like so amiable a dog, Clark scrubbed the broad head absently until, content with his greeting, Seaman flopped on the floor near the crackling fire.

Clark's thoughts returned to Lewis. How was he getting on with the touchy Spanish governor? Damn all, the Spaniard knew the days of his nation's sovereignty were over in this territory, but he wouldn't let himself be rushed. Men have to have their ceremony, Clark mused. Perhaps especially when they have lost the game.

That reminded him once more of his shooters. He sipped his whiskey-laced tea and reflected that men shot straighter when they aimed with eyes that were not bloodshot and squeezed the trigger with fingers that did not shake.

114

Camp Wood was not Seaman's first encounter with winter's sharp bite. A year ago, on a farm just outside of St. John's, he had known the howling of Atlantic Ocean gales, the sleets and snows of a Newfoundland winter. That winter, however, had been relatively mild compared to the season Seaman now experienced along the Mississippi River bottom.

During his first weeks at the camp, while the clearing rang with the whack of axes biting into wood, while the men filled every dry moment with cutting and hauling, pounding and sawing, Seaman was left largely on his own. He was always alert for Meriwether Lewis's return—reassured now by experience that Lewis *would* eventually reappear—but he was free to explore the deep surrounding woods, to splash across the shallow creek, to follow any scent that lured him.

When, on a January morning, he found a cold skin spread over the surface of the stream where he had gone for a drink, the big dog sniffed at the ice and explored along the bank, searching for a break or hole. The zero-cold air was sharp in his throat. It cut even through his thick winter coat. Shivering, he snapped, teeth clashing, at the white frost his breath made on the morning air.

After a few moments of curious exploration, Seaman stepped tentatively onto the skirt of the ice-covered creek. Nothing happened. Yet he felt uneasy, perhaps because the slick surface was so treacherous, offering no grip for his pads. He had already learned that much about ice.

When no misadventure occurred, he stepped farther away from the bank.

Several of the men were watching, interrupting their activities. Grinning with anticipation, a few of them moved closer to the riverbank as the dog stepped gingerly out onto the sheet of ice. George Shannon started to call out, but Reuben Fields put a hand on his arm. "Let 'im be," Reuben urged. "He's got to learn."

They all saw what was coming before Seaman had any warning. The thin new sheet of ice began to bow, too weak to bear his considerable weight.

The creaking of the ice caused him to halt. He started to turn back, floundering on the slippery surface. The veins of myriad small cracks ran away from him in every direction like living things, and he felt the first tremor of fear.

The ice caved in under him, plunging him into icy water.

Shock!

The cold froze his brain. In those first seconds there was only blind instinct, a wild-eyed thrashing in the water. But the creek was never deep, and after a moment his paws found the bottom. He hurled himself toward the shore, trampling the thin sheet of ice all the way to the bank.

Safely on solid footing, panting and shivering, the big dog was aware of two things: the men above him on the riverbank, laughing and shouting, and the bone-deep cold, harsh as slashing teeth, as ice formed on his coat and on his eyelashes and even between his teeth.

William Clark pushed through the ring of recruits, whose raucous good humor over Seaman's icy dunking was, in a perverse way, a mark of their growing attachment to the dog.

"Here, bring him this way," Clark ordered. "Fun's fun, but he'll be frozen stiff if we don't get him warm in a hurry. Shannon, bring him to my hut."

Shaking uncontrollably, and chagrined by the men's laughter, as if it told him that he had made a fool of himself, Seaman allowed himself to be hustled over the crusty snow to William Clark's cabin, where York had built up the morning's fire to a welcome blaze. York took one look at the shivering dog, at the icicles formed in the wet strands of black coat plastered to his body, and dove immediately into a trunk. His big hands emerged a moment later with a couple of thick towels.

York and Private Shannon set to work at once, briskly toweling down the dog until his violent shivering had diminished to an occasional quiver.

Seaman submitted to their pummeling in his docile fashion. "Get his feet warm and dry," Clark warned. "We don't want frostbite. He has a long way to walk with us."

116   Clark had recent personal experience behind his urging. Earlier that week he had broken through the ice of a frozen pond he was crossing. His feet and legs were immediately soaked to the skin. By the time he returned to camp his boots were frozen to his feet, and there were anxious moments while he warmed his feet and worked the boots free, all the while goaded by the worry that frostbitten feet or toes could cripple him.

When York and Shannon had got the worst of the water squeezed from Seaman's dense coat—the undercoat was surprisingly dry—the dog gave a vigorous shake, sending a shower in all directions that drew mock protests from the three men. He then paced the room in a circle before nosing all three men in gratitude. He shook himself again, the spray causing sparks to flare in the stone fireplace. Though the memory of that first shock of cold when he'd plunged through the ice still lingered, Seaman had recuperated quickly, thanks to Clark's prompt intervention.

"We're not so different, boy," Clark murmured to the

dog. "But I should know better." His tone conveyed reassurance where the words themselves had no meaning for Seaman.

The next day the creek was filmed over again with ice formed during the night. Once again Seaman made his way down to the edge of the stream. This time he tested the thin ice near the bank with one huge paw, gradually increasing the pressure until he broke through to the cold water running beneath the ice. After scratching the opening to create a wider circle, Seaman peered closely into the icy water. He took a tentative lap with his tongue. It tasted cold but good, and he drank a little more, cautiously standing on the solid ground of the bank.

One of the watching soldiers chuckled. "He learns quick, that one."

William Clark had also observed the dog approvingly. Though he had not said as much to Lewis, he had had some misgivings about the usefulness of having the dog along, not to mention adding the equivalent weight of another 150-pound man to the keelboat's burden. The last of his doubts finally disappeared. "He'll do," Clark murmured.

"Drouillard says the Indians will think he's good medicine," George Shannon said.

"If so," said Clark pointedly, raising his voice so that others would hear, "he'll be worth more than a soldier who can't shoot straight."

The lesson of the frozen stream stayed with Seaman from that time on, not so much learned as remembered, as if the original knowledge was already there in a primitive core of his brain, the knowledge hard won by his ancestors, the Bear Dogs of the northern plains.

Meriwether Lewis spent six weeks in St. Louis before rejoining his command at Camp Wood at the end of January. In the interim he had made friends everywhere in the city and used his new relationships to learn everything that was known about the Missouri River and the interior of Louisiana. He talked to

117

traders, trappers, merchants, rivermen. He sought out maps of upper Louisiana from every available source. He crafted voluminous questionnaires about the territory and the Indian Nations inhabiting it and badgered his informants for their answers. He corresponded tirelessly and wrote lengthy reports of his activities and findings to Thomas Jefferson, adding detailed thoughts and suggestions for the government of the new territory.

At the same time Lewis was also acquiring goods that might prove useful on the expedition, from kegs of tallow to the friction matches invented by one of his new friends, Dr. Antoine Saugrain, a French chemist and physician who had settled with his family in St. Louis. Instant fire, Lewis was convinced, would rival his air gun as another kind of magic with which to impress the Indians.

Early in February William Clark was given a break from camp routine, Lewis taking his place while Clark enjoyed the hospitality of Charles Gratiot, Pierre Chouteau, and others among Lewis's newfound St. Louis friends. Through the rest of that month and into March, the two captains traveled back and forth across the river frequently, while the level of urgency in the preparations for the voyage increased at the camp.

On one of Lewis's trips to St. Louis, Seaman, with a bark of enthusiasm, accepted Lewis's invitation to jump into the pirogue with him. Seaman rode across the icy river to St. Louis with his head high, nose to the wind.

As it happened, however, that week was stormy without letup. Rain, snow, or sleet fell each day, turning the city's streets into a muddy quagmire. While Lewis and Captain Amos Stoddard, over from Fort Kaskaskia, were meeting with prominent St. Louis citizens over the impending ceremonies that would transfer governing authority over Upper Louisiana from Spain to the United States, Seaman was left in the care of friends. He stayed at their lodgings during the day, gazing out the window like one in mourning. By the end of the week he was glad to return to camp and the jocular company of the soldiers.

Louis Charbonneau

On March 9, 1804, Spanish troops turned out in full military regalia before the government house, with Governor Don Carlos Dehault Delassus at their head. Captain Stoddard had been given authority to accept the transfer of power for both France and the United States. Meriwether Lewis and William Clark were over from Camp Wood for the occasion, Lewis as the representative of the President.

It was a blustery March day, the wind sharp enough to make the troops involuntarily hunch their shoulders against the chill. Delassus gave a gracious speech—brief for a Spaniard—releasing the citizens of Louisiana from their pledge of loyalty to the Spanish crown.

Through Meriwether Lewis's intercession, a delegation of St. Louis citizens, led by Charles Gratiot, had persuaded Captain Stoddard to allow the largely French-speaking citizens of the city to have the French flag flown over the fort for one day. Accordingly, a small detail of American troops from Stoddard's company, acting as proxy troops of Napoleon, marched up to the fort to take symbolic possession in the name of the French emperor. When the Spanish flag fluttered down, it was the French tricolor that rose over the fort.

One day later, March 10, the French colors were replaced by the Stars and Stripes. The transfer of sovereignty over all of Louisiana was complete, the last concrete act that made Thomas Jefferson's purchase of the territory a formal reality on the western frontier.

In the spring of 1804, when river traffic was becoming active, a heavy barge, down from the Ohio, put in toward Natchez Landing. The craft was overladen, low in the water, and heeling badly in the Mississippi's pounding current.

A sudden squall caught the barge's sail. The boat swung broadside to the current, momentarily out of control. The helmsman tried to bring her around, but some of the boat's cargo shifted as a big wave rolled against the side of the boat.

She leaned badly, shipping water, and rolled massively against the wharf.

There was a grinding, splintering crash. A gaping hole appeared in the planks on the larboard side below the water line. In seconds the cargo hold had filled with water. Again and again the battering waves threw the barge against the pilings of the wharf. She began to break up.

The helmsman joined the crew in the water, swimming for their lives. The cargo spilled into the river—boxes, bales and chests, some swept away in the current, others breaking open and spilling their contents into the river like blood gushing from a wound.

Within a few minutes it was over. What was left of the shattered barge lay on her side against the bank below Natchez Landing, a torn red fragment of cloth flying from a broken rib like a desolate flag.

Amongst the cargo had been several chests shipped down the Ohio River from Cincinnati, intended to be transshipped to an oceangoing vessel bound for Richmond, Virginia. Only one of these chests, thrown onto the rocks below the Landing, survived the shipwreck intact.

Two days after the barge sank, a crew from the Tennessee Militia, then stationed at Natchez, scoured the riverbank below the Landing on assignment to retrieve anything of value from the lost cargo. They broke open the wooden chest, whose shipping label had been lost. A litter of white bones spilled onto the sand.

After a few moments of joking and horseplay, in which one private chased another with a large jawbone held next to his own chin, the soldiers moved on. The last of the ancient bones collected by Meriwether Lewis for Thomas Jefferson at Big Bone Lick lay scattered on the beach.

One day early in April found both captains back in camp. The Mississippi was rising rapidly. Even Wood River was running fast, swollen with spring runoff. Meriwether Lewis stood impatiently on the east bank one afternoon, staring across the way at his ultimate challenge, the Missouri, which still disgorged huge chunks of ice into the Mississippi, making a crossing below the junction of the two rivers hazardous. The Mississippi could be crossed upstream, however, and Lewis finally called for a small crew of men to join him and William Clark in the red pirogue, which had been freshly caulked and painted for the upcoming journey. On a last minute impulse Lewis whistled for his dog, who bounded forward joyfully to take his place in the dugout.

It was a cold, wet, turbulent, stomach-lurching voyage across a single stretch of muddy water, but Seaman felt a new excitement communicated wordlessly by the men in the boat.

It was a typical spring day, clouds scudding swiftly before blustery winds and exposing patches of brilliant blue sky. They beached the boat in a tiny cove above the Missouri's angry mouth. Lewis left the crew in charge of the pirogue while he and Clark strode inland. Seaman bounded along with the two captains, intrigued by the fresh mysteries promised on this far side of the river.

They emerged from a wooded bottom onto an open slope. As they climbed slowly, Lewis grumbled about some of the problems he had faced in St. Louis. He fretted over Clark's description of insubordination among the recruits, some of whom had defied Sergeant Ordway's orders during the captains' absence. He brooded aloud over the many long delays of the winter months and the inadequacy of the information he had been able to gather in St. Louis. "By the Lord, I feel like Columbus! It is an unknown ocean we set out upon. Beyond the Mandan villages it is absolutely uncharted. The maps we have are guesses only, not to be relied on at all! We shall have to draw our own—you shall, Clark! You're better at it. By the Lord, we'll ride rivers and climb mountains where no white man has been before us. We'll be the first!"

"That we will," Clark murmured.

121

Their eyes met in a moment of silent communion, sharing the dream. "There's no man I'd rather be there with," said Lewis, impulsively gripping Clark's shoulder.

"Nor I." And Clark added with a grin, "By the Lord!"

They came to the top of the knoll, and both men caught their breath when the land suddenly opened out before them, an astounding reach of open, rolling grassland stretching as far as the eye could see under that turbulent sky, with the muddy Missouri coiling and twisting through it like a brown rope. They stood silent, for a moment speechless.

Beside them, Seaman lifted his muzzle to the wind. It came not with a familiar rustle of leaves or a sighing of branches, but as a long, rolling rush across the undulating grasses. It brought a bewildering chorus of strange smells.

The young dog had come from a bleak, winter-bare island farm to the tidy hills of Virginia, a place of green forests, streams darting out of shadows into bright valleys, skies that seemed close and contained. On his journey over the Alleghenies with Meriwether Lewis, he had explored caves of darkness and dappled light in the woods, hunting in close thickets of brush, chasing small, furry, frightened creatures who escaped into holes or darted up trees out of reach, while he barked at them exuberantly, enjoying the chase more than the victory. Now he faced a world both wilder and grander than anything he had experienced. Everything opened out before him. The land marched away from him in a rolling sprawl, wave upon wave, extending beyond the reach even of his keen eye. Its vaulting immensity awakened a strange yearning. What he experienced was not fear, or the simple fascination of the unknown, but a whispering in his blood, of voices calling down through the centuries, the voices of dogs resembling him who had roamed the high country long before the coming of the white man, who had lifted their heads at night in a darkness as limitless as space and howled like wolves.

Unable to contain the feeling that welled within him, Seaman began to moan far back in his throat, until his excitement burst out of him in a thunderous bark.

"Listen to him!" exclaimed Meriwether Lewis. "He feels it, Clark."

"He knows that's where he's going." William Clark squinted as the setting sun burst from behind the clouds and lit up the far horizon as if it were on fire. "Now I know what George felt when he first came down the Ohio. It's like . . . like . . ."

"Like Adam on the first day," said Lewis.

Part two

the

missouri

12 I set out at 4 o'clock, P.M, in the presence of many of the neighboring inhabitents, and proceeded on under a jentle brease up the Missourie . . .

—WILLIAM CLARK, May 14, 1804

William Clark was a methodical man. That trait had helped to make him an excellent scout, engineer, at times even a spy, for the army on the western frontier. He was able to carry a mass of detail in his head, but he was also proficient at ordering it on paper in plans, sketches, maps, and reports.

As early as January, in his cabin at Camp Wood, Clark had been busy working out on paper an itinerary for the coming expedition. He estimated the miles, days, and months that would be required to reach the Mandan villages, to gain the "rock mountains," to descend from these unknown heights to the western ocean. From these calculations he attempted to break down the trip into miles per day and a probable time-table.

Clark made the same minute calculations with regard to the men and materials to go on the journey. If there were thirty-six men attached to the expedition, how many should be assigned to the keelboat? The white pirogue? The red pirogue? How should these numbers be adjusted if there were only thirty men? Or forty? As the roster expanded with new recruits, Clark adjusted his lists, creating squads under each of the three sergeants, changing assignments from day to day until he was satisfied.

There were also extensive lists of provisions and supplies. The quantities were prodigious—fourteen barrels of parch-meal, twenty barrels of flour, seven barrels of salt, fifty kegs of pork, fifty bushels of meal, twenty-one bales of "indian presents," boxes of candles, pails of soap, kegs of whiskey, plus clothing, medicines, weapons, and ammunition. With the exception of food and drink, the cargo was distributed in mixed bales, so that the loss of one would entail only the loss of a small quantity of any particular item, rather than, for example, all of the mosquito nets or all of the Indian beads. And almost daily Clark had to adjust his packing and distribution of these tons of baggage to accommodate new finds Meriwether Lewis sent from St. Louis, where Lewis continued to spend much of his time. In addition to his con-stant search for information and needed supplies, Lewis had been working with Captain Stoddard on an Indian Council, making known to the Delawares, Shawnees, Sauks, Abanakis, Omahas, Missouris, and other Indian tribes of Louisiana that their allegiance was now to the United States, not Spain or France.

Now it was May. Once more Lewis was delayed in St. Louis, this time making arrangements with his friend Pierre Chouteau, a prominent citizen of that city, to send a dele-gation of Osage chiefs to Washington, D.C. to sign a treaty of peace with their new Father in Washington. Pierre Chou-teau and his brother Auguste had not only been helpful to Lewis all winter, they had also come up with a group of nine French *engagés*, led by their *patroon*, Jean Baptiste Des-champs, all experienced rivermen who had signed on to take one of the pirogues up the Missouri as far as the Mandan villages and to bring the keelboat back in the spring.

All of the men were impatient to be under way. Not counting the two captains, York, and Drouillard, the per-manent party included twenty-three privates and three ser-geants. Two of these were French rivermen, reputed to be among the best on the Mississippi, who had taken the rare step of enlisting in the American expedition as privates. Pierre Cruzatte, who had but one eye, and that one weak, would share the bow oar of the *Discovery* with Francois Labiche. The *engagés* would row the seven-oared red pirogue, with any extra hands being assigned to the keelboat. The third boat, the smaller, six-oared white pirogue, would be manned by Corporal Richard Warfington and six soldiers from the St. Louis garrison. According to Lewis's plan, they would be sent back downriver before winter, carrying scientific specimens, information, and letters for the eagerly waiting President of the United States.

Sitting at his field desk each evening, William Clark studied the sheafs of plans, lists, and notes he had prepared so painstakingly over recent months. It was always easier on paper, Clark thought. But such plans could never allow for the rogue element in events, in the muddy river across the way, or in the men who now sought to challenge her.

Lewis and Clark had agreed on May 15 as the tentative departure date from Camp Wood. If Lewis could not be there, Clark was to set off on his own and Lewis would join him by traveling overland to St. Charles.

The afternoon of May 14, 1804—one day earlier than planned—everything was ready, and Clark decided to wait no longer. The day was cloudy and gray with intermittent rain. It had also rained that morning, dampening some of the goods packed aboard the three boats but not the men's spirits. After a dreary winter of training and drilling and camp chores, the Corps of Discovery experienced a tremendous lift simply from the action of setting out.

To a rattle of gunfire from the country people who had come to see them off, the three boats pushed out across the swift turbulence of the Mississippi and slowly forced their way past the mouth of the Missouri, which, true to its reputation, was muddy, rapid, and clogged with driftwood.

Though the men were fresh and strong, William Clark chose not to test them too far that first day. They proceeded under sail a little over four miles to the upper point of the first island in the Missouri. There they made their first camp.

The eager excitement among the men, even more than the thrust of the boats up the unfamiliar river, told Seaman that the journey for which he had been waiting was under way. He explored the point of the island and aped the action of the sentries in circling the camp. He got in the way while the men tried to light fires with damp wood. When the men were struggling to erect tents where the ground was not too sodden, the curious dog got a paw tangled in one of the ropes and pulled a tent down in the mud.

Rain returned with darkness. Caught in the open, Seaman knew enough to sniff out the captains' tent. He snuffled and scratched at the closed flap until York let him in out of the rain, which sounded like musket fire against the tent. Seaman stopped inside the entrance to give a vigorous shake. As the spray flew, William Clark swore and York jumped backward, crying, "If you shake one more time, Seam'n, you're gonna shake outside!"

130

Unconcerned by the threat, the Newfoundland searched out a dry patch of turf and flopped down. The rain continued to drum against the roof of the tent.

By morning the campfires had been swamped. The breeze was strong, however, and after the rain let up the boats beat their way upriver under sail for nearly ten miles. Three times the keelboat—the men had taken to calling it the barge—rode up on a submerged log with a grinding, shuddering impact. Once Seaman was thrown off his feet from the forward deck. He skidded into the runway on the starboard side and had to scramble to avoid being thrown over the gunwale into the muddy river.

By the end of the second day Seaman had begun to reach an accommodation with the two Frenchmen who alternated at the bow oar. The dog had been accustomed to riding on the forward deck during the trip down the Ohio, but now he was often in the way. Both Cruzatte and Labiche rode in the bow, one taking the oar, the other acting as bowsman or pilot, crouching on the deck and scanning the river to watch for logs, driftwood, sandbars, and other obstacles; sudden warning shifts of the current; or, up ahead, the plunge of a part of the soft riverbank into the rushing current.

Finally William Clark ordered the dog back toward the stern. Used to his station up front, Seaman was puzzled by the order. "Go back!" Clark commanded, pointing the way.

George Shannon, manning one of the oars near the stern, tried to help by calling Seaman to him. The confused dog went reluctantly. "It's all right, boy, you can see as well from up there," Shannon encouraged him, indicating the deck over the stern cabin. "Go on now, lie down."

This last command was clear enough, and Seaman hopped up onto the deck. He quickly discovered that his new situation, elevated above the two runways where the men heaved at their oars, was nearly as strategic as his familiar post in the bow, and he had soon cheerfully adapted to his new outlook as the boat continued up the river.

At noon on May 16, the little flotilla reached the French settlement of St. Charles, a cluster of about a hundred poorly made houses on a shelf at the foot of a small hill. Here they would wait for Meriwether Lewis's arrival.

For the next four days the boats lay over. The villagers were friendly and hospitable; for them the arrival of the boats was the event of the season. The crew were anxious to sample their hospitality—a bit too eager, Clark thought, though he relented that first night, when a ball was held in honor of the members of the expedition.

By morning his reluctance was confirmed. Three of the soldiers—William Werner, Hugh Hall, and John Collins—had not returned that night. When they stumbled down to the dock in the gray of the morning, they found their commander waiting for them, uncharacteristically stone-faced. At

131

this early stage of the journey, Clark felt no challenge to the detachment's discipline could go unchecked. "Ye were told to be back here at midnight," Clark said grimly. "Not only are ye absent without leave, but ye disgraced the entire party by your conduct last night. Ye'll stand for a court martial this afternoon."

Werner and Hall were sheepishly apologetic; only Collins was unrepentant. He had a feisty disposition and a reckless spirit that all too easily spilled over into defiance. All three miscreants were found guilty, but at the last moment Clark forgave the twenty-five lashes decreed for Werner and Hall. Collins, however, as much for his intractable response as for his misconduct at the ball, received fifty lashes administered by his peers with willow switches. He would find duty at the oars a painful chore for some days.

Seaman was restive during the days the boats remained at St. Charles. He sensed that this was only a temporary stop, that the wide, muddy river beckoned. Then, late in the afternoon of the fifth day, after another awesome display of thunder and lightning and heavy rain, some riders appeared, hunched over their horses' necks, drenched and weary. One of them turned away from his companions and rode down the hill toward the dock. Seaman felt a surge of joy that brought him bounding forward as the rider swung down.

Meriwether Lewis could only laugh as two huge, muddy paws were planted firmly against his chest.

The rain continued most of that night. Seaman lay happily in the officers' tent, listening to the pounding of the rain, contentedly aware of the murmured conversation of the two captains who shared the tent with Clark's servant. The dog had no notion of a somber note in the discussion.

"Your rank is not such as I wished, or had reason to

expect," said Meriwether Lewis apologetically. "I would give anything if the matter could be changed. You know I wished you to have equal rank, to be equal with me in every way."

"Mm."

"It was Mr. Jefferson's wish as well. He requested the captaincy for you—damn Dearborn, anyway! He didn't like having his fence bridged, that's all, not even by the President. He could've found you a captain's ranking in one of the corps if he'd wished."

"It doesn't matter," said Clark, though clearly it did.

Clark had received the keenly disappointing news in a letter from Lewis a week before leaving Camp Wood, but this was their first chance to speak of it directly. Instead of the captain's rank he had been promised, Clark had been appointed a lieutenant in the Corps of Artillerists. His pride had been stung. He had felt deceived and ill-used—not by his friend Lewis but by the Secretary of War, Henry Dearborn. For one gloomy night, while rain drummed against the roof of his cabin, he had even contemplated the unthinkable: withdrawal from the expedition. By the next morning, when the skies had cleared, his angry impulse had also passed. Even had he been willing to give up his part in the great adventure, he could not at that late date have allowed its success to be jeopardized by any action of his.

Lewis placed a hand on Clark's arm. His clear blue eyes were concerned. "Dearborn has withheld the rank, and there's nothing we can do about it now. But that shall stay with us, Clark. No one else shall know. As far as this expedition is concerned, and every man who is a part of it, you will share the command equally with me, and your rank and pay shall be the same. Agreed?"

For William Clark, there had never really been a choice. The slight he felt would not be forgotten, but Lewis's genuine distress and Clark's own eagerness for the journey made his response inevitable. "Agreed!"

"Let's have a toast to our firm partnership." Lewis

153

poured a gill of whiskey for each of them. He cocked his head as rain lashed at the tent, spilling through the flaps that covered the entrance. "To wet throats and dry land!"

They grinned at each other.

The Corps of Discovery was complete. Their journey had begun.

13 nothing Remarkable to Day   water verry Strong   past one place whare the water Roles over the Sand with grait fall and verry Dangeris for Boats to pass ...
—CHARLES FLOYD, June 16, 1804

*I*t had been a rainy spring, wet enough to cause concern even before the three boats of the Corps of Discovery edged away from the dock of St. Charles—to three cheers and a shot from the bow gun—and pushed upriver. In the days that followed, the skies continued to open. The river rose—as much as a foot in one night—and the current in the main channel was so strong that the *Discovery* could make no headway at all by oar or pole, some of the crew having to plod along the bank, hauling the barge by rope.

But these banks presented their own hazard. They crumbled and slid and frequently collapsed in huge sections into the river, with a roar like distant cannon. The boats had to pass warily when forced close to the banks. Even when the tumbling walls of mud themselves presented no immediate danger, they hurled their weapons into the rushing current: tangled brush and even whole trees that sailed down the river, their higher branches held aloft like masts and sails, their stout lower branches projecting outward like spears, their earth-laden roots riding below like battering rams.

Even worse than these threats were the rolling sands,

always treacherously on the move under the force of the swift water; the thick tangles of driftwood that broke loose and filled the channels; or the submerged logs the rivermen called saw-yers or "planters," hidden beneath the Missouri's murky sur-face, often discovered too late, only after one of the boats had struck or ridden up on the unseen barrier.

The river was full of surprises.

On the second day out of St. Charles, at the urging of the French rivermen, the boats pulled in close to a wall of rock at the base of some high cliffs. Here the soldiers were astonished to see a huge cave open into the cliff. With his usual exactness Clark noted its measurements, which he estimated at "120 feet wide 40 feet Deep & 20 feet high."

"She be the beegest cave you evair see, eh?" Cruzatte said reverently. Both the French and the Indians—Cruzatte was both, his father having lived among the Omahas and married an Omaha woman—regarded the huge cave above the Mis-souri's bank with awe, more because of the ancient pictographs painted on the walls than because of its unique size.

"Why's it called the Tavern?" one of the soldiers asked.

Baptiste Deschamps had clambered out of the red pirogue onto the ledge with many of the *engagés*. Deschamps never seemed in awe of anything but he studied the faded images on the wall with thoughtful attention. He said, "Rivermen used to cache their furs here. And whiskey," he added.

"Any of that still around?" John Collins asked with an irrepressible grin. The lacerations on his back, a legacy from his recent court-martial over his drunken misconduct at St. Charles, were not yet healed. "We be good customers."

By now most of the soldiers had got out of the boats to explore the cave and to leave their marks on the damp walls, William Clark among them. Their voices echoed hollowly in the huge cavern. Even the clomp of their army boots was mag-nified into the steps of behemoths.

Following Meriwether Lewis as he drifted away from the

group, Seaman was glad to see him move toward an opening at the side of the cave. Like most dogs, he welcomed a dim hole or shelter to crawl into to rest or lick a wound, but such refuges were chosen to be close and confined. Not a great, damp and gloomy cavern like this one, with dripping walls and a pervasive chill no body warmth could ease.

Lewis spoke to Clark. "I'll be climbing these cliffs, I think, to see what observations I might make of the land."

"And the river," Clark suggested, thinking of the hard water they had encountered that morning and a log on which the keelboat had been hung up for an hour.

Already eager to be about his observations, Lewis nodded agreement. "Wait for me a mile upriver, then."

As Clark called the others back to the boats, Lewis and Seaman left the cave, the voices of the men quickly falling behind. Lewis began to climb toward the top of the cliffs, pausing along the way to examine the plants and bushes until they thinned out to bare rock. Outside the cave the day was warm, but after some minutes of climbing they discovered a steady breeze on the heights.

Lewis stopped on a promontory, directly over the center of the Tavern, which offered a panoramic view up and down the river. There was smoke far off to the east where St. Charles was hidden behind its modest hills and more plumes rising at the Femmes Osage settlement, little more than a mile away, where the expedition had stopped briefly that morning. To the west the river coiled and twisted, forcing its turbulent way between crumbling banks, with a string of islands set into the muddy brown current like emeralds. And there the boats toiled, the setting poles flashing in the sunlight as they rose and fell.

Lewis moved forward for a better view. Seaman shied a little from the rim. When he looked down, he felt a moment's dizziness, the illusion that the earth was moving swiftly under his feet, though in reality it was the waters far below that moved.

A gust of wind caused Lewis to stagger. He turned to step

back from the edge of the precipice. A chunk of granite gave way. Lewis gave an involuntary shout, which was lost in a rattle of gravel as a piece of the cliff broke off. Lewis dropped over the edge as if falling into a chute.

Lewis's hands clawed at the rim. Seaman darted forward, instinctively trying to catch Lewis's sleeve with his teeth. The fingers slipped and dropped out of sight.

The dog peered over the edge. Meriwether Lewis hung spread-eagled against the face of the cliff about twenty feet below the rim. In the act of falling he had whipped out his knife and plunged it into a fissure in the rocky wall, breaking his fall.

The top part of the cliffs jutted outward. Beneath Lewis was a long, straight drop nearly three hundred feet down to the river.

Seaman began to bark excitedly, dancing along the rim and even making tentative moves as if to try to climb down the steep face. Lewis turned a strained glance upward and shouted, "No! No, Seaman, go back!"

The Newfoundland did not jump. Instead he ran back and forth along the edge, barking furiously. But the boats had already moved well upriver, and his deep-voiced alarm went unheard above the roar of the hard water.

The dog went back to the rim where Lewis had fallen and, despite his uncertainty about his footing, peered over the edge.

Lewis was closer.

Using his knife, he had held his balance until he could shift his body over to his left, where the cliff face presented some of its ragged features. His boots found cracks and miniature ledges. His free hand found a projecting rock that was firmly in place. He shifted his knife to another, higher position.

Foot by foot Meriwether Lewis dragged himself upward toward the rim. And at the top he felt something grab his sleeve and pull, making the going easier. He came over the edge, Seaman's teeth fastened firmly to his left sleeve.

As Lewis knelt on the solid rock to catch his breath, Seaman happily licked his face. Lewis grabbed the big head and held it with both hands.

That night, when the story of Lewis's close brush with disaster was told, the Newfoundland was made much of, York even giving him extra tidbits from the captains' mess for his evening meal.

Clark also grumbled about unnecessary risks. "To risk all before we've fairly begun . . . it won't do, Lewis."

"No lectures!" protested Lewis. "Even if I deserve one. It was an accident, that's all."

"If ye hadn't had your knife . . ."

"Aye," Lewis admitted. "And my dog as well."

"Do I have your word," Clark pressed him, "that we won't be doing any more climbing?"

"Agreed," said Lewis with a grin. "That is, until we come to the next tall rock where you'll want to scratch your name!"

By the next day the incident at the Tavern and its possible consequences were forgotten. The Missouri reasserted her claim to complete and lasting attention. The current was swift, the water so dark that Seaman could see nothing beneath its surface. He could only sense the river's power. Watching the men heaving at their oars and poles, the sergeant sweating at the helm, the two captains alert and watchful, those of the crew who were frequently put ashore leaning hard against the towline, Seaman learned respect for the river by vicariously sharing in the men's struggles.

About midafternoon, after the boats had passed several islands and small creeks, there was a perceptible quickening in the current. Quiet eddies along the left bank disappeared in a rush of water.

Above the rushing sound Seaman heard Cruzatte's warning. "Damn the Mizzou! Ha! You know what dees place be name'? De Devil's Racegroun'. By'm by, you see. Wait—hear dat? She's comin' now!"

The steady roaring up ahead grew louder. The *Discovery*, leading the way for the two smaller boats, inched slowly along a channel, Cruzatte leaning precariously over the prow and

guiding the helmsman with signals to keep clear of the larboard shore, where the river roiled over projecting rocks. The water ran so hard that rowing was useless. The crewmen aboard bent to their setting poles, working in a sweating rhythm, while those on shore slipped and stumbled in the clay of the banks, hauling on the cord. Seaman paced back and forth on the small platform that formed a deck over the rear cabin, caught up in the battle while kept apart from it. Foot by foot, yard by yard, the heavy barge plodded up the river. The roaring rocks on the left persisted for a full half mile before their jagged teeth could no longer be seen snarling through the foam.

Beyond the Devil's Raceground there was no time to lean back and grin and exchange congratulations. Here islands were strung along the river. The keelboat tried to pass through a narrow channel on the left side of one of these islands, but with a series of thunderous crashes parts of the south bank began to fall into the river. The boat turned above the head of the island, seeking to escape the disintegrating banks and their dangerous debris by attempting to cross to the starboard side of the river between the island and a sandbar in the middle of the river.

Suddenly Cruzatte was frantically signaling. The boat pulled hard against the rope that still tied her to the men on the shore. And Seaman felt a deep shudder as the bow ran up on sand.

What followed was a blur of images: the men in the boat on their feet and poling furiously, the barge wheeling against the sandbar and turning broadside to the current, the captains both shouting orders, Clark's face as red as his hair, the men on the riverbank still hanging on while portions of the bank collapsed under them, the long rope stretched taut over the water, and—

Crack! With a sound like a gunshot the towline broke.

Hung up on the sandbar, the hard current striking her broadside, the barge began to lift and topple. The men spilled out on the high side, officers and all. They threw their weight on that side to keep the boat from tipping. Heedless of danger, filled not with the panic that showed in some of the men's faces but with excitement, Seaman jumped into the river after them.

The power of the current kept the sands moving, and in seconds the sand under the boat had washed away, freeing her. But in an instant the same current wheeled the boat again, driving her toward the sand once more.

And then Seaman lost sight of the boat and the crew. He was in his own fight with the damned Missouri now. The swing of the boat away from him had pushed him out into the main channel. The hard water swept over him, pushing him down and holding him like a giant hand.

He began to swim, his broad webbed feet driving against the water's resistance, propelling him upward. His head burst above the surface into a babble of noise and blinding light. Like the debris from the falling banks he was swept swiftly downriver.

His rolling eyes glimpsed a flash of green—the willows on the island! Without hesitation he struck toward that glimpse of safety. His lungs were bursting. His body felt like a stone that could only sink to the bottom. But the pride and determination and courage that had been bred into his line for generations past overrode any temptation to give up.

He edged closer to the island. Felt his paws strike the bottom, lose their footing as the current tugged him away, find it again. A final lurch with all of his remaining strength and he was out of the Missouri's pull, stumbling onto the shore of the island.

For only a few moments he lay flat, drenched and weak and trembling with exertion. Then the thought of his companions in the boat drove him back to his feet.

On shaking legs, Seaman ran along the island toward its head. Now he could see the red pirogue out in the channel, the *engagés* furiously poling, making headway with their smaller, lighter craft against the current. And as the dog reached the tip of the island, there was the *Discovery*!

Some of the crew, turned swimmers, had tied a new line

to the boat's stern and struck for the south bank of the river. Just as Seaman reached the head of the island, the first of the men reached the shore. Those who were already on the bank joined them, and as the boat wheeled once more the rope caught her and the stern swung away from the sand.

In seconds the boat rode free in the deep water of the channel.

The men back on board sprang to their poles. Those on shore hauled on the line. Turning away from danger, the *Discovery* edged back toward the south bank of the river, once more passing across the tip of the willow island. One of the men pointed, and Meriwether Lewis shouted.

Seaman needed no command. He splashed out into the river, pushed into deep water, and within moments felt strong, willing hands seize him and haul him up into the boat.

The big dog lay exhausted on the cabin deck while the struggle went on. Back toward the south shore with its collapsing banks. Into the narrow channel, a second cord now attached to the bow. The men on shore slipping and falling, breaking through thick brush and bramble along the bank. The rhythm of the poles on board, each man planting his pole and thrusting, then pulling back and retreating to the end of the line, while the next man took his place, and the next . . .

Seaman watched and listened and panted, and the strength slowly seeped back into strained muscles. After what seemed a long while, he saw Lewis point toward the shore. The bow of the keelboat turned in the direction he indicated. The crew thrust and pulled harder now, knowing that this day's battle was nearly over, this one day on the river.

As the keelboat nosed in toward the shore Seaman stood, panting. He felt someone clap him on the head, heard someone else laugh, and knew an inarticulate happiness.

14

*A*s summer came on and temperatures climbed, Seaman gradually came to sense a growing apprehension among the men. Although he had no way of comprehending the source of this nervousness—as much excitement as fear—the dog understood it without explanation or reason. There was in his heritage a deeper knowledge beyond reason, a knowledge of danger that could strike without warning, of the enemy hidden in the tall grass or behind the blanket of darkness.

During the day, when the men fought their unending battle with the river, there was little time for other fears or worries, real or imagined. Moreover, out in the boats, every man was awake and alert and, except for those on shore, reasonably immune to surprise attack.

At night it was different. Then there was time for thought. For rumors and speculations. For the latest information about the Kansas Indians, said to be out on the Plains hunting buffalo. For stories about the warlike nature of the Osages or the Sioux tribes, who would surely be encountered further up the Missouri. Many of the soldiers had fought Indians in Kentucky or Tennessee or in the Old Northwest Territory, or their older

brothers and fathers had. Some of them expected hostilities; a few looked forward to the possibility of such confrontations. All, in particular their leaders, Meriwether Lewis and William Clark, knew that they had to be prepared for sudden attack at any time.

Such concerns were not idle as the expedition struck deeper into the ancestral lands of Indian Nations whose friendliness was by no means assured. For that reason, when an island was not too densely overgrown or so sandy that the shifting current might rearrange or relocate it during the night, the two leaders preferred such waterbound isolation for a campsite. Here the Missouri itself, so treacherous and turbulent an adversary by day, became a welcome buffer against any enemy. By contrast, when the nature of the terrain dictated a choice of campsite on land, along either bank of the river, the expedition's isolated little beachhead seemed dangerously vulnerable, as feeble as a single star flickering in the vastness of the dark universe.

144   Early on, Lewis set forth the daily duties of the sergeant of the guard and the sentries. The sergeant who drew the day's assignment in the middle of the keelboat was also responsible for the sentries whenever the expedition stopped to eat or rest, or when they made camp at night. Immediately upon landing during the day, the sergeant and the two men who had drawn sentry duty made a sweep of the immediate area to a distance of a hundred paces. The two guards were then posted, one to watch the landward side of the location, the other to guard the boats. At night, a similar sweep of the perimeter of the camp was made both on landing and at each changing of the guard, to a distance of a hundred and fifty yards out.

Seaman was curious about this ritual and the wary attitude of the men while carrying it out. From the first day on the Missouri, padding after the guard detail and observing the cautious circling of the camp or landing place, he sensed its protective purpose, his guarding instincts requiring no further information.

Louis Charbonneau

During the first weeks some of the men, especially Corporal Warfington's detail of soldiers and those of the permanent party who had been recruited from active army units, joked about the captain's black dog following the sentries around like a shadow. Sergeant Ordway tried to discourage the Newfoundland, believing the dog an unwanted distraction for the guards from their sentry duties. But after a while, as nervousness about Indians increased, the men stopped laughing at the dog. Obviously Seaman took his assumed responsibilities seriously. Moreover, his alertness, keen hearing, and acute sense of smell soon convinced the men that he might detect an unwanted presence in the vicinity and give the alarm more quickly than any sentry.

Seaman became a familiar part of the regular sentry sweeps about each camp. Even that didn't satisfy him. The big dog habitually undertook his own last private check of the perimeter each night, just before lying down to sleep by the entry to the captains' tent.

"By gar, dat dog, he t'ink he guard us all," observed Cruzatte one night, closing his one good eye in an exaggerated wink.

"Might be he do just that," Drouillard said.

On May 25, during an overnight stop at the tiny settlement of St. John's, Lewis and Clark eagerly sought information from Regis Loisel, a trader who had just returned from Sioux country more than a thousand miles upriver. Loisel provided a fresh, firsthand account of conditions on the river and what the explorers might encounter. He had seen no Indians on the Missouri, he said, below the Poncas Sioux village.

St. John's was the last white settlement on the river. As the Corps of Discovery proceeded on, now and again they met rafts carrying trappers or traders downriver who, depending on their luck, came empty-handed or laden with valuable furs. From one such party Lewis purchased three hundred pounds

of buffalo tallow. The men were soon smearing the animal fat on their arms and necks, or on their upper bodies when they went shirtless, as protection against mosquitoes and other insects.

One raft carried trappers in the employ of Regis Loisel, bound for St. John's. One of the trappers, a white-haired Frenchman named Pierre Dorion who worked for Loisel as an interpreter, had lived among the Sioux for twenty years. Lewis and Clark questioned him far into the night before at last persuading the old man to accompany them back up the river to serve as an interpreter with the unpredictable Sioux.

In the days that followed the men of the crew continued to pester Dorion with questions. When he spoke of the warlike nature of the Sioux, dwelling on their savage practices in dealing with their enemies, his listeners exchanged uneasy glances. At night the sentries were more alert than before, more sensitive to the shadows beyond reach of the campfires, more conscious of the sounds that reached them from the dark, surrounding wilderness.

146

The days became hotter, an oppressive kind of heat that drained the strength out of the men laboring in the boats or heaving on a tow rope along the riverbank. Sometimes they had to rest in the middle of the day while the sun was overhead. Sometimes, fighting the falling banks and shifting sands, they made only a few miles in a day.

For Seaman the heat was an enemy more real than any threat in the woods by day or in the shadows of night. While riding in the keelboat, he sought out the shelter of the cabin during the heat of the day. When he went on shore during one of Lewis's many forays into the interior, he would retreat into any patch of shade while Lewis tirelessly examined flowers and shrubs, or tasted strange new berries growing wild on bushes at the edge of the Plains. And as often as not, retreating from the heavy burden of heat that sapped his energy, Seaman encountered tormenting mosquitoes.

June 26 was another hot, grueling ordeal on the river. At sunset, exhausted and short-tempered, the men hauled the *Discovery* around a sandbar. The boats came to at a point above another broad river, the Kansas, nearly half as wide as the Missouri itself, which here measured five hundred yards across. Recognizing the men's depleted state, Lewis and Clark decided to stop for three or four days to rest the crew, to make observations, and to allow the hunting party to catch up.

At break of day the men were set to work building a breastwork across the full width of the point between the two rivers, piling heavy brush and logs to a height of six feet. When they had finished, with the two waterways on their flanks and the thick barricade before them, they had made the camp into a kind of fortress.

The Corps of Discovery remained behind its redoubt at the junction of the two rivers for three days, drying out their gunpowder, repairing and drying one of the pirogues, sunning some of the goods that had become damp during the first month's journey on the Missouri. Then they set off once more.

The land was beginning to change, and with it the animal life along the river and on the prairie. Game was becoming more plentiful, and where there was game there were also wolves prowling. On the last day of June, riding in the barge, Seaman felt a jolt of excitement when he found himself staring across an open expanse of the river toward a full grown adult wolf, standing motionless on a sandbar.

The wolf had been walking across the sand after a flock of wild turkeys, which kept scuttling nervously before him. He stopped suddenly, as if just becoming aware of the boats in the river, of the men at their oars and poles, and of Seaman, standing rigid on the rear deck of the barge.

The men in the keelboat ceased paddling. One soldier

nudged another with an elbow, directing his gaze toward Captain Lewis's dog as a low rumble, more excitement than warning, grew in Seaman's throat. "Dat wolf," cried Pierre Dorion excitedly, "he t'ink he see one dam' big ghost, eh?"

While no one was certain of the old trader's meaning, there was no mistaking the flash of recognition that passed between the dog and the wolf in that frozen moment, like an unexpected confrontation of old enemies—or old friends.

A tremor went through Seaman's body. The rumbling growl became a kind of whine, and he was on the brink of leaping into the muddy river. His front feet danced in excitement, like the French rivermen hopping to Pierre Cruzatte's fiddle.

Meriwether Lewis took in the scene at a glance. "Stay!" he commanded. "Easy, lad . . . easy . . . it's only a wolf."

The wolf was a large one, as tall and rangy as the Newfoundland, its thick, coarse coat yellowed with soil. Seaman saw not a strange, alien creature but what might have been an image of himself in an earlier time, when common ancestors ran in yelping packs across the snow-crusted tundra of the high country, wild and free.

And then the wolf was gone. It dipped into a hollow and vanished. The abundant grass of the Plains stirred with its passage . . . or perhaps only with the wind.

July 4, 1804, was hot in the Missouri River valley. When some of the crew of the *Discovery* had to go ashore with the towline, a number of them went barefoot. Stepping onto the hot sand, they immediately began to swear and jump from one foot to another. Within minutes, as the sand scalded bare feet, some were forced to abandon the rope. Others returned to the boat for the moccasins most of them were adopting in place of their heavy shoes, Joseph Fields had even worse luck, surprising a rattlesnake dozing on a sandbar. It struck quickly, sinking poisonous fangs into Fields's leg.

Louis Charbonneau

Lewis treated Fields's bite with a poultice of his own concoction, made of bark and powder. That evening, in honor of Independence Day, the expedition fired its swivel gun in the bow of the keelboat, and an extra gill of whiskey was doled out to each man. Cruzatte broke out his fiddle, and the warm night air of the river bottom heard strange new sounds celebrating a young nation's day of independence.

The following day on the river was a bad one—hard water, broiling heat, sandbars that came in parallel rows and defied passage, a huge drift upon which the barge turned around three times before it was brought under control. By midday, when the boats came to at a beaver dam, the men were in no mood to find another landing place or to share their dinner hour with the busy builders of the waterways.

This time Meriwether Lewis gave Seaman his head. Shackled by Lewis's command during his recent encounter with the wolf, now the big dog's energies exploded. He dove into the river and swam eagerly toward the intricate structure of logs and brush and branches. At his approach several sleek, dark-coated animals slipped into the river. One of them peered from behind a thicket, hesitated, and retreated only when Seaman was almost upon it.

The beaver was a fat, heavy animal, and on the dam its movements seemed ponderous and slow. It reached the water an instant before Seaman caught it. He jumped in after the beaver and, to his astonishment, found himself pursuing a swift, graceful, and powerful swimmer that easily outdistanced him. The beaver found a hole deep under the dam and disappeared into it.

When the frustrated dog clambered out of the water onto the dam, he found the men on the boats grinning and cheering him. "Son of a bitch," yelled Collins, "you see that beaver run?"

Francois Labiche and Pierre Cruzatte did not join in the general cheering. "Dat beaver," Labiche muttered to

his fellow riverman, "she one damn t'ing you no catch so easy."

"She like *Francaise*," answered the one-eyed fiddler. "Wit' de French woman, de trouble come when you catch her."

15 We Lay be for to See the Indianes who we expect Hear to See the Captains. I am verry Sick and Has been for Som time but have Recoverd my helth again   the Indians have not Come yet this place is Called Council Bluff.

—CHARLES FLOYD, July 31, 1804

GEORGE SHANNON'S JOURNAL

July 12, 1804

rested today   the men are much fatigued. our two capts. took observations. Capt. Clark went walking with 5 Men, the land verry rich. Many berries grow wild, grapes, and plumbs and wild Cherries, which supplements our meals and is delicious. A Court Martial held today for Pvt. Alex. Willard, who was caught asleep at his post last night. He denied his guilt, claiming that he was only lying down but had all his senses about him. He was found Guilty by his Peers and is to receive 100 Lashes, which will be administer'd 25 Lashes every night for four consecutive Nights. This punishment is very light, for it is a Serious Matter for a sentinel to sleep on his post, endangering us all. The first 25 Lashes given at sunset, in which no one took any pleasure.

July 13, 1804

hard rain last night. We was able to proceed under our Sail most of the day, the wind blowing strong from the South relieves the heat som what, which afflicts all the men severly. Many have boils, tumors, &c., which Cap. Lewis attributes

to the water. Capt. Clark took a Measure below the Kansas R. he declared that for each pint of water he took from the Missouri R. he found half a wine glass of mud. Skies in the N.W. appears verry stormy tonight.

July 14, 1804

Delayed this A.M. by rain and wind. when this slackened at about 7 A.M. we set out, but had proceeded only a short time when the sky becom verry black and the winds blew hard, sand stung our faces and got into our eyes. The Boats were near the upper point of a Sand Island, crossing over because of the bank opposit falling in, when the Storm struck the keelboat broadside, nearly over-turning her. all Hands leap'd overboard and was hanging onto the boat to hold her upright, the anchor was Dropp'd to keep her from being smashed on the sand Island. The Storm continued to blow, no Relief for about 40 minutes, the Wind so strong that it blew the waves over the side of the boat. Only the tarpalin which Cap. Lewis had ordered placed over the Lockers prevented the boat from filling with water, which rolled off the tarpalin, as it was there was two barrels of water in the Boat. The Pirogues was in a similiar distress on the River above us, the men holding on to keep their boats from being swamped. This continued for what seemed like an Eternity but was less than an hour, when of a sudden the storm quit and all was quiet, the River being as smooth as glass. We bailed out the water and proceeded on

July 21, 1804

I have not Writ for several days, being out Hunting. It has been verry hot and the going hard. Today we passed opposit. the mouth of the Great River Platt. It is a tremendous strong current which makes extensive sand bars about its mouth and throws sand all the way across the Missouri onto the far bank. This River is shallow, being no more than 5 Ft. at its deepest part, but is very wide at this place. It appears verry smooth in spite of the violence of its Current. It is verry hot hear, all men much fatigued so it is necessary to lay over during the middle of the day until we can proceed on. We pass'd the River Platt and continued on 4 Miles and camped on the South Side of the Missouri R. a great number

Louis Charbonneau

of Wolves howled about our camp all night, the men's sleep much disturbed, and Cap. Lewis's dog was kept awake and prowling about the camp all night. He is much agitated by the presense of these Wolves.

July 23, 1804

this day fair, the wind from the South and steady, it brings relief from the Heat. It being determined that we are close to Indian towns, we lay over. The prairies was on fire to the S.W., which is a sign that Indians are present, they use this as a signal, the smoke being visible over a great distance. Cap. Lewis sent G. Drewyer and P. Cruzat to the village of Otos to invite them to a Council. We put goods out to dry, examin'd our powder and guns, in readiness for whatever comes.

July 25, 1804

The Men busy making new oars & poles to replace those broke or lost. G. Drewyer & Peter Cruzatt returned today from the Oto village. There was sign of recent habitation but no Indians was present. We do not know if they have left because they are afraid of us or are out hunting the Buffalo. The Plains from the river to the village is open prairie all the way. the musquiters excessive bad tonight, we stay behind our musquitar bars. R. Fields says they are the size of Kentucky horse flies. Cap. Lewis's dog is sore afflicted with them. a Fair day, the wind continues from the South.

July 28, 1804

Yesterday we completed making our new oars & poles after dinner proceeded on and made 15 Miles. this morning was dark with a steady drizzle all morning. Shots was heard off to the S.W. G. Drewyer was hunting in the priarie, this eve. he returned with an Indian he met while he was hunting. This savage is of the Missouri Nation, which has been much reduced by Wars, &tc, and he now lives with the Otos. His people are only 4 Miles from the river and consists of 20 Families. All are curious about this savage. He wears only a

leather apron over his Privates and a buffalo robe, otherwise he is nakid, but the musquitors do not seem to be troublesom to him. His people hunt with bows & arrows, but Drewyer says they have also some old muskets, they would like some Powder & Ball from us. The Captains decided to send one of the French, la Liberty to go with the Indian to invite his people to come and Council with us at the next bend of the River. Liberty speaks some sign language which is common among these people. it begun to rain at dark and continues. Sgt. Floyd feeling poorly. Many of the men have Boils and dyssenterey, but all are ready to meet the first Plains Indians to be encountered.

On July 30, 1804, the Corps of Discovery came to a clear, open prairie on the south side of the Missouri and made camp to wait for the return of La Liberté with the Oto Indians. The situation of the camp, which they named Council Bluff, was one of remarkable beauty. The bottomland was rich and green. The camp was set in a small grove of timber at the foot of a gentle rise. In the bottom about the camp grew tall grass and an abundance of flowers and fruit, the latter including blueberries, gooseberries, cherries, raspberries, plums, currants, and grapes, all of which the men picked eagerly to supplement a diet now heavy with meat. The highland at the top of the rise was covered with a shorter grass and extended as far as the eye could see. Here a bluff overlooked a beautiful prospect of the Missouri meandering through the Plains, each point in the river covered with tall trees, the highlands on either side rolling back from the river breaks in wave upon wave of grasses like an endless sea.

During this layover, on August 1, William Clark celebrated his thirty-fourth birthday. For his dinner, he ordered a saddle of venison, an elk fleece—the fat meat from the shoulders of an elk—and a dessert concocted by York of cherries, plums, raspberries, currants, and grapes.

As a golden sunset turned the prairie on fire the next evening, the sentry called out an alarm. Lewis and Clark moved to the edge of the camp. At the top of the rise, pausing to peer down at them, was a party of a dozen Indians on horseback. "By the Lord, Clark," Lewis said, "we have our Indians at last!"

As if in response, the Indians fired several shots in the air. Black smoke spurted from their ancient muskets, and the echo of the shots racketed across the prairie.

"Give them an answer, Sergeant!" Lewis called out to John Ordway, sergeant of the guard that night. "From our cannon—hop to it!"

The cannon's boom shook the evening air. On the rise the Indians' horses shied and danced nervously. But their riders quickly controlled them and a moment later began a slow descent toward the river bottom.

"Peaceable Indians, it would appear," Clark murmured.

"We'll be on our guard tonight all the same, I think."

"And in the morning you can immobilize them with the Speech."

Meriwether Lewis laughed aloud as he stepped forward, raising his right arm in friendly greeting.

155

Among the visitors were a half-dozen Otos and the same number of Missouris, accompanied by a white man, a French trader named Fairfong who was living with the Otos. The Indians had brought gifts of watermelons, in return for which the captains presented them with roast meat, flour, and meal to enjoy that first evening, and tobacco for their peace pipes—the universal gesture of friendship on the Plains.

The council began the following morning at nine o'clock. The men of the detachment were curious and a little on edge after a sleepless night, but the Indians proved to be sober and peaceful. Lewis and Clark met them under an awning made of the keelboat's square sail. For the occasion the enlisted men were in uniform. Most had grown beards during this summer on the river, but during their three-day wait they had had time to bathe and clean themselves up, and they made an impressive show in their wrinkled blue jackets.

With the Indians sitting on the ground before him, Lewis gave the Speech, as he and Clark had come to call it. He had practiced it before, in his tent at night and in the early meeting with the Shawnees and Delawares on the Mississippi, and he had written out a more formal, polished version. But this morning, Lewis felt, was historic. This first council with the Plains Indians was one of the purposes Thomas Jefferson had set forth for the expedition, and Lewis spoke with genuine fervor while the French trader, Fairfong, translated. "Children!" Lewis said. "Listen to these truths. Let your wisest men, and the warriors whose stout arms have protected you from danger in times past, council together on these truths, which alone can perpetuate the happiness of your Nation . . .

"We have been commissioned and sent by the Great Chief of the Seventeen Great Nations of America to council with you, and with all of the red men who hunt and live along the borders of the Missouri. We have come to inform you that a great council was held between the Great Chief of the Seventeen Nations of America and your old fathers, the French and the Spaniards. And at this council it was agreed that all of the white men of Louisiana, all who inhabit the waters of the Mississippi and the Missouri, should now obey only this one Great Chief. He has adopted them all as his children, and they are now one family with us. Your old traders are among these men who are now no longer subjects of France or Spain, but citizens of the Seventeen Great Nations of America, and are bound to obey the commands of their Great Chief the President, who is now your only Great Father . . ."

The old fathers of the red men, Lewis went on to say, the French and Spanish, had withdrawn their soldiers and surrendered all their forts and lands on the Missouri and the Mississippi, and they had gone beyond the great lake toward the rising sun. Here Lewis's arm waved in a stiff gesture toward the east. The morning was already warm, and the sol-

156

diers were beginning to feel hot in their uniforms. The Indians listened impassively. The speech was long, but they were accustomed to long speeches, which were a mark of respect and seriousness. "Your old fathers will never return to visit their red children or display their flags," Lewis said. "From now on no vessel shall pass on these great rivers, or pass the mouths of all the rivers through which the traders bring goods to the red men, except those that sail under the protection of the Great Chief's flag which you see here, the flag of the Seventeen Nations of America . . ."

The cities of this nation were as numerous as the stars in the heavens, and the Great Father's people were like the grasses on the red men's plains. But the Great Father had sent Lewis and his friends to offer the hand of friendship, to make the way to the setting sun a road of peace between the Father and all the red men along that road. He wished to know his children's wants, that he might relieve them.

Lewis's voice droned on, much of its oratorical fervor grown hoarse. The men sweated in their uniforms. The mosquitoes buzzed around them. The Indians' attention began to wander at last, or their heads grew heavy on their necks. But Meriwether Lewis was oblivious to the heat, the whining mosquitoes, the slow climb of the sun in the sky. He was experiencing an almost religious exaltation, born of the knowledge that, on this morning, on this bluff overlooking the muddy Missouri, he was taking a significant step toward fulfilling the dream Thomas Jefferson had invited him to share. Looking at the broad, open countenances of the Otos and the attentive faces of the smaller Missouris, Lewis had a sense of being touched by his personal destiny as he had never been before.

For Seaman, this first encounter with the red men of the Plains was a source of puzzlement. They wore strange garments. They smelled of smoke and grease and dried blood. Yet they had

come in the manner of friends and had been accepted as such by Lewis and the others of the detachment, which meant that Seaman also must accept them.

The Indians had bedded down at the edge of the camp on the night of their arrival. Sensing the mixture of wariness and curiosity in his companions, Seaman dozed fitfully during the night, awakening every time one of the strangers stirred in his blanket or, as one man did, spoke in his sleep.

The ceremonies of the council meant little to the Newfoundland, whose interest perked up only when the speeches were over—Lewis's long speech and the replies of each of the half-dozen Indian chiefs. Then the parade of soldiers broke up, and the red men milled about, examining their gifts. They cried out in astonishment when Lewis demonstrated his air gun, and they stared in open curiosity at Clark's black servant, whose color of skin they had never seen before. And more than one of the Indians, especially one wrinkled old Missouri who was a second rank chief, stared in wonder at the huge Bear Dog who accompanied the white men and sat at his councils.

158

When the Indians left after dinner and the camp was struck, Seaman took his customary place in the keelboat with his curiosity about the strangers unsatisfied. As he watched them climb the rise on their horses and disappear onto the highland, there was in him no sense of an encounter ended, but of something only begun.

Although their daily battles with sawyers and sand bars on the Missouri came to seem almost commonplace for the men of the expedition, the river continued to astonish them. In the days following the meeting with the Indians at Council Bluff, banks fell in at every bend of the river. William Clark noted the remarkable twists and turns of the river's course. One night he walked back along the shore below the evening camp and then crossed a neck of land. He reached the riverbank again within 370 paces. Clark stared at it in wonder. Early that evening he had made his calculations for the distance the boats had traveled that day around the bend, putting it at twelve miles on the river . . . to accomplish actual progress of 370 yards!

But, in the aftermath of the Oto council, it was not the river that most disturbed the two commanders of the detachment. La Liberté had not returned . . . and one of the enlisted men was also missing.

On August 4, Moses Reed had reported to Clark that he had forgotten his knife, leaving it behind at Council Bluff. A knife being one of a man's most valuable possessions in the wilderness, Reed was granted leave to return for it.

The boats crawled up the river. Two nights later the camp huddled under a violent storm of wind and rain. Neither Reed nor La Liberté had returned.

The following day, after a late start because of the storm, the boats pulled in at noon to a sheltered beach on an island. Over dinner Lewis and Clark conferred. "Reed should have caught up by now," observed Lewis.

"Aye, it's been three days." Though generous by nature, Clark was also a realist. He had had experience with the occasional deserter during General Anthony Wayne's wilderness campaigns a decade ago, and his suspicion of Reed's absence had begun to harden into conviction.

"The rains might have delayed him."

"Aye."

The two men stared at each other. Lewis read the answer to his unspoken question in William Clark's eyes. For all of his experience with men, Lewis remained an idealist who sometimes mistook his own fidelity to principle for the appearance of it in others. Slower to believe that Reed was guilty of outright desertion, Lewis felt the more betrayed—and angry. It was one thing for La Liberté to be missing—the Frenchman was only an *engagé*, after all, a hired hand—but Reed was an enlisted soldier in the permanent party.

Abruptly Meriwether Lewis turned toward the mess of

Sergeant Pryor, to which Reed had been assigned. He called Pryor over to the captains' mess. "The missing man, Sergeant . . . did he leave anything behind? Any of his possessions?"

"His knapsack is here, Cap'n. I been holdin' it for him. He should catch up with us any time now, sir."

"Let's have a look at that knapsack, Sergeant."

A quick examination confirmed what Lewis and Clark both suspected. Reed's few items of clothing, his rifle, powder, and balls, all were missing. He had evidently cached them out of sight before coming up with his excuse of the missing knife, and had then taken them with him.

"He has deserted," said Lewis coldly. "The Frenchman, too."

Clark agreed. Although Reed had given no indication of his unhappiness or intention to desert, the evidence was undeniable. "He'll have headed for that Oto village."

Desertion could not be ignored. Lapses in discipline had been remarkably few during this summer on the river. If anything, the daily struggle united the detachment in their common purpose. But it was still early in the journey. The greatest challenges and hazards were still ahead. To fail to deal firmly and decisively with this first attempt at desertion risked the future of the entire expedition.

160

"I'll go," William Clark said grimly.

"You're needed here."

"Drouillard, then."

Meriwether Lewis nodded. With little discussion, the two captains quickly agreed on the selection of three others to accompany George Drouillard—Reuben Fields, William Bratton, and Francois Labiche. Lewis gave the four-man detail their instructions in blunt terms, concluding, "If they try to resist or refuse to return with you, you will shoot them, is that understood?"

The men exchanged sober glances. Drouillard answered for the others. "They be deserters, *Capitaine*. We bring 'em back."

Louis Charbonneau

Ten days later Francois Labiche straggled into camp in the evening, tired and hungry. He had become separated from the others, he told Lewis and Clark while he wolfed down his first good meal in days. Using a drag, the men of the crew had caught upwards of eight hundred fish the previous day, mostly catfish and bass. Labiche put away three large fried catfish before he slowed down enough to answer questions.

"I see your fire," he said, picking a bone from between his teeth. "That is what bring me to you."

"We set fire to the prairie as a signal to the Indians," said Clark. The captains hoped to bring any Omaha or Sioux Indians in the vicinity to the river to council with them.

"Some of de Otos is come with Drouillard. They be here quick, I think."

"What about Reed and Liberty?" Lewis asked impatiently.

"*Oui*, we catch them. They, how you say, take refuge with the Otos. But Liberté, he quick give us de slip again. We no catch him, I think."

"But Reed? He was caught?"

"*Oui*. They bring him soon."

The following day, August 18, 1804, was Meriwether Lewis's thirtieth birthday, but its celebration was delayed. Early in the afternoon the detail sent after the deserters reached camp, and Lewis wasted no time convening a court-martial. The party with their prisoner was accompanied by several Oto chiefs, including their grand chief, Little Thief, and a number of warriors. The captains welcomed the Oto chiefs, offered them food, and politely informed them that it was necessary for the captured man to be brought at once to trial.

The court-martial was swift. Reed admitted his guilt, including his attempt to desert as well as the theft of "a public Rifle Shot-pouch Powder & Ball." He asked for mercy. He

was sentenced to run the gauntlet through the assembled soldiers four times, with each man in the line provided with nine
switches to punish him. In addition, Reed would no longer
be considered a member of the expedition. At the earliest
opportunity he would be sent back to St. Louis.

When the three principal Oto chiefs perceived the nature
of the punishment that was about to be given, they showed
alarm. Patiently, Meriwether Lewis explained the customary
nature of military discipline among his people and pointed out
the harm that Reed's desertion could bring to the entire expedition. Then he turned toward the waiting soldiers, who had
formed the parallel lines of the gauntlet. His gaze met that of
Reed, who seemed more resigned than sullen. "Carry out the
punishment!" called Lewis firmly.

It was a hell of a way, Meriwether Lewis thought, as Reed
bent his head and stumbled along the gauntlet, the switches
whistling in the air before they bit into his naked back, to
celebrate a birthday.

162

Cruzatte, whom the men had taken to calling St. Peter, got
out his fiddle that night, and the soldiers and *engagés* danced
with foot-stomping enthusiasm before the astonished assem-
blage of Indians. After resting for several days to wait for
Drouillard and his party to return with Reed, the men were
feeling lively. Their celebration of Meriwether Lewis's thirtieth
birthday was a way of putting the harsh necessity of Reed's
punishment behind them. Even Sergeant Floyd, who had been
sick off and on for several weeks, rose to his feet to pound his
heels to Cruzatte's energetic music, until he was short of breath
and had to stop, laughing and coughing and holding his side.
Clark ordered an extra gill of whiskey for each man in honor
of his friend's birthday. The Otos crowded forward, eager for
their share.

The next day, after the morning's speeches, after the
giving of medals and presents, after the shooting of the air
gun, after a demonstration of one of Dr. Saugrain's sulfur

matches to light a fire almost instantly, and in the midst of the friendly interchange with the visiting Oto chiefs, Sergeant Charles Floyd gave a sharp, involuntary cry and doubled over in agony.

He fell writhing to the ground. Clark was immediately at his side, and he ordered several men to carry Floyd to the captains' tent.

The sudden, alarming turn in Floyd's illness dampened the mood of this second Oto council. Throughout that afternoon and evening, while the sick man lay in the captains' tent, every man in the party came around at some time for a word of encouragement. York prepared a broth, but Floyd could keep nothing on his stomach, vomiting whatever he swallowed. Lewis, who had tried everything in his limited medical kit to relieve Floyd's recurrent illness, despaired even of easing the poor man's pain. William Clark finally persuaded Lewis to get some rest himself.

Clark sat up with Floyd through the night. So did York, who sponged Floyd's face with a damp cloth periodically and spoke soothingly in his deep voice to the sick man whenever Floyd cried out or stirred.   163

In the morning the Indians left. The Corps of Discovery, its mood somber, took the boats several miles up the river, past a willow island and to the foot of a bluff on the south side. There they came to, with the idea of preparing a warm bath for Sergeant Floyd to lie in, hoping that it might relieve his condition.

Floyd had fallen silent during the brief passage upriver in the boat. When he spoke suddenly, Clark, who had remained close to his side, was startled. Though Floyd was very pale and sweat stood out on his drawn features, his voice was calm and composed. "I'm goin' away, Cap'n," he said. "I was wonderin' . . . would you write a letter for me?"

"Of course I will, Sergeant." Clark swallowed hard. "But don't be in too much of a hurry to leave us. A warm bath will do wonders for ye, I'm thinking."

Floyd smiled, as if reassured.

Several of the men had lined a hollow in the ground with the hide of a large elk, which would hold water. After a few minutes enough water had been heated over a fire to warm the river water used to fill the hollow. One of the men called out to Floyd in the keelboat. "Bath's near ready, Sergeant!"

William Clark looked up with tears in his eyes. Relief had come too late.

16 The Seoux is a Stout bold looking people, (the young men hand-som) & well made, the greater part of them make use of Bows & arrows ... the Warriers are Verry much deckerated with Paint Porcupine quils & feathers, large leagins and mockersons, all with buffalow roabs of Different Colours.
—WILLIAM CLARK, August 30, 1804

*A*s the Missouri River wormed its way northward into the high country, Seaman and his companions welcomed drier air and cooler mornings and evenings. The High Plains were more open, the vistas grander, the winds more sweeping across the long, rolling highlands covered only with short grass.

But the most striking change toward the end of that summer on the river was the increasing numbers of all kinds of birds and animals. Along the river bottoms and prairies below the Platte River valley, the herds of deer had been of modest size. In the daily effort to find enough game to meet the voracious demands of the detachment, Drouillard and the other hunters had frequently been absent for days at a time, often straying far from the river.

North of the Platte there was a steady increase in the animal life of the plains and rivers. In the tributary streams beaver became plentiful. On the plains elk were a common sight. Prairie hens and wild turkeys were almost daily fare. Once, from their congregation on an island in the Missouri that Meriwether Lewis named Pelican Island, thousands of

those exotic, large-billed birds filled the sky, flying ahead of the boats for an entire day.

Prairie wolves—coyotes—began to appear. They would stay beyond the range of the campfires at night and bark like dogs, and their presence agitated Seaman until he became accustomed to seeing and hearing them. Now, too, large gray wolves filled the vast chambers of the night on the open prairie with their calls, which kept the Newfoundland awake and prowling restlessly about the camp.

And there were the buffalo.

On August 23, 1804, Joseph Fields had the first encounter. Now one of the expedition's best hunters, Fields came upon a huge buffalo bull in the open plain. The shaggy animal, apparently little disturbed by Fields's sudden appearance, stared at him, head down.

Slowly Fields brought his rifle to his shoulder, taking careful aim. His hands were sweating and the long rifle shook a little. Up close, the buffalo was much larger than he had expected. These animals were said to be easily spooked, more prone to run than to charge, but he wondered if this received wisdom was always true.

He squeezed the trigger. The rifle slammed into his cheek as it fired. With a kind of surprise he saw the buffalo's front legs buckle as if he had been tripped. Fields loaded and aimed again, his hands no longer shaking. The second shot put the huge animal down.

Fields circled the buffalo with a feeling of awe. Then, realizing that he couldn't drag the carcass or even carry a fair portion of its meat by himself, he hurried back to the river. When the boats appeared around a bend, he hailed them eagerly.

Fields's news of his kill caused great excitement. The boats were sent upriver to the point nearest the plain where he had shot the buffalo. Meriwether Lewis, Sergeant Ordway, and ten other men struck overland along the hunter's trail.

It took all twelve of them to drag the dead buffalo across the prairie to the river. Much of the meat was jerked or pickled, but choice portions were held out for supper that night. All in the party agreed that buffalo meat, properly grilled, was highly palatable, on a par with elk or deer.

For the two commanders of the expedition, the day was an important landmark. They had reached buffalo country at last.

At first there were only a scattered few of these great, shaggy beasts so precious to the Plains Indians, so strange to the eyes of men from east of the Mississippi. Then larger herds of several hundred were seen drifting across the prairie, followed by slinking packs of wolves waiting to prey upon the old, the weak, the lame. At last, on the High Plains, the buffalo multiplied into the vast herds of which Indians and traders had spoken so eloquently that their words seemed to be the exaggerations of men accustomed to speak in tall tales. Now the buffalo spread across the prairie like a shaggy brown carpet, not hundreds but thousands of them, one enormous herd succeeding another, awakening awe at the prodigality of nature.

167

The teeming life of the High Plains kept Seaman in a constant state of excitement. Each new encounter brought a strange mingling of wonder and recognition, like that moment when the yellow wolf on the sand bar returned his gaze across the roiling water. The Plains were new to the dog, but they were not alien. He had a unity with nature few humans could approach. The bounding antelope had been chased in forgotten dreams. The buffalo was an adversary known, quickly accepted, unfeared. The coyote had run from the Bear Dog's ancestors and howled its frustration at the night.

And the gray wolf was both brother and enemy, as he had always been.

Meriwether Lewis was no stranger to arduous journeys. He had undertaken many of them during his active duty in the army, especially during the last two years when he was acting

as paymaster, frequently traveling, alone or with a small detachment of soldiers, from Fort Pitt in the East as far as Fort Kaskaskia on the Mississippi and Fort Detroit in the north. He had approached this summer on the Missouri with the stubborn determination that was part of his nature—and with a desire to be Thomas Jefferson's scientific surrogate, bringing the wonders of this uncharted land into the realm of human knowledge.

As summer waned, Lewis rose each day with increasing eagerness. The expedition was in Sioux country now. Home of the most feared warriors of the High Plains.

The expedition's relations with the red men of the Plains were, in Lewis's mind, one of his most important charges. The Sioux were a key. A true Nation, the Sioux were actually eight major tribes, some more peaceful than others. One or more of the tribes always seemed to be at war with their neighbors, a state of unrest Thomas Jefferson was anxious to change. As an avenue of trade to the Pacific, the upper Missouri would be of little practical value if the way could only be won through open warfare with the Indians, or even if the white men were caught in the middle of endless intertribal warfare. "In all your intercourse with the natives," the President had instructed Lewis, "treat them in the most friendly & conciliatory manner which their own conduct will admit; allay all jealousies as to the object of your journey, satisfy them of it's innocence, make them acquainted with the position, extent, character, peaceable & commercial dispositions of the U.S., of our wish to be neighborly, friendly & useful to them, & of our dispositions to a commercial intercourse with them . . ."

But no members of the great Sioux Nation had yet appeared.

Lewis did not then know that, although he had not seen the Sioux, the Sioux were watching him. A general council had been called of the several tribes to debate the coming of this invading army of whites. Though no direct action had yet been agreed upon, word had gone out from the council, calling all wandering bands of warriors to converge near the Missouri.

Louis Charbonneau

On August 27, 1804, three Indians appeared on the river-bank. Lewis felt a jolt of excitement.

The Indians waved. They appeared friendly. And, through old Pierre Dorion acting as interpreter, they quickly revealed that they were Indian members of the Yankton Sioux, living on the River Jacques about nine miles from the Missouri.

One of the Indians recognized Dorion, who had stayed in their village. Lewis quickly decided to send Dorion, Sergeant Pryor, and one of the French *engagés* to the Sioux village to invite the chiefs to come to the river for a council.

The next day the main party stopped by a hill on the south side of the river that they named Calumet Bluffs. The camp was made in a handsome bottom with thick groves of timber. The red pirogue had run onto a snag that day, smashing a hole in her bottom. While the pirogue was unloaded and the cargo dispersed between the other two boats, a flagpole was raised, a canopy formed of the keelboat's sail, and the Corps of Discovery settled down to wait.

Lewis's impatience was finally ended on the afternoon of August 29. After a hard storm of driving wind and rain had washed the plain, Pryor, Dorion, and the Frenchman appeared on the opposite bank. Ranged about them, some on foot and others on horseback, was a band of about seventy Sioux Indians—old men and boys, and muscular, painted warriors.

Lewis promptly sent the white pirogue across the river with a present of tobacco, corn, and kettles for the Indians to use in cooking their evening meal. The white chiefs, he informed them, would council with their Indian children in the morning.

No one slept much that night. Seaman, catching the nervous excitement of the men, was as alert and watchful as the sentries on duty.

Pierre Dorion surprised everyone when he introduced his son, whom he had found trading at the Yankton village. Sergeant Pryor was quizzed over and over again about what he had seen. He described the handsome, conical tipis in which the Sioux lived, made of hides painted white and red. He told

of the Indians' attempt to carry him and his companions into their village on ceremonial robes until he had made it clear to them that he was not a chief. "I wasn't gonna give 'em the Speech, Cap'n Lewis," he said with a grin.

Lewis, elated by this promising encounter with the Sioux, turned to William Clark with a mischievous smile. Lewis had given the Speech to the Otos. "Now it's your turn, Clark. I'll greet them. You'll give them the Speech!"

Clark worked late that night by candlelight on his own written version of the Speech. He was still at it in the morning before and after breakfast.

Clark finished it at noon. By then the pirogue had been back and forth across the river several times, ferrying the Sioux chiefs and warriors across.

The council was held under an oak tree with the canopy overhead and the United States flag flying from a staff. The morning had been foggy, but now the sun had burned through, dissipating the mist. A beautiful day, Clark thought.

After Lewis greeted the Sioux visitors, William Clark rose, a tall and imposing figure. When he spoke, acting the orator, his voice boomed like his brother George's. He told the Sioux that his red children had a new Father now, the Great White Father in Washington, that all of the red men were under his protection, and that the Father wished all of the Indian Nations to be at peace among each other and with the white men, who would now come from beyond the long river to trade with them and bring the goods they needed. Clark warmed to his task as he spoke, moved by the colorful scene before him— the warriors dressed in their decorated buffalo robes, the sun sparkling on the river, York standing off to the side and beaming at his master, the men of the expedition trying to appear solemn and attentive to words that had already become familiar. A moment to remember, Clark thought. A moment to dream of.

Louis Charbonneau

After the speeches on both sides were over, five of the Sioux were officially recognized as chiefs—one Grand Chief, one second chief, and three third-ranked chiefs. All were given medals, tobacco, and other presents. The Grand Chief, whose name translated as Shake Hand, was soon parading around wrapped in an American flag while wearing a red-and-blue army coat with gold lace and a cocked hat with feathers.

Soon it was time for demonstrations of the white man's powerful medicine, such as Lewis's air gun. When he shot it at a tree, many of the warriors ran to inspect the target and, when they found bullet holes in the trunk, shouted and danced with excitement.

Old and young, the Sioux were also fascinated by Lewis's dog, and he allowed Seaman to join in the Indian boys' fun. Seaman romped with the Indian boys just as he had with William Clark's nephews in the meadow before George Clark's cabin. He chased sticks for the young Sioux boys and brought them back in his mouth. They vied with each other to throw things for Seaman to carry, while they mimicked Lewis's command, crying "Fetch!"

Seaman even tried to chase down the boys' arrows when they shot against each other for the coveted blue beads offered as prizes, and Lewis had to call his dog away. He ordered Seaman to sit. The Indians marveled at the way the black dog obediently sat, patient and motionless, like a wise man sitting at a council.

Seeing how impressed they were, Lewis then commanded Seaman to stand up and walk on his hind legs. With his full black coat, when the Newfoundland reared up to his full height, standing on his back legs with his front paws dangling before him, his resemblance to a black bear was so remarkable that the Indians shouted and pointed and slapped their sides. Shake Hand, an old chief with a long memory, was deeply moved. "The Bear Dog!" he cried over and over. "The Bear Dog! The Bear Dog!" For he was old enough to remember the Bear Dog known in the ancient stories of his people, long before

the coming of the horse, when the People lived and fished and hunted and killed their enemies near the headwaters of the great Mississippi River.

After dark Meriwether Lewis gave the Indians a grained deerskin, which they stretched over an empty half keg to form a drum. While two braves beat on the drum, ten others accompanied the beat by rattling skin bags filled with beads or pebbles. The young warriors had painted their faces and chests, some with the faces all white, others with white daubed around the forehead or on their chests. They whooped and danced in turn and chanted of great deeds, while their chiefs looked on with solemn dignity and the white men watched in fascination.

The Indians danced until exhausted. When the festivities finally came to an end and the Indians returned to their camp across the river, the two captains at last were able to retire to their tent, dead tired but satisfied that they had had a successful day.

"I believe it was your speech won the day," said Lewis.

Clark grinned. "I don't know about that, but they seemed friendly enough. And pleased with their presents, I think, though it's hard to tell what's in their heads."

"No doubt it helped, having old Dorion with us." Lewis paused reflectively. "I've talked to him about staying behind. He knows these people, and they know him. If anyone can get all the tribes together and act as peacemaker, I can think of none better."

"Aye, they trust him, it appears."

After a moment's silence Meriwether Lewis observed, "You noticed there were no women amongst them."

"This bein' a hunting party, I suppose that's natural enough."

"Young Dorion, who's been living with the Indians these past months, has heard other rumors—that the Sioux are preparing for war and accordingly they have removed all of their squaws and their young children to safety, while the warriors gather."

"War with whom, I might ask," William Clark murmured.

"With an invading army of white men coming up the river."

Pierre Dorion and his son remained behind with the Yankton Sioux band. The old man had been commissioned by Lewis to encourage peace among the various tribes and to collect as many of the chiefs as he could to go downriver in the spring to St. Louis. From there they would be taken to Washington to visit their new Great Father.

The Corps of Discovery returned to the battle with the muddy Missouri.

The river's level had fallen steadily as summer waned. The shallower water meant even more trouble with shifting sands and bars. Sometimes the boats could make no headway at all, by oar or sail or rope, and all hands had to get waist deep in the water to haul the boats along.

Meanwhile, in the week following the council at Calumet Bluffs, a new source of anxiety festered. George Shannon was missing.

173

GEORGE SHANNON'S JOURNAL

A u g u s t   2 6,   1 8 0 4

This day Patrick Gass was elected Sergeant to take the place of our deceased friend Sgt. Floyd, he rec'd 19 votes. Drewyer and Myself was sent to find our 2 Horses which is used by our hunters, they strayed off while grazing. Drewyer went into the prairie to look for the horses, but they came to the River and I collected them. It being late I stayed out all night.

August 29, 1804

Taken shelter from a hard storm, much wind & rain. It is 3 Days I have been surching for the Expedition. I came upon a place where the Prairie was set on fire, but there was no sign of Indians or the Party. I am able to ride one of the horses so am confident of overtaking them. Thunder this eve.

August 31, 1804

A Fair day no sign of the Party. I shot my last ball and have no others for my gun. Ate some Plumbs & Grapes for my supper, the prairies is plentiful with such berries. There are no trees except in the bottoms and the points of the River. It is now 5 Days since I have spoke to any Man. A violent wind this eve. with rain.

September 2, 1804

sheltered in a cave last night, hard wind & rain, and verry cold. Wind strong from N.W. this morning, bringing more rain, with Thunder and lightning. The Missouri R. verry brown and filled with Trees & Sawyers which drop into the River from the falling banks. No sign of the boats yesterday or today.

I shot my last bullit two days ago. I Whittled a wooden one with my knife and used it to kill a Rabbit, which I cooked and eat the last of for supper. This is a high Prairie with bluffs on both the North and South side which come close to the river. It has plumbs & grapes aplenty so I will not starv. I waited out the rains which come and went all day, Proceded on this eve. when it let up, a verry cold night. I have High Hopes to rejoin the Party tomorrow.

September 3, 1804

Set out at Day light a verry clear day but cold. This morning pass'd an old trading post on N. side of the river. I swam a very wide River on the South side, it measures 150 Yds. acrost. No sign of the Party.

Louis Charbonneau

September 4, 1804

Very cold wind from the South it kept up all day, no rain. I crossed a beaver dam but could not catch any. The prairie has many Deer, Elk, goats and Buffalows but as I am without bullits for my gun I cannot Hunt them. I cannot explain how the Boats can be so far ahead, there is no sign of their fires. One of the horses came up Lame. I ate some grapes and wild Cherries for supper, this is all I have had to eat for 3 Days. This Prairie is a lonely place for one Man.

September 6, 1804

Am verry hungry, nothing to eat but Grapes. Tried to run down a Turkey but as I am weak from not eating it was able to get away. A Bad Storm this A.M. and verry cold winds makes it unpleasant. This day I come to a verry high Hill which raises above the prairie. I climbed the Hill and was able to see for a great Distance a butiful Prairie, no trees except by the river bottoms, there are many Buffalows feeding on the grass. I did not see the Boats. It is clear I am lost and like to Starve except for grapes & berries. I feel myself fortunate that I have not encounter'd any Savages. I was compelled to leav the Lame horse behind when it gave out. I am wondering if Cruzat is playing his Fiddle tonight and the French & Others dance a jig A Cold Night.

175

September 7, 1804

This morning clear, I could see for a verry great distance from the top of a Hill, but I could not see the Boats. I thought I heard Guns on the Prairie Saw two goats with horns that run like Deer. The gangs of Buffalow are immense, they came within 30 Yds. of my fire this eve. They are not Afraid of me. Ate some Grapes, which is all I have had.

September 9, 1804

I have give up hope of finding the Party. The Hills where I have my camp are verry high. Below is a slope where a Town of little Dogs lives. They

are very numberous. They sit outside their houses, which are under ground, and whistle. When anything comes near they give a warning and jump down in their holes. They are about the size of a Squirrel. They are the only Company I have.

I will stay at this place, as I am verry weak from having no food but a few berries each day. Some of our French spoke of a trader who will be Coming down the River in a boat and I will wait for him. It is a great Sorrow to me if I am not to continue with the Party of North West Discovery. Heard guns today, but am not sure if they was Real. I put my Trust in the Good Lord.

For a week, after Drouillard returned to camp alone without finding the horses, search parties were sent out each day to locate Shannon. They came upon his tracks and campfires, and it was soon evident that, having become lost, the young man had mistakenly concluded that the boats were ahead of him on the river. Hurrying to catch up, he had moved faster on land than the boats could proceed on water, putting himself ever further out of reach.

The morning of September 11, 1804, was an ordeal on the river. The Missouri was now only a few feet deep in many places, and several times that morning the keelboat ran aground. Twice the crew had to get down in the water and drag the boat along.

Then, as the boats steered cautiously along a narrow channel past three islands, Sergeant Pryor, acting as bowsman in the keelboat, looked up at a sloping hill to the left and called out, "Someone up on that hill, Cap'n Lewis! A man on horseback, looks like."

Quickly Meriwether Lewis drew his spyglass from its sheath. The glass swam over the slope, past a prairie dog village, and jarred to a stop as a figure leaped into view. "By the Lord!" Relief rang in Lewis's voice. "It's Shannon!"

The name became a question, then a shout, at last a cheer. The prodigal had been found!

Thank God, thought Lewis gratefully. I have lost one good man. I have no wish to lose another.

It was left to William Clark, writing in his journal that evening, to sum up Shannon's near tragic experience. "Thus a man had like to have Starved to death in a land of Plenty," Clark wrote, "for want of Bullitts or Something to kill his meat."

Patrick Gass told Shannon about the escapade that had led, after an all-day siege, to the capture of a "barking squirrel."

The little animal was in a cage of Gass's making. He joined four magpies and a prairie hen, also kept in wooden coops whose neat fittings, smoothly working hinges, and sliding wooden bolts attested to the Irishman's woodworking skill.

As Shannon knew, Patrick Gass had recently been elected—the election being a surprisingly democratic gesture by the two commanders of the expedition—to take Charles Floyd's place as a sergeant in the Corps of Discovery. Gass was a short, burly man of thirty-three with curly black hair, bright blue eyes, and hands whose blunt fingers, nicked and scarred, offered no hint of their dexterity. Gass had been with Captain Russell Bissell's company at Fort Kaskaskia when the expedition reached that post, but before his enlistment in the regular army he had served a long apprenticeship to a carpenter. He was the first volunteer from Bissell's company for the western expedition, but his captain, reluctant to lose both an experienced soldier and his best carpenter, had refused to release him. Gass was determined. The adventurous spirit that had lured his father across the Alleghenies in the 1780s to what was then the far western frontier burned in Pat as well. He took his plea directly to Meriwether Lewis. After hearing him out, Lewis overruled Captain Bissell and signed Gass on. The Corps of Discovery could also make good use of a carpenter.

Four days before George Shannon's famine ended when

he was reunited with the detachment, Gass told him, they had come upon a whole village of prairie dogs. "*Petite chién* is what the French calls 'em. Well, nothin' would do but we should catch some of 'em. There was hundreds in that town of theirs—covered about four acres, it did. Cap Lewis had every man of us go up the hill, with every kettle and cookin' pot and empty keg we could carry filled with water. The captain figgered pourin' water down one of them holes would just sorta float the little fellers out.

"They'd pop up all around us, whistlin' and yelpin' like they do—you've heard 'em, lad?" Shannon, watching the little creature in its cage, nodded. It seemed calm enough now, he thought. "But any time we'd make a move, they'd just jump down their holes and disappear. Capt Lewis's dog there, Seam'n, he was fit to be tied. He'd run after one of them little bitty dogs and it would dive into its hole. He'd dig and dig without gettin' anywheres close to it. Then another one would pop up and yap at him, and Seam'n, he'd go after it like a terrier after a rat, and the same thing'd happen." Gass shook his head with a grin. "He kept that up until his tongue was hangin' down to the ground, and he never did get close to catchin' one."

"How'd you catch this one?"

"It weren't easy, lad. We kept it up the whole day, pourin' water down one or another of them holes. We poured five barrels into one hole without fillin' it! We tried diggin', too. After we got maybe six feet down, we used a pole to plumb the bottom, and we found out we still had as far to go as we'd already dug!"

One of the men nearby, listening to this account, chuckled. Ignoring him, Gass said, "Hell, it was dark, and we was near givin' up when we finally washed this little feller out of his house. Near drownin', he was, so he couldn't give us no trouble. I built him this new house, and he's gettin' along just fine, as you kin see."

"What's gonna become of him?"

"Why, don't y' know, lad? Along with them birds and the

prairie chicken, and whatever else the Cap'n finds . . ." Patrick Gass paused to consider the fact that his finely crafted coops and cages would be going on a journey almost as far to the east as the Corps of Discovery would travel in the opposite direction. "He's goin' back, lad . . . to see the President of the United States!"

17

*I*n the last week of September the Corps of Discovery came to the villages of the Bois Brulé. The warlike People of the Burnt Woods were a branch of the Teton Sioux living near the mouth of Bad River, which William Clark decided to call the Teton River after the natives found there. Since this was the largest concentration of Indians the expedition had yet encountered, Lewis and Clark approached the meeting with their customary friendliness tempered by an alert and wary caution.

But the expedition's first contact with the Bois Brulé went badly. On the afternoon of September 24, John Colter, who had been on shore hunting, appeared on the south bank, waving his arms. "Them thievin' savages! They stole the goddam horse!"

Colter was brought aboard, fuming with anger. The anger was at least partly directed at himself for losing the detachment's last horse. While he was busy dressing a deer he had shot, several Indians had sneaked up behind him where the horse was grazing, grabbed the trailing reins and fled.

Undoubtedly the horse could be replaced at the Mandan

villages, Meriwether Lewis said to William Clark. But the hostility of the theft could not be ignored.

A short distance farther on, within sight of the smoke rising over the Sioux villages, five Indians appeared on the bank. Lewis had the keelboat brought close to the bank. Using an Omaha who had come up the river with the expedition from the meeting at Council Bluffs as an interpreter, Lewis spoke firmly. *We have come as friends, but we come without fear of any Nation of the red men. Some young Sioux braves have taken our horse, which belongs to the Great White Father. We wish to council with our Sioux children, but we will not speak until the horse has been returned safely.*

It turned out that the Omaha Indian's knowledge of the Sioux language was limited to only a few words, but the Indians on the bank seemed to understand his attempt at translation. They withdrew, talking animatedly.

The boats came to at the mouth of the Teton and waited. Most of the party stayed on board, anchored safely offshore. The men conversed among themselves in low voices. Colter's voice rose above the others, still angry.

181

At dusk a young warrior appeared on the bank, leading the horse. He stared at the white men in the boats for a long moment before he dropped the reins and immediately trotted off toward the nearest village.

"That's an encouraging sign," Meriwether Lewis murmured.

William Clark grunted, his expression truculent. "At least they're willing to talk."

In the morning after breakfast the white pirogue brought Lewis and Clark to a sandbar in the middle of the river. There they had the keelboat's sail raised as an awning, and a flag flown on a staff. The *Discovery*, with most of the crew aboard, remained anchored about seventy yards from the meeting place.

The first and second ranked chiefs of the Bois Brulé,

whose names translated as Black Buffalo and The Partisan, arrived at eleven o'clock that morning. Lewis and Clark, both in full uniform, greeted the chiefs with ceremonial courtesy. They offered pork and meal to their visitors from their own provisions. In return, the buffalo-robed chiefs had brought a present for the white fathers consisting of great quantities of buffalo meat, packed in animal skins. From the packs came the high odor of spoiled meat.

"Look at your dog, Lewis," said Clark. "He doesn't think much of their meat."

Lewis had ordered Seaman to sit near his right hand, for he was well aware that both the Bear Dog and his obedient responses constantly astonished and impressed the Indians. Seaman's nose was in the air, quivering and sniffing as if in disdain.

The chiefs stared at the Newfoundland, but what they were thinking, about Seaman or the white chiefs, soon became a matter of guesswork. Although usually he could communicate effectively with signs, George Drouillard spoke no Sioux. In his place Pierre Cruzatte, who spoke a smattering of Omaha and other Indian languages, had joined the Omaha Indian to serve as an interpreter for the council. He tried his best, but the Sioux language was also strange to him. Lewis regretted having had to leave Pierre Dorion behind with the Yanktons.

The council began at noon with the customary smoking of tobacco. The crew had been brought in from the boats, and Meriwether Lewis rose to his feet. This time he had his speech written out. It was a fair day. The light breeze from the southeast lifted the colors of the flag, whose flutterings reminded Lewis of the sound of pigeon's wings in a loft.

As Lewis's voice droned on, the chiefs' attention wandered—to the Bear Dog sitting patiently at Lewis's side, to the men of the Corps, to the three boats rocking in the water. In the midst of a rhetorical flourish about the Great Father in Washington and his wish to see peace among all the red men of the Missouri basin, Lewis suddenly realized that the chiefs didn't understand a word of his speech or the halting attempts of his interpreters.

He cut the speech short. Clark climbed to his feet and added some words of his own. Turning to Lewis, Clark said, "What now? We're talking into the wind with these fellows. They don't have a glimmer."

"They understand presents."

Lewis kept the Indians waiting a bit longer while he had all of the Corps parade before them. Then he and Clark passed out gifts—medals to the chiefs, including a large Jefferson medal to the Grand Chief, Black Buffalo, and other presents. They seemed to be received well enough, and the two captains began to relax.

All continued to go well when the chiefs were invited on board the *Discovery* to witness at first hand such curiosities as the cannon in the bow, the corn mill attached to the gunwale, and, of course, Lewis's mysterious air gun. The chiefs were also eager to sample a quarter-glass of whiskey each, which one of them called "white man's milk." Downing their drinks with enthusiasm, they passed the bottle, sucking on the neck even after it was empty, one chief jerking it away from the other until all were disappointed.

The Partisan began to laugh and lurch about the boat, but his laughter lacked good humor. Seaman, brought back aboard with the chiefs, growled. He was quicker than his human companions to sense malice behind a false smile. He didn't care for these strangers with their loud voices and their animal skins that smelled of sweat and smoke and dried blood.

Laughing loudly, The Partisan elbowed Black Buffalo. He pointed at the air gun. He stumbled toward it, but Meriwether Lewis had placed the rifle out of reach. The Partisan reeled drunkenly, making a joke of his grab.

"Better get them off the boat," Lewis said to Clark.

"Aye, I'll go with them."

The white pirogue was standing by with several of the soldiers from Warfington's detail. However, the chiefs showed

no disposition to leave. With loud words and gestures that needed no translation they begged for more whiskey. Clark got them into the pirogue with some difficulty. "Take us ashore," he told the three soldiers at the oars. For what they were worth, he also took the two would-be interpreters along.

The pirogue knifed across the river to the south bank. As soon as it was within reach, three braves on shore waded into the water and seized the boat's tow line. One painted "soldier"—a special class of personal warriors attached to each chief—jumped aboard and hugged the pirogue's mast, as if by so doing he could prevent the boat from moving.

William Clark disembarked with the Indian chiefs. As soon as they were ashore, The Partisan staggered up against him. Clark felt a rough hand clawing at his sleeve and smelled what to his mind was the stink of treachery. Either the chief was drunk or he was playing the part—and Clark was angrily convinced that it was all an act. The Partisan's words were slurred and incomprehensible, but Clark caught their meaning from the man's blustering tone and insolent gestures. *The white man's presents are nothing! The men of Washington come to The Partisan with empty hands, promising much and giving little. Their gifts are an insult, not worthy of a squaw.*

When Clark tried to pull free, The Partisan grabbed his coat and hung on, so close that Clark felt his hot breath. The Indian's grin became a leer. "Chief Red Hair not go!"

The Partisan's hold became a drunken pawing. Clark's temper flared. Jerking away from the chief's grasp, he drew his sword. In the same motion he signaled with his free hand to Lewis in the keelboat.

Everyone reacted. The Sioux warriors lining the riverbank seemed to move as one man, arms flashing. There was a whirring sound like a gust of wind among autumn leaves as scores of arrows slid from their quivers and leaped to their strung bows. In the pirogue the men who had accompanied Clark brought their rifles up, ready to fire. And in the keelboat, still anchored out in the river, Meriwether Lewis saw his friend's predicament and ordered all men to arms. The swivel gun in the bow was swung about, bringing it to bear on the shoreline.

Seeing the white soldiers ready for battle, The Partisan backed off about twenty yards to a band of his followers. His words were loud and boastful, their meaning plain. With a sweeping gesture he embraced the line of warriors along the bank with their drawn bows, their arrows fitted to the strings. *My soldiers are great warriors! They are a match for the soldiers you have in your boats!*

William Clark's retort was contemptuous. "I have men and medicine on board that would kill twenty such Nations in one day!"

A pile of twigs, warm and smoking, could erupt into fire with a single spark from a pair of flintstones. William Clark recognized that the situation on the riverbank had reached that incendiary moment. Black Buffalo, Clark noted, had taken no part in the angry exchange with The Partisan. Clark's judgment of the man told him that the Grand Chief was caught in a dilemma, not wanting conflict with the white strangers but unwilling to show fear or weakness before his own people, who might perceive any act of conciliation as cowardice.

185

Though Clark was now surrounded, he saw that the pirogue and its crew had been left unhindered while the Indians crowded around him. "Back to the barge," Clark ordered the men.

"But Cap'n, we can't leave you—"

"That's an order. The interpreters can stay. The rest of you go—now!" For all the good the interpreters are doing, Clark thought.

The pirogue pulled away. Though William Clark now appeared extremely vulnerable, left on the shore surrounded by a ring of scowling faces, he felt no fear. What moved him instead was a stubborn anger that brought heat to his face and neck. He could not back down, not at this first meeting with a hostile band of Sioux. A soldier's instinct told him that retreat or any show of weakness now would only embolden the ag-

gressive, unfriendly members of the tribe—and possibly jeopardize the safety of the entire expedition.

The Partisan and Black Buffalo had been exchanging heated words. The Partisan gestured toward Clark, his tone and manner threatening. But his words were no longer slurred, Clark thought, confirming his opinion of the man's duplicity.

At that moment all of those grouped along the riverbank seemed simultaneously to hear the rub and squeak of oars. Everyone turned toward the river.

The white pirogue was heading back toward the bank. But now there were not three men in her but a dozen, all armed and obviously ready to do battle. In the keelboat the cannon was aimed at the riverbank. All men aboard her and the red pirogue were at arms, staring toward the shore.

As the small pirogue with its twelve men neared the bank, the Indians fell back. In a moment the two chiefs were left with only their personal soldiers to face Clark.

Seizing the moment, Clark ordered the Indian soldiers away from the pirogue. There was a further retreat from the riverbank by the other warriors who, only moments before, had lined the bank with their bows and arrows ready to shoot.

Sensing that the time of immediate danger had passed, William Clark chose a diplomatic way out of the situation. He extended his hand toward the two chiefs.

The Partisan turned away scornfully. Black Buffalo hesitated, but he, too, declined Clark's gesture of friendship.

"Have it your way, then," Clark said curtly. He turned and stepped into the bow of the pirogue. "Take us back," he snapped. The heat still rode his face and neck.

Then something happened that startled William Clark and the other men with him. They had not drawn ten yards from the riverbank before Black Buffalo, a lesser chief, and two of their soldiers came wading into the river after the pirogue, calling out in very loud voices.

At Clark's order the oars were raised. The pirogue hove to. By exaggerated gestures the Indians begged to be taken aboard. After only a moment's hesitation Clark relented. Once more he held out his hand toward Black Buffalo. This time the Grand Chief of the Bois Brulé seized it eagerly, and Clark helped him clamber into the boat.

Moments later they reached the keelboat, where the savages were brought aboard amidst silence and suspicious stares.

Without delay Meriwether Lewis ordered the anchor raised, and the boats proceeded upriver. Most of the Indians on the riverbank were left behind, though some continued to follow them along the bank. Aboard the boats, as the excitement of battle readiness drained away, there was a kind of letdown. A few of the men joked about how close they had come to pulling their triggers, but the presence of the Sioux chiefs on board constrained them.

The men rowed on in silence. A hawk circled high overhead. The Indians who had come aboard the keelboat were also subdued. When one of the red men moved toward the stern, Seaman was instantly on his feet, a rumble starting in his throat. The warrior fell back in alarm.

A mile up the Missouri River from the mouth of the Teton, the boats of the Corps of Discovery dropped anchor off a willow island in the middle of the river. For safety the two pirogues were attached by lines to the larger keelboat. The cooks, accompanied by a guard, went ashore to build a fire. Another guard was posted in the keelboat. The immediate threat might have passed, but the two captains judged that the hostile members of this Sioux tribe were not to be trusted. At this time less than fifty men were attached to the expedition. Clark estimated the numbers of Indians in the villages immediately surrounding them at fifteen hundred.

Over supper, still disgruntled by his experience, William Clark said, "I'll call this island Bad Humored Island."

Meriwether Lewis smiled. "You're surely in bad enough humor, old friend. And with good reason."

Both men glanced toward the four Sioux who had accompanied them. They sat quietly by themselves, having shared the white men's evening meal. They had drawn their buffalo robes about their bodies against the evening chill.

The Grand Chief, Black Buffalo, had taken a pipe from a polecat's skin he wore under his robe. He stuffed the pipe with a mixture of bark and root scrapings the Indians called *kinnikinnick*, their version of tobacco. He lit his pipe with the end of a stick from the cooking fire.

"Vile smelling stuff," said Clark, himself a confirmed pipe smoker.

"An Indian is said to be at peace while he smokes," Lewis murmured. "And our chief seems peaceable enough now."

William Clark grunted. "Let's see what tomorrow brings."

The following day, September 26, Clark wrote in his field notes that the chiefs who had come upriver in the keelboat "appeared disposed to make up and be friendly." The chiefs were also eager to show off the boat and its marvels to their wives and families, who, as it turned out, lived in the second Teton Sioux village, one of some sixty lodges about two miles upriver from the first village. When the Indians were put ashore, Meriwether Lewis went with them amid general signs of friendship.

Three hours later he had not returned, and Clark was worried. He called Sergeant Ordway. "Take some men and go into that camp, Sergeant. I want to make sure nothing is amiss with Captain Lewis."

"Yes, sir."

If John Ordway entertained any misgivings, they did not show. With three men, including Pierre Cruzatte to act as interpreter, he climbed the bank and disappeared in the direction of the village. Cruzatte, who was half-Omaha himself, was surprised to see a number of captured Omaha prisoners in the camp.

Ordway was back far sooner than Clark expected. His relaxed manner conveyed his message ahead of the welcome words. "Cap'n Lewis says he's bein' treated fine, Cap'n Clark. He says the Indians want the white chiefs to stay over for the night so's they can show us they mean well. They's havin' a dance tonight."

A short while later Lewis himself returned, and it was Clark's turn to experience Sioux hospitality. Immediately on landing ashore, he was met by a group of ten young braves, each man smeared with grease and blacking, wearing a buffalo robe and a headband decorated with hawk feathers. The braves laid a large, dressed, and elegantly decorated buffalo robe on the ground, insisted that Clark sit on it, then bore him up on the robe and carried him in triumphal parade to the center of the nearby village.

Clark was carried into a large tipi, a conical shelter made of decorated skins sewn together, and lowered to the ground on his buffalo robe. The young warriors immediately withdrew, and Clark looked around curiously. Within the tipi, evidently a council house, about seventy men sat in a circle. The chiefs sat together. In front of them, in a cleared space about six feet in diameter, a peace pipe rested on two forked sticks. Swan's down was scattered on the ground around the peace pipe. On either side of this small circle the flags of Spain and the United States were planted. Nearby, meat was cooking in a large pot.

189

Within a few minutes the warriors had returned, this time bearing Meriwether Lewis on a similar ceremonial buffalo robe so that his feet would not have to touch the ground.

The two friends grinned at each other. "Looks like we're getting a king's welcome," William Clark said.

"A bit better than yesterday. Have you see that angry chief, the one called The Partisan?"

"Not yet."

"I don't think we've seen the last of him."

But this day proved to be harmonious. The Sioux chiefs gave ponderous speeches in turn. Black Buffalo took the pipe of peace from its cradle before him, pointed to the heavens and the four quarters of the earth, lit the mixture of tobacco and *kinnikinnick* in the bowl and passed the pipe around the circle. Everyone smoked.

After the smoking, a feast was offered: portions of dog, *pemmican*—buffalo meat jerked, pounded, and mixed with raw grease—and ground potato. The smoking and feasting lasted until dark. Then everything was cleared away, a large fire was built up at the center of the lodge, and the white men from beyond the long river were treated to a spectacle of music and dance. There were musicians playing on a kind of tambourine made of hoops and stretched skins, others beating drums or shaking long sticks with hoofs tied to them to make a jingling noise. The men danced and sang while they played. Young women also participated in this dance, comely girls with black flashing eyes and raven hair, dressed in handsome deerskin dresses and robes, their faces daubed with color. They held up captured enemy weapons as they danced or carried sticks or poles from which dangled scalps and other trophies of war.

The musicians and dancers seemed tireless. When some dropped out to rest at last, others took their places. Their chanting and jingling and rattling filled the tipi, and the sound was carried on the night air down to the riverbank where the men of the Corps listened in wonder.

The celebration went on until midnight. By then Lewis and Clark could honestly claim fatigue from all the entertainment. Wearily they retreated to the boats, accompanied by four friendly chiefs, who insisted on spending the night with them on the river. All the men of the expedition were also on board, and the boats anchored about a hundred yards off shore. Though all seemed to be going well, Meriwether Lewis ordered a double guard. There was less than the usual grumbling in the night. The men were in good spirits, convinced that the worst was behind them.

Seaman did not sleep. Unfamiliar smells were strong in the keelboat, smells of animal fat and stale sweat and smoke. One of the Indians aboard talked in his sleep in a loud, gutteral voice. The red men lay wrapped in their buffalo robes in one

190

of the runways. From his accustomed perch on the rear cabin deck Seaman was able to observe them. He lay on his stomach, his head between his front paws, his eyes watchful and alert. The boat rocked gently in the restless current of the Missouri, and one of the pirogues tied to the mother boat occasionally bumped into it in the darkness, causing a stirring among the sleeping men.

The guard changed halfway through the night. Seaman watched.

The third day the Corps of Discovery spent among the Bois Brulé was a repetition of the previous day's round of ceremony, music, and dancing. Sergeant Gass and a group of the men accompanied Lewis on an early visit to the village. Clark and some of the others went in the afternoon. That evening, both of the captains and some of the men were present for more feasting and dancing, which went on even longer than the night before, well past midnight.

191

At last the visitors begged off. They did not have to feign weariness. Their eyes were bleary, and their heads ached from too much smoke and too many songs and too many boastful speeches they could not even understand.

The Partisan, to the captains' surprise, had joined in that night's festivities, and he accompanied Lewis and Clark to the river along with a "principal man" from the village—a status just below that of a chief. "The Partisan wants to sleep on the boat with us," Lewis told Clark. "What do you make of it?"

"At least we can keep an eye on him there."

There was not enough room for everyone in the single pirogue that met them, so Clark escorted the two Indians out to the keelboat, while Lewis and a small guard remained on shore. The crewman steering the pirogue—in the darkness Clark could not see who it was—had a clumsy hand, or he was sleepy. Nearing the keelboat, he cut too close across its bow. The pirogue struck the larger boat's cable. The anchor line snapped with a sharp crack.

Instantly the barge began to swing about into the current. Clark bellowed out an order: "All hands up! Man the oars!"

There was consternation on the keelboat. Men scrambled in the darkness. Seaman gave a deep bark. Next to Clark in the pirogue, The Partisan reacted to Clark's sharp command and the flurry of activity. His cry of alarm carried a tremor of panic. Too quick to panic, Clark thought fleetingly, but there was no time to dwell on the perception.

"What's he saying?" Clark demanded of Pierre Cruzatte, who was leaning over the bow to see what had happened to the anchor cable.

"He say, de Omahas, dey come! He say dey are attack!"

"Damn fool!"

While the crew got the keelboat under control and began to row it toward the south bank, there was action along the bank. More and more warriors appeared. By the time the *Discovery* drew near the shore—less than ten minutes, Clark judged—the entire bank was lined with armed Sioux warriors, the Grand Chief Black Buffalo at their head. There was an ominous threat in the way so many warriors had suddenly materialized in the middle of the night, all of them appearing wide awake and ready for battle.

Lewis came aboard the keelboat. Cruzatte appeared out of the shadows to stand beside the two captains in the bow. "We no find de anchor for de barge before light, I think."

"Can we hold her where she is?" Lewis asked.

"*Oui.*"

After conferring with Clark briefly, Lewis decided that the boats would have to stay close to the shore, even with the threat of a falling bank—and the looming menace of scores of Sioux warriors staring down at them.

Black Buffalo had come aboard the keelboat to join The Partisan. Watching them, Cruzatte said in a low voice, "*Capitaine* . . . I talk with de prisoners in de village."

"Who . . . oh, you mean the Omahas." Cruzatte, who had learned the Omaha language from his mother, had been able to move about the Sioux village that day, encountering many of the captured Omahas. Lewis's curiosity was aroused. "What is it? They can't hear you"—he glanced toward the two chiefs in the runway—"and couldn't understand you anyway."

"Dey say, we no can go upriver. De Sioux, dey stop us."

"Why? We've been nothing but friendly."

Cruzatte shrugged. "De river, she is their river, eh? Dey want to decide who come and go."

"We'll see about that," William Clark snapped.

"I think we'd better be on our guard tonight," said Meriwether Lewis. "I don't like the way The Partisan gave that alarm."

"Too quick by half," said Clark, remembering his own suspicion.

"Alert the sergeants," Lewis told Cruzatte. "Be quiet about it, but we want a double guard. And every man sleeps with his gun at hand."

Cruzatte slipped away silently in the darkness. A small portion of the riverbank crumbled into the river and Clark glanced at the bank with a crease of worry.

"No sleep tonight," Lewis murmured.

Clark grinned in the darkness. "What do you want, Lewis, more dancing girls?"

In the morning the keelboat's anchor could not be found. Not wanting to delay any longer in his vulnerable situation, Meriwether Lewis ordered all hands ready to get under way.

The Sioux chiefs protested, reluctant to leave the boats. Lewis was insistent, however, and after some palavering the Indians were finally put ashore with the exception of the Grand Chief himself, Black Buffalo. He wished to go up the river a short distance with his new fathers, he said. While he was pleading his case with William Clark, one of the members of the Sioux soldier class grabbed the barge's cable and refused to release it. Clark heard a rising note of anger in Meriwether Lewis's voice. "Those are men of your Nation," Clark warned the chief. "They've set on our cable."

Black Buffalo left the boat and spoke to the young warriors. Turning to Lewis, he pantomimed filling and lighting a pipe and said, "They are soldiers. They wish tobacco."

On the shore The Partisan was speaking loudly. He also craved more tobacco and a flag like the one that had been given to Black Buffalo.

Lewis's expression tightened. To Cruzatte, he said, "Tell him I will not be forced into anything. No tobacco, no flag, nothing, not while my boat is held!"

Cruzatte stumbled through an attempt at translation, which was hardly necessary. The men in the boats, seeing their captain's anger, were tense, ready for anything. Black Buffalo spoke to his soldiers, who stubbornly clung to the keelboat's cable.

Seeing the stubbornness on both sides, William Clark sought to defuse the situation. He tossed Black Buffalo a carat of tobacco. "Take this," he said contemptuously, "for your soldiers who are not men but children who must be bribed with gifts." Then Clark stepped deliberately over to the swivel gun on the port side. "And tell them to release the boat—that is, if they still listen to their chief."

Stung, Black Buffalo, who had seemed anxious all along to avoid a more serious clash, passed the tobacco over to his soldiers, jerked the rope from them and handed it up to the bowsman, Francois Labiche. "Go in peace," he said.

The boats moved quickly away from the bank, the crew working the oars in silence, all watching the receding shore and the line of Indians clustered for some distance along the bank. Everyone knew that a moment of real danger had been faced and overcome, by patience and firmness and perhaps a little luck. They felt their own mettle had been tested, even more the toughness and determination of their commanders. Tested and proven.

In the stern, standing on his feet with his nose lifted to the river breeze, Seaman felt a nameless pleasure in the familiar rolling of the boat, the lift and squeak of oars, the return to the pattern of life on the Missouri.

Louis Charbonneau

Meriwether Lewis had cautiously kept the Newfoundland on the boat during the three days at the Teton Sioux villages, recognizing the Indians' fascination with the big dog. "I don't want them trying to steal my dog the way they stole Colter's horse," he had confided to William Clark.

Seaman had seen only the throngs of red men who crowded the banks each day, staring and pointing at him in open curiosity, and the chiefs who had been brought on board the keelboat. The suspicion they had awakened in the dog still lingered.

He was glad to be back on the river.

18

a curious custom with the Souix as well as the rickeres is to give handsom squars to those whome they wish to Show some acknowledgements to. The Seauex we got clare of without taking their squars, they followed us with Squars two days. The Rickores we put off dureing the time we were at the Towns but 2 [handsom young] Squars were Sent by a man to follow us, they came up this evening, and pursisted in their civilities.

—WILLIAM CLARK, October 12, 1804

*A*lthough the Arikaras were largely surrounded by the Sioux and Crees to the north, the Cheyennes to the west, the Pawnees and Omahas to the south, they had held their own on the Northern Plains. Rather than remaining nomadic buffalo hunters, like most Plains tribes, they had adopted stationary villages, like the Mandans a little further up the Missouri. And in time these had become effective trading centers.

There were three such Arikara villages when the Corps of Discovery reached them on October 8, 1804. The villages numbered some 2,000 souls, of whom about 500 were able-bodied warriors. When the expedition made camp late in the day just past the upper end of an island, the voyagers saw cultivated fields scattered across the island and a village at the center. The dwellings were distinctive, dome-shaped earth lodges, large enough for several families to share. The men were prepared for peace or war, Clark noted in his journal. Instead, among the many Indians who crowded the riverbanks, they saw only friendly faces.

Meriwether Lewis, with two men and two interpreters, took a pirogue across to the island and walked to the village.

Louis Charbonneau

Clark waited with the main party. While reassured by the apparent friendliness of the Indians, he remained on the alert.

Before long, the pirogue reappeared. This time there were two strangers in the boat with Lewis. They were not Arikaras, to Clark's surprise, but bearded white men.

The two men were traders, Antoine Tabeau and his assistant, Joseph Gravelines. Tabeau worked for Regis Loisel, whom Lewis and Clark had met at St. John's early on their journey. The traders had been left at the village to pursue Loisel's interests among the Arikaras. Gravelines was able to converse with fluent ease in the peculiarly difficult Arikara language, one so afflicted with numerous dialects that some Arikara bands had trouble communicating with each other. Whether the presence of the white traders and Gravelines's skill as an interpreter had smoothed away any difficulties, or whether the Arikaras were simply at that time disposed to be friendly, Meriwether Lewis reported to Clark that his reception had been cordial and the Arikara chiefs were eager to council.

After the recent prickly encounter with the Teton Sioux, the news was welcome.

On the day following the expedition's arrival among the Arikaras, the chiefs and many others came in a steady parade all day long to view the white men of the big boats. Seaman provoked great interest among them, for no Arikara, not even the oldest among them, could claim to have seen such a dog before. But the object of greatest interest and admiration to the Indians proved to be Clark's manservant, York. And York, being in one of his playful moods, outdid himself.

Like his father before him, York had been a Clark family slave since birth. Though he knew his place, York did not always stay meekly in his role. For one thing, he and William Clark were of an age, and as boys they had been more companions than master and servant. Moreover, he had an exuberant, fun-loving nature, at times irrepressible, and Clark would sometimes grumble that York didn't think he was a

slave at all, he was just tolerating the fiction because it offered him an amiable life with no responsibilities.

To which York would grin and say, "Yes, suh, Cap'n Clark, suh!"

On the journey up the Missouri, York's stature among the men had grown. At first reserved with the soldiers, he had gradually opened up until he was giving free rein to his predilection for boasting and pranks and the rough-and-ready horseplay they all enjoyed.

Though as Clark's aide he was exempt from the regular duties of the enlisted men, York had learned to handle a long pole and a towline, and his remarkable strength had served the party well in several emergencies with the boats. York's readiness to go into the river with the men when willing hands and strong backs were needed had not gone unnoticed. The men had cheered York on when he swam the Missouri's torrent to a willow island just to collect some greens for the captains' dinner. Lately he had even demonstrated formidable hunting skills; on September 9, 1804, York had shot and killed two buffalo.

Moreover, the tall, broad-chested, big-bellied black man had been good-humored about being on display for the Indians who had come to council with the white men. He had even begun to enjoy the obvious awe and admiration he inspired in savage eyes.

Now, standing at the center of the Arikara village near the lodge of its principal chief, Kakawita, York was the center of attention. Speeches had been given, presents had been exchanged on both sides, and the general mood was one of great good humor and cheerfulness.

York grinned at the wide-eyed wonder of the Indians, young and old, and roared, "I'm an animal!" He thumped his chest with his fists. "My master set a trap and caught me in it . . ."

Nearby, Joseph Gravelines enthusiastically interpreted York's dramatic shouts into Arikara. York took gleeful delight in the frightening impression he was making. Among the Indians, he seemed a true giant. The Arikara men, though taller than the stocky Teton Sioux warriors, were slender, and the women were universally small. York towered over them, naked to the waist, his chest and belly glowing with sweat.

"He brought me out of the jungle and tamed me. He taught me to walk like a man and talk like a man. He even taught me to dance like a man!"

The Arikaras shrieked in amazed delight when the black-skinned, self-proclaimed man-beast nimbly stomped before them in one of the lively dances the white men had demonstrated earlier. Cruzatte, who had his fiddle with him, promptly added a raucous tune to accompany York's remarkably agile romp. It was not the dance itself that caused the Arikaras to marvel aloud, but the fact that so large and heavy a man could disport himself with such fluid grace—as if a buffalo could leap like a deer.

"Hoo-ah!" York roared. "I'm wild and fierce, and a dancin' fool!"

Watching this performance with mixed feelings, William Clark grew more and more uncomfortable. The Indians all along the river were fascinated by York, no doubt of it. They couldn't believe his color wasn't painted on, and in their curiosity they had touched and pinched and even rubbed his skin to assure themselves that the ebony color was genuine.

"Your man has won the day, Clark," observed Meriwether Lewis beside him. The two stood near the entrance to the lodge of Kakawita.

"He's gone too far," Clark growled. "It's all well and good to put on a show, but he's making himself out to be more terrible than I like. A wild animal, indeed!"

"Maybe it's not such a bad idea to put a little fear in these Indians' minds. The word will spread."

"Caught and tamed!" Clark said, unmollified. "I'll tame him when he's done with this foolishness."

But York was not finished. He seized one of the buffalo-hide containers of corn presented by the Arikaras as a gift and effortlessly lifted it with one arm. Then he flipped the heavy

199

load from one arm to the other as the Indians gasped. The men of the expedition, used to York's boasting and his feats of strength, shouted approval.

Suddenly the black man swooped upon two Indian boys who had been watching him with wide eyes. With a roar York lifted one in each arm and held them up, wriggling in momentary terror. Several of the Arikara warriors were on their feet instantly, alarmed. But the boys, quicker than their elders to realize that the giant meant them no harm, began to shriek and giggle with delight. Hoisting one boy to each shoulder, York whirled and danced to his viewers' astonishment, carrying the two boys like feather adornments on his shoulders.

"What the devil is he going to say or do next?" William Clark grumbled. "That's what worries me."

"Whatever it is," said Lewis, "he's made himself powerful medicine for us, as far as these savages are concerned. And that's all to the good."

York went on to new demonstrations of strength and agility, each more impressive than the last. When he had finally had enough and, grinning, waved off more encouragement, there was a general roar from the delighted Arikaras. The men who had come up the river with him joined the cheering. The Indians, laughing and shouting, gathered around the beaming, sweating black man, reaching out to touch and pinch his skin, his muscular arms, his magnificent belly, his glowing back and shoulders.

Lewis clapped William Clark on the back. "You might as well accept it, Clark. He'll be chief of these people if we don't watch out!"

The councils with the Arikaras continued to be amicable. The Indians seemed genuinely receptive to the white chiefs' message of peace. Lewis and Clark used their diplomatic skills to soothe jealousies among the chiefs of the three villages, their solution being to recognize each leader in turn as a chief and award appropriate medals and presents.

Pleased with the outcome, Lewis prevailed upon one of the Arikara chiefs, Ar-ke-tar-na-shar, to accompany the expedition up to the Mandan villages, where he could join the white chiefs in initiating peace between the two Indian Nations, as the Great Father in Washington had urged.

After three days among the Arikara Indians, the Corps of Discovery once again pushed out into the Missouri. The river was now shallower than it had been all summer, and the voyagers had to seek out each passable channel, sometimes backtracking when shifting sandbars blocked their way. Now there was cold to endure as well, at night and in the early morning, and a growing weariness from the long struggle of that summer. At times tempers became short.

On October 13, 1804, Private John Newman's control broke.

That morning the keelboat, attempting passage over a shallow bottom where the current ran hard, had been unable to proceed by oar, pole, or sail. Observing the difficulty from the bow of the boat, Meriwether Lewis ordered Newman ashore with the towing party.

"No," Newman said, a stubborn set to his jaw.

"What's that?" Lewis was startled, disbelieving. "You heard me, Newman—we're aground. Get ashore and give a hand on the rope."

"God damn you, you officious bastard! Pull it yourself. Leave me alone!"

Newman was a burly Pennsylvanian, an army regular who had been recruited from Captain Daniel Bissell's company while at Fort Massac. A hard worker, he had also become known among the crew for his quick temper. Those within earshot in the keelboat were thus appalled by his sudden defiance of their captain, but not surprised.

"Newman—"

"Why me? Damn it all, Cap'n, I been on the tow more'n any man here! I jes' won't do it, is all."

"You'll do as you're ordered as long as you're a member of this party," said Meriwether Lewis coldly.

Trail

"Go to hell," Newman muttered.

He was tired, he was fed up, he felt aggrieved over too much sentry duty, too much oaring, poling, and hauling, too many mosquitoes. In brief, too much unrelenting hard work with no real relief. What's more, Newman had taken a fancy to one of the two Arikara squaws who had been following the boats up the river. The warrior accompanying the comely Indian women had, to put the most honest face on it, offered the enjoyment of either of them outright to anyone man enough to want her. And just last night old preacher-faced, pursemouthed Captain Lewis had ordered the Arikara and the two squaws away, leaving Newman and several other men frustrated and angry. It had been a long summer of too much labor and too little recreation, and Newman felt personally abused.

"You'll stand down, then, Private Newman," Lewis said with crisp formality. "Consider yourself confined to the boat. You will surrender your weapon and remain a prisoner until you face a court-martial, which shall be as soon as our circumstances permit, agreeable to the Articles of War. Is that understood?"

202

Newman understood. By then his anger was cooling, leaving behind it the first wish to take back his words. But it was too late. He had put the rope around his own neck and kicked open the trap door.

The trial was held that night. Private John Newman was judged by nine of his peers, a group that included two of the detachment's sergeants, Gass and Ordway. The severity of Newman's mutinous conduct was reflected in the swift but troubled verdict. Guilty of mutiny, the prisoner was sentenced to "75 lashes & disbanded from the Party."

Six men, fully two-thirds of the court, concurred in the nature of the punishment, which could hardly have been more devastating. Newman was to remain with the expedition only as a common laborer, relieved of guard and other military duties. In the spring he would be sent back to St. Louis with the keelboat, deprived of the honor and privilege of remaining a part of the Corps of Discovery.

The first part of the sentence was carried out the following day at one o'clock, much to the alarm and dismay of the Arikara chief accompanying the expedition to the Mandans. Arke-tar-na-shar recognized the necessity for a chief to give example to his men, but his people never whipped anyone, he said, not even their children. If he had to give such an example, which the chief agreed that he had done on occasion, he made it not by such humiliation, but by death.

A week after Newman felt the sting of the lashes, on the twenty-first of October, a cold rain began during the night. Before dawn it turned to a driving sleet that froze on the ground. At daybreak the storm became a fall of snow.

By the time the boats were ready to get under way, the highlands on both sides of the river were covered with a mantle of white. Meriwether Lewis stood on the bank with William Clark, powdery snow clinging to his sandy eyelashes. He brushed the snow away and said, "We'll have to put up for the winter very soon now."

"Those Mandan towns can't be far ahead, from what we've been told." They had been seeing abandoned old Mandan villages on the prairies and in the bottoms for several days, mute testimony to past Mandan glories. "Mr. Tabeau has been amongst them, and he says they're friendly."

"Yes, and he's not the only trader they've welcomed, from what I hear. I expect we'll find English traders there as well. Their posts aren't that far north." Lewis's gaze over the snow-bound prairie was reflective. "Mr. Jefferson is proved right in sending us here in the most expeditious manner to assert our rights."

The two men were silent for a moment. The earth itself seemed muted and muffled by the softly falling snow. In this high country, both men knew, winter came early and with a fierce cold such as Virginians had never known among their

gentler hills and valleys. The Corps of Discovery would have to build shelters, stock provisions, make peace with the natives and, if such were possible, obtain additional stores to see them through the long harsh winter.

Meriwether Lewis felt the wind bite through the hide of his coat. He shivered. "Let's be off, then . . . and pray we find a channel open in this damned river!"

The season's first snow continued for three days. For William Clark it was not a welcome event; it brought on an attack of rheumatism in his neck so violent that he could not move. Meriwether Lewis treated it with hot stones wrapped in flannel, which gave his friend temporary relief.

And they proceeded on.

On the third day of the storm, with Clark's rheumatic seizure beginning to ease, the boats turned into the bank at the point of an island separated from the east shore of the Missouri by a narrow channel. Almost immediately a party of Indians appeared on the island. They approached the boats with their hands raised in greeting.

By good fortune, the Indians were a hunting party led by Black Cat, the Grand Chief of the Mandans, accompanied by a small band of lesser chiefs and warriors. It was an auspicious meeting, for soon both the Indians and the white men were seated on blankets in a cleared place, facing each other and ceremoniously smoking the pipe of peace. Much to the relief of Lewis and Clark, Black Cat welcomed the Arikara chief, Ar-ke-tar-na-shar, with great cordiality.

After puffing the ceremonial pipe passed over to him by the Mandan chief, Meriwether Lewis handed it to William Clark with a smile, as Black Cat nodded approval. In Clark's eyes, Lewis read a satisfaction that matched his own.

In reaching the Mandans, they had gained their first objective. Here they would winter amidst a peaceful and friendly people.

Their first season on the river had ended.

204

Louis Charbonneau

As the first snow of November dusted the gray Potomac, Thomas Jefferson celebrated his reelection as President of the United States. Though all of the electoral vote would not be counted until year's end, it was already clear that he had won a resounding victory, losing only Connecticut and Delaware —two states where electors were chosen by the legislature, not by popular vote.

It had been a trying year, both for Jefferson and for the country. In the spring he had lost Maria, one of his two daughters—"half of all I had," he wrote. Then, in July, Aaron Burr, Vice President during Jefferson's first term, had killed Alexander Hamilton in a duel—a barbarous solution to disputes, in Jefferson's view. Though Burr was a Republican, of Jefferson's own party, and Hamilton a Federalist, the President mourned the latter's death far more than Burr's fall from grace and rejection by both public and party. Though he had strongly opposed Hamilton's monarchist, antidemocratic politics, he had respected his brilliant rival as a man. He could not say the same of Burr.

And now there were whispers, unverified but disturbing, of a secessionist plot encouraged by Burr's followers. And Burr himself? Would he shatter the Union for his own ends?

The plot would not succeed, if plot there was. Jefferson had a profound and growing faith in the young republic he served as President.

He retired early. The White House—still more generally called the President's House—was a huge, drafty mansion of thirty rooms, much of it still unfinished, all of it cold in raw weather like this. He remembered joking with Meriwether Lewis, his first private secretary in office, that they were like two mice in a church, sharing this great house alone, with just a few servants.

Lewis . . .

Jefferson felt deeply the scarcity of news of the expedition. The last had been word, filtering down the Missouri, Indian

to trapper to merchant, that on August 4 Lewis and Clark had reached the River Platte and that they had held a great council with Otos and Missouris.

Since then, silence.

Had they reached the Mandan Nation before the river froze? What of the troublesome Sioux? What of the river itself and all its obstacles? Had any men been lost?

He thought of Burr and the plotters. Petty men, jealous, envious, ambitious, might dream of dividing the Union. Ardent men like Lewis and Clark, ambitious only for their country, thought of duty and sought adventure. They would not cripple the Union but extend its reach.

It was not only commerce with the Indians, the fur trade of the mountains, a water passage to link with the Columbia, and thus to the Far East, that Jefferson envisaged as fruits of the expedition he had fathered. He saw another gain. A young nation, crossing the Mississippi, leaping rivers and mountains, would swiftly grow too strong and proud to be shaken by small men.

206

Three months with no news. And winter lay ahead. The River Platte was six hundred miles from St. Louis. The Mandans were another thousand miles. It might well be a year before he would know the expedition's fate and the unknown perils in which those sturdy explorers were now engaged.

So long to wait and wonder, here in his drafty church. Perhaps, before sleep, a white-haired mouse's prayer might yet be heard . . .

Part three

"I shall vanish and be no more.
But the land over which I now roam
Shall remain....and change not."

Warrior Song

mandan

winter

19 The near approach of winter, the low state of the water and the known scarcity of timber which exists on the Missouri for many hundreds of miles above the Mandans ... determined my friend and companion, Captain Clark, and myself to fortify ourselves and remain for the winter in the neighborhood of the Mandans, Minnetarees and Ahnaharways ... who are the most friendly and well-disposed savages we have yet met.

—MERIWETHER LEWIS, S p r i n g, 1 8 o 5
LETTER TO HIS MOTHER, LUCY MARKS

*T*he Mandans were a light-skinned tribe, many of them appearing more tanned than redskinned. Fair hair and light eyes were common among them. This gave rise to the legend that they were descendants of an ancient tribe of Welshmen who had crossed the great ocean and settled here in the middle of the North American continent. The story was a white man's myth. The Mandans were true Indians in origin—their own mythology said that they had come from underground—but the white men had come to trade with and dwell among them for so long that there was in their blood a strong mixture of white and red heritage.

As late as the mid-eighteenth century the Mandans had been one of the most powerful Indian Nations on the Northern Plains. They lived in stationary villages along the Missouri River—nine large villages, each numbering several hundred warriors, and an equal number of smaller villages, scattered along a broad reach of the muddy river.

Even among the Sioux, the Mandans were feared enemies. Their women were among the most admired beadmakers on the Plains. They also dressed leather better than most tribes

and were expert at fashioning furs and feathers into clothing and decorative artifacts. They traded their painted buffalo robes, their dressed and ornamented skins of deer and elk and antelope, their furs and peltries, and their handsome beadwork for muskets and powder, axes, and kettles from the Omahas, Pawnees, Sioux, Assiniboines, Gros Ventres, and other tribes.

Then came the white trappers and traders, a few of whom chose to dwell among the Mandans. Those who came up the river were Frenchmen from the lower Missouri and the Mississippi River settlements. Those who came overland from the north were British and French Canadians of the Northwest Company and Hudson's Bay Company, both of which had built trading posts on the Assiniboine River.

The white men brought the smallpox.

Within two generations most of the Mandan villages stood abandoned, empty and desolate shells, their earth lodges filling with dust or falling in upon themselves, their stockades reduced to bones, like the skeletons of buffalo bleached white upon the prairie. As their villages were decimated by the disease, which sometimes wiped out entire bands almost overnight, the Mandan Nation became weak. And their enemies, especially the Sioux, became bolder.

In the autumn of 1804, when the Corps of Discovery came up the Missouri River after leaving the Arikaras, only two Mandan villages remained. Although they were home for only about twelve hundred people, numbering about 350 warriors, these villages remained the most important trading center on the upper Missouri. They existed in a loose confederation with three other villages in the immediate vicinity. One was Mahaha, on a bluff opposite the mouth of the Knife River, home for a small band of about fifty Ahnahaway warriors and their families, who were related to the Minitarees, or Gros Ventres of the Missouri. The latter tribe, often called the Big Bellies by white men, lived in two larger villages a short distance up the Knife River from the Missouri and within sight of the Mandans. The two Minitaree villages housed about twenty-five hundred people. Like the Mandans, the Minitarees lived in stockaded towns with permanent earth lodges, and they had established themselves as traders.

The Mandans were accustomed to white visitors, but they had never seen anything like the small army of whites who arrived in the big boats. Crowds came down from the villages to watch the boats move slowly past them.

Meriwether Lewis had walked overland with Black Cat to the Grand Chief's village. William Clark led the boats up the river. Stopping at the lower Mandan village, he met its chief, She-he-ke. Light-skinned even for a Mandan, She-he-ke was as friendly as Black Cat. A fat, loquacious, and good-natured man, he expressed a cordial welcome, speaking through a bearded white man who was in his lodge when Clark arrived.

The white man was René Jessaume. He was a French Canadian who had been living among the Mandans for about ten years. He was short, slope-shouldered, with a round pot belly, a greasy beard, and restless eyes that always seemed to be looking over Clark's shoulder or down at his feet. His manner seemed more cunning than trustworthy, and Clark was struck by the fact that, although the Indians around him were uniformly clean, Jessaume had the dirty, unkempt appearance of one who washed neither himself nor his clothes.

But he spoke the Mandan language. His wife, Clark learned, was a Mandan. He had made himself useful as an interpreter both to the Indians and to traders of the Northwest and Hudson's Bay companies. Jessaume was the kind of man, Clark thought, who would insinuate himself into a situation to his own benefit. He was also talkative, quick to describe and evaluate the various Mandan chiefs and what the white visitors might expect of them.

Clark hired him as an interpreter on the spot.

Cold winds delayed a council with the Mandans for a day. On October 29, 1804, the council was held near the second Mandan village, with Jessaume acting as interpreter. The

213

Mandan chiefs listened gravely, if with some evidence of impatience, to the speeches. There were also chiefs present from the Ahnahaway and lower Minitaree villages. Only the Grand Chief of the Minitarees, who was called Le Borgne, or One Eye, scorned the council—although the white men were told merely that he was out hunting.

Winter was a promise in the cold winds blowing across the Plains. After the council both Mandan chiefs, Black Cat and She-he-ke, whom Lewis and Clark soon began to call Big White because of his size and his light color, were anxious to help the visitors find a suitable place for a winter camp. Big White showed them a sheltered bottom near the mouth of the Knife River, protected by a bluff from the full force of winter storms and close to the upper Mandan village. He was disappointed when the white chiefs shook their heads. The site was not suitable, they explained through the interpreter, because there was little timber nearby. And the white men intended to build winter lodges entirely of wood.

214   "Are you going to stay above our village or below, then, this cold season?"

"We need more wood to build our huts," Clark explained.

"You will also need corn," the Indian chief said, "when there are no buffalo to eat. If you go down the river, it will be too far to send corn from my village."

"By the Lord," murmured Lewis, "he's worried about us!"

"If we eat, you shall eat," said She-he-ke. "If we starve, you must starve also."

The next day the detachment went downriver to a wooded bottom on the north side where there was an abundance of timber, most of it cottonwood. There they pitched tents and immediately began to fell trees for a fort.

In the lower Minitaree village of Metaharta a young girl heard stories of the white men who were building a wooden village and wondered. She herself was not an Hidatsa, or Minitaree. She had come from the land of the Snake People, who were also called Shoshoni. They were not of the Plains but of the mountains. To her, they were the People.

Out of necessity, the People sometimes came down from their high meadows to the valley of many rivers to trap beaver, or they rode out on the prairie to hunt the buffalo, for there was little meat to be found in the mountains.

Five winters ago, in the autumn of the year, a band of the People had come to the place where three rivers met, not far from the huge rock formation that could be seen at a great distance and resembled the head and shoulders of a beaver swimming in the river.

The Minitarees found them there by the Three Forks.

The People had many enemies, rivals in pursuit of the buffalo. They were almost always at war with the Blackfeet and the Gros Ventres of the prairie, nearly as often with the Crows, and sometimes with the more distant Nations such as the Minitaree and the Mandan tribes. In such warfare it was as common to capture young women and children as to steal good horses; all contributed to the well-being of their captors.

When the Minitarees attacked, the People were outnumbered and fled. Most retreated up the westernmost fork of the river toward the mountains and hid themselves in the brush and among the trees. The Minitarees pursued them into the woods.

Warriors were not captured, for such captives could not be trusted. The old were not taken, for they were useless. The girl saw one of her People's chiefs hurled from his horse, but she did not know what became of him. She saw a Minitaree brave crush her grandmother's head with his battle axe. When her grandmother was struck down, the girl panicked. She tried to follow the others up the western stream, hoping to lose herself in the willows on the far side. While she was in the middle of the river, crossing over, a brave on a brown-and-white horse swooped down on her, leaned over, and scooped

her up in one arm. Hysterical with grief and terror, she screamed and kicked, but the warrior rode off with her, laughing.

The Minitarees had killed four of the People's warriors, she later heard them boasting, as well as four women and a number of boys. Besides stealing many fine horses, they had captured four boys and all the surviving women and girls. One of the children was the same age as the girl captive, a friend with whom she had laughed and played in the mountain meadows.

The Minitarees rode for seven days and nights. They left the mountains behind and entered an endless expanse of naked prairie, treeless and barren. There were no grassy meadows, no pure mountain streams sparkling over rocks. Everything was brown, the streams were muddy, dust hung everywhere in the wake of great herds of buffalo.

The girl's terror slowly ebbed, and her grief became a dull ache of the spirit, a shadow of the aching of her body from the endless pounding she endured as she rode.

After a week her captors joined a larger group of hunters from their village. The prisoners were paraded, and there was much shouting and laughter. The girl was poked and pinched and prodded, and the warrior who had captured her seemed to make a great boast of his success.

At last they came to the main village of the Minitarees on the Knife River. It was the kind of village the girl could not have imagined in her wildest dreams. These Hidatsa lived not in airy skin tipis that could easily be erected in the best places but in dome-shaped lodges made of poles and mud, very spacious inside but dark and smoky and crowded.

Eleven years old when she was captured, the girl lived among the Minitarees for the next three years. She was given a Minitaree name, Sacajawea, which meant Bird Woman. The warrior who had captured her, Running Bear, sold her to another, a principal man of the village, for a horse and a painted buffalo robe. The principal man, who was called Ka-wi-ta, had recently lost a daughter to sickness. His wife, Blue Cloud, needed someone in the lodge to clean and fetch and carry, to look after her youngest child, to soften and sew skins, and to cook. Sacajawea became part of Ka-wi-ta's lodge, and though she was a slave she was treated well.

One day in the spring of her fourteenth year, a white man came to the village during the trading time, when there were many ceremonies and games. He was astonishingly hairy to her eyes. Hair grew over his arms and the backs of his hands, tufts of it peeped from his shirt where it opened at his throat, and hair covered his entire face. Though the People in times past had traded for horses with bearded white men from far to the south, she herself had never seen one. This white man was short, powerful-looking, and as boastful as an Indian. She thought him very ugly. Yet he fascinated her as well, for she had never imagined that a man could truly have such pale skin and be covered with hair like a bear.

Sacajawea learned that the white man lived in the lower Minitaree village. He had an unpronounceable name. Once she saw him staring at her and she looked away, her eyes cast down, as was expected of an Indian woman, and especially of a captive.

During the trading fair, there were shooting and riding contests, games of chance, feasts, and dances. Sacajawea, who had become almost like a daughter in Ka-wi-ta's lodge, was allowed to join in the Buffalo Dance. The young men were the featured dancers, wearing buffalo head masks that covered their heads and shoulders. The young women formed a circle around them and danced, shaking their rattles and chanting.

The hairy man with the unpronounceable name watched her during the dance, causing her to shiver without knowing why.

He played in a game of hands. Sacajawea was at the side of Ka-wi-ta's lodge, helping to prepare food for the ongoing feasting. She could hear the men's outbursts of excitement and laughter. There were many men from her village as well as from the lower village. Even the terrifyingly ugly Grand Chief of the Minitarees, Le Borgne, was there, with his one milky

eye and gross features and long, powerful arms, his laughter a roar that drowned out all others.

Suddenly Sacajawea's arm was seized by a warrior. She was dragged toward the center of the lodge near the fire pit where the men were gambling. Ka-wi-ta had placed a rug on the ground in front of him, and he told her to sit on the rug.

She did so, frightened but obedient. All of the men were looking at her and grinning, all except the hairy one, who did not smile but glared as if he were angry.

Sacajawea did not understand the game, but after a few minutes she saw that the hairy one was holding out his right hand with two fingers showing, and this matched the hand that Ka-wi-ta held up. The white man grinned through his beard. He stood and, to Sacajawea's bewilderment, held out his hand to lift her to her feet. She stumbled up. She saw Blue Cloud, who had become mother to her for the past three years, watching her from the back of the lodge with the shining eyes of sadness.

She learned that the hairy one had won her in the game, that she now belonged to him and must go with him and obey him, just as she had obeyed Ka-wi-ta. Sacajawea felt ashamed, for Ka-wi-ta had received nothing for her, as if she had no value.

Then the hairy one did a mysterious thing. He went away for a short time and returned with a fine spotted horse. Over the horse's back was a blanket of many colors, and in a skin bag attached to the horse's neck were the pelts of many beavers. Sacajawea understood that the white man had brought presents to exchange for her, not relying only on the game of hands but making her a person of value.

Sacajawea learned to say her husband's name, which was Charbonneau. Her life with Charbonneau, as the youngest of his three squaws, was not an unhappy one. Though he was often away for long periods, he provided well for his lodge. He always came back with many skins or pelts to trade or with goods he had obtained in the north from the white traders in the land of the Assiniboines. Charbonneau's second wife, Otter Woman, was also of the Shoshoni, and she still remembered some of the words of the People. Otter Woman had one child who was called Tess because his French name, Toussaint, could not be spoken easily. Charbonneau's first wife, Corn Seeker, had grown fat and lazy in his lodge, for he was not as demanding as an Indian husband. But she was not mean to the newcomer. As long as Otter Woman and Sacajawea did all the work of the lodge, she was content. When they didn't, her tongue scalded like water from a hot kettle.

Sacajawea was sixteen years of age and had been with Charbonneau for two years when she heard about the white men who had come up the river in large boats. She did not believe all of the stories she heard, such as the tale of a giant among the strangers who had a skin not of white but of ebony. Still, she was a curious and intelligent girl, and she wondered.

Charbonneau had been away from the lodge on one of his long absences. When he returned, at the beginning of the cold time of year, he seemed almost angry to hear his women babble excitedly about the men who had come up the river in the big boats. He told them not to tell stories when they knew nothing of the things they spoke of.

He left the lodge for a while. When he returned that evening, he was quiet and at the same time fidgety, as if he were excited. At last he said, "I have spoken to Jessaume," mentioning the name of another squaw man who lived among the Mandans. "He has been hired by these strangers to inter- pret for them among the Mandans." After another moment's silence he added, "Jessaume does not speak Minitaree. Maybe I will interpret for these whites." And he looked at Sacajawea.

Immediately her interest quickened. The little Shoshoni girl had proved quicker to learn than Charbonneau's other wives, and he had come to rely upon her in his communications with the Minitarees. Even though he had lived among the Indians for many years, he spoke their language badly, often mixing in words of French or English, or resorting to signs.

Sacajawea now spoke the Hidatsa language better than he did. Whenever he had to speak of important things to the leaders of the village, or when he was interpreting for the white traders from the Assiniboine posts, he now relied on Sacajawea to translate his words into Minitaree or to tell him what the Indians said. She had learned some of his French words and expressions and understood his garbled version of Minitaree. In a real way she was *his* interpreter.

"Charbonneau will go see these strangers tomorrow," he said at last. "Maybe this be important thing."

On November 3, 1804, the day after construction of Fort Mandan began, René Jessaume moved to the camp with his Mandan wife and their child. The next day another Frenchman arrived. His name was Toussaint Charbonneau.

Charbonneau was introduced to the American captains by Jessaume. Also a Canadian, Charbonneau was a stocky, black-bearded man in leathers and furs. He had a prominent, fleshy nose and a large head. The large features, wide shoulders, and bulky furs created an impression of a much bigger man than he actually was. Sharp brown eyes peered from under bushy black eyebrows. His beard, like his long hair, was black streaked with gray, greasy and tangled. He pawed stubby fingers through his beard while he studied Meriwether Lewis; his fingers acted like thick tines of a very coarse comb.

"You speak Minitaree, then?" Lewis asked, on hearing that Charbonneau lived among the Big Bellies.

"*Oui, oui,* Charbonneau speak Minitaree ver' good, *m'sieur.* Live wit' dese people long time. You need good Big Belly interpret', eh?"

"Maybe."

Lewis didn't much care for the man or his command of English. But he had been little more impressed with Jessaume, and the latter had already proved himself useful as a Mandan interpreter. Obviously, someone who could interpret for the expedition with the Minitarees would be equally valuable.

Louis Charbonneau

Charbonneau was what the French rivermen called a squaw man, one who preferred living among the savages to staying with his own kind, who bedded with their squaws and survived by trapping and trading. A lazy man, some said, who liked living among the Indians because his squaws treated him like a god, doing everything for him in slavish fashion, scurrying to carry out his slightest wish.

But a man of the wilderness, Lewis thought, whatever else might be said of him. A survivor who had lived off the land, adapting to its harsh demands, hunting and trapping and using his wits, learning to live with the people of the land. It was easy to underestimate such a man.

And an interpreter of a language impenetrable to the members of the expedition. The encounter with the Bois Brulé Sioux had forcibly taught Lewis and Clark the hazards that might threaten them where communication failed. They had brushed close to an outbreak of hostilities, at least in part for lack of someone who could adequately interpret the Sioux language.

"You go to de Rock Mountain," Charbonneau said suddenly.

"That's right. In the spring."

"Two of Charbonneau's squaws are of de Snake people."

Lewis's attention immediately sharpened. "You mean the Shoshoni?"

Charbonneau nodded vigorously. "*Oui, oui,* from de mountains. My youngest squaw, she speak Shoshoni good. She was stole from her people, *comprenez?*" He shrugged, as if such an event were commonplace among the Indians. "She very young *femme* den, maybe eleven, maybe twelve year. But she remember good. You go to de mountain, eh, *Capitaine?* Maybe you take Charbonneau. Maybe you take my squaw, she of the Shoshoni, to interpret for you."

Lewis and Clark exchanged glances. Some sawdust blew toward them and Lewis had to look away, but not before Clark had seen the excitement in his eyes.

Lewis drew his friend aside. "What do you think, Clark?

If nothing else, this Shoshoni wife of his might be able to supply accurate information about her people and the route to their lands."

"Mm. Still, to take a woman along . . . we won't even have the keelboat. It will be hard going."

"These people are accustomed to hardships we don't even dream of. And their squaws, let's face it, do most of the work. I hardly think this one will be a burden."

Weighing the idea in the judicious manner that Thomas Jefferson had hoped would temper Lewis's impetuousness, Clark finally nodded. "We need the man. Perhaps in the end the woman will be even more useful."

Lewis turned back to the two Frenchmen. "All right, Charbonneau, let's see how you work out." He glanced at Jessaume. "Tell him we'll take him on as an interpreter with the Minitaree. If it goes well with him, then he and his Shoshoni squaw can go with us to the mountains in the spring."

When Jessaume had translated, Charbonneau grinned, showing tobacco-stained teeth with a gap between the two upper front teeth. He glanced at the activity all about him, the foundation already laid for the first row of cabins, the logs stacked ready for building, Patrick Gass directing two men who had begun splitting some of the long logs with their axes. "You build you fort, Charbonneau move in pretty damn quick, *Capitaine*. Dis winter, she be a hell-raiser, you'll see!"

"This squaw of yours," William Clark interjected on impulse. "What is she called?"

The Frenchman beamed with an almost parental pride. "She have Minitaree name. Sacajawea—it mean Bird Woman."

Oh hell, thought Clark. That's one I'll never be able to spell.

The first weeks of November were fortunately mild, though the winds blew ceaselessly across the treeless highlands. The skies were a brilliant blue, achingly bright, and the nights brought an immensity of darkness that closed around the feeble campfires in the bottom.

The scent of new wood and the din of saws and axes and hammers filled the bottom from dawn until after dark each day. Then the night would shut down with its eerie silence, until, somewhere in the dark, a wolf keened softly and the hairs would rise on the back of a man's neck. Or Seaman's.

Meriwether Lewis had deferred to William Clark's experience in the design of the fort. Pat Gass, carpenter and sometime house-builder in civilian life, was in charge of the actual construction.

The walls went up quickly, forming two rows of huts, four in each wing, joined at one end and open at the other to form a rough "V" shape. In the angle where the two wings met, two extra rooms were added; one would serve as a storeroom, the other as a smokehouse. Above them a lookout tower was raised with a catwalk. From the lookout a sentry could oversee the interior of the fort as well as the approaches to it.

The huts faced inward. The backs of the two long rows presented an unbroken wall rising eighteen feet above ground. Steep shed roofs slanted downward to the inside wall, which was seven feet high. Within each room, at a height of seven feet, a ceiling was raised of puncheons—long cottonwood logs split and hewn to form one flat side—to create a warm sleeping loft. 223

The work went swiftly, proceeding with a sense of urgency, for ice had begun to run in the Missouri.

Charbonneau returned to the camp on November 11, 1804, bringing with him not one but two of his wives. They brought presents of four buffalo robes for the white men. Both squaws, the interpreter confirmed, were of the Snake Indians who lived in the Rocky Mountains. The older of the two, though still obviously in her teens, was a shy girl with a prematurely worn expression. She seemed frightened of the white strangers, keeping her eyes cast down, her shoulders hunched as if against a blow. Her name was Otter Woman.

It was the other squaw who caught the eyes of both Lewis

and Clark. She was young, hardly more than a child, Clark thought, not entirely approving of the Frenchman who was said to have won her in a game of chance. A small, sturdily built girl, she had a deep red color, a slant of eyes, and a neatness of features quite different from the flat-faced, light-skinned Mandans. Pretty in her way, Clark thought.

And pregnant.

When Charbonneau went over to one of the men's camp-fires to cadge some coffee, calling out, *"Bonjour, mes amis, bonjour!"* Lewis and Clark stood aside and exchanged glances of dismay. "That foxy devil!" Clark said. "He said nothing about his woman being pregnant. And she's the one he means to take with us!"

"We can't have a baby along," Lewis said, but his words seemed to express more doubt than conviction.

The two men were silent. The young wife of Charbonneau chose that moment to lift her eyes. Her gaze was direct and inquiring without being bold—a look of intelligence, Meriwether Lewis thought grudgingly.

A Shoshoni. When the expedition reached the high mountains, they would have to abandon their boats and proceed overland. To cross the mountains and reach the head-waters of the Columbia on the far side, they would need more than friendly faces; they would need horses. From what Lewis had been able to learn from the Mandans, confirming what he had heard in St. Louis, the Shoshonis possessed fine herds of horses. And what kind of advantage might a band of white strangers gain among the Snakes if a Shoshoni girl was with them? Someone to greet the Snake chiefs in their own tongue, to allay their fears, to assure them of the strangers' good intentions . . .

William Clark's thoughts had taken another turn. "If she's to stay here, even temporarily while Charbonneau is with us, she must have proper shelter."

"I believe we have little choice, then. We'll have to make room for her."

"In our cabin, in the room adjoining ours."

Louis Charbonneau

Lewis shrugged. "There will be no place for her in the other huts."

Clark contemplated the awkwardness of arrangements, and his thoughts ranged ahead to the arduous struggle with the Missouri River that would begin again in the spring. He thought of a woman with a newborn child facing those torrential currents in one of the pirogues . . .

"Impossible," said William Clark.

"I know, I know. But we need her. When will the child be born?"

"I can't say—I'm no expert in these matters."

"You've had enough nieces and nephews, surely, from what I saw at Louisville."

"Well . . . yes." Clark sighed. "It's early yet, as far as I can tell. But she'll have the baby before spring."

"Soon enough to travel with us?"

Clark stared at him. "By God, Lewis, you mean to have her along no matter what—and her child, if needs be!"

"I mean to reach the Pacific Ocean," said Meriwether Lewis.

20 This day was very cold: an experiment was made with proof spirits, which in fifteen minutes froze into hard ice.
—PATRICK GASS, December 7, 1804

ne morning in mid-November when the men of the Corps of Discovery stepped shivering from their tents, feeling a harsher bite in the air, they stared about them in wonder.

The shelf on which Fort Mandan had been raised was a crystal palace. Every tree was coated with ice, and the glitter in the morning sun was that of a thousand chandeliers.

Though their huts were unfinished, the men moved into them that morning. Working feverishly, they raised the last of the heavy roof beams and began to enclose the huts. In the next few days cracks between logs were stuffed with rags, grass and mortar, covered over with mud. Grass and clay were layered over the loft floors. Doors were fitted. As the main structure neared completion, details of men were sent out to collect rocks for chimneys.

They were ready for winter.

On November 19, 1804, the day the roofs were completed over the rows of huts at Fort Mandan, a group of weary riders plodded across the windswept plain north of the Mandans.

They hunched inside their heavy coats and thick buffalo robes against the searching wind and the driving snow. At times they had to feel their way blindly, and only their familiarity with the trail kept them from wandering off into the endless prairie.

They had been eight days in the saddle, covering the 150 miles from their trading post on the Assiniboine River. Among the men were Francois Antoine Laroque and Charles Mackenzie, agents of the Northwest Company, their assistant Baptiste Lafrance, and four French voyageurs from the post.

The horsemen passed the small Ahnahaway village and descended the slope to the banks of the Missouri River. A border of ice crept out from the bank, and there was ice running in the main channel, but the river was shallow, and the horses had no trouble fording it.

The riders followed the Knife River for a short distance. It was growing dark when they came in sight of the stockade and hump-backed lodges of Metaharta, the lower Minitaree village, squatting close to the ground as if huddled against the storm.

In the warm lodge of Black Moccasin, the old chief of the village, the white men were welcomed with cordial familiarity. They gathered around the fire pit in the center of the lodge to bake the cold from their bones and hear the latest gossip. Indians, they knew from experience, loved to gossip.

Antoine Laroque inquired after Toussaint Charbonneau, whom he had found useful in the past as a Minitaree interpreter. Black Moccasin smiled. The old chief seemed to be enjoying himself, a man hugging some secret knowledge. His gnarled fingers toyed with a medal suspended from a leather chain around his neck, drawing Laroque's gaze to it.

"The squaw man is not here," the chief said. "He has gone down below the Mandan towns to the wooden village the Americans are making, for he is to work for them."

Mackenzie, eating some pemmican offered to him by one of Black Moccasin's wives, stopped chewing, his mouth open. "Americans!" he blurted.

The news was a shock. The trading party had left their

Assiniboine posts before news had arrived about the white men in the vicinity of the Mandan and Minitaree villages.

Laroque was the first to recover. "So," he murmured, "they have come at last."

The fur trade, he knew with a sudden, chilling clarity, would never again be the same.

During the night of December 6, 1804, the Missouri River froze solid opposite Fort Mandan. Shortly after breakfast the next morning Big White and a band of Mandans appeared before the fort on horseback. "The buffalo have come in answer to our prayers!" the chief announced. "It is time to hunt."

Meriwether Lewis promptly assembled a hunting party and rode out with the Indians. That day the white hunters shot ten buffalo, the Indians many more. The next day it was William Clark's turn, and his party was successful in killing eight buffalo and a deer.

228

The hunts were not easy, for the snow was deep, the weather bitterly cold. Two men hurt their hips slipping and falling on the icy ground. Several others returned to the fort with frostbitten feet. York, who had gone out with Clark, even had his penis "frosted a little," occasioning merciless taunting and jocularity among the soldiers.

These minor problems were counted a small enough price, for the men of the Corps of Discovery were learning what the Plains Indians had always known.

The buffalo meant survival.

Winter was a happy time for the Plains Indians, a time to relax and to rest, to visit friends, to enjoy games and dances and ceremonies, and tell stories of past glories—for they were great storytellers. But it was also a lean time, when many went hungry because of the scarcity of game, when even the buffalo were rarely seen on the snowbound plains.

Louis Charbonneau

When the shaggy beasts came, often in response to the ceremonial Buffalo Dance, everything stopped for the hunt.

For the Mandans, as for other Indians, the buffalo was far more than a principal source of food. He was ikon, giver of life, supplier of virtually every need. Every part of him became a part of the Indian's existence.

In its rawhide state, the buffalo's hide provided durable moccasin soles, drums, belts, pad saddles (the latter filled with buffalo hair), ropes, and thongs. Even the unique, tub-like bullboats the Mandans used to cross the river were made of rawhide skins sewn together over a willow pole frame.

The unmarked parts of the hide were tanned into softer, more pliable buckskin. This made comfortable moccasin tops, shirts, dresses, leggings, breechclouts, winter robes, and bedding, as well as decorative objects both ceremonial and functional such as pipe bags, weapon covers, quivers, and baby cradles. The more attractive, decorated hides also formed handsome tipis. Though the Mandans lived in permanent earth lodges, they carried the familiar Indian tipi with them when hunting or visiting another village.

Besides padding for saddles, the buffalo's hair was used in ceremonial headdresses, pillows, halters, and—in the form of hairballs, often found in the stomach and greatly prized—medicine balls.

The horns were crafted into cups, spoons, and ladles; the hooves and feet became glue and rattles; the tail yielded whips, switches, and decoration for clothing. The skull was a religious object, displayed in ceremonies and dances, during which food and drink was served from buckets, cups, and dishes made of the stomach lining. In the same ceremonies, the hair of the buffalo's beard could be seen on weapons and garments. The bladder carried porcupine quills, bedding, beads, and buttons. And buffalo chips provided fuel for the fire.

The buffalo's bones were formed into arrowheads, war clubs, scrapers, splints, tools, even dice for gambling. And its

sinews were treated and woven to make thread for sewing, string for bows, cinches for saddles.

The rest was eaten.

On December 9, 1804, Meriwether Lewis stepped past the half-finished palisade of pickets rising across the front of Fort Mandan and walked along the low bluff that overlooked the Missouri River. Seaman followed him. It was another crisp, cold morning. There was little wind, though no day on these high plains advanced very far without wind. The temperature hovered near zero. The silence was almost eerie. The cry of an Indian boy romping far up the river in the direction of the nearest Mandan village was like glass breaking.

Seaman bounded along the edge of the bluff, putting his nose down to sniff at the snow-covered ground or lifting his head to gaze across the frozen river. For a moment Lewis stood watching him, idly enjoying his dog's inexhaustible capacity for finding interest in each day as he found good in all people.

Even the British traders, Lewis thought.

To be truthful, he held it only as civility when Seaman permitted himself to be admired and petted by Larocque, Mackenzie, and the other traders. Lewis himself had been, in his own view, more than civil. On his arrival at the Mandans he had met one of the Northwest Company's agents, Hugh McCracken, at one of the villages. Finding that McCracken was to leave shortly for his post to the north, Lewis acted swiftly, sending a letter for McCracken to deliver to his superior, Charles Chaboillez. The letter extended the hand of friendly cooperation, but it also carried a bold assertion of American dominion over the upper Missouri.

When Larocque and Mackenzie had arrived from the north in November, Lewis had lent Charbonneau to Larocque as an interpreter among the Minitarees. He had undertaken to repair Laroque's compass. The generous-hearted Clark had volunteered to corral Mackenzie's horses at Fort Mandan so they would be safe from theft.

Louis Charbonneau

That said, Lewis's nationalism and his old dislike of things British, rooted in childhood memories of British raids in Albemarle County during the Revolution, were never far from his thoughts. William Clark good-humoredly pointed out that, of the "English" traders they had met, McCracken was Irish, Mackenzie a Scot, Larocque and his assistant Baptiste Lafrance both French, but Lewis was not swayed. When he learned that Lafrance was spreading false rumors among the Indians about American intentions, he stiffly confronted Larocque and warned him that the rumors must stop. And when Laroque expressed an interest in joining the expedition when it left in the spring, Lewis was quick to discourage him. "He wishes only to spy upon our venture for his company," Lewis said to Clark. "There's no doubt, the English trading companies have no wish to see us reach the Pacific."

Lewis took seriously his role as representative of American power. He knew that American and British interests in the fur trade would inevitably be in conflict. And he knew that he and Clark, should they be successful in finding a route across the continent to the Pacific Ocean, would confirm and extend a sovereignty that until now had existed only on paper.

Diplomatic and civil, he would be with the traders from the Assiniboine posts, helpful and cooperative, insofar as he deemed reasonable and prudent. But Lewis would leave no doubt in their minds about the changing of the guard.

It was the American flag that would fly over Fort Mandan.

Behind him the stillness of the morning gave way to sudden commotion as a contingent of men of the Corps of Discovery spilled out of their huts, their steps crunching on the frozen ground. They slapped their hands together, stamped their feet and squinted against the sun's glare, blindingly white off the snow. A horse whinnied. There were four horses, one that had survived the journey upriver and three others borrowed from the Mandans.

Lewis ended the milling around with a crisp order to fall in. The hunting party crossed the frozen river on foot. They walked past the expedition's three boats, now locked in a grip

of multilayered ice. Upriver, smudges of smoke smeared the brilliant blue sky above the Mandan and Minitaree villages. Lewis thought of recent visits to the smoky earthen lodges with their blackened interior walls, their fire pits that were always kept burning.

On the prairie beyond the river, the snow lay everywhere, a foot to eighteen inches deep, and even though it was a light, dry powder, it slowed the men's progress, dragging at their legs and feet. Seaman dodged back and forth across the snow-pack, excited to be out of the fort after being cooped up for days at a time during the early winter storms that had raged across the plains. The snow reached almost to the Newfoundland's belly as he carved out his own path.

Meriwether Lewis marveled at his dog's adaptability. By this time more than two years old, Seaman had reached his maturity. He was full grown. Lewis estimated his weight at over 150 pounds, the equal of at least half the men in the party. After a year and a half on the trail, his muscles had hardened to the toughness of hickory. He had also gained confidence and self-assurance, meeting the constantly changing circumstances of the expedition without a hitch. Yet he retained his playfulness, his ready amiability, his loyalty.

The cold did not seem to faze him. Lewis felt it seize his own extremities as he walked, snipping at his toes, his fingers, his ears, his nose. Seaman padded along through the snow with his jaws open in evident pleasure, his nose lifted to the crisp cold air. The hardened pads of his feet seemed impervious to frostbite. His coat, with the onset of winter weather, was as thick and dense as a good buffalo robe.

One of the latter, Lewis thought, he meant to have for himself this day!

The buffalo were not close to the river—the day before William Clark had had to range seven miles from the river before finding the herd—but a wide trail was soon found in the snow. Less than two miles from the Missouri and meandering slowly toward the river, the herd came into view. It moved like the purple shadow of a cloud across the white landscape.

From a low rise the men of the hunting party stopped, staring at the spectacle. The Mandans had gone out hunting early.

The Indians hunted on horseback, displaying remarkable skill. Their hunting horses, Lewis had been told, were specially chosen and trained. They had to be swift, because a buffalo in his prime could outrun a mediocre horse. They had to be quick to dart in for the strike and leap aside to escape a raking horn if an enraged buffalo turned on them. The hunting horse could not shy from the sight and sound and smell of the herd or panic in the confusion that often accompanied the chase. And it had to learn to respond to its rider's knee pressure only, for a hunter had to have both hands free for his bow and arrows. Above all, the horse had to be surefooted and nimble, for the prairie was pocked by innumerable fissures and gullies, rocks and brush and burrows—all now hidden beneath the deceptively smooth surface of the snow.

There were about two hundred buffalo visible at a glance in the nearest herd. Against a hill to the southwest was a smaller group of about twenty-five or thirty bulls. Most of those in the larger herd were cows and youngsters, for at this season the mature bulls kept to themselves. Also visible, never far away, were the slinking forms of the wolf pack.

But the Mandan hunters on their painted ponies were closer. Behind them, running to keep up, were the women and boys too young to be hunters, carrying their skinning knives.

"Watch that rider, lads!" Meriwether Lewis exclaimed in admiration.

An Indian on a pinto raced toward a cluster of bison. Sensing danger—though they had poor eyesight, the huge animals had excellent senses of smell and hearing—the buffalo tried to run, but they floundered badly in the snowdrifts. The Indian's pony closed swiftly on a full-grown cow with a thick winter coat, almost black in color. As he drew near, the Indian

233

had his bow and an arrow ready, fitted to the string. He used only his legs to guide his horse and keep his own balance. The rider darted between two animals toward his chosen target. The hunter was almost on top of the cow when he shot the arrow straight down from a distance of only a few feet. The force of the blow, behind the left shoulder and into the buffalo's heart, was so strong that the arrow was buried up to the feathers.

And in the instant the arrow flew, the Indian's horse leaped away, escaping from danger. It was like a dance, Lewis thought, a breathtaking and beautiful dance of speed and skill, courage and risk.

"Let's not leave them all to the Mandans!" he shouted. "Get in close and don't waste your powder!"

The men all started running then, through the sculptured white drifts toward the ponderously moving buffalo herd.

Suddenly another Indian hunter somersaulted as his horse stumbled in an unseen hole. The Mandan rolled in the snow while his horse righted itself. In an instant the thrown rider grabbed a rope that trailed from the bridle. At the end of the rope, the horse jerked to a stop. The Indian raced nimbly toward him and leaped onto his back. Within a few seconds the hunter was once more in the chase.

By contrast to the Indians on horseback, the men of the expedition lumbered along awkwardly on foot, slipping and struggling through drifts. It was like trying to run in knee-deep water.

But the buffalo also moved slowly. Their great weight became an enormous burden in the snow. They ran with a rolling gait and resembled a dark wave undulating across the sea of white.

Plunging through the drifts beside the men, Seaman was caught up in the excitement of the chase. As he and Meriwether Lewis drew close to one of the buffalo, a bark of excitement burst from the dog's throat. Lewis had taken aim, and Seaman's roar startled both him and the buffalo. Lewis's shot was a jerk rather than a squeeze, the buffalo veered in panic, and

234

the shot went wild. The whole herd was startled by the dog's
bark into a stampede.

The run was short-lived. The huge animals soon exhausted themselves in the snow, and the hunt was on in earnest. Rifle shots cracked in the dry cold air. Animals were
falling from the white hunters' bullets as well as the Indians'
arrows or from lances driven deep into the vulnerable cavity
behind the buffalo's last rib. For the Mandan hunters, their
women and children moved in with their knives as soon as an
animal fell. A fallen buffalo could not be left behind even for
a few minutes or the wolves would close in.

Seaman became aware of the wolf pack skulking behind
him, of the plunging horses with their vivid slashes of red and
yellow paint, of another stain on the pure white snowpack
where the knives flashed in the brilliant sunshine, of his own
companions slipping and falling as they ran, cursing, lifting
their rifles and shooting, the powder smoke spurting like gusts
of black breath.

A huge cow charged straight at the dog, red eyes rolling
in panic. Seaman saw the bulk of hair and muscle and bone
and leaped to the side, ducking clear as the buffalo ran past
him. At that moment, off to the right, George Drouillard's gun
spoke. His aim was true, and the buffalo went down as if a
rope had caught her front legs and thrown her.

The herd moved on across the snow. Some of the men of
Lewis's party went back to claim their kills, one of which had
already been lost to the snarling wolves. They began cutting
away the hides and butchering the carcasses on the spot. The
four horses were brought up, the best sections of meat packed
onto the horses. The hunters were disappointed in several of
the buffalo they had killed, for the animals were thin, all bone
and muscle, the heavy autumn layer of fat burned away during
winter's search for ever scarcer food.

Around noon the horses were laden with all they could
carry. By this time the buffalo herd had disappeared over a
rise in the direction of the river bottom, and all that could be
seen on the plain were the splashes of red on the snow where

an animal had fallen, the clusters of activity where the Indian skinners still worked—their hunters had killed several times as many buffalo as Lewis and his men—and the wolves swarming over the fallen carcasses they had claimed.

Meriwether Lewis sent a detail of a half-dozen men to accompany the horses back to the fort. After an hour's rest the remaining hunters regrouped and resumed the chase.

In the afternoon they closed on some of the buffalo in the river bottom. The men were slower now, their legs heavy from pushing through the snow for hours, their hands and feet and faces numb with cold, and their successes were fewer.

By the end of the day the white hunters had killed nine buffalo, but three of these and part of a fourth had been lost to the marauding wolf pack. Meriwether Lewis estimated the Indians' total at forty killed, and they had lost few of these because their women and children were so numerous and so efficient in following up each kill. It's our first winter hunt, Lewis thought. It's been their way of life for untold generations.

236

That night the hunting party, save for those who had returned to the fort at noon with the horses, made camp in the river bottom, sheltered a little by the bluff at the edge of the highland. They joined two men from Clark's party who had remained in the bottom overnight to guard the meat from the previous day's hunt. Their fire seemed cold, unable to warm them. It burned with so little heat that, only a few feet away from its heart, the men shivered in their blankets or buffalo robes. They added wood to the fire and hunched closer, but in the end they could only endure the darkness and the cold, waiting for morning.

Seaman slept by Meriwether Lewis's side. At intervals he lifted his head when he heard the wolves howling. Once when the cloud cover parted and the river bottom was bathed in moonlight, he saw the dark shapes skulking across the snow and flowing among the trees like shadows blowing on the wind, and he remained awake, alert to danger.

Louis Charbonneau

During the night Meriwether Lewis shivered in his sleep. He lay huddled under the skin of one of the buffalo killed that day, his only covering. Though he was reluctant to be next to the fresh hide, Seaman shifted closer to Lewis, who instinctively rolled over in his sleep toward the new source of heat. Seaman lay beside him, his nose quivering at the sharp scent of blood. The dog had shown an unexpected fastidiousness about freshly killed game. He would bring down an animal when commanded to do so, but he would not gorge himself on the carcass like a wolf. Nor would he even enter the new smokehouse at the fort where meat was hung. He waited— "like a gentleman," Meriwether Lewis said—for his share when the meat had been cut and cooked and portioned out.

This night, however, he lay close against his master, and gradually Lewis's shivering ceased as he drew warmth from the big dog's body.

By morning the temperature stood at ten degrees below zero.

Meriwether Lewis, the nine men still with him, and Seaman breakfasted on bone marrow. Afterward Lewis improvised a travois for Seaman, Indian fashion, with two long poles cut from a willow in the bottom and secured, one on each flank, by strips of hide across Seaman's shoulders. The trailing poles formed a platform on which packs of the buffalo meat were laid.

Five men stayed behind to guard the remaining meat. Lewis and the rest of the party set off along the river bottom toward the fort, Seaman pulling the travois easily across the frozen ground.

Coming past the point, the party pulled up at Lewis's signal.

In the distance the buffalo herd walked across the Missouri.

The men stared at this remarkable sight, expecting at any moment to see the layer of ice begin to sag and crack.

But the herd passed sedately over the ice and in a few minutes had reached the north side. The leaders began to plod up the bank.

Above them, along the riverbank, the Mandan hunters appeared. Waiting.

21 Had I these white warriors in the upper plains, my young men on horseback would soon do for them, as they would do for so many wolves . . .

—LE BORGNE, MINITAREE CHIEF, QUOTED BY CHARLES MACKENZIE

For Seaman the Mandan winter settled into a new kind of routine, limited by the winter storms and by Meriwether Lewis's reluctance to have the dog stray far from Fort Mandan in view of the Indians' fascination with him. During severe weather the men left the compound only on specific errands or on recreational forays to the Indian villages, excursions on which Seaman was not invited. Except for the occasional walk with Lewis along the river or the excitement of a hunt, Seaman remained at the fort.

Lewis and Clark, meanwhile, were preoccupied with establishing friendly relations with the Mandans and the Minitarees. Only Le Borgne, Grand Chief of the Minitarees, remained aloof, professing disdain for these "strangers." Lewis's sometimes touchy relations with the British traders improved dramatically in December with the arrival of Hugh Heney, who brought a warm reply from Charles Chaboillez to Lewis's letter. Heney was a gregarious and friendly man with whom Lewis immediately got along well. He was also generous and cooperative in offering information on the country to the

west, even providing Clark with sketches for his tentative map of the upper Missouri.

The Indians were almost daily visitors to Fort Mandan. Though Seaman had not forgotten his suspicions of the Teton Sioux chiefs, he found these visitors friendlier and gradually became less wary of them. They came to watch the men work on the huts, often staying on in the evenings for the nightly entertainment the men of the Corps provided. The men were also invited to perform at the Mandan villages, where their novel form of dancing was a source of great amusement and delight to the Indians.

At Fort Mandan dancing was virtually the only form of recreation that winter. Seaman frequently got into the spirit of the music—the fiddles of Cruzatte and Gibson, sometimes accompanied by a tin whistle or a tambourine, always by clapping hands and pounding feet. The dog would bound around the circle of dancers, barking and prancing. One of those who amazed and delighted the Indians was Francois Rivet. The slim, agile *engagé* had perfected the art of dancing on his hands to the lively French folk music, and so swiftly did he move amidst the clapping and heel-thumping of the others that he created the illusion in the eyes of the savages of "dancing on his head." As word of Rivet's prowess spread among the villagers, his became the performance most often requested by visiting Indians.

It became common practice for some of the chiefs and principal warriors to stay overnight at Fort Mandan whenever they came there to visit. Slowly Seaman came to accept their presence and their good nature. For their part the Indians were fascinated by the Bear Dog. Once Big White approached Meriwether Lewis to ask if the Bear Dog might be purchased. Lewis promptly turned him down, assuring the Mandan chief that Seaman had been especially chosen for his great journey to the western ocean.

But there was one at the fort who had already become the Newfoundland's first true Indian friend.

When Charbonneau and his squaws moved to the fort,

Louis Charbonneau

Seaman seemed to understand at once that there was something different about Sacajawea. Nervous at the first approach of the huge Bear Dog, unlike any she had ever seen, the young Indian girl retreated. "Ah, by gar, woman, *le chién*, he no bite you!" Charbonneau scolded her.

While the girl stood rigid, Seaman sniffed her, making what seemed to be a remarkably thorough inspection of the entire hem of her deerskin dress. The cold nose touched her leg, and she shivered. Then Seaman gazed up at her—he did not have to look far, for she was small, scarcely five feet tall—and pushed his muzzle against her hand.

Tentatively, then with growing confidence, Sacajawea touched his broad skull with her fingers. After a moment she began to fondle his ears.

When she lay down on her blanket that afternoon to rest, the black dog stretched out on the dirt floor of her room near her feet.

The dog's attachment for the young Indian girl did not go unnoticed. "Your dog seems to have taken a fancy to the interpreter's squaw," William Clark observed one evening.

"Dogs and children," Lewis said absently. He was busy writing in his journal, making up for the many months he had left most of the recording of events to Clark. Then, his curiosity piqued by the question, he asked with interest, "Do you suppose he knows she's pregnant?"

"Well . . . I don't know about that."

William Clark paused, struck by the mystery Lewis's query unlocked. Who could answer such a question? The bond that linked man and dog, forged over measureless time, had a strength and intimacy that was beyond logical analysis. That instinctive partnership had created in the dog a loyalty toward man that, in most instances, was truer and more reliable than man's loyalty to man. Why couldn't that bond include other forms of intuitive understanding? Who had not heard the mournful howl of a dog who had lost his master, or known of one so torn with grief that he cared not to survive?

"In any event, she's good with him, and he's very pro-

tective about her, so I suppose he does have some kind of understanding about her condition." Clark paused a moment to reflect. "York likes her, too. And he tends to hover when anyone is sick or in need."

"Hover?"

"Hover. When the girl was sick last week, he was around with soups and stewed fruits and I don't know what all. Like a mother hen."

"So that's what that business with Jessaume was all about!"

"Yes," said Clark testily. Jessaume's squaw had been staying at the fort, along with Charbonneau's wives, and somehow the story of York's attentions to one of the squaws who was feeling ill became garbled in the telling. An ill-natured man at best, Jessaume had jumped to the conclusion that it was his wife who was involved and that Charbonneau was in complicity with York. The two interpreters had quarreled over the misunderstanding, and Jessaume had stalked out of the compound. "He misunderstood and didn't bother to find out the truth. If he'd taken a hand to his wife . . ."

"Perhaps I should speak to York," Lewis said gravely, although a hint of a smile lurked behind his expression.

"To what purpose?"

"Why . . . I shall advise him not to hover!"

December was cold. Temperatures dropped to as low as forty-five degrees below zero. The work on the pickets at the front of the fort went on, along with daubing the interiors of the huts to make them more livable. Meat brought in by the hunters was stored in the new smokehouse. John Shields got a forge and bellows working, and word of his skill in repairing or making metal tools, weapons, and utensils raced through the Indian villages. Soon there was a daily traffic in Indians coming to Fort Mandan to exchange corn for the work of the blacksmiths. It took the work of three smiths, William Bratton and Alexander Willard joining Shields, to meet the demand.

Louis Charbonneau

On Christmas Eve the picket line was completed. A wide gate was set in place. Fort Mandan was now a complete enclosure. Examining it, one of the visiting traders, Antoine Laroque, observed that it appeared so impregnable it was almost cannonball proof.

To help celebrate Christmas, Meriwether Lewis passed out flour, dried apples, pepper, and other articles to the several messes. He instructed the interpreters to pass the word to the Indians that this was a very special Medicine Day for the white men and no one else would be allowed inside the fort. With the exception of Charbonneau's wives, no Indians would be present that Christmas Day.

Christmas began with a salvo from the swivel gun, which awakened William Clark and brought him stumbling from his hut. The men were in a holiday mood, quickly enhanced when Clark doled out a dram of whiskey to each. Another discharge of the swivel followed, and the rattle of a round of small arms rolled across the prairie to the wonderment of the Indians who heard it. The American flag was run up the staff for the first time, and the men of the Corps, in that moment proud of themselves both as explorers and builders, saw the hoisting of the flag as a suitable reason for another glass of spirits. Their two captains agreed.

One of the rooms was cleared out for dancing. Music rang through the fort. Outside, beyond the high walls, the curious Indians who had come down to the river bottom listened to the sounds of the white men's medicine. At ten in the morning Meriwether Lewis doled out another glass of whiskey to each man, and more dancing followed, the men feeling warm and snug in their new fort, the spirits warming their bellies.

At one o'clock a gun was fired as a signal for dinner. The cooks had prepared roast turkey, deer, elk, and buffalo meat, corn seasoned with salt and pepper, apple tarts baked with flour and cinnamon, hot tea with sugar. After the feast another salvo served as a notice to resume the dancing. The merriment went on all afternoon and into the evening until, exhausted, one by one the celebrants began to collapse. By eight that evening, in the long winter night of the north, the holiday celebration was over.

In January Seaman made his second Indian friend.

Meriwether Lewis's reputation as a skilled medicine man had spread among the Mandans and Minitarees, and a steady stream of patients began to show up at the fort for treatment of various ailments. One day early in January the temperature dropped to twenty-one degrees. But buffalo had again been sighted in the vicinity, and the Mandans were out hunting in spite of the cold. During the night a man and a boy became separated from each other and the other hunters; they did not return.

That night was one of the worst of the winter. In the morning the temperature was forty degrees below zero. When the Indians went out in search of the missing man and his son, it was with the gloomy expectation of finding both of them frozen to death. The father, however, was found unharmed. Only the boy remained missing.

At ten o'clock that morning, he limped into Fort Mandan. He had lain out on the prairie through the cold night without a fire, wearing only a pair of antelope leggings and moccasins with a buffalo robe for covering. His feet were frozen.

Meriwether Lewis immediately had the boy soak his feet in cold water. He was also given hot food and a shirt to wear, and placed near the roaring fire in the captains' hut. After a while some needles of pain offered hope that his feet might be saved.

In spite of his affliction the young Indian was a cheerful boy, and he was much taken with the Bear Dog. He was not surprised to find Seaman living in the captains' lodge, for among the Mandans their valuable animals, whether horses or dogs, were brought into the earth lodges with the family at night. A horse within one's own lodge could not be stolen.

The boy was soon hobbling about the compound. As he

came to know Seaman's amiable nature, the Indian became strongly attached to the Newfoundland, and the two were often together. With Meriwether Lewis away from the fort much of the time, cementing relationships among the Indians and the frequent visitors—who included a party of Assiniboines as well as the British traders—Seaman spent much of his time with the Indian boy and with Sacajawea, who was rapidly approaching the time she would give birth.

On January 27, with great reluctance, Meriwether Lewis amputated the Indian boy's toes. After that, however, the boy's full recovery was rapid. His father came to the fort to express his gratitude. "My son will walk and ride and hunt," he said. "And he will remember the medicine of the white father, and the Bear Dog who lives in his lodge."

Sacajawea's pains began two weeks later, on the morning of February 11, 1805.

William Clark had left the fort with a hunting party a week earlier and had not yet returned. Toussaint Charbonneau, who had also been out hunting, had reached the fort the night before. He told Meriwether Lewis that he had left two men with the meat to protect it from wolves. Early on the morning of the eleventh he left once more with Drouillard, taking two sleighs along on which to transport the meat.

Charbonneau had been gone about an hour when Meriwether Lewis, returning to his hut, heard a stifled cry from the interpreter's room. He went immediately to the connecting door.

In a corner of the dim room Sacajawea lay in her blankets. Otter Woman and Corn Seeker, Charbonneau's other wives, were with her. And, standing near the door with a bowl of broth, Clark's servant York. Hovering, Lewis thought.

"This be her time," York said softly. He had been many times a witness to both birth and death. He suspected that the little Indian woman, who was both young and small, would have a difficult labor.

"Do what you can for her. I imagine the other Indian women will take care of things."

"Might be, Cap'n Lewis, suh, she be needin' you."

Lewis felt a momentary dismay. On this journey he had done things of a medical nature he had never tried before, from concocting an ointment for pleurisy to amputation, but he was not prepared, he thought, to be a midwife.

"Yes, well . . . we'll see."

Lewis was busy in the compound through the morning but found time to stop at his hut periodically and peer inquiringly at York, who always seemed to be checking the kettle to make sure he had hot water ready. Each time York shook his head.

Distracted, Lewis had not noticed his dog's absence that morning. Any other day Seaman always seemed to be tagging along wherever Lewis went about the fort.

The next time Lewis looked in on the interpreter's squaw, he stepped into the room—and almost stumbled over Seaman. The Newfoundland lay full length across the room's entrance, just inside the doorway, as if he were guarding it. When he saw Lewis, he thumped his tail against the wooden floor—the only finished floor in the fort, Lewis was reminded, a gesture on the part of the men who had installed the floor for the interpreter's wives shortly after Christmas—but he remained where he was when Lewis left.

Charbonneau returned in the afternoon with the meat-laden sleighs. As soon as he heard that his squaw was about to give birth, he hurried to the hut where she labored. Almost immediately he emerged from the room, looking ashen and shaken. "*Mon Dieu!*" he gasped. "Why she take so long?" He staggered outside and showed no inclination to return to the room where the Indian girl shuddered with agonizing spasms.

Observing the incident, Meriwether Lewis reflected that the interpreter might not be one to rely on in a crisis. He seemed to prefer to pretend that it didn't exist. He even sounded petulant over his woman's failure to produce his child without pain or fuss.

Louis Charbonneau

Outside, however, Charbonneau turned the problem into a boast. "She is small, *ma femme*," he said to some of the soldiers, "and *le bébé*, he is boy, sure, eh? A big boy, a Charbonneau!"

The pains became worse. Jessaume, who had arrived to offer support for his fellow interpreter—this being one of the times the two Frenchmen weren't quarreling—spoke as if this were only in the nature of things. "De squaw, she be young, an he be her first *bébé*, eh? He is hard, alway." He nodded sagely at his own words.

By this time Meriwether Lewis was seriously concerned. The Indian girl's labor seemed to him to have gone on much too long. The pain she was enduring had left her sweating and weak, her whole body torn by the spasms. Charbonneau's wives, even the oldest one who had come from the Minitaree village for the event, seemed as helpless as Lewis himself. Only York, bathing the girl's face with wet cloths, soothing her with his rumbling voice, seemed to know what he was doing.

Jessaume entered the hut and peered into the room just as Sacajawea was racked by another spasm that wrenched a cry from her—though she had drawn blood from her lip through trying to hold back her cries. "*Capitaine . . .* Jessaume, he have *idée*, I think."

"What is it? At this stage I'd try anything."

"Many time I have done this. Is old Indian *médicin*, de rattle of a snake."

"It works?" Lewis asked dubiously.

"*Oui, oui*, it nevair fail, I swear! It bring de *bébé* quick, like dat!" He skated one palm off the other.

At that moment another stifled cry from the Indian woman ended Lewis's indecision. He had several rattles in his chest, trophies from a night when the expedition had made camp in a rattlesnake-infested bottom. He dug the rattles out of his chest and handed two of the rings to Jessaume.

Taking a small dish from York, the Frenchman crumbled the two dry rings between his fingers, breaking them into small pieces and powder. He added a small quantity of water from the kettle and stirred until the mixture dissolved into a milky liquid.

It was York who helped Sacajawea drink the potion. Gently he lifted her head. She responded with docile trust, too weak to resist, Lewis thought. She swallowed a little of the liquid, gagged and coughed, but accepted more when York patiently brought the bowl to her lips.

When the dish was empty, Sacajawea fell back on her blankets. The dark eyes seemed huge in her drawn face. She cannot endure much more, thought Lewis.

Ten minutes after Sacajawea drank Jessaume's prescription, there was a loud shriek from the room where she lay, as if she had been driven to a final extreme of agony. Then, after a brief silence, came a babbling from the other Indian women, pierced by the thin, unmistakable bawl of a newborn baby.

York appeared in the doorway, his round face beaming. "That done it, Cap'n Lewis, suh! You tell Chabono, he be the poppa of a fine new boy!"

When Meriwether Lewis entered the room a little later, both mother and child had been cleaned up. The Indian girl looked small, wrapped now in a buffalo robe, a child herself holding a miniature version, his wrinkled face lost in folds of soft white doeskin. Lewis, who had lived so long in the isolation of a man's world, could only stare.

Charbonneau was less awed by the miracle of birth—he was already a father, *n'est-ce pas?*—and he strutted back and forth, grinning through his beard. "By gar, Charbonneau, he make good sons, eh, *Capitaine*? Is not so?"

"He's a fine looking boy," Lewis agreed.

Sacajawea lay quiet, utterly spent. Yet in the dark eyes now was not pain or confusion but a serenity that moved Lewis far more than Charbonneau's elated boasting. The Indian woman's eyes sought Lewis's, and her expression deepened.

By the Lord! Lewis breathed. She means to carry him all the way to the western ocean. And I'm blessed if I don't believe she can do it!

The boy, who was named Jean Baptiste, was the last new recruit to the Corps of Discovery.

22 a fine Day I am ingaged in Copying a Map, men building perogus, makeing Ropes, Burning Coal, Hanging up meat & makeing battle axes for Corn.

—WILLIAM CLARK, March 1, 1805

GEORGE SHANNON'S JOURNAL

February 17, 1805

Some of our Men was attacked by the Seoux two days past. These men had been sent after Meat which was left by our Hunting Party. They were Geo. Drewyer, Frazure, Goodrich and Newman (who has done much to Redeem himself, tho he is no longer one of the Permanint Party). They had 3 Horses with them to pull the slays carrying the Meat, when they were attacked by more than a hundred Indians. The Seouxs took two of the horses and two of the men's knives, and would have made off with the 3rd Horse if our Men did not protest vigorously and show'd themselves ready to fight.

When our men returned to Fort Mandan Cap'n Lewis sent word to the Mandan Villages at once inviting the chief and their Warriors to join us in pursuit of the Thieves at first light. At Midnight the Chief of the 2nd Village came to us, with another chief and a few men. But said that all of the young warriors were out hunting, and they had most of the guns which these Indians possess.

Louis Charbonneau

We set off at Sunrise, notwithstanding that the Thermometer was at 16°
below zero and verry cold. We went down the River to the place where the
men was attacked. One of the Mandan Chiefs had to go back, haveing become
Blinded by the Snow. We found the meat which Cap. Clark had left at his
last camp had been stolen by the Indians. We pursued them but they have fled
and we could not catch them.

February 21, 1805

After we left the first deposit of meat which had been taken or destroyed
by the Savages, we continued on to the next lower camp, and found that the
Indians had overlooked it. We packed this meat and were forced to give up the
pursuit, but we hunted for 2 Days and killed 36 Deer and 14 Elk, so we were
able to fill our two Slays. One of our slays carried about 2400 lbs. of meat,
and was pulled by 16 Men along the ice. All were exhausted and glad to return
to our fort, and listen to St. Peter play his Fiddle & the Frenchmen danced.

February 23, 1805

A Fair Day, warm and pleasant after so much Cold. All hands busy
cutting the boats from the ice. Even the keelboat, which we pulled on to the
lower bank in November past, is locked in layers of ice. We cut as much as
possible with our axes. We have tried using hot stones, which is an Indian trick,
heating the stones in a fire and dropping them onto the ice in the bottom of the
boat and around the sides. but all the Stones we could gather exploded in the
fire. Cap'n Clark says it is the type of stone to be found in these parts, none
of which is able to withstand the Fire.

We have fixed some axes on long poles. When the first ice is cut through,
the water rushes in from below and fills up the space, there being another layer
of ice below. We use our long handle axes to pick through the ice beneath this
water. It is hard work, but on this day we cut one of the perogues loose and
the 2nd nearly ready. Many Indians come to watch us at our work. The Father

of the boy who had his feet froze last month came to fetch him today. Cap'n Lewis's dog followed them to the Gate and barked after them. Seamon has been friendly with the boy.

February 25, 1805

We fixed up a Windless and after much exertion drew the 2 pirogues up on the upper bank, where they will be safe when the ice on the river begins to break up, which would put the boats in great peril. We made a strong rope of elkskins, but when we tried to use it to haul the Discovery up the bank it broke several times. We worked at this all day until darkness coming forced us to give up the attempt. More Indians come to watch. They have not seen anything like our boats, for these people use only canoes and small Bullboats. These are round boats made of Buffalo skins stretched over a lightweight Pole frame, and in the water they bob like teacups afloat. They are so light the Squaws can carry them easily. In the water the Bullboats wobble and roll and turn in circles, but the Indians paddle them across the river with great speed and dexterity. They are a very superstitious people, and they believe our large Boats are a sign of powerful Magic.

February 26, 1805

a fine day, we started to work at daylight on pulling the Keelboat ashore and kept at it until nightfall. As it was coming Dark and we were making our greatest effort, Sgt Ordway yelled and some of the Men jumped back. With a great roar the ice gave way near us all along the bank for a Distance up to 100 Yds. All hands then gave every effort, and the boat was pulled onto the bank. Now all the boats are free of the threat of being smashed to kindling by the ice, which is said to come tumbling down the Missourie like a White Avalanche, crushing everything in its way.

February 28, 1805

A fine Day. Mr. Jos. Gravelines returned to Fort Mandan from the Arikara village with two French, who spent the winter there. He tells us the

Louis Charbonneau

Seous who attacked our Hunters intend to wage war upon us. One of the Canadian traders is said to be putting rifles in the hands of these Seoux which they could use against us. The Arikaras are disposed toward peace with us and with the Mandans, which our Captains have encouraged them in. These Arik. refused hospitality to the Seoux thieves who stole our 2 horses. This refusal is the greatest insult they could give without going to war.

March 6, 1805

Our smiths are busy mending and makeing axes for the Mandans. All other hands work on the boats, fixing up the Perogues and making canoes to take us up the River. The Indians are busy getting ready for their Spring buffalo hunt. They burn the grass to encourage the Buffalo to feed on the early crop of grass that will follow. It makes the whole day cloudy from the smoke. I cut my foot with an ads [adze—Ed.] while working on a new boat in the bottom where we fell our trees.

253

March 9, 1805

A cold and windy Day. I am laid up made lame by my foot, but Cap'n Lewis has treated it and informs me that it will heal well enough before we are ready to leave this place. Many Indians visit us at our Fort. The Chief of the Metaharta village of the Big Bellies stayed overnight, his name is Black Moccasin. He stayed with 2 of his Wives. Today Cap'n Clark walked up to the bottom where the Men work on the boats and he met One Eye, Head Chief of all the Big Bellies, whose French name is Le Borgne. He is a very big man for an Indian & Ugly with his white eye and a scar on his face, & is said to be terrible in Battle. He has refused to visit us before but now agrees that we are to be his Friends. Cap'n Clark sent him on to the Fort, where he was met by Cap. Lewis. Mr. Chabonaux the Minetaree interpreter came also and spoke for the Chief. One Eye smoked a pipe with Cap'n Lewis, and he rec'd many Gifts, a Medal with the likeness of the President such as we give to Big Chiefs, a shirt, a Flag, cloth & other things with which he was very pleased. We fired 2 of our Guns for this Chief to show his importance.

March 11, 1805

The Day cloudy and cold, with snow blowing in the afternoon. My foot gives me trouble. Our French Interpreter who has been helping the traders from the North West Co. rec'd many gifts from them including 200 Balls & Powder, knives and presents for his Squaws. He says he will not do all that is required of any man who is in the Permanint Party. We fear we will not have him with us or his Squaw, who was to go with us to the Snake Indians which are her People. Our Captains give him a night to think about this and decide. All hands busy on the boats.

"When is he coming?" Impatience edged Meriwether Lewis's tone.

"Drouillard just came in through the gate. It seems our interpreter needs another interpreter to speak for him."

Lewis was silent for a moment, staring into the blazing fire in the stone fireplace. March had turned cold again after the deceptive warmth of late February. All the same, spring was not far off. Time was running short. And the abrupt turn-about of Toussaint Charbonneau was an unexpected and unwelcome complication.

254

"What do you suppose got into him?" William Clark mused.

"It's obvious enough, isn't it? Those English traders have corrupted him. It wasn't enough that one of them tried to poison the Indians' minds against us—it's taken us all winter to win the Minitarees over. Let's face it, Clark, they have no wish to see us cross the mountains and reach the Columbia River. They're the ones who put ideas into Charbonneau's head."

"I doubt Mr. Heney would have been party to any such scheme," said Clark with his customary impulse toward fairness. "Or Mackenzie or Larocque, for that matter."

"Who else, then?" asked Lewis skeptically. "In any event, our interpreter is a vain man. Perhaps too full of his own importance. If he persists in balking over our conditions . . . well, we shall go without him."

"Agreed."

Without warning the door burst open. Charbonneau, bulky in his furs dusted with snow, stamped into the room, bringing a gust of cold with him. Drouillard silently followed him into the hut, nodding at the two captains without comment. Their arrival roused Seaman from his comfortable sleep before the fire, and the big dog wagged his tail lazily as he greeted familiar friends.

"By gar, she is cold, eh?" Charbonneau planted himself before the fireplace, holding out his stubby-fingered hands toward the fire and rubbing them briskly. "How is my papoose behave? He no keep you awake with him bawling, eh?" Yellow teeth gleamed like dull gold through the black tangle of Charbonneau's beard as he grinned.

"He's no problem—sleeps like a baby," said Lewis with unintentional humor. Then, without preamble, he confronted the Frenchman with a sharp question. "You've considered our talk last evening?"

"*Oui, oui, mon Capitaine* . . ." Charbonneau glanced at Drouillard. "I have consider this . . ."

"He want me translate for him," Drouillard said. "He no wish any . . . how you say, misunderstan'?"

"I see," said Lewis dryly. Charbonneau's English was execrable, but Drouillard's was not all that much better. Still, the two had worked together effectively that winter, often with the help of Charbonneau's young wife, who seemed to have a surer grasp of Minitaree words than her husband. She would explain the Minitaree to Charbonneau in a mixture of French and Big Belly languages, Charbonneau would in turn translate what was said into French to Drouillard, who would complete the chain by offering an approximate English rendition. It occurred to Lewis that he would regret losing the little Shoshoni woman more than losing the husband . . .

"You know our terms," said Lewis. "Any man who goes

with us from this place must enlist as a member of the party and pledge to do his share in assuming all duties." Turning to Drouillard, Lewis added, "Make sure he knows exactly what I've said."

Drouillard spoke to the interpreter in French. Charbonneau nodded and assumed a grave expression. The little Indian woman, hearing Charbonneau's voice as he gave his reply, came to the door of the room, carrying her red-faced baby wrapped in his doeskin robe, only the wrinkled face and lank black hair visible. Seaman came over to greet Sacajawea, pushing his head against her hand. She petted him absently, her dark eyes very large as she listened to her husband. Charbonneau talked vigorously in his manner, pursing his lips importantly, using his hands in quick, emphatic gestures. Damned if he doesn't think *he's* setting the conditions, thought Lewis.

Drouillard said, "He say, he no do work, Cap'n. He is interpreter, is all. He say he no stand guard. If he have, how you say, quarrel with any man, then he must be free to go when he please. An' when he go, he must carry any t'ing with him he want, meat and corn and such. These are what he say."

"Why, the nerve of him!" Clark exploded.

"By the Lord!" Lewis was more incredulous than angry. Observing at once from Clark's reaction that they were in complete agreement, he nodded at the redhead.

Clark spoke for them without hesitation. "Drewyer, you tell this Frenchman his conditions are inadmissible! Make damned sure he understands that clearly. If he's to be with us, he'll go under our terms, with the same responsibilities as every other enlisted man, or he can pack his gear and get out whenever he's ready!"

At Clark's tone, which made Drouillard's translation superfluous, Charbonneau stiffened. Even before Drouillard had finished speaking, the bearded Frenchman began to shout excitedly. "Charbonneau, he no go wit' dese people! He is important man, he no *soldat*! You no want him as interpret', dat is fine, *c'est bon*!"

"Tell him to clear out," said Meriwether Lewis crisply.

"The squaws can stay if they wish until he has made arrangements to transport their baggage. But our agreement is canceled."

With that Lewis stalked out of the hut, his icy calm making his dismissal of the interpreter more devastatingly final than Clark's heated words.

Charbonneau stared after him, his mouth open in disbelief. Slowly his defiant posture seeped out of him. For a long moment there was silence. Then Charbonneau turned to glare at Sacajawea in the doorway, at Otter Woman behind her. "You pack up everyt'ing," he growled. "We no stay here, not one damn night!"

He left immediately. Only William Clark saw the understanding in Sacajawea's eyes, and the fleeting look of dismay. She wants to go home, he thought. She wants to go with us to find her people.

Three days after Charbonneau had moved out of Fort Mandan in a huff, taking his squaws and their meager possessions across the river, Drouillard entered the captains' hut quietly in the evening. During the few seconds the door was open, the sound of a fiddle could be heard, accompanied as usual by clapping hands and stamping feet. The men were amusing themselves as they did nearly every night, watched by an audience of Mandans.

William Clark, who had just lit his pipe, nodded a greeting as he puffed. Meriwether Lewis glanced up from his field desk, where he was busy cataloging the items that would shortly be shipped back to Thomas Jefferson. He said, "Come in, Drewyer. You look as if you could stand a dram. What do you say? Captain Clark and I will join you."

"I no would refuse it, *Capitaine.*"

York, who seemed to have had too much time on his hands since Sacajawea, Otter Woman, and their children had moved out, quickly produced the whiskey and poured a draft for the three men. Drouillard sniffed the spirits appreciatively, took a swallow with obvious satisfaction and said, "Charbonneau, he wish me to speak for him."

"I believe he has said quite enough," Lewis snapped.

"I figgered ye had somethin' to tell us," Clark said mildly.

"He be sorry, *Capitaine.*" Drouillard addressed Lewis's obvious anger. "He say he foolish man, his tongue wag before he think. He wish *les capitaines* give him one more chance, maybe. Is possible, *n'est-ce pas?*"

"I don't know," Lewis replied, slightly mollified. "We can't have men deciding what they will or won't do or changing their minds along the way if something displeases them."

He was silent for a few moments, and William Clark knew that Lewis was thinking about the young Shoshoni woman, so quick and bright, and of the inevitability that, reaching the mountains, the expedition would be forced to abandon its boats. Then they would need horses—horses that, according to Sacajawea and others, her people had in abundance.

When Drouillard had finished his drink, he peered inquisitively at his two commanders. Exchanging a glance of perfect understanding with his partner, Clark said, "Tell him we'll think on it. Tell him . . . this time he may have gone too far."

On March 17, 1805, Charbonneau sent a second Frenchman, Baptiste Lepage, a trapper who had been at the Mandan villages when the expedition arrived and who had promptly signed on to replace the banished Private Newman in the permanent party, to intercede for him with the captains. This time the humbled interpreter was summoned to the captains' hut. He shuffled into the room without arrogance, his grin sheepish through the black beard, his quick eyes anxious and pleading.

Drouillard translated for him. Charbonneau was sorry for acting such a simpleton. He was anxious to accompany the expedition to the western mountains. He would join in total agreement with the terms laid down for him by the captains and would do all that was asked of him.

"Including guard duty?" Clark asked sternly.

"*Oui, oui,*" said Drouillard, while Charbonneau nodded vigorously.

"And towing the boat, or rowing, or anything else required by our circumstances?"

"*Oui, mon Capitaine,* what you say."

"All right, then . . ." Lewis and Clark had agreed upon their decision before the Frenchman's arrival. "Tell him he can go with us, and he will be duly sworn in as a member of the Corps of Discovery."

In the doorway to the back room York stood listening. A broad grin spread across his face. The little squaw and her baby would be moving back into the hut.

The ice in the river was breaking up, sometimes with a grinding and crackling that went on all through the night, a sound of awesome power. During brief lulls in their busy preparations for departure, the men of the detachment would stop to gape at the Mandans hopping from one ice cake to another in the Missouri—these frozen stepping stones were often no more than two feet across—to retrieve the floating carcasses of drowned buffalo. Many of the animals had died some time past, to judge from the rank odor of decaying meat, but the Indians regarded the spoiled meat as a rare delicacy.

The nights remained cold, but the days were warm and pleasant whenever the sun came out. Great flocks of ducks and geese passed overhead on their northward pilgrimage, honking at spring.

By April 1, 1805, all of the boats—the keelboat, the pirogues, and six new canoes—had been caulked and pitched. Early that morning a storm moved in. Thunder rolled, and lightning flashes lit up the prairie, already blackened from the Indian practice of setting fires. A harsh volley of hail bounced off the steep roofs of the huts at Fort Mandan. When the rattling died away, there was a lull, followed by a gentle rush of rain. For the men of the Corps of Discovery, eager to be

under way after their long winter hiatus, even the rain was a welcome sign of spring. It was the first real rain, they said, since last October.

Late in the afternoon, between intermittent showers, the boats were let down the riverbank into the swiftly moving current of the Missouri River. The men stared down at the empty boats riding high in the water, and there was not one among them who did not feel a quickening of anticipation.

For the next few days the work of packing and loading went on from first light until well after dark. In the past Meriwether Lewis had left most of the supervision of the loading to William Clark, who had gained considerable experience at it at Camp Wood. But now Lewis fussed over a collection of boxes and crates that were being carefully packed and placed aboard the keelboat.

The first box contained the skins and skeletons of antelope, the horns of a mule deer, the bones of a coyote, a Mandan bow and a quiver filled with arrows. Another was packed with buffalo robes, many of them heavily adorned, along with other skins, either mementoes of the detachment's own hunts or gifts obtained from the Indians. In this box there were also the horns of a bighorn mountain sheep obtained from the Mandans. This was a new species the explorers looked forward to seeing for themselves.

One box held samples of soil, salts, and minerals; still another carried the specimens of plants that Lewis had laboriously gathered along the route up the Missouri River valley, carefully pressed and numbered from one to sixty, each specimen labeled as to where and when it had been found and its properties as far as they were known from observation or from the reports of Indians. And other boxes held earthen pots, Indian utensils, furs and skins, skeletons, and more painted robes.

Sheltered on the deck of the *Discovery* were three cages built by Patrick Gass for this journey downriver. In one was the prairie dog that had been flushed from its hole that memorable autumn day after a daylong seige. Next to it in another cage were four magpies, and the third cage contained a prairie hen. All had been kept alive and healthy through the winter at Fort Mandan.

Along with the artifacts and animals, skins and bones and specimens went William Clark's maps and journals and a long essay by Meriwether Lewis summarizing his findings and perceptions. Clark's maps accurately charted the course of the Missouri and its tributaries with an exhaustive detail that defined the land for all who would come after him. He also included a map of the Missouri country west of the Mandan villages, drawn from the reports and sketches of traders and Indians. Finally, he sent a voluminous chart of all the Indian tribes inhabiting the Missouri River valley, fifty-three in all, with such information as he and Lewis had been able to gather about each.

All these were secured aboard the keelboat, to be shipped down to St. Louis and from there sent on to "the Seat of Government."

By nightfall on April 6, 1805, all was ready. There was dancing again that night in one of the rooms at Fort Mandan. Some of the men lay in their lofts, listening to the scratching of Gibson's and Cruzatte's fiddles, to the shouts and laughter, thinking of what lay behind them—and what might lie ahead. They stared at the puncheons of the ceiling, perhaps remembering the cuts they had made with their own axes . . . recalling with a grin that time in December when York had his penis frozen a little, to his great consternation . . . the day Sergeant Pryor threw out his shoulder and it needed four tries to get it back in place . . . the times Joseph Whitehouse and others stumbled back to the fort with frozen toes and feet . . . the night Thomas Howard came back late from an amorous adventure and, finding the gate locked, simply climbed the stockade wall, earning Meriwether Lewis's wrath when an Indian followed his example . . . or the scrape John Ordway got into over a Mandan squaw whose husband beat her after she had

been with Ordway, causing her to flee to the fort for safety—
the captains had ordered Ordway to give presents to the husband as recompense and to avoid the woman in the future . . .

Now the long wait was over. Now there would be challenges enough each day to keep every man busy, and sufficiently exhausted when he fell into his solitary blanket at night to find instant sleep.

Lewis and Clark looked on their detachment now with a feeling of pride and confidence. They saw a disciplined unit that little resembled the sometimes unruly, even rebellious lot that had left Camp Wood a year ago. Most of the time now the two commanders did not even need to give specific orders—and never had to repeat them. For the most part the men knew and understood their duties and performed them cheerfully. They might joke or grumble in the manner of soldiers everywhere, but their goal was a common one, shared by officers and men.

They had signed up for various reasons—for adventure or glory, for a piece of land, or for escape from whatever it was they had. What they shared now was a determination not only to survive but to achieve what they had set out to do, something no white men had done before them.

They would ascend the Missouri to its source.

They would climb the Stony Mountains and cross the Great Divide.

They would reach the rim of the known American continent, and taste the salt of the western ocean.

Part four

to the

rocky

mountains

23 This little fleet altho' not quite so rispectable as those of Columbus or Capt. Cook, were still viewed by us with as much pleasure as those deservedly famed adventurers ever beheld theirs; and I dare say with quite as much anxiety for their safety and preservation.
—MERIWETHER LEWIS, A p r i l 7, 1 8 o 5

*A*s the *Discovery* edged out into the Missouri River, Corporal Richard Warfington, standing in the bow of the barge, self-consciously saluted his two captains on the river-bank. Warfington's feelings were as crowded as the deck on which he stood. Part of him was excited by the prospect of returning to St. Louis in charge of the keelboat; the other part felt the wrench of separation from his companions of the past year, fellow soldiers now bound for even greater adventure.

With Warfington were two of the French *engagés*, five of the six soldiers he had had in his original detachment (the sixth, Robert Frazier, had enlisted in the permanent party), and John Newman and Moses Reed, who were being sent back. The trader Joseph Gravelines was also aboard, having been employed by Meriwether Lewis as pilot for the keelboat, with the added charge of taking one or more of the Arikara chiefs to St. Louis and arranging for their visit to the Great Father in Washington.

The men who now made up the permanent party of the Corps of Discovery were already in their boats. At the moment the barge pushed out into the current, William Clark bellowed his own order. "Cast off, lads! Westward it is!"

The little flotilla, consisting of the two pirogues that had come up the Missouri River from Camp Wood and six newly crafted canoes, started upriver against the familiar drag of the current. The river was so wide at this point—during the winter William Clark had paced it off at 500 yards walking across the ice—that the buffalo-robed natives on the far bank were faceless puppets.

Fretful over his lack of sufficient exercise, Meriwether Lewis walked along the bank with Seaman. The men in the boats watched them until they were out of sight. The soldiers took an unvoiced pride in the sight—the captain with his brisk, muscular stride, the black dog loping easily at his heels; the one a commander each soldier would unhesitatingly trust with his life, the other a friendly companion to each of them.

In the eyes of the detachment both Lewis and Clark had amply proven their mettle. They had led the way up the Missouri, conquering every obstacle. They had bested the truculent Sioux. They had dealt in fair and friendly fashion with the Otos, the Arikaras, the Mandans and Minitarees. They had directed the building of the fort, which had seen their men safely through the harsh winter. At each stage the men's confidence in their leaders had grown and with it their belief in themselves and the destiny of their expedition.

In addition to the two commanders, the permanent party included three sergeants—Ordway, Pryor, and Gass—and twenty-three privates. Besides Pryor there were seven others of the original nine "Kentuckians,": Bratton, Colter, the Fields brothers, Gibson, Shannon, and Shields. Only Charles Floyd was missing. The two rivermen, Cruzatte and Labiche, remained indispensable in the boats. Another Frenchman, Baptiste Lepage, who had replaced the banished John Newman on the roster, had won the captains' confidence, as had Robert Frazier, enlisted from Warfington's detail. Three early troublemakers, Collins, Hall, and Willard, who had experienced the bite of switches on their backs as the result of courts-martial, had seasoned into dependable soldiers. The others had also proved themselves—Hugh McNeal, John Thompson, Richard

268

Windsor, Goodrich, Howard, Potts, Werner, Whitehouse, and Wiser—all, as Clark wrote in his journal, "possessing perfect harmony and good understanding towards each other."

Rounding out the corps were the two interpreters, Drouillard and Charbonneau; Sacajawea and her baby; and Clark's manservant, York—turned cook, hunter, and voyageur. All were in high spirits, rested, and ready for anything. Even, as Cruzatte said, for "dat damned Mizzou!"

For the first week above the Mandan villages, the going was easy. The current was moderate, the channels clearly visible, the banks not falling in as they had the previous summer. The mornings were cool, the days fair with little wind. After some early mishaps—one canoe was swamped the first day out and two-thirds of a barrel of gunpowder lost—the men became accustomed to handling the canoes. William Clark slapped his first mosquito of the season. Sacajawea, at one dinner stop, dug up some wild artichokes stored in a gopher hole. Four days out, fresh bear tracks were seen, so large that Meriwether Lewis concluded they must have been made by the "white bear," or grizzly, so feared by the Indians.

At the end of the first week the expedition stopped overnight above a creek where Charbonneau had once camped with a hunting party of Indians. As the two commanders were pursuing a practice of naming creeks and rivers after members of the expedition, Meriwether Lewis found the interpreter's past association with this stream sufficient reason to call it Charbonneau's Creek.

Baptiste Lepage had once ascended a few miles further up the Missouri on a trapping expedition. Beyond that point no white man had ever ventured.

Ahead lay only the unknown.

As the expedition moved farther from the hunting grounds of the Mandans and Minitarees, game became more abundant

269

and remarkably tame. Ignorant of hunters, they would allow men to pass within a few feet without shying away. Even the beaver were tame, showing themselves by daylight as they watched the fleet of boats passing by. The men began to shoot them in the water by day and to set traps for them at night, for they now considered beavertail a delicacy.

Shortly after mid-month the boats' easy progress changed with the arrival of hard winds, roiling the waves into such turmoil that it was dangerous even to put the smaller canoes into the water. For several days the fleet was grounded. Whenever the winds temporarily abated, the Corps proceeded up the river, sometimes only a few miles at a time. Blowing sand became a daily irritation, a sand as fine as smoke that got into everything—food and drink, eyes, mouth and throat. Among the men, sore eyes became the most common complaint.

One evening when the wind moderated, Meriwether Lewis went ashore with Seaman and walked along the bottom. Everything interested him—the rocks along the shore, coal or lava or other minerals in the face of a bluff, a shrub or a berry he had not seen before, the beaver feeding along the verge of the river, larger and fatter and thicker-coated than any beaver he had seen before, and the immense herds of buffalo, deer, elk, and antelope feeding on the plains. And always the thought beat into his brain: *No white man has observed this leaf before, or walked this bluff, or seen the fertile meadow that opens out beyond this bend.*

In a wooded point Lewis and Seaman came upon a small herd of buffalo. Surprised by the intruders, the buffalo trotted away from them. One calf lagged behind and was soon separated from the others. Curious, Seaman circled the calf. Bolting from him in fright, the youngster ran down to the riverbank. When Seaman, more playful than aggressive, bounced toward the buffalo calf, it gave a bleat of fear and headed straight toward Meriwether Lewis.

Lewis could not help laughing. The calf stayed close to him as he walked. Whenever Seaman drew near, the frightened animal got behind Lewis like a child hiding behind its mother's skirts. "No closer," the captain told his dog. "You're frightening the poor creature."

Lewis started back along the bottom toward the bank where he had left his canoe. Although the distance was more than a mile, the calf continued to follow at his heels. It had attached itself to him as tenaciously as it might have to its parent. Seaman trotted along behind them, keeping ten yards or more away as Lewis had commanded, accepting the situation with equanimity.

The wind gusted, blowing sand off a bar in the river toward them, forcing Meriwether Lewis to duck and protect his eyes. When he could safely peer around, the buffalo calf was still there.

Lewis ordered Seaman into the canoe. Then he hesitated. He was carrying his rifle, and for a moment he considered the calf's fate. Separated from its mother, it stood little chance of survival in the wilderness. And he had noticed that a cow would not leave the herd to search for her young if wolves were in the vicinity. Still, the herd might drift back this way along the bottom before nightfall . . .

And Lewis had made a point of shooting only unfamiliar specimens he wanted record of or what was needed for the expedition's consumption. Neither he nor any of the Corps' hunters killed without reason.

He stepped into the canoe and shoved off. The calf tried to follow, advancing into the shallow water at the river's edge before stopping. Lewis dipped his paddle deep and moved out into the current, striking across the river towards the encampment. In the bow Seaman sat happily looking ahead, eager now to rejoin his companions of the detachment.

Behind them a plaintive bawling drifted over the water, until another swirling cloud of dust hid the calf from view on the receding shore.

For the next two days the winds were so violent that the canoes could not be put into the water. On April 24, 1805, the winds

did not let up all day, and there was nothing to do but lay by, dry some of the cargo that had been dampened, and wait. In the afternoon a hunting party was sent out for meat.

The hard winds blew until about seven in the evening. Sand rose over the river in clouds that obscured the far shore and made life miserable at camp. At dusk the hunters returned with meat, and the winds died down enough for supper to be prepared.

During the afternoon Meriwether Lewis had been preoccupied with protecting the articles in one of the pirogues that had got wet. Over his meal he asked Drouillard if he had seen Seaman.

"*Mais non, Capitaine* . . . he was wit' us early." The interpreter frowned. "He no come back?"

"We thought he'd headed back to camp," said Gibson, who had been hunting with Drouillard.

"I haven't seen him for several hours."

"Maybe he's gone back after the calf of yours, Cap'n," one of the men suggested.

There was a little laughter, but it died away. Seaman's absence was not a laughing matter. No one could remember him ever being away from camp for any period when he was not in the company of one of them. But everyone was accounted for. It was growing dark. The dog had been out on the prairie with the hunters for a time, and he hadn't returned.

As dark came, Meriwether Lewis walked along the river and climbed to the top of a low bluff. He could see a considerable distance, but the darkness was thickening even as he stared across the plain. He saw the dark mass of a buffalo herd less than a mile away, a scattering of other game. There were also wolves in the area, he thought. The hunters had brought several cubs back to camp that evening, and where there were young wolves, the pack was not far away.

He felt a chill. The evening had cooled, but it was not the temperature that made him shiver.

Back at camp Lewis accepted a mug of coffee in silence.

William Clark said, "He'll show up any time now, nothing the worse for wear."

"It's been too long," said Lewis somberly. "He should have returned by now, unless . . ."

The possibilities for disaster were innumerable. As the hours of that evening dragged by with no sign of Seaman, Lewis's worry became fear, and the fear became reluctant certainty that his dog was lost forever.

It was a quiet camp that night.

Coming off the winter months of rest at Fort Mandan, Seaman was full of energy. He had also, in the middle of his third year, reached his prime. He stood about twenty-eight inches at the shoulders and weighed about 160 pounds, not an ounce of it fat. His coat was thick and glossy, his muscles hard, his bones strong, his mind agile and quick, his senses sharp.

Like Meriwether Lewis, Seaman was infinitely curious. His walks with Lewis and others on shore had heightened his curiosity about the wilderness through which he traveled. He had come to know that the buffalo were not his natural enemy, that elk and deer and antelope would run from him. Like the men of the expedition, he had come across the tracks and scent of huge bears, and, without knowing why, he had felt the hackles rising on his neck.

It was a rabbit that led him away from the hunters.

Seaman had been casting about on his own, following up the bewildering array of scents at every turn, and discovering that much of the prairie was now covered with the short grass on which the great herds browsed and with ever-increasing quantities of prickly pear, a diminutive cactus as well-armed as a porcupine. Seaman was learning to tread carefully, for his pads were readily pierced by the sharp spines of the cactus. Before long he was limping, and he became separated by some distance from the hunting party.

The rabbit broke from a hole, startled by Seaman's ap-

273

proach. In swift bounds it raced across the prairie, Seaman in hot pursuit. The prickly pear and his lacerated paws were momentarily forgotten. For the best part of a mile the chase went on, veering this way and that until Seaman lost all sense of direction. And in the end the rabbit dove along a shallow gully, dodged into a thicket and disappeared.

Seaman prowled around the thicket, his jaws open, chest heaving like a bellows, excitement racing in his blood. He could find neither the rabbit nor its hole.

When he was finally ready to abandon the search, Seaman was brought back to familiar reality by the distant rattle of gunfire. It told him the hunters were busy but he could not clearly place the direction of the shots. They seemed to have come from far off to the west, the direction of the sunset— now a dazzling celebration of gold and red and pink against the horizon. But that was not the way to the river, which Seaman readily identified by the band of greenery along its borders, perhaps a mile to his right.

274

Still, he had come out with the hunters. He started off to the west, ears alert to more gunfire. But all he heard as he trotted along was the whining and scouring of the winds blowing across the plains, stirring up clouds of dust and sand, obscuring the sunset, blurring the contours of the land and blotting out such identifiable features as the river bottoms until you were almost upon them.

And the light was beginning to fade.

Animals were all about him in bewildering numbers. The huge herds of buffalo seemed to accept his presence among them, the elk hardly stirred as he passed by, even the antelope only trotted a few yards away. Never hunted, knowing only a few natural enemies such as the bear and panther and wolf, the herds merely hunched against the winds and watched the large black dog go by.

Nearing a low rise, Seaman smelled blood and death, mingled with the strong scent of an animal he had not yet met but whose smell he knew. He slowed to a walk as he neared the top of the rise.

Below him, in a little hollow, a huge grizzly gorged himself on the carcass of a dead buffalo. His great head lifted as he became aware of an intruder, and he reared up on his hind legs, towering higher than any man. He gave a warning roar. But his feast was too tempting to leave, and he let the roar suffice. No animal in his world dared challenge him.

Seaman had no wish to confront the bear. He moved around the scene of the feast in a half-circle that carried him away from the river. He was so intent on the giant bear, all of his senses tuned to it, that he did not see or hear or smell the wolves.

Past the grizzly, turning back toward the line of treetops that defined the river bottom, he came to a halt.

The wolf pack had got between him and the river.

They had been behind him, downwind, so that he had had no warning, stalking him for some time. There were about a dozen adult wolves in the pack. None was close to Seaman's size or bulk, and they were uncertain of this animal that resembled a black bear but walked on all fours like a wolf. But they had confidence in the pack, and they were accustomed to attacking animals they were able to isolate from a herd. They were in no hurry. They wanted to know more about this creature, to detect any sign of weakness, to be certain of their superior strength in numbers.

They moved when Seaman did, blocking his route to the river. With each passing minute they became bolder—and more impatient. They glided through the short grass of the prairie, slinking with bellies low to the ground, watched, and waited. Waited for their leader to decide when to attack.

Dusk washed over the wide valley like a wave soaking up the light. In the gray twilight Seaman's instincts took him toward the great buffalo herd drifting across the table. The wolf pack followed. But as he had before, Seaman was able to weave among the grazing buffalo without disturbing them. When the wolves came close, however, a huge buffalo bull swung toward the pack and charged. The wolves scattered before him. The thick-coated, big-headed beast wheeled around and rejoined the herd.

Seaman had trotted on. By the time the leader of the wolf

pack had spotted the black dog again, Seaman had slipped past them toward the river, his way no longer blocked.

They came after him faster then, and the dog's pride kept him from breaking into flight—pride and the instinctive knowledge that such a display of fear would erase any last restraint among his stalkers and bring them flying after him. He was intelligent as well as courageous, and he recognized the unequal odds he faced in the impending battle. He would therefore choose his time and place to turn and fight. He would—

Out of the corner of his eye he saw the ravine. It was a deep cut slashing into the bluff that overlooked the river, and it funneled out onto the wooded bottom below. Seaman trotted behind some brush at the edge of the ravine and, without hesitation, dove over the edge.

He slipped and slid down the steep wall of the canyon. When it leveled out he was immediately on his feet. He ran down the crease, slashed through thick undergrowth close to the base, and emerged onto the lush floor of the river valley.

Down in the bottom the night was already dark, the day's dimming light cut off by the bluff. Dense shrubbery yielded to copses of trees and then a deeper wood. As Seaman wove among the trees, he could hear the wolf pack spilling down the ravine in his wake, yowling and snarling.

The Newfoundland chose a place to make his stand back in the woods, with the steep wall of the bluff directly behind him, brush to conceal him until his enemy was close, and cottonwoods before him to break up any mass attack into single lanes.

There Seaman crouched on his stomach, head up, ears pricked, heart drumming in his deep chest.

He heard the wolves at the edge of the wood.

One of them began to whine, a sound of pain—or fear.

As minutes dragged by, Seaman's puzzlement grew. The wolves prowled about the edge of the wood but would not enter it, as if they were afraid to penetrate the gloom. And after a while even the whining and snarling and snuffling ceased.

With full darkness came a deepening silence. It was broken only by the lapping of the waves against the riverbank and the moaning of the wind in the tops of the cottonwoods. Seaman knew that the wolf pack had withdrawn—he had heard them scrambling up the ravine the way they had come—but he did not understand why.

For a long time he lay in his place of concealment. At last he rose and was immediately aware of the cut pads on his paws. He limped toward the edge of the wood. A low rumble like distant thunder stopped him.

The sound was not distant. It was close at hand. Close enough to make the hairs rise on the back of Seaman's neck, to bring every sense to a quivering pitch.

He stood motionless. His eyes were accustomed to the darkness, yet he saw nothing. Certainly no animal large enough to account for the deep, menacing growl he had heard.

Then a long shadow moved. It did not rise from the ground but separated from the stout branch of a tree about twenty feet from where Seaman stood and ten feet above ground. It moved with a slow and heavy grace, making almost no sound except for the sudden rake of claws on bark.

277

The animal dropped swiftly to the ground, stretched out its great length, turned its head once toward Seaman and strolled out of the wood.

In a patch of moonlight a large male cat—cougar or mountain lion, Seaman had no way of knowing—ambled to the edge of the river to drink. Then the big cat, evidently well-fed and indifferent to Seaman's presence, walked east along the river bottom, its long tail swaying languidly, its huge feet leaving deep impressions in the sand at river's edge.

Seaman sank back into his shelter of brush near the bluff. He no longer trusted the darkness. For a long time he lay still. He thought of the wolf pack's unwillingness to enter the wood. He licked his sore pads and rested. And at last he slept.

Meriwether Lewis had had a restless night. He was up early, and in the first light of dawn he climbed to the elevated plain south of the river bottom where the hunters had gone the

previous day. Sprawling herds of buffalo and elk fanned out over the prairie. Below him and a quarter mile downriver, a small group of deer trotted timidly through a stand of cottonwoods, pausing to browse amidst the tender green grass of a clearing. Although the wind this morning was not violent, it blew steadily, and there were already swirls of blowing sand. The air was very cold.

There was a bleakness to the morning in spite of the surrounding beauty, reflecting the sadness in Lewis's heart.

He went back down to the river and signaled the sergeant of the guard to rouse the camp. The wind, he thought, was moderate enough to permit the canoes to enter the water safely. They could not linger.

When they started up the river, the water froze on the oars. They shone like silvered paddles in the morning sunlight.

After an hour Meriwether Lewis had the boats pull in to the point of a woodland a little over two miles from the night camp, and the men sat down to breakfast.

At about eight o'clock, a half-hour after they had stopped for breakfast, Richard Windsor, the guard on the point overlooking the river in both directions, gave a shout. "Cap'n Lewis, sir! Look there!"

The crew was instantly alert. Many of them reached for their weapons; the others wished they hadn't left them in the boats. Lewis strode briskly to the edge of the river and looked in the direction Windsor indicated.

He felt a thump in his chest like a blow, then a surge of joy. He tried to call out, but could not make a sound. A thickness clogged his throat.

Seaman limped along the bottom toward him, footsore and weary. He saw the familiar, bowlegged figure standing on the riverbank, saw Lewis start toward him, and his steps quickened to a run.

24 these bear being so hard to die reather intimidate us all; I must confess that I do not like the gentlemen and had reather fight two Indians than one bear . . .

—MERIWETHER LEWIS, May 11, 1805

alking overland, Meriwether Lewis reached the Yellowstone River about two miles upstream from its conjunction with the Missouri. He took celestial observations to fix the longitude and latitude of this important location. When he rejoined the main party that evening where they had camped by the mouth of the Yellowstone, he found everyone in a cheerful mood. The Yellowstone was the first of the major landmarks west of the Mandan villages that the Indians had spoken of. Finding it as described had produced a general satisfaction. "What do you say we reward the men with a dram?" William Clark suggested, and Lewis quickly concurred.

The portion of spirits, enhancing an already happy situation, had the predictable result. St. Peter got out his fiddle, George Gibson tuned up his instrument to join him, a space was cleared at the center of the encampment, and soon the river bottom rang with squeaky music, ragged and raucous singing, the pounding of moccasined feet on the sparse turf, and the general sounds of merriment.

This strange babble silenced all other animals in the vicinity.

One evening William Clark spotted two giant bears at a great distance. Lewis was out hunting, and the crash of his rifle when he shot an elk echoed across the plain. The noise alarmed the two animals on a hillside at least a mile off. Although they were too far away for Clark to see them clearly, he was startled by the ease and speed with which creatures so large were able to run up the hill and disappear over the top. Watching them, he felt uneasy. Anything that big and fast was an adversary to approach cautiously.

Meriwether Lewis's first encounter with a grizzly did not induce the same respect. Lewis blundered upon him unexpectedly coming around a clump of brush, and the bear was so startled that he instantly bolted in apparent fear, escaping before Lewis could fire upon him.

A few days past the Yellowstone, Lewis was walking on shore with George Drouillard. The wind was moderate, the morning bright and cool. As usual Lewis carried his Harpers Ferry rifle and his espontoon, the latter an archaic weapon no longer standard army issue but one he was fond of carrying. Drouillard was armed with his long rifle.

Drouillard suddenly gestured. He had spotted two large bears in the river bottom. They were more yellow-brown than white, but there was no doubt of their identity. These were the redoubtable grizzlies. In spite of the stories he had heard, Lewis was more excited than intimidated.

One of the bears was rolling on his back on the ground, enjoying a mud bath. The other, who was standing erect, saw the two men as they fanned out across the bottom, Lewis to his left, Drouillard veering toward the river on the right. The grizzly reared up to his full height and roared.

Each hunter selected the animal nearer to him as his target. Lewis fired a split second before Drouillard. Both bullets found their mark. The bears bellowed in pain and anger. Drouillard's target, not mortally hurt, turned and retreated rapidly along the river bottom. Lewis's bear, however, shook off his bullet and charged.

With startling speed the huge animal closed on his attacker. Lewis ran back along the bottom. When he glanced over his shoulder he saw the grizzly stumble on the low sandhill where Lewis had knelt to fire upon him. From that quick glimpse Lewis took heart. The bear was badly wounded.

For about seventy yards the grizzly kept up the chase without narrowing the gap. When Lewis saw him stumble a second time, he turned and quickly reloaded. While he was pouring his powder the bear started toward him again. Coolly, Lewis finished loading, took aim at the lumbering animal, and, from a distance of no more than fifty yards, shot him in the throat. At the same instant Drouillard fired at the bear from the riverbank.

Struck by both balls, the grizzly wobbled, righted himself, and kept going for another ten yards before he fell.

He was a young male—"Not growed up," Drouillard observed in his laconic way. Meriwether Lewis estimated his weight at about three hundred pounds. Though young, the bear had impressive talons and teeth. Still, after all the tales of the grizzly's ferocity he had heard that winter from the Mandans, Lewis was feeling quite euphoric about bringing down his first white bear. Armed only with their bows and arrows and poor muskets, it was small wonder the savages feared this bear and would attack him only when there were many hunters in a band. But for a skilled rifleman, Lewis thought, the grizzly was not as invincible a foe as he had been painted.

"At least we shall have a taste of white bear meat," said the captain cheerfully, poking the carcass with the point of his espontoon.

Drouillard said nothing.

Trail

May arrived not with warm breezes but with hard cold winds. The boats had to take shelter at midday from high waves. That night the winds continued to howl about the camp, and the men woke often to the pounding of the waves and thrashing of trees in the river bottom.

At sunrise it began to snow.

The blizzard continued until about ten that morning, and the winds did not subside until afternoon. When silence finally came to the river bottom, the men crawled from under their blankets or buffalo robes to stare about them in wonder. Although the sun emerged briefly, they were still chilled. Lewis and Clark had been reasonably comfortable during the storm in the warm skin lodge they had obtained from Charbonneau, and which they shared with the two interpreters, Sacajawea and her baby, and York.

Shivering against the cold, the two captains climbed a slope to the foot of the rising plain on the south side of the river. With the coming of spring, the bottoms had been green with grass and the prairies painted in yellow and purple and blue flowers. Now these splashes of color stood out as bright as paint against a canvas of white. As far as the two men could see in any direction, the new-fallen snow lay an inch deep over the treeless plain.

Shaking their heads at such a spectacle to usher in the month of May, the Corps of Discovery set out late in the afternoon, determined to gain at least a few miles up the river while the winds abated. The air remained cold. The water froze on the oars.

A few days later the weather cleared, and the boats began to make good progress. Lewis and Clark took turns walking on shore. Game was all about them in greater abundance than they had ever seen.

Early one evening William Clark, rowing one of the canoes with Drouillard, saw a huge grizzly lolling on a sandbar

282

at the edge of the river. "Put ashore!" Clark urged. "Look at the size of him!"

Drouillard ran the canoe onto the sand, and the two men hopped out, rifles in hand. They were no more than thirty yards from the bear. Clark's heart pounded as he stared at it. It was at least twice as large as the young male Meriwether Lewis had killed.

"Keep shooting, *Capitaine*," Drouillard said softly.

They began firing at the grizzly, taking turns shooting and reloading. Fortunately, the grizzly did not charge. It began to roar with pain and rage as the lead balls slammed into its body at close range. At last the bear turned away and plunged into the river.

In the middle of the Missouri the grizzly stopped on a sandbar. He made no attempt to attack his tormentors but kept up a terrible roaring that went on for at least twenty minutes, while the two hunters gaped at him from the shore.

When the bear finally collapsed, Clark and Drouillard rowed out to the sandbar. They were soon joined by the men in the red pirogue, who had witnessed the attack from the river. Everyone stared in amazement at the enormous creature. It lay on its back with its jaws open, revealing huge teeth yellow and worn blunt with age. Clark took the bear's measurements. It was more than eight and a half feet tall, five feet ten inches around the chest, almost four feet around its neck. Its arm was nearly two feet in circumference, and its deadly talons, five on each foot, were measured each at four and three-eighths inches. Its weight, Clark estimated, was about six hundred pounds.

What impressed the men most was not the bear's size but the sobering realization that this animal was very hard to kill.

On examination the grizzly proved to have no less than ten lead balls in him, five of them in the lungs. Yet he had swum halfway across the turbulent Missouri River with the bullets in him and then taken twenty minutes to die.

283

The cavalier confidence that Meriwether Lewis had gained from his first meeting with the white bear was now badly shaken.

"I would feel myself equal to the gentleman if I met him in the woods," Lewis mused one evening to Clark, who was smoking while Lewis wrote and Cruzatte picked idly at his fiddle nearby, testing strings which had got wet in the boat. "But I wouldn't want to meet him in the open prairie."

"Nor I. Everything we heard about them is true. They fear no creature, it would seem, and have a very ferocious temper when attacked."

"I think, in the open, I would not seek a confrontation with him alone, and I will urge the men to act with the same prudence."

"After what we've seen, it will take little urging," said William Clark.

284 When he was not hunting, George Drouillard regularly spelled Cruzatte in steering the white pirogue. On May 14, 1805, Drouillard was taking aim at a grizzly downstream, and—a rare circumstance—both Meriwether Lewis and William Clark were ashore at the same time. In the boat with Cruzatte were Toussaint Charbonneau, Sacajawea and her baby, and three other men as crew.

Cruzatte had been at the helm of the boat for most of the day and was taking a short respite. He had turned the rudder over to Charbonneau with a sense of unease and finally a shrug. He was well aware of the interpreter's timidity on the water and his shortcomings as a helmsman, but the wind was moderate, there was no sign of trouble. What could go wrong?

But the winds of the High Plains were capricious. Less than an hour after Charbonneau began to steer the pirogue, the breeze unexpectedly quickened. Cruzatte, sitting in the bow, felt the cool breath of it on his cheek. He peered with his one eye upriver, watching for the high waves or blowing sand that would warn him it was necessary to head quickly toward shore. At this time the pirogue was well out in the river, at least three hundred yards from the south bank where Lewis and Clark were walking along with Seaman.

Abruptly the wind shifted. A violent gust caught the square sail. Charbonneau panicked. He threw the tiller over to the right. Instead of putting the boat before the wind, he luffed her up into it. The wind was so strong that it jerked the square sail out of Thomas Howard's hands amidships. The boat lurched onto her side. Only the resistance of the canvas tarp kept her from turning completely over.

Charbonneau bleated in terror. *"Ah Jesu—merci, merci!"* In his fear he let go of the rudder.

The others in the boat were hanging on. Charbonneau cried out to God for pity on him. Cruzatte yelled at him to take the rudder again.

On shore, Lewis and Clark felt the sudden violence of the wind and saw the pirogue turning over on her side. Both men fired their rifles to try to catch the attention of the belea- guered crew in the boat. "Cut the ropes! Haul in the sail!" Clark bellowed. In the blowing of the wind and the noisy waves, his cry went unheard. Lewis impulsively dropped his gun and pouch and began to strip off his coat.

"Don't be mad!" Clark yelled at him. "Look at those waves—and the water's near freezing!"

Lewis sensed the folly of his gesture. The waves were too high, the current too strong, the water too cold, the sinking boat too distant. But he felt a stab of anguish as he stared in despair out over the choppy waves, for, in addition to the people 2whose lives were now threatened, everything most vital to the success of the expedition—the irreplaceable instruments, books and papers, Indian presents, all of his and Clark's journals, his plant specimens, medicines, clothes and provisions, kettles and pans—all were in the white pirogue, all in danger of spilling into the river. We're lost! he thought in despair.

In the boat Pierre Cruzatte roared at Charbonneau. "Take the rudder, you miserable excuse for a weasel, or by gar I'll

shoot you now! Take the rud' and do your duty, or go to meet your devil, not your God!"

Cruzatte's rage penetrated Charbonneau's hysteria. The sight of Cruzatte's gun aimed at him and the fury in St. Peter's one eye jolted the interpreter out of his panic. His hand groped for and found the rudder.

"To the wind, man—no, no, de other way!" Cruzatte screamed above the turmoil. "*Oui, oui!* Now you men, take in de sail! An' grab dose kettles! Quick, or we all sink wit' her!"

The men reacted with alacrity. A slashing knife cut down the square sail. The boat began to come around to the wind as she righted herself. But she had shipped so much water that it nearly filled the boat, coming within an inch of the gunwales. Frantically the crew began to bail out the water. In their concentration no one noticed the little Indian squaw in the stern.

Sacajawea alone had seen the pirogue's precious cargo begin to float away as the boat filled with water. Calm amidst the storm, as articles swept by her she scooped them up— sheafs of papers, leather bags, glass vials, tins and cartons, everything she could grab and hold before it was lost to the river.

Now, while two men bailed and the others rowed, the boat crept toward the shore, wallowing low in the water but somehow not going under. Sacajawea crouched in the stern, her arms filled with waterlogged articles. Charbonneau crossed himself and prayed but kept hold of the rudder. Slowly, slowly, the shoreline inched closer.

Later, setting the goods from the pirogue out on the sand to dry—"We will have to lay over tomorrow to see what can be saved," Lewis said with initial pessimism—the captain gradually realized that most of the cargo had been recovered. The heavier boxes and bales had remained in the boat. And the cool-headed, courageous, and determined Indian woman, unmindful of the wind and waves and the child she carried on her back, had plucked from the water and retrieved almost everything that tried to float away.

The most serious losses were some medicines that had been spoiled. Otherwise, the losses were minor, and Lewis took note in his journal of the principal credit that was due. "The Indian woman to whom I ascribe equal fortitude and resolution, with any person onboard at the time of the accedent, caught and preserved most of the light articles which were washed overboard."

If he had had any lingering doubts about the wisdom of taking the Shoshoni woman along on the expedition, they had been put to rest.

Charbonneau was another story. How in the devil could a man spend much of his lifetime on the river without ever learning to swim or handle a boat!

25 the flesh of the beaver is esteemed a delecacy among us; I think the tale a most delicious morsel, when boiled it resembles in flavor the fresh tongues and sounds of the codfish, and is usually sufficiently large to afford a plentiful meal for two men.
—MERIWETHER LEWIS, May 2, 1805

ike the wolves, who could always be heard at night, the white bears often came near the camps after dark, perhaps curious about the fires. Seaman always knew they were there, and on some nights he had little sleep, constantly being roused by noise or scent, nosing the sentinels to see that they were awake or patrolling the encampment on his own. But the grizzlies made no attempt to attack the sleeping camps.

As with the men of the detachment, who were proving to be excellent hunters, Seaman found his hunting instincts sharpened and intensified by life on the High Plains, passing amidst game increasingly more abundant than ever. Swans and geese were commonplace, beaver were in every bend, deer populated every bottom, and herds of elk, antelope, and buffalo at times appeared to cover the entire prairie.

The Newfoundland also turned out to be a fine retriever. Once in April he swam the river to bring back a goose Joseph Fields had shot. A week later he caught an antelope in the water. Meriwether Lewis had observed the wolves taking an antelope in the river as it tried to swim across, and, when he spotted one swimming, he sent Seaman after it.

Louis Charbonneau

There was no contest. So swift and graceful on land, the antelope was a clumsy swimmer. This one was also a pregnant female, and in poor condition. Seaman outswam the antelope, caught it, and drowned it in a turmoil of thrashing water.

Later Meriwether Lewis heard some of the men jokingly disparage the achievement, pointing out that it was hardly a fair encounter. Lewis remembered, and, when he was out hunting one day early in May and spotted an antelope separated from the herd, he could not resist the challenge on his dog's behalf. Lowering his rifle, Lewis glanced down at Seaman and pointed toward the antelope, which was about thirty yards away. "Fetch!" he commanded.

Seaman was off in a bound. Startled, the antelope stood frozen for a few seconds as Seaman ran toward her. At last she bolted, and the chase was on. Six soldiers, along for that day's hunt, were soon cheering Seaman on. Lewis heard at least one excited wager—"A carat of tobacco she gets away!" "Sure, it's candy from a babe"—Pat Gass's voice—"Come on, Seam'n! Take her, you black son of a bitch!"

The antelope veered sharply, Seaman's jaws snapping at her flanks. For an instant the maneuver opened space between her and the pursuing dog. Then Seaman began to close the gap between them from ten yards to seven, six, five . . .

He heard the shouts urging him on, felt his blood racing and the excitement of the chase. He ran with long, powerful strides, and where the antelope began to tire he ran faster. In her panic the fleet "goat" of the prairie made the mistake of running in a straight line.

The last two yards of space closed like a gate slamming shut. Seaman caught her. The two rolled on the ground in a boiling cloud of dirt and grass, and in an instant it was over.

Among the watching men, there was a moment of silence. Then the soldier who had lost the bet to Pat Gass—it turned out to be Peter Wiser, the youngster from Pennsylania—said, "She's carrying her young, and she's poorly at that. Else he'd never have caught her."

"I'll enjoy smokin' yer tobacco," Gass said cheerfully, "however lame it comes to me."

That night William Clark took note in his journal of Seaman's adventure. "Our dog caught an antelope a fair race," he wrote, pausing a moment before he added, "this animal appeared verry pore and with young."

No one had reason to see Clark's entry or to remark on the singular change expressed in that brief entry, a change that had taken place unnoticed. Until now, in their talk as well as in the various journals being kept by the men, Clark included, Seaman had always been "Capt. Lewis's dog." He was still that, but he had become something more. In the minds and hearts of the detachment he was one of them.

Our dog.

290 Though he accompanied Lewis most often when he was on land, Seaman was a comfortable companion with all of the men by now, and he often went out with others. Hunting with George Drouillard he learned an Indian's way of silent stalking, learned to cut and follow sign, learned an infinite patience.

Frequently the dog walked ashore with Clark, Charbonneau and Sacajawea, or he went afield with the Indian girl while she gathered herbs and roots. On the latter occasions he was alert and vigilant, an instinctive protector, as if both the girl and her baby had been adopted as his special charge. Charbonneau sometimes grumbled about the dog. "He no want you go anywhere wit'out him," he told his Shoshoni squaw. "Is no good for *bébé*." But the girl, grown fond of her amiable protector, would hear nothing against him.

During this time Seaman had also learned to ride in the smaller boats with a sailor's ease. The two pirogues were no problem, being larger, but even in the long, narrow canoes the big dog was comfortable, sitting up with the spray in his face and the strong winds of May buffeting him, his mouth open in joyful anticipation of each bend in the river.

For the men, however, the river became a harsher challenge in the second half of May. The river hills became steeper, shelving into perpendicular cliffs that shouldered close to the river on both sides, leaving only narrow bottoms or none at all. Rocks and gravel from these steep precipices had tumbled into the river or lined the shores. When the winds and hard current forced the men to the cords to tow the pirogues, they had to go barefoot—their moccasins either disintegrated or kept coming off when they tried to wear them in the water— and the sharp stones and gravel cut and bruised their feet until they could scarcely hobble.

The current was especially strong around the wooded points in the river, and at the bottoms of gullies, which had thrown stone barriers out into the river as much as forty or fifty feet, over which the water boiled with great force.

The country beyond the bluffs was high, broken, and barren, treeless except in the deeper gullies and the points of the river. Only the spiny prickly pear flourished, as punishing to the feet of the moccasined hunters—their boots had been universally abandoned for the comfortable and easily replaced Indian footwear—as the rocky shoreline was to the men towing the boats.

Beaver remained plentiful. The men set traps at night, schooled by Drouillard and Lepage in the techniques of baiting and setting the traps, or when the surprisingly tame dam-builders showed themselves during daylight, shooting them in the water. When that happened, as with other games, Seaman was sent into the river to retrieve the prize.

Late in the afternoon of May 19, 1805, the white pirogue, in which Seaman was riding, was making good progress when a beaver dam was spotted near the mouth of a creek. Drouillard, who was steering, handed the rudder over to Pierre Cruzatte and scrambled toward the bow with his rifle. Quickly taking aim at a beaver that paused at the foot of its intricately

woven thicket of branches and mud, Drouillard fired. He saw
the beaver move in the instant he squeezed the trigger. The
bullet missed its mark by a few inches, only wounding the
animal in the water. Drouillard immediately sent Seaman after
it.

A few times on the way up the Missouri, Seaman had
jumped into the river after a live beaver, but he had never
really come close. He had been sent to retrieve several after
they were shot, and he approached this wounded animal without hesitation, his strong legs and broad, webbed feet driving
him powerfully through the water. The beaver plunged beneath the surface to escape. Blood stained the water in his
wake. Seaman dove underwater after him.

A full-grown beaver was a formidable adversary in the
water. It was about four feet long—a third of that being the
wide, flat tail—and had both strong claws and large, powerful
teeth. Moreover, like any animal, a wounded beaver became
doubly dangerous.

292

Seaman saw the beaver swimming away from him toward
the opening of its chamber beneath the dam. With a surge
Seaman lunged toward the animal and caught the broad tail
with his teeth.

The beaver, very much alive, spun in the water, its big
teeth slashing like razors. They cut across Seaman's left hind
leg, slicing through flesh to the bone, severing an artery.

In pain and shock Seaman released his hold. The water
was suddenly dark with blood. The compact, muscular beaver
slipped away into the darkness.

As soon as he saw the widening stain on the surface,
George Drouillard guessed what had happened and he had
the boat brought close to the spot. They were nearly there when
the dog surfaced. Drouillard caught and pulled him into the
boat. Blood was spurting from the cut in Seaman's leg, and
the dog twisted around, trying to reach the wound. "Get us
ashore!" Drouillard told the men on the poles. "Fire a shot to
warn the captain!"

Walking on shore, Lewis came toward the river when he

heard the shot. Drouillard tersely explained what had happened, and Lewis climbed into the pirogue. "Don't move him," he said. "I'll treat him where he is."

The severed artery seemed to have a life of its own. Each time Lewis thought he had stopped the bleeding, it would spring up again. He used compresses to bind the leg tightly and stop the flow temporarily, but each time he released the pressure the bleeding began again unabated. While he was attending to the dog he had the pirogue continue upriver in search of a suitable place to stop for the night.

Late in the day the crew had to get out of the pirogue with the towlines to pull past some rapid water. Beyond the rapids, at a wooded point on the north side, Lewis had the boat pulled in to shore.

Seaman was carried to a level patch of turf. Lewis was gravely worried now. The dog was obviously much weaker from loss of blood, and Lewis had not been able to stop the loss. He used one of Dr. Saugrain's matches, husbanded throughout the expedition, to build a quick fire. As soon as it was hot, he heated the point of his knife in the flames.

293

He laid the hot blade across the artery, hoping to both seal and cauterize the wound. George Shannon, stricken with fear over Seaman's condition, was holding the dog's head and shoulders at Lewis's direction, and he winced as Seaman convulsed and whimpered in pain. There was a strong smell of seared flesh and burning hair.

A half-hour later the seepage of blood began again. Lewis repeated the cauterizing treatment. By then he was afraid for his dog's survival, feeling helpless to staunch the draining away of Seaman's strength and life. He used a gut string from Cruzatte's violin to sew up the wound, drawing the folds of skin tight. He had done all he could.

Now he could only wait.

Through the night Seaman lay limp on a blanket near the fire, watched by one or more of the men in turn—Lewis and Clark, Drouillard, Shannon, York, and others. Even Charbonneau came to stand over the dog, shaking his shaggy head

and combing his beard with his fingers and muttering about "Dat damn beaver!" For a long time Sacajawea knelt near Seaman's head, her hand stroking him soothingly, murmuring a kind of chant in what Lewis presumed was Shoshoni.

In the morning York tried to feed Seaman some meat and broth, but the dog seemed to lack the strength to swallow. He was placed in the white pirogue, and the party proceeded on, fighting the rapids and sawyers, which were now becoming more frequent, worried about their dog but hiding their concerns in activity—in the harsh demands of the cord, in the punishment of the stones that bit into their feet and left them bruised and bleeding.

Not long after starting out, the boats pulled past a creek infested with clouds of flies. They settled on the meat when the men tried to eat their breakfast, forcing them to brush the flies away from their portions. And the insects swarmed around Seaman, seeking to cover his wound, which was protected by a blood-soaked bandage. The captains named this Blowing Fly Creek from the enormous numbers of these flies, and everyone was happy to get back on the river.

At eleven that morning they came to a picturesque stream entering the Missouri from the south known as Musselshell River. William Clark measured it at a little over a hundred yards wide at its mouth. The boats pulled in at the wooded point formed by the junction of the two rivers, and Lewis decided to stay there the rest of the day to take observations, to explore the Musselshell—and to rest Seaman.

At dinner Lewis carried a small portion of jerked buffalo meat over to where Seaman lay, remembering York's fruitless attempt to feed him that morning. He lifted the big head with one hand and held the meat toward the dog.

He thought Seaman's tail twitched but could not be sure. The dog's eyes rolled toward him. Then Seaman's tongue lapped tentatively at the meat.

"By the Lord," Meriwether Lewis whispered, but his throat thickened and he could not speak.

Behind him York said huskily, "He hungry now, I make him some fine soup!"

The Corps of Discovery proceeded on. During the day Seaman lay in the white pirogue, hardly aware of the heaving efforts of the crew or the pounding of the waves. When Seaman's leg swelled up on the second day after he was bitten, Meriwether Lewis applied a poultice to the wound but was afraid to bleed it. "He has no blood left to give. I don't know what to do if it doesn't heal now," Lewis said gloomily to William Clark that night.

"He appears better to me tonight. And York tells me he ate a little more this evening. York tempted him with a bit of Charbonneau's white pudding."

Lewis responded with a surprised grin. Charbonneau's version of a sausage he called *boudin blanc*—buffalo meat pounded and packed into a long intestine, dipped in the Missouri, boiled in the kettle, and fried in bear's oil until sizzling brown—had become one of the most prized items on the expedition's menu. "I'm surprised he was able to hide a portion of it from the men."

"They all knew," said Clark.

And in the morning Seaman was visibly improved. He did not lie motionless but attempted to hobble about. From then on his appetite improved prodigiously, and with it came a slow resurgence of his normal strength and liveliness. Cruzatte joked that, since Seaman's leg now contained a string from his violin, when the leg was completely healed, he would play a tune upon it.

Meanwhile, the boats struggled up the river. The bluffs remained close to the water on both sides, very high and steep. On the bluffs the bighorn sheep, an animal much prized by the Mandans, began to appear. They inhabited fissures and crannies in the faces of nearly perpendicular cliffs, where neither wolves nor bears could reach them. They leaped about these rugged bluffs with remarkable speed and agility.

Down below, the boats slogged along with neither ease

nor alacrity. They were encountering a lot of hard water in this part of the Missouri. One churning rapids with a sharp but fortunately shallow fall proved very difficult to get over. Those of the crew who were not on the ropes had to take to the river to keep the boats from filling with water. By means of a combination of wading and towing, they succeeded at length in lifting the boats safely past the barrier. When they collapsed on shore beyond the rapids, legs quivering and arms aching, they wondered what other surprises lay ahead. This had been a drop of only a few feet. The Indians at the Mandans had spoken of a "Great Falls" not far ahead.

A week after Seaman had hovered near death from his severed artery, he was able to walk on shore with Meriwether Lewis. Only a slight limp betrayed any evidence of his accident.

On the morning of May 26, 1805, William Clark on his morning walk saw snow-covered mountains about fifty miles to the northwest. As soon as camp was struck that evening, Lewis set out to climb the river hills, determined to seek the highest vantage point he could find. Seaman accompanied him with little trouble, although Lewis noted that he did not bound along with his usual exuberant energy. That would come, Lewis thought, greatly relieved by his dog's recovery. If Seaman could handle this climb, which even Lewis the energetic walker found fatiguing, then he was well on the way back to normal.

They came to a high promontory. The stiff breeze buffeted Lewis, and he had to brace himself, legs widespread. Shielding his eyes with one hand against the setting sun, he peered off toward the northwest, across the long and level plain north of the river.

His heart thumped.

With shaking hands Lewis brought his spyglass from its scabbard and trained it on the horizon. *There!*

Above the horizon only the peaks of some mountains were visible, covered with snow.

Certain that he beheld the Rocky Mountains for the first time, Lewis felt an exultation that shook his very being. There, somewhere in those rocky heights, the seemingly boundless Missouri had its source. And in that moment all of Lewis's dreams and hopes, all of the struggles and anxieties of the expedition, found their answer.

He lowered the glass, no longer able to see clearly.

The weather turned dark and cloudy with a threat of rain. The elkskin cords, weak and rotting from exposure to sun and water, frequently gave way, threatening to throw the boats upon projecting rocks. Somehow each rocky threat was avoided. New ropes were made, a deeper reservoir of strength was plumbed, and the corps proceeded on.

On the night of May 28, 1805, they camped on a point of timber on the south side of the river. Late that night only the two sentinels were awake, John Thompson watching the boats with his eyelids heavy, Hugh Hall posted where he could observe the inland perimeter of the camp.

No one saw the massive head and shoulders held above water as a huge buffalo bull swam across the river from the north shore. In the darkness he lost his way. When he came to the bank, he found an unexpected obstacle in his path.

The buffalo blundered up the bank. Clambering across the white pirogue, he stepped on a rifle, bending it, and smashed the stock of a blunderbuss. He came up the bank to the level bottom and charged into the middle of the camp.

By then the beast was alarmed, and his panic was fed by the sentry's shout, the smoke from the fires, the smell of strange creatures all about him. He crashed blindly through the camp at full speed.

All about him men lay on the ground in their blankets. By some miracle the pounding hoofs missed heads and arms and backs, sometimes coming within eighteen inches of a sleeping man. As some of them began to rise up and an uproar grew louder, the buffalo veered away—directly toward the captains' tent.

And suddenly, out of the darkness, the stampeding buffalo was confronted by a large black shape hurtling at him with a roar.

Seaman had been sleeping just outside the entrance to the captains' tent. He slept lightly, instantly awakened by the slightest disturbance. He heard the sounds of splintering wood and heavy blows at the edge of the river. He was rising to his feet, hackles up, when the buffalo reared above the bank and plunged through the camp.

Within seconds the charging animal was close and veering toward the tent that Seaman guarded. Without hesitation he threw himself at the buffalo's throat.

His jaws closed on thick fur. A massive weight knocked him aside. Seaman hit the ground, rolled to his feet and attacked again, this time nipping at the buffalo's flan as it passed him—turned away from the tent by the dog's ferocity.

The buffalo blundered on through the woods, disappearing into the darkness. The camp was in turmoil. Out of the captains' tent came first William Clark, then Meriwether Lewis, then Charbonneau and York, while Sacajawea crouched protectively over her baby inside the shelter. Soldiers everywhere were on their feet, rifles in their hands, sleep in their bewildered eyes. "De white bear!" Charbonneau wailed. "*Sacre bleu!* De bear!"

"Look out—it's back!" someone shouted.

Hugh Hall, the sentinel at the edge of the camp, turned toward the new threat, but his rifle never reached his shoulder. He recognized Seaman as the dog emerged from the woods after giving chase. Seaman trotted back into the camp, so plainly at ease that any remaining panic among the soldiers quickly subsided.

And by then John Thompson, the sentry on duty by the boats, had spotted Sergeant Ordway and reported to him. "It weren't no bear, Sergeant—that was a goddam buffalo!"

26 *Set out & proceeded on with great labour we were obliged to make use of the tow rope & the banks were so muddy & slippery that the men could Scarcely walk notwithstanding [this] we proceeded as well as we could, wind hard from the N.W.*
—JOHN ORDWAY, M a y 3 o, 1 8 o 5

They came past white cliffs that formed majestic cities sculptured out of stone. The spectacle of these edifices overlooking the river moved Meriwether Lewis to imaginative descriptions in his journal. "The water in the course of time in decending from those hills and plains on either side of the river has trickled down the soft sande clifts and woarn it into a thousand grotesque figures . . . eligant ranges of lofty free-stone buildings, having their parapets well stocked with statuary; columns of various sculpture both grooved and plain, are also seen supporting longer galleries in front of those buildings." Pausing to read what he had written, Lewis wondered wryly if he had been in the wilderness too long. Then he added, "As we passed on it seemed as if those seens of visionary inchantment would never have an end . . ."

Although the scene left a profound impression on Lewis's imagination, the men towing the boats against the hard current were less rhapsodic. They bruised and cut their feet, wore their callused hands raw on the elkskin ropes, threw out a shoulder or aggravated a pulled muscle, and kept slogging on. They had little energy to spare for the raw beauty of the river's course.

Trail

On the evening of June 2, 1805, they came to a fork in the river road.

The width of the south fork was measured at 372 yards; that of the northern branch, 200 yards. Which was the Missouri? Which would take them on to the Rocky Mountains?

The north fork was deeper, its current more turbid, its waters as muddy as the Missouri had always been. By contrast the south fork was clear and rapid, its surface unruffled. It *looked* different.

The argument went on long into the night. Feisty John Collins was belligerent in his conviction. "It's the north branch—that's the Missouri! Ye've only to look at it."

Pat Gass and John Colter were equally certain, and the other two sergeants, Pryor and Ordway, were not long in seconding Gass's opinion in favor of the northern branch. Before long it became clear that among the men there was little disagreement. Still, no one pushed the matter too hard. The most knowledgeable voice among them had remained silent through the evening, Pierre Cruzatte keeping his own council. Nor did Cruzatte bring out his violin. With so much at stake, this was not a night for fiddling.

"*Quién es?*" Charbonneau demanded of the French riverman, the most experienced of them all with the ways of the river. Charbonneau shared the view of the others; he had no doubt. "What you think, eh, St. Pierre? Is it not so, by gar?"

And at last Cruzatte put down his pipe, tapped out the ashes against a rock, and sucked at it once or twice. He pointed toward the north with the stem of his pipe. "Is dat way. Dat is de Missouri."

As far as the men were concerned, that made it unanimous.

In their tent Lewis and Clark had heard scraps of the debate. Sacajawea and her baby slept in a corner, causing the two captains to lower their voices as they weighed their decision. In the end it was theirs to make; not the men's.

"If we choose wrong," said Meriwether Lewis, "we risk not being able to cross the mountains before winter."

"Aye, too much time will be lost. We are a good two months into the traveling season already."

"It's not even the loss of time I fear so much as what the men will feel if they go on, only to find out we have embarked on the wrong road and must turn back."

"They're good men. They'll go on."

"I fear it would take the heart out of them."

Both men contemplated the hardships the men had endured to come so far. If they lost their determination—or their faith in the men who led them—how long before they would give up the struggle as hopeless?

"They're all convinced it's the noisy, muddy north fork."

"Aye." William Clark considered his own judgment. Perhaps he could not find convincing arguments in favor of the south fork, but he knew that his choice was not blind. He had an instinct for geography. He trusted it. "It's the south branch," he said firmly.

Slowly Meriwether Lewis nodded. He believed that Clark's choice was correct. Nevertheless, the men had been asked to voice their opinions. These, and the evidence supporting them, should not be dismissed out of hand. That also would damage morale.

"I believe we must explore both rivers," Lewis said finally. "I'll take a party up the north fork, you go along the south."

"How far?"

"What do you think? Forty, fifty miles? That should be far enough to make a determination. About two days each way. That's four days if we leave early in the morning—I don't wish to lose more time than that."

"The men will be pleased we take their vote seriously."

After a silence made comfortable by the knowledge that, as usual, they were in agreement, Lewis said thoughtfully,

"There's another matter. We spoke of sending a boat back with some of the men."

"Aye . . ."

"There's been considerable Indian sign these past weeks, even though the savages have avoided us."

"Ye're thinkin' we shouldn't deplete our party?"

"Yes."

"Mm. I believe we need every man for the boats in any event, the way the river has been. It won't get easier, I'm thinkin'."

"We've never spoken to any of them about going back."

"Aye, and I doubt there's one amongst 'em would go willingly, save perhaps our French interpreter." He glanced toward the sleeping Sacajawea. The Indian girl was feeling sick, but it was the husband who had tired of the journey.

"Then we're of a mind?"

"Aye. We all go on together. And starting at dawn, we'll explore these two rivers!"

302

Early the next morning, accompanied by five men, William Clark walked up onto the plain and followed the south fork. The land was barren, dusted only with short grass and prickly pear. The latter were so numerous and their spines so sharp that they easily pierced the men's moccasins and had them walking gingerly. After two days Clark had advanced forty miles and decided to turn back. Nothing he had seen altered his conviction that the river he followed was the true Missouri.

Meriwether Lewis did not return to camp until two days after Clark. With six men and Seaman, he had traveled over sixty miles along the northern branch, far enough to conclude that its course bore too far north to match the descriptions of the Missouri he had received from Indians at the Mandan villages. He acknowledged it to be a handsome river and— taking his cue from Clark, who a week earlier had named a fine stream Judith's River in honor of a young Virginia girl whose image remained lively in his thoughts—Lewis named the new stream after his cousin, Maria Wood. Maria's River, he noted gallantly, did "but illy comport with the pure celestial virtues and amiable qualifications of that lovely fair one; but on the other hand it is a noble river."

Back in camp the two captains conferred once more. The men of the corps remained unanimous in favoring Maria's River as the Missouri. Trusting their own judgment, Lewis and Clark overruled them.

Being too large and heavy for an overland portage, the red pirogue had reached the end of its journey. On an island opposite the point where Maria's River entered the Missouri the boat was lashed into place between two trees and covered with brush, to be reclaimed on their return.

Some of the baggage was then redistributed among the canoes, and a cache was dug under Pierre Cruzatte's supervision. In it were placed some articles that could be spared for the continuing journey, or would be needed on the return passage, including powder and lead, saws, axes, utensils, skin packs, and buffalo robes. The items were placed in layers and covered over with dirt and brush, topped by a layer of sod that had been carefully removed and, put back in place, would soon blend into the terrain, making the cache undetectable even to the sharp eyes of passing Indians.

On June 11, 1805, Meriwether Lewis set out with George Drouillard, George Gibson, Joseph Fields, and Silas Goodrich in search of the falls of the Missouri. Seaman, fresh from a sixty-mile hike up Maria's River, trotted along with them.

The main party, facing severe rapids, proceeded on up the south fork of the river they continued to call the Missouri.

When his hunters spotted a herd of elk in the river bottom, Meriwether Lewis led the men down from the plain. They shot four elk before the rest could flee. They butchered the meat and hung it in plain view by the riverbank for the oncoming party in

303

the boats to find. Lewis decided to have dinner here by the river, but of a sudden he was seized by violent intestinal cramps that doubled him over in agony. While his companions dined on marrowbones, Lewis crouched over his pain.

The pain persisted through the afternoon. Lewis was unable to travel. By nightfall he was perspiring heavily with a fever.

He had brought no medicine with him for this brief excursion, but he was nothing if not enterprising in such matters, the extensive herbal knowledge he had learned from his mother having been supplemented by his wilderness experience and his innate curiosity. He had the other men gather a parcel of small twigs of chokecherry, a bush abundant in the river bottom with whose medicinal powers he was familiar. Following Lewis's instructions, they stripped off the leaves and cut the twigs into two-inch pieces. These twigs, boiled in water, produced a thick black substance. "Hell's fire!" exclaimed Goodrich. "Who'd have thought there'd be so much sap in them little twigs?"

304 At sunset Lewis drank a pint of the strong decoction, which had a bitter, astringent taste. An hour later, while his companions made faces of sympathy as they watched, he downed another pint.

By ten o'clock Lewis's pain was gone. The fever abated, and, lying on some willow boughs, he rested comfortably. The next thing he knew the sun was filtering through the leaves of the cottonwoods overhead, and Goodrich, tireless fisherman, was walking up the bank with a string of a half-dozen fish he had caught that morning. "They's good eatin', Cap'n," he called out encouragingly, uncertain of his captain's condition.

"Give me one more swig of my elixir," answered Lewis cheerfully, "and I'll eat half those fish myself!"

The small party returned to the plain, veering inland to avoid the ravines that cut into the highland for a distance of one or two miles from the river. The men marveled at Lewis's brisk pace after his affliction the previous day. Seaman cavorted happily ahead, responding to Lewis's cheerful mood—which brightened even more when, from an elevation in the plain, Lewis had a clear view of the Rockies, rising layer upon layer until the last snowy peaks were lost in clouds.

By day's end, with only one two-hour rest before noon, they had covered twenty-seven miles. That night, while Seaman sorted out the smells in the river bottom, Lewis amused himself trying out Goodrich's bait. Within a few minutes he caught upwards of a dozen fish. He was feeling quite himself again.

Halfway through the morning of June 13, 1805, Lewis was walking alone with Seaman. Fearful of missing any sign of the falls while walking inland from the river, Lewis had sent Fields off to the right, Drouillard to the left. Gibson was with him but, unable to match Lewis's pace, he had fallen behind. Lewis saw his dog's ears prick at a rumbling sound. Then he saw what appeared to be smoke rising from the plain, disappearing almost instantly.

Within a short distance the rumble had become the roaring of a great mass of water, and the wisps of smoke became clouds of spray from the riverbed two hundred feet below the plain. "By the Lord!" Lewis muttered aloud. He began to run. Excited, Seaman barked as he ran ahead.

3o5

The sound of the falls became a tremendous thunder as the two neared the river. Lewis came into sight of the falls at noon, the sun directly overhead, its rays slanting through the rising mists and painting an extraordinary rainbow.

As excited as Seaman, Lewis clambered down the steep slope with the Newfoundland scrambling ahead of him. Seaman followed Lewis out onto a tumble of rocks about twenty feet high that projected far out into the river channel. The two stopped at the point, almost opposite the very center of the great falls of the Missouri. Seaman lifted his face to the wind and the spray. Lewis stood beside him, a chaos of sound all about, grinning as he took in the scene.

Off to his left, for about a hundred yards into the river from the south bluff, a smooth even sheet of water fell more than eighty feet in a straight drop from a precipice. The remaining two hundred yards of the cascade, most of it to Lewis's right from his rocky point, was of the same height, but huge, irregular rock formations at the bottom dissolved the thundering falls into white foam that leaped and soared in a thousand sparkling shapes. Water and foam struck the abutment where Lewis and Seaman stood and, carried on the powerful surge of the current, rolled into tremendous billows that swept past the rocks and disappeared downriver in an instant. And over all this the dazzling rainbow arched through the spray that rose as high as the cliffs on either side.

"Magnificent!" Lewis exulted aloud. To see such a thing, hidden from the beginning of time from the eyes of civilized man . . .

He clapped his dog on the shoulder and shouted aloud. Far above them, just arriving at the edge of the bluff, Silas Goodrich stared down at Lewis and Seaman on the rocks below and felt the very earth shake beneath his feet.

306

While Lewis was in search of the falls of the Missouri, for the boats struggling upriver against ever more frequent and difficult rapids, every foot was a battle won.

And in the white pirogue, still and pale, Sacajawea lay helpless, fighting her own silent battle against a sickness that saw her becoming weaker and weaker.

During the first two months of travel up the Missouri River from the Mandan villages, the little Indian woman was determined not to be the burden the white chiefs feared. Almost daily, when the boats stopped for dinner or to make night camp, she went out on the plains or along the river bottoms to gather wild onions, licorice, or whiteapple to add to the expedition's meat-heavy diet. When the captains began to consult her regularly about Indian signs they came upon—abandoned lodges, a pair of worn moccasins left behind by a hunter, even a football that floated down the river one day—she was quick to identify artifacts of those Plains tribes with which she was familiar, and she took quiet pride in the sense of importance such questions gave her. Whether cooking or cleaning up or helping to load the boats each day, she was tireless and uncomplaining, all the while carrying her baby in his cradleboard strapped to her back between her shoulder blades. And when the white pirogue nearly overturned in the river, she had remained calm, though her heart beat like a drum as she fished precious cargo from the water.

She took special pleasure in those days when she walked on shore with Charbonneau and William Clark. Clark had taken a fancy to the sunny-natured child whom his mother called "Pomp," a Shoshoni word for firstborn. Neither howling winds nor churning waves seemed to bother the baby, who seldom cried or whined. With Sacajawea, Chief Redhead was genial and unfailingly courteous. What he called her "jawbreaker name," he shortened to the more familiar "Janey." Even Charbonneau, whose timidity as a waterman in contrast to his boastfulness had earned him the scorn of many of the soldiers, fell within the embrace of Clark's generous nature.

For a week, however, Sacajawea had had severe abdominal pains accompanied by increasingly high fever. She was pale and weak and could neither help in the boats nor with the cooking. Meriwether Lewis gave her a dose of Dr. Rush's pills—specific for almost any ailment—with little effect. She accepted them because she had seen the soldiers take the same medicine, and she was convinced from the months at Fort Mandan that Lewis had great medicine. But when Lewis himself came down with severe dysentery, and then left to search for the falls, it was left to Captain Redhead to treat her. Clark, who had sat up with Charles Floyd on the last nights of his life, could not help remembering Floyd's stomach pains . . .

He tried bleeding her to reduce the fever and aches. The treatment made her weaker. Next he gave her a dose of salts. He was running out of ideas, and Sacajawea was failing.

The following day, lying in her blanket in the pirogue, too weak to move, Sacajawea heard excited voices. Joseph Fields had arrived downriver with a letter from the captain. Lewis had discovered the falls—five major cascades in all,

307

with wild rapids and lesser drops in between. Sacajawea listened, half understanding. Her husband came to her and explained what Lewis had discovered and what it meant. The boats could not pass the falls. The expedition must look for the best place to halt and prepare for a grueling portage.

Sacajawea made no response. She tried to nurse her four-month-old baby, but there was little milk. "You must get well," her husband said crossly. "*Mon Dieu!* What is become of *le bébé* if his mama die?" Charbonneau made the sign of the cross, muttering to himself. To her surprise Sacajawea saw tears run from his eyes into his beard. She was greatly moved.

"I'll stay with her," Meriwether Lewis said, two nights later. "We'll camp here below the creek. That idea of yours, Clark, making carriages for the canoes and using them as wagons for our baggage is a good one. Pat Gass will see the men started making wheels. We need you to go ahead to measure the falls and stake out a trail for us across the plain."

Clark looked toward Sacajawea, stirring restlessly where she now lay inside the captains' skin lodge, sweat on her brow. "I would not care to lose her."

"It would be a great loss for all of us."

Lewis was as dismayed as his partner over the Indian woman's sickness. True, he had been counting heavily on her presence when the expedition met her people. Beyond that, she had become a part of the expedition, one of his charges. He had lost but one man, he thought grimly. He would not lose this loyal woman.

Calling on his mother's skills as a herbalist, as he had throughout the journey whether treating his men or Indians, Lewis tried both bark and laudanum to relieve Sacajawea's pain. A sulphur spring had been found on the point opposite Portage Creek, and after tasting the water Lewis promptly had two kettles filled and brought to camp. When Sacajawea turned her head away from the evil-smelling potion, Lewis spoke firmly to Charbonneau. "Wringing your hands will do no good, Chabono. You must convince her to drink it. It will ease the devils inside her."

Finally, prevailed upon, Sacajawea accepted a full mug of the sulphur spring water from Lewis. In spite of gagging and a coughing fit, she held the mug in her two small, brown, shaking hands and drained it. Then she fell back, breathing hard. Her dark eyes gazed up at Lewis with perfect trust.

Lewis left the tent and joined Clark before the fire, which etched the gloom on Clark's face. "She is a fighter," he said. "I doubt those women we knew in our former station could endure such a trial, but . . ." Lewis left the thought unfinished. It was hardly just, he reflected, to fault the drawing room ladies of Washington or Virginia, unused to hardship more severe than choosing between a red or violet piece of cloth, because a little wilderness savage's strength of will impressed him. "You've done all you could, my friend. She is too weak to be bled again so soon. Perhaps the sulphur waters will be beneficial."

"We'll just wait, then . . ."

One of those who waited was Seaman. Like most dogs, he had an instinctive sense of distress in those to whom he gave his loyal friendship. Through that evening he lay near Sacajawea's feet, watching as the string of beads she wore around her neck rose and fell with her labored breathing. Pomp's customary serenity had changed to restless complaining, for the child was hungry. Without rising, Seaman crawled closer on his belly until he was within the baby's reach. A tiny brown hand clutched at his ear. He put his head between his paws and rested, while the radiant warmth of his body soothed both mother and child.

Toward midnight, checking on his patient, Meriwether Lewis thought her breathing more relaxed, the film of perspiration on her brow lighter and cooler.

By next morning the Indian woman's fever had broken. Although she remained pale and weak, by evening Lewis was able to feed her some broiled, well-seasoned buffalo beef along with a savory broth from the same pot. The next day, dipping once more into his medical kit, he prescribed fifteen drops of oil of vitriol. During the day Sacajawea was able to move about, the crisis apparently past. At bedtime she guided Pomp's eager mouth to the nipple of her milk-laden breast, and both slept content.

So rapid was Sacajawea's recovery that on the following day, while Lewis was busy sorting out cargo for the portage, she ate heartily of some of her favorite foods, dried fish and whiteapple. Almost at once she was violently sick. Lewis confronted Charbonneau in an uncharacteristic rage. "God damn you, man, I told you what she should eat! Why did you let her gobble up whatever she wanted?"

"*Merci, mon Capitaine* . . . I did not know! *Ma femme*, she seem so *bonne* . . ." He wrung his hands and pawed his beard in distress. "*Mon Dieu*, I mean no 'arm!'"

"You never do! But by the Lord, it has a way of following you!"

Another hearty dose of sulphur water proved efficacious, however, and this time Sacajawea's recovery was much quicker. By June 20, 1805, when William Clark returned to camp after staking out and flagging the portage route, when the wheels had been finished for the carriages, when all preparations were complete, when the fiddles of Cruzatte and Gibson were produced and a lively session of music and dance followed, Sacajawea sat at the edge of the circle and clapped her hands. Pomp gurgled happily in his cradleboard, and the Indian woman's dark eyes sought out Captain Redhead and Captain Lewis, the two chiefs who had coaxed the devils from her and made her whole again.

310

27 We all believe that we are about to enter on the most perilous and dificuelt part of our Voyage, yet I see no one repineing; all appear ready to meet those dificuelties which await us with resolution and becomeing fortitude.

—WILLIAM CLARK, J u n e   2 0,   1 8 0 5

*T*he eagle stood at the edge of her nest, talons hooked around a stout branch. Around her swirled the mist from the nearby falls, which thundered down from a precipice just west of the island in the middle of the river. The falls broke upon some rocks and swept past the island in a long, racing curl of white foam. She hardly noticed the turmoil. She had first begun to build her nest here in a tall black cottonwood four years ago. The scene was as familiar and natural to her as the sunshine or the blue sky.

Her nest was nearly eight feet across, set securely in the fork of a thick limb about eighty feet from the ground. She had made it with the help of her mate, placing a great mass of sticks with painstaking architectural care to form the shell. Each branch was interlocked with others for strength. Spaces between branches had been filled with weeds, sod, sprays of leaves, or earth. The resulting nest was now so strong that, in winter, it was capable of supporting a ton of snow. The cavity, in which two large white eggs now rested, had a nearly flat floor. The eagle's mate, smaller than she and the only male she would ever accept, would remain in the nest this morning to protect the eggs while she was away. He fluffed his feathers to warm himself, for in the shadows and mists of the river canyon it was still cool.

But the sun was up. They were daytime birds, and it was her time to hunt.

Like a mythical bird, she rose almost lazily out of the mists. With a smooth, powerful beat of wideswept wings she climbed above the bluffs on either side of the river, above the mists that rose even higher, into the bright sunshine.

As she flew, her keen black eyes swept the broad and level plain. It stretched away from her toward the mountains that framed her world to the north, the west, and, more brokenly, the south. Her gaze missed nothing. She saw the enormous herds of buffalo that frequently blotted out the prairie, the smaller clusters of elk and deer, the wolf packs, the occasional lumbering bear.

These were of only passing interest to her. None threatened her or her mate, or the fledglings that would soon break out of their shells. No land creature could swim safely across the roaring rapids below the falls or defy the walls of water that swept past her island. And nothing that flew dared challenge her isolated domain.

She rode the currents of air, using her feathers to brake, the fingerlike petals on her wings for lift. Now, cruising, she did not even have to flap her wings, for she used the thermal updrafts and soared effortlessly above the plain, seeing the sunlight bright on the water and the foaming cataracts below, seeing the strange creatures who labored like ants upward from the river bottom to the highland.

For days she had watched these newcomers off and on, for her gaze was always sharp to any change in the landscape below her, especially anything moving on the river. She was a fish eater, and some of these creatures, as she had observed, were also hunters of fish. They had plodded slowly up the river, pausing to rest now and then but always moving closer to her island.

Louis Charbonneau

Now they were leaving the river.

Their progress slowed to a crawl. She watched them for a long time before she began to lose interest. Then she wheeled in a long, slow, lazy circle that brought her over the river once more, over the tumbling cascades of the falls. Her concentration was total, her hooked beak open as if ready to tear. In the boiling rapids she spotted her morning meal, and she launched herself in a long, angled dive straight toward the river.

George Drouillard, another hunter, saw the white head of the bald eagle as she hurtled downward, and thought of a spear in flight.

The night before the portage began, Meriwether Lewis and most of the men of the party hauled one canoe and a load of baggage up the steep hill to the plain, advancing their burden about three miles along the eighteen-and-a-quarter-mile portage route to give them a good jump on the next day's run.

In the morning Charbonneau, Sacajawea and her baby, John Ordway, Silas Goodrich, and York remained at the lower camp. Drouillard, Reuben Fields, and George Shannon had been dispatched up the river to hunt for elk, whose skins were now urgently needed to cover Lewis's iron-framed boat—which, according to Lewis's grand design, would now replace the two pirogues that were being left behind. Everyone else in the detachment, including the two captains, climbed out of the river bottom to the highland. The sun felt good that morning, for the air was cool.

The long canoe on its cumbersome carriage waited where they had left it, next to one of the stakes William Clark had set out to mark the route. Everyone felt fresh and eager. Their activities in recent days at the portage camp—digging caches, cutting and drying meat, mending and sewing clothes, making wheels and carriages, packing baggage—had been light duty compared to their backbreaking struggle past the Missouri's rapids.

Taking their places, a half-dozen men hauling at the front of the carriage, the others ranged along both sides, they put their weight and shoulders into it and heaved.

Their wagon hardly budged.

There were a few chuckles, glances exchanged. This might be harder than they had bargained. Still, the plain was mostly level, wasn't it, they thought, peering westward along the route? There were a few gentle rises, several gullies and washes, but none of them too deep. Nothing they couldn't handle.

Clark, acting as pilot, was a few yards ahead. He glanced over his shoulder. "All right then, lads, let's put your backs into her."

They did, and the carriage creaked forward a few feet, all the men digging their moccasined feet into the earth and pushing or hauling with eye-popping effort. For the first time they experienced a feeling of dismay, a perception of the real challenge they faced. They felt, too, the cutting edges of the plain. Beaten into points and peaks like a merengue by the hoofs of buffalo passing after recent rains, the earth had hardened into sharp edges as it dried, and each point cut into the men's feet. They felt, slicing through their moccasins as if through paper, the spines of the prickly pear. But most of all they felt the dead weight of their awkward carriage groaning on its wide wooden wheels. Pushing it was like shoving against a stone wall.

After a little while there was no more of the usual joking and talking. The Frenchmen even forgot to swear. Every man needed all of his breath and strength and force of mind for the task. Soon they were bathed in sweat in spite of the coolness of the morning air. The sweat ran down their foreheads and into their eyes; it made their hands slip on the twisted elkskin ropes or caused them to lose their grip on the sides of the carriage.

Every few minutes they had to stop to rest. They would kneel where they paused, silent, their chests heaving, eyes peering through a film of sweat at the deceptive plain that had seemed so level before they started out but was now cursed by one rise after another.

Halfway through the morning, at one of the rest stops, Meriwether Lewis rigged up a harness for Seaman. The men needed all the help they could get. When the earthbound ship began its voyage once more, Seaman was harnessed up ahead with the men hauling the wagon. The dog's Newfoundland ancestors had been used to haul wagonloads of wood or ice, and he fell to as if by instinct, his hard muscles taut, his webbed feet digging in, all of his weight thrust forward and driving.

All through the morning the crew labored, Seaman along with them, as the air grew warmer, the sun hotter overhead, the resisting weight of the carriage more and more intolerable. Yet they plodded on, grunting and straining. Now when they stopped—Clark halted them at frequent intervals—many of them collapsed in their tracks and were asleep in an instant, near total exhaustion. When they started up again, they were sometimes on hands and knees, leaning forward to grasp at clumps of grass, spiny knobs of earth, or imbedded rocks to gain some small purchase in dragging themselves forward an- 315 other foot, another yard.

At noon they came up to a creek lined with willows. There was a steep ascent just before the gully along which ran the creek. There the coupling tongues of one set of wheels and one of the axletrees—made of an old mast from the white pirogue—broke. The carriage sagged forward and tilted. Some of the cargo pitched over the side. Alexander Willard leaned against an angled wheel with a sob.

They rested by the creek, which they named Willow Run after the only trees growing along the wash. These had to do for new tongues and an axletree. Pat Gass didn't think much of his choice, but the willow was all he had.

Two precious hours were lost while the replacement pieces were made and fitted to the carriage.

If the morning had been a test, the afternoon was torture. They were all badly fatigued now. Their muscles were sore,

their eyes dull. Most of all their feet were cut and bruised, making every thrust an act of will to push past the pain. A quarter-mile climb from one creek, steep and rough, would have been a matter of a few minutes to a man walking. For those pushing the carriage it was thirty minutes of agony. Shallow gullies turned into appalling ravines. The slightest dip into which a wheel might sink demanded every man's backbreaking effort to free the wheel.

The stops became more frequent, the pauses longer. Men snatched fragments of sleep while they stopped, lifted themselves like blind men when they dimly heard the gentle urgings of Lewis or Clark to push forward again. "That's it, lads . . . one more gully after this, and then it's all downhill!"

The sun went down, and the air felt chill against their sweat-drenched bodies. In the gray of dusk they labored, while darkness crept toward them across the prairie, its progress swifter than theirs.

The darkness of the plain had enveloped them, and they were still a half-mile from the site chosen for their camp when a willow tongue gave way.

It could not be repaired that night. They left the canoe on its wheeled carriage where it was and parceled out the baggage among them, each soldier, Seaman, and the captains taking what he could haul or carry. They stumbled down the last long incline toward the river, too exhausted to feel triumph or relief or even curiosity about their new camp.

The first day of the portage was over.

"Cap'n Lewis, sir," Nathaniel Pryor said, "I think you'd best have a look at Seaman's feet."

The Newfoundland lay quietly near one of the fires, steadily licking his paws. Lewis squatted on his haunches to inspect Seaman's feet. When Lewis lifted his left front paw the dog gave an involuntary jerk. All of his paws were cut and bleeding. The pad on his left hind foot had been badly sliced open by a stone or cactus spine. And, on testing the left shoulder, Lewis found the reason for the muscular spasm in a sprained or pulled muscle.

"Kept right on haulin', he did," said Peter Wiser, who was tending the captains' fire in York's absence. "That's our dog fer you."

"So did all of you."

Gently Lewis's hands probed the dog's body, searching for other areas of pain. Like all of the men who had been out on the plain this day, Seaman was no doubt sore all over. But it was his feet that would have to heal. "I believe you've done your duty," Lewis murmured. "You'll stay with me here, and rest, for we can't make moccasins to fit those paws."

Seaman lay on his side and slowly thumped his tail against the ground.

Pat Gass, John Shields, and Joseph Fields also stayed with Meriwether Lewis at White Bear Island camp—named for the grizzlies inhabiting an island just opposite the campsite—and Lewis quickly put them to work on preparations for his iron boat, making cross straps and horizontal bars of willow, shaving elkskins, sewing skins together to form the outer covering of the aptly named *Experiment*.

Meanwhile, William Clark returned to Portage Creek with the rest of the men to prepare for another portage. Late in the day he had two canoes taken up to the plain to be ready for an early start in the morning. That night the men repaired their moccasins, double-soling them as added protection against the prickly pear and the serrated surface of the prairie.

There were two canoes riding in their improvised carriages the following day, and the ordeal of the first portage was repeated twofold. But in the afternoon strong winds rose from the southeast. With typical ingenuity Clark had the men raise the sails on their land barges. The brisk winds ballooned the sails and gave a surprising amount of help in carrying the canoes forward. "By gar, I never thought to see such a t'ing!" Cruzatte joked. "Dese boat go sailin' on dry land!"

At dusk, while they were still three miles short of the White Bear Island camp, a hard rain lashed the prairie. The voyagers saw it coming a long way off, the sky dark and lowering, huge clouds piling atop one another to an enormous height, the rain marching toward them like a gray army. It came with a thunder that puzzled them until the storm arrived and they felt the sting of hailstones.

The wooden wheels of the carriages were quickly choked with mud. The ground underfoot became a slippery morass. In minutes the entire plain was covered with water. They struggled on, slipping and falling, picking themselves up from the mud, heaving at their carriages, the heady exhilaration of the afternoon's brief spell of dry-land sailing now forgotten.

Long after dark they stumbled into the upper camp, soaked and caked with mud, near collapse. Meriwether Lewis took one look at his bedraggled corps and, as each man collapsed on the ground near one of the fires, he received from his captain's hand a dram of whiskey.

318

In the morning the crew rested, most of them revived enough to tease and cajole Seaman, who had been awake most of the night—and had awakened many of the sleeping men—patrolling the perimeter of the camp and barking furiously whenever one of the neighboring grizzlies prowled too close.

Shortly after their noontime meal William Clark roused his men and they trudged across the muddy prairie toward the Portage Camp below the falls. They brought with them the two empty carriages, and they arrived late that afternoon in time to take one canoe and a load of baggage up to the plain. Then they went back down to the river bottom and collapsed on their blankets. Most of them were instantly asleep. The vaulting stillness of the evening was undisturbed except for the rushing of the river over rocks and the nearby thunder of the Great Falls.

Charbonneau was acting cook at the base camp, and after a while some of the men stirred, as the tempting smell of his *boudin blanc* penetrated their exhausted stupor. One by one they roused themselves for their supper. They ate in a general silence, without the usual joking and camaraderie.

Still later Pierre Cruzatte got out his fiddle, not so much to play as to test its strings lovingly and reassure himself that the instrument was undamaged by its latest travels. A tentative squeak of a single string trembled in the night air like a lonely bird call. Then, almost by reflex, Cruzatte drew the bow across the strings as he tuned them. Idly his random bow movements became purposeful. A tune formed.

Some heads lifted as the fiddle music picked up its tempo. After some minutes Toussaint Charbonneau, well rested at the base camp, hopped up and gave an impromptu dance. Baptiste Lepage, scornfully summing up the interpreter's gyrations as "dat damn rooster strut," proceeded to demonstrate a much more energetic, foot-stomping reel. That goaded Hugh McNeal into dragging himself up to prove that an Irish jig would make a Frenchman's strut seem like child's play any time. And pretty soon Goodrich and Collins were on their feet, Willard and Werner and the others, clapping hands and lending nasal voices to the music of St. Peter's fiddle. Before long the entire clearing rang with merriment.

Even Sacajawea, recovered at last from her lingering illness, was able to smile and clap as she watched the men, and Pomp brought his fingers together in imitation. Toussaint Charbonneau finally plopped down beside them, pawed his beard with his greasy fingers, and thrust his face close to the baby's. Pomp, trying to focus, reached out with small fingers for the beard.

Charbonneau stared at the men in the clearing who, such a short time ago, had been too exhausted to eat, and he could not deny his affinity with them. Only a week ago, when Sacajawea had been so sick, he had been anxious to abandon the expedition. "We no go back," she had said in Minitaree, even as she shook with fever. "You gave your word." She was Shoshoni, and a Shoshoni's word was good.

Stubborn Indian, he thought.

But it was a great thing they were doing, making a trail

for others to follow across the Rocky Mountains to the western ocean. A thing that would be spoken of and remembered. And he was part of it . . .

The men of the Corps of Discovery brought the last canoe and all of the remaining cargo up to the plain from Portage Camp on the morning of June 28, 1805. In spite of their exhaustion, by this time the men, like Charbonneau, were feeling proud of themselves. They had survived three harrowing trips over the eighteen-and-a-quarter-mile portage. In their minds the ordeal was already the material of story and myth, a tale they would be able to tell in numbing detail to their grandchildren.

Because there was too much cargo for the lone remaining canoe and its carriage, some of the baggage had to be left behind on the plain. It was a blustery day with scudding clouds but a lot of blue sky showing. As the men labored, the day became hot and humid. Most of them were stripped down to leggings and moccasins, and their bodies glistened with sweat.

Starting late after breaking up the lower camp, they were compelled to halt at Willow Run, the eight-mile mark, late in the afternoon. At dark the plain was swept by rain driven on a violent wind. With little or no shelter available, everyone hunched down miserably against the storm, unable to do anything but wait it out. "One more day," William Clark said encouragingly into the sodden, dripping darkness. "Ye have reason to be proud of what ye've done. Tomorrow will see us all at the end of this portage."

But in the morning the prairie was saturated from the heavy rain. The overburdened canoe could not move through the mud. Trying to make the best of a lost day, Clark sent most of the men back across the prairie for the remaining cargo that had been left behind at the top of the hill. They would have to carry it up to Willow Run on their backs. Then Clark decided to use the day himself to explore the river once more and measure the falls. His initial notes and measurements of the falls had been lost in a windstorm, and he was anxious to renew them.

Sacajawea and Charbonneau, who had remained at the base camp until now, were also eager to view the spectacle about which they had heard so much. York tagged along, but he was more interested in hunting than sightseeing. While Clark led the others to a bluff overlooking the river and the great falls, York took himself off across the muddy plain, his rifle over his shoulder.

Sacajawea stared with pounding heart at the awesome cataract that plunged down through foam and mist onto the rocks far below. Even Charbonneau, who often affected a worldly indifference to nature's wonders, gaped at the scene as if struck dumb.

In the few minutes after their arrival at the river, however, an ominous black cloud appeared, swiftly filling up the western sky. Off to the east the plain was still splashed with bright sunlight, but where Clark and his companions stood on the bluff, the day became as dark as night. The wind howled across the treeless plain with a force that threatened to hurl them over the precipice into the river just above the eighty-seven-foot falls.

Looking about him, Clark sought some kind of shelter from the fast-approaching storm and the fierce gale. Quickly he led his small group to a deep ravine that cut into the bluff about a quarter-mile above the falls. The walls of the canyon cut off the force of the wind, and there was shelving rock under which they would be protected from the rain.

Clark guided Charbonneau, Sacajawea, and Pomp—the boy happy in his cradleboard despite all the turmoil about him —to the upper side of the ravine just as the first rainfall reached them. It was moderate, creating no anxiety. Clark set down his gun and compass on the ledge, along with the umbrella his brother George had given him as a parting gift, his shot pouch and horn, placing them under the protective canopy of rock. Sacajawea took the opportunity to slip her baby from his cradleboard and bathe him with rainwater.

With no warning other than a rolling rumble that William Clark mistook for thunder, a cloudburst struck. It came like a wall of water pouring out of the sky—like a heavenly cataract,

Clark thought, numbed by the sudden fury of the storm. The downpour became a deafening artillery salvo as some of the rain turned to hail.

Out on the plain the men returning to Willow Run with baggage on their backs were caught in the open and battered by hail. It whipped them in chunks as large as musket balls. Most of the men were nearly naked, stripped down as they labored in the warm, muggy air. The wildness of the wind blew them about like leaves, and the hailstones lacerated them like sharp stones as they stood defenseless. Soon the men dropped their burdens and scattered in every direction, demoralized and lost in the center of the chaos. One man was knocked down three times until he finally huddled where he had fallen, helpless to resist the battering.

In the partial shelter of the ravine, William Clark suddenly felt water rising around his feet.

He stared along the ravine where it cut into the plain. Water boiled down the fissure, rising even as he glanced in that direction. Alarm stabbed through the sense-drugged stupor created by the storm. He grabbed Sacajawea's arm. "Get out of here!" he shouted. "Hurry!"

Without waiting for her response, he lifted her up, urging her upward along the face of the canyon wall.

Charbonneau, who was a little above them, saw the urgency in Clark's actions and reached for Sacajawea's hand to pull her up. He followed Clark's glance up the ravine and froze in terror. An avalanche of water and mud and rocks raced toward them. Clark shouted at him to help Sacajawea, herself now terrified and clinging desperately to her naked baby—for the cradleboard, along with Pomp's clothes, had been swept off the ledge where she had placed them. But Charbonneau crouched motionless just above them, paralyzed by fear.

With his left hand Clark grabbed his gun and shot pouch. With his right he pushed the little Indian woman ahead of him as he began to climb. In an instant the water covered his knees, his thighs, reached his waist, and pulled at him with a powerful drag, rising as fast he could climb.

322

At last Charbonneau's spell broke. He scrambled toward higher ground, pulling Sacajawea after him as Clark pushed her from below. They climbed frantically in a race against the rising torrent. In seconds they reached the rim of the bluff, as the flash flood boiled down the ravine just beneath their feet— a torrent of debris-filled water now fifteen feet deep and carrying away everything in its path.

Clark and his companions lay limp at the edge of the plain, Sacajawea huddled over her baby to protect him, while the rain and hail beat down upon them.

After a few moments that seemed like an hour, Clark thought the roar of the storm was diminishing, but it was some minutes more before there was any perceptible relief from the pounding he and his companions endured. He thought with fleeting anguish of his precious compass, carried away in the flood. But it might as easily have been the Indian woman, he thought. Or little Pomp! And a chill prickled his flesh, making him shiver.

Suddenly he heard a shout through the diminishing noise of the storm. At first he could see nothing. Then the call was repeated. Out of the curtain of rain York appeared. His round face was shining wet and furrowed with anxiety. "Cap'n Clark, suh! Oh thank the Lord! I was feared for you and the little squaw. I couldn't find you nowhere!"

When York reached them, his gaze was drawn toward the ravine. Involuntarily he fell back a step. "Oh my! I didn't see you go down there . . ." His eyes rolled skyward, crescents of white showing. "Oh thank you, Lord! Thank you for the cap'n and for the little woman and her babe!"

"Eh, what is dis?" Charbonneau complained. "What about me?"

William Clark felt the lingering vestiges of fear drop away, and he burst out in laughter, lifting his face to the rain. Thank God for Charbonneau!

28 We begin to feel considerable anxiety with rispect to the Snake Indians. if we do not find them or some other nation who have horses I fear the successful issue of our voyage will be very doubtful or at all events much more difficult in it's accomplishment.

—MERIWETHER LEWIS, J u l y 2 7, 1 8 o 5

*T*he Corps of Discovery celebrated Independence Day, 1805, at White Bear Island camp with a feast of beans and bacon, buffalo beef and Lewis's suet dumplings, followed by music and dancing on the riverbank. The captains drained the last of the whiskey kegs—"An historic moment!" William Clark declared—pouring out a dram for each man, though it meant leaving the expedition bereft of spirits for the rest of the journey, save for a small amount in Lewis's medicine kit. The men toasted their young country and themselves. The portage was behind them. Surely, they said, as the whiskey burned its way to their bellies, nothing they would face in the months ahead could be worse.

All were now busy on Meriwether Lewis's iron boat— sewing elk and buffalo skins, making stays, building a tar kiln to produce pitch. But in the next few days the project—so dear to Lewis—became more and more uncertain. With no pitch pine available, the kiln failed to produce tar. The needle used for sewing had a sharp edge that cut the skins around the holes. Lewis kept trying to improvise. Without pitch, he tried a substitute mixture to caulk the seams and holes. The sticky

coating, made by pounding charcoal and blending it with beeswax and tallow, seemed to work.

On July 9, while Lewis beamed, the *Experiment* was
launched. Gracefully proportioned and remarkably light in
spite of its size, the iron-framed boat "lay like a perfect cork
on the water," Lewis exulted.

A sudden storm drove everyone to shelter. When it passed
and Lewis inspected his prize creation once more, his enthusiasm turned to dismay. His composition coating had separated. The seams of the skin covering lay exposed to the water.
The boat leaked badly.

He had nothing else with which to seal the leaks. The
disastrous conclusion was inevitable. He could waste no more
time on his precious *Experiment*.

Though dubious about the iron boat from the start, William Clark had refrained from questioning the venture. Over
the past two years he had acquired too much respect for his
friend's ingenuity. In Clark's view, Lewis's foresight and
judgment—whether in selecting boats for the journey, defining
the kind of men who would man them, or choosing and obtaining the immense quantities of supplies that had served
them all so well—had made the expedition's success to this
juncture possible. If his iron boat sank like a stone, the failure
did not diminish one whit Clark's admiration for his partner's
inventiveness or faith in his judgment. *Had he not the imagination for this journey into the unknown, we would never have
come so far, we would not now be camped almost in the shadow
of the Rocky Mountains.*

On July 13, 1805, while the Corps of Discovery prepared once
more to ascend the Missouri, on the other side of the continent,
in his downstairs study at the President's House, Thomas Jefferson closed the doors and shutters, as if he sought to hide a
precious secret. Only candlelight flickered, throwing shadows
across the jumble of wooden crates in the center of the room.

Scientist, naturalist, and philosopher, author of his nation's bold Declaration of Independence, twice elected its President, in that moment Jefferson felt more like a youngster sneaking down the stairs on Christmas morning to a quiet room before anyone else was up, to open a surprise gift with trembling hands.

The crates and boxes Pat Gass had nailed shut in April had arrived in St. Louis aboard the keelboat early in June, in the care of the dependable Corporal Richard Warfington. One of Lewis's friends of the city, Pierre Chouteau, had taken charge of the cargo. He had divided it into two shipments. The bulky items, including almost all of the skins, skeletons, Indian artifacts, robes, soil, and plant specimens, and the live birds and animals were sent by boat to New Orleans for transshipment to Baltimore. The second part of the cargo went overland directly to the White House. It included all of the documentation Lewis and Clark had assembled as far as the Mandans—Lewis's long letter and summary of the voyage, Clark's detailed journals and maps, notes on Indians, their numbers, customs, and languages.

The arrival of the crates had caught Thomas Jefferson on the eve of his departure for Monticello on his annual summer vacation. Using an iron bar and a hammer, Jefferson opened the boxes with his own hands. Memories rushed in of long evenings he had spent in this room with his ambitious young secretary. Holding sheafs of documents in his shaking hands, the President thought, By God, he's done it! Opened the continent! Extended our reach halfway up the Missouri!

He found a listing of the contents of the crates coming by ship. Scores of plant specimens for Dr. Barton! Strange animal skins and skeletons, Indian weapons and clothing and artifacts—even live animals, by heaven!—enough to keep Mr. Peale busy in the back rooms of his museum for months. But, above all, the crates Jefferson beheld and those still to come carried knowledge. Descriptions of the people of the Plains, before now a mystery. Information that defined the shape, texture, and dimensions of the land and all of its inhabitants.

Louis Charbonneau

A long finger traced the route of the Missouri on Clark's general map. An old man's hands, bony and spotted, quivering like leaves in the wind. Small matter! The lines these hands once drew in speculation were now fixed, charted with admirable detail.

The finger moved on past the Mandan villages on another map, this one conjectural. Where were Lewis and Clark now? The long silence while the expedition moved beyond the reach of civilization had been a trying time for Jefferson, beset by whispers of his Louisiana project's disaster, spread by his Federalist rivals in the midst of his successful reelection campaign. He had been worried far more than he would permit himself to acknowledge over the fate of the men he had sent into that vast unknown.

Now the voyagers—Lewis, Clark, all those stalwart young soldiers—were once more advancing into an uncharted wilderness. What new marvels were opening to their wondering eyes? How Thomas Jefferson envied them!

Taking up the iron bar and hammer again, Jefferson fitted the point of the bar into the top panel of the last crate and struck a blow. A nail screeched in the wood. In its cage, Jefferson's pet mockingbird fluttered in agitation, as if it heard the cry of the wilderness.

327

The prickly pear, so troublesome on the portage, was in full bloom at mid-July when the eight boats of the expedition—two dugout canoes had been carved to take the place of the abandoned *Experiment*—set off up the Missouri River from White Bear Island.

The mountains were now close at hand. Even the air was different. For Sacajawea it carried the scents of her childhood, of sage and pine. Everything began to look more familiar to her—the clarity of the Missouri's waters that had been so muddy below the falls, the forested slopes crowding close to the river, the snow-clad peaks beyond them. Only a week after leaving the White Bear Island camp, she spoke tentatively to William Clark of her conviction. "My people have lived on this river," she said.

"Are you certain, Janey? It's important."

She nodded vigorously. "The place I have spoken of, where the three rivers meet, is not far."

The Missouri River entered the first range of mountains. The river narrowed, forcing its way through spectacularly high, steep cliffs of solid rock for a distance of nearly six miles. In this dark gorge there was hardly anyplace beside the river large enough to camp. At last the bluffs appeared to draw apart as the boats rounded a bend and poled toward them, walls of rock opening up like giant gates. Lewis named the singular passage the Gates of the Mountains.

Past the bluffs the river became wider, slower-moving, spreading out to the aprons of verdant meadows on either side. Here, excitedly, the young Indian woman showed Meriwether Lewis where she had gathered wild onions as a girl. *And there! See, my captain? That red earth on the bank? My people use it to make the red paint which they smear on their cheeks and on those of strangers, as a sign of peace.*

Later, when they were walking ashore, he had Charbonneau ask her, "What other signs of peace might I give? How will your people know we are not their enemies?"

"You must show them your blanket—like this." Sacajawea slipped her blanket from her shoulders, held it by two corners, and flapped it above her head. Then she let the blanket settle before her, as if she were spreading it out on the ground in invitation. Kneeling on the edge of the blanket, she looked up at Lewis. "The blanket is a sign that you wish to speak in friendship."

Lewis nodded thoughtfully. "Is there anything else?"

She pondered the question. "You are white men. But they will think you are Pahkees who have come to kill them." She had previously told Lewis that Pahkee was the Shoshoni name blanketing both the Blackfeet and the Gros Ventres of the prairie, who were often in league with each other and always enemies of the Snakes. Sacajawea smiled a little. "You no look like *tab-ba-bone*. The sun make you dark, like Indian."

Lewis recognized the accuracy of the observation. In their greasy, water-darkened leather garments, their hair grown long and lank, their skin deeply tanned, the men of the expedition could readily have passed for Indians at any distance. Lewis pressed Charbonneau on the word Sacajawea had used, wanting to be sure of its meaning. "That word *tab-ba-bone*. That is the word for a white man?"

"Is word for stranger," Charbonneau confirmed after talking to his wife. "Is same for white man." It did not occur to Sacajawea that a stranger might also be an enemy, and the word not always reassuring. "She say you must show where you skin is pale like ash, so dey believe an' not be afraid."

There were signs—some old, some new—of Indians along the river. They passed a large abandoned village of many lodges. They found pine trees where the bark had recently been peeled away, and Sacajawea explained that her people found the soft, sap-filled inner bark a nutritious food. In the mountains there was little game, she explained. Unlike the Pahkees, her people did not have guns to shoot deer and antelope. Often they went hungry . . .

Both Lewis and Clark—the former with the boats and the latter walking ahead on shore—saw signal smoke climbing against the sky. Though Lewis at first mistook the smoke for Clark's campfires, it was soon evident that these were Indian signals. The smoke meant that the approach of the detachment up the river had been seen.

In response to the signals Meriwether Lewis hoisted flags on the boats, which no Indian war party would do. William Clark, while marching overland, reconnoitered three miles ahead of his hunters before he would permit them to shoot, fearing to alarm any Indians in the vicinity.

But there were no Indians to be found.

Pushing on ahead, wearing out the men with him, Clark reached Three Forks in advance of the boats. In spite of sickness and exhaustion, he explored the tributaries, seeking to

329

identify the true source of the Missouri. Two of the men now
with him became disabled, Toussaint Charbonneau with a bad
ankle, Joseph Fields with foot problems; Clark pressed on in
spite of a tumor growing on his ankle. Hot, tired and feverish,
he became sick after drinking too much from a cold spring
and was forced to turn back.

On their way back toward Three Forks, Charbonneau, in
a careless moment, slipped on the riverbank. Instantly he was
in the water. He went under and came up choking and crying
for help. The strong current pulled him downstream.

Sick as he was, Clark went into the river after the interpreter. He grabbed Charbonneau by the hair and—ignoring
the Frenchman's yelps of pain—dragged him by the hair to
the safety of the bank. "Ye're more trouble than ye're worth!"
he snapped. Charbonneau swallowed his reply. He knew that
it was Clark's sickness and fatigue that spoke.

Meanwhile, Meriwether Lewis and the rest of the detachment had arrived at Three Forks. All were exhausted by
the strenuous poling up the last stretch of the Missouri River.
Even Lewis had been obliged to lend a hand, and the men
acknowledged that the captain could "push a tolerable good
pole." That modest praise meant enough to Lewis for him to
record it in his journal.

Lewis climbed a flat-topped bluff overlooking the junction of the three rivers. He sketched the pretty scene, slapped
at mosquitoes, gazed in silence that could not mask his elation
at attaining this goal.

Here the Corps could stop and rest. They had earned it.

"Dis is where it happen," Charbonneau said, translating his
squaw's words. "Sacajawea, she be in de middle of dis *riviere*,
de one you call Jefferson. She run, she try escape from de
Minitaree, but is no good, dey catch her quick."

Here, where three beautiful streams came together and
the Corps of Discovery rested, the Shoshoni woman had been
captured and taken from her people. Her story was a gory one,

of men and women and even children murdered on this spot. As Meriwether Lewis listened to her tale, he searched her impassive face for some sign of emotion. In vain he sought to hear a tremor in her voice or to detect the trace of a tear in her black eyes. Nothing. No sign of emotion, no hint of re-membered terror, no sorrow over those of her people who had been murdered, whose blood had stained the clear waters of the Jefferson River. Nor, he thought, did she exhibit any joy over returning to the land of her people—now, by her own account, so close. By the Lord, she feels nothing! She is a child. If she has enough to eat and a few trinkets to wear on her arms or about her neck, she is content.

Studying the young Shoshoni woman, Meriwether Lewis was misled by her Indian restraint. He saw only the stoic face, not the beating heart.

In truth this return to the Three Forks had left Sacajawea in turmoil. Many parts of her childhood had become dim in her memory, as if seen through a mist, but every detail of her capture by the Minitarees was as vivid as a slash of fresh paint on a white buffalo skin.

She remembered the heat of that morning, the feel of the sun on her arms and the side of her neck when she knelt by the stream. She remembered forming her hands into a cup and dipping them into the stream and the sharp, delicious taste of the icy water when she carried it to her lips. She was kneeling there when she heard the first ear-piercing shrieks of the Minitaree warriors.

Of course she did not then know who they were, only that they were enemies. She saw the fright in her grandmother's loved face. She heard the warriors of her People shouting in alarm and the small thunder of the weapons in the hands of their attackers—each crash of a rifle struck the girl's ears like a blow.

Her people had no such weapons. They scattered like antelope before the hunters, but the enemy rode them down. Sacajawea could still remember the sickening thunk of the battle axe crushing her grandmother's skull, the scream of terror from one of her childhood friends when an enemy warrior seized her, the thrashing of men and horses in the tangled willow brush beside the river, and the wild beating of her heart when she tried to flee across the shallow stream and looked up to find a mounted warrior bearing down upon her. She thought his painted face a mask, his grin that of a wolf. Only much later would she know that it was only the face of a man, a warrior triumphant.

But Sacajawea's return to Three Forks had awakened not only the rush of remembered terror, but many other emotions and memories associated with this place. The excitement of a young girl riding with the People over the mountains. The eager talk of finding the buffalo and feasting on its flesh after the long meat-fast of winter. The profusion of beaver among the streams that meandered here across the lush green meadows. The sweetness of the dark gooseberries she had discovered on a bush and tasted for the first time. The warm, close companionship in the lodges and the music of the People's songs . . .

None of this was visible to Meriwether Lewis. None of it showed in her face.

The white chiefs questioned her about the mountain pass through which her People traveled to reach the Missouri and the buffalo hunting grounds, but she could not help them. Although Three Forks was so familiar to her, she was unable to say which of the three streams that here formed the headwaters of the Missouri River would take them to the river's ultimate source in the mountains. When she had come over the mountains, she had been a child. Though she recognized landmarks enthusiastically, she was weak on direction.

She could assert only one thing with conviction. "Just over the mountains is the place where my People hunt and fish and raise their lodges. It is not far."

The captains made their decision. They had named the easterly arm of the three forks Gallatin's River, after the Secretary of the Treasury; the middle fork Madison's River, for the Secretary of State; and the most westward branch Jefferson's River, in honor of the President, author and architect of their expedition. They chose to follow Jefferson's River.

Early on the morning of August 8, 1805, a week after leaving Three Forks, Sacajawea surprised Meriwether Lewis by a show of emotion. Jumping up and down in apparent agitation, she tugged at William Clark's sleeve. She pointed toward a large, distinctively shaped rock formation that thrust abruptly above the level river valley. In her excitement she spoke rapidly in Shoshoni, and Charbonneau was called over to interpret. "She call dat rock de Beaver's Head," he translated. "De Snakes, dey t'ink it look like beaver, eh? My woman say, she seen dis rock. She know it well."

Lewis and Clark exchanged glances. Though both men thought it required considerable imagination to find a beaver's head in the formation, that did not diminish their enthusiasm. They had chosen the right stream to follow. They must be close to the mountain pass!

Sacajawea smiled happily. She saw the elation in the eyes of the white chiefs. It was a reflection of the joy that beat so quickly in her breast.

333

That night Lewis and Clark conferred. They were now well into August, and both men were acutely aware of the necessity of getting through the mountain passes before they were blocked with snow. "Snow will come early to these parts," Clark said worriedly. "We have a month, no more."

Their situation, if not yet desperate, soon would be. Game and food of any kind were becoming scarce. They had used up most of the meat they had been able to pack and bring with them up the river. The men were generally in a bad way— Clark himself now crippled by his ankle tumor. The Indians, who certainly knew of their presence, continued to avoid them, hiding in the mountains.

"They're obviously afraid of us. But the Indian woman says we'll find them on this river, or west of its course. If she's right, their village can't be far away."

"I believe her," said Clark.

"Then I will go ahead and find them, if it takes all of that month you give us."

"Will ye take the woman?"

Lewis had pondered the question, weighing the advantage of having a Shoshoni woman with him should he find her people against the critical need to travel fast over difficult, mountainous terrain. "She cannot leave her child for a month," he said finally. "And carrying him, she would be unable to keep up. We must move quickly."

"Then ye must go without her."

"I won't come back until I've tracked down these Snakes and found a way over the mountains!"

334 Seaman was delighted when he saw Meriwether Lewis, George Drouillard, John Shields, and Hugh McLean preparing to set off early in the morning on foot. He danced around them, barking in his enthusiasm.

The past month had been a troublesome time for the Newfoundland. All during the stay at White Bear Island camp he had been agitated by the presence in the area of an uncommon number of grizzlies. Especially at night the bears disturbed him. They prowled close about the camp. He could hear and smell them. A nervous excitement kept him awake, pacing the perimeter of the camp, barking furiously whenever one of the huge animals came near.

He was relieved to get back on the river. If each day in the boats for the men brought the certainty of hard work on oar or pole, for the dog it promised new adventure. One day, shortly after the corps started up the Missouri once more, Drouillard shot a deer in the river bottom. The wounded animal ran into the stream. Drouillard shouted at Seaman. Without hesitation the Newfoundland leaped into the river. He was exhilarated by his plunge into icy water, the dimly heard shouts of the men in the boats, the excitement of pursuit. Though the deer was still strong enough to swim, Seaman swiftly closed the distance between them. In the middle of the river the chase ended. Seaman finished the hunter's kill.

That night, as the men enjoyed venison for supper, Seaman was given a hearty share in honor of his achievement. Around the campfires a lively debate ensued over the relative prowess of retrieving a pheasant from a field, a duck from a pond, or a deer from the turbulent Missouri River.

But in the days that followed, there was only the plodding journey up the river. Seaman was confined most of the time to the boats or the night camps, even when Lewis or Clark went ahead on foot. When the dog did get ashore, he was plagued by the ever-present prickly pear and by a new demon, a barbed grass whose pointed seeds penetrated the men's leggings and moccasins. The seeds pierced Seaman's pads, got in between his toes and dug into his coat, and he was constantly biting and scratching at them in an extremity of pain. One barbed seed sneaked into his left ear. When an infection set in, Meriwether Lewis had to probe for the offender and extract it.

During the trip upriver and again while the expedition lay over at Three Forks, the mosquitoes were worse than ever, whining about Seaman and the men both day and night, joined by a tiny eye gnat that swarmed about everyone's eyes.

There were also rattlesnakes. Several were killed each day. William Clark shot one that appeared between his legs while he was fishing. On another occasion Seaman unexpectedly stepped upon a large, coiled rattler. He jumped back. The snake, sun-dazed, struck too late. Seaman danced around it, barking while the snake angrily whirred its rattles, until Clark killed it with a single shot.

Now, as the Jefferson River became increasingly narrow and shallow, and the boats encountered one rapids after another that kept the men toiling in the water on the towlines, Seaman was eager to join Lewis and his companions on another trek across country. He too was tired of the river.

Meriwether Lewis regarded Seaman with a fond but skeptical appraisal. Although he had taken little notice of the dog's appearance lately, now he was struck by Seaman's ragged, unkempt state. Rather than glossy black, the long coat was dull, filled with burrs and barbed grass seeds, caked with mud and tangled into thick mats. Moreover, Seaman walked with a decided limp, a condition he shared with most of the men of the corps.

Reluctantly Lewis shook his head. Turning to William Clark, he said, "I'll leave Seaman here with you. Have young Shannon take a comb to Seaman's coat. It'll keep the lad busy so he doesn't wander off and become lost again."

George Shannon had made such a practice of disappearing that the men of the expedition were becoming used to it, worrying less when the youth failed to appear. Just this past week he had missed the boats while returning from a hunting foray. Taking the wrong turn at a forks, he had been lost for three days before catching up—by then a worried young man.

336

"I want Seaman to look presentable for these Snakes. He makes a strong impression on the red men, and I want to make the most of it."

Clark ran a loop of elkskin rope around the dog's neck and held him by it as Lewis turned away. Seaman stamped his feet and whined in frustration. At the edge of the camp Lewis paused to look back. He hesitated before giving a rueful sigh. "Oh hell, Clark, turn him loose." And as Seaman bounded joyfully toward him, Lewis added, "There's a comb, I suppose, among those Indian trinkets. I'll see to his grooming myself. Come along, then, Seaman—let's go find those Indians!"

Early on the morning of August 10, 1805, Meriwether Lewis and his companions came upon a well-traveled Indian trail leading toward the mountains. The absence of fresh tracks did nothing to diminish Lewis's excitement. This had to be the Shoshoni road, the path to the land of Sacajawea's people.

Falling in with the Indian trail, the party followed it upriver. After about fifteen miles the land opened out to a handsome valley. But here, once more, the river divided. One fork swung to the southeast, the other to the west, and there were visible Indian tracks beside each.

Lewis explored the southeast fork for a short distance until it became choked with brush and the trail petered out. Returning to the forks, he left a note for William Clark, telling him to stop here and wait. This was as far as the boats could travel. The thought was inescapable: Without horses, this is where the expedition must end. There was no way the men could carry all their baggage on their backs across these mountains.

The little group of explorers started up the valley toward the west, Seaman foraging ahead with his endless curiosity but keeping a watchful eye on his companions. Soon they entered a beautiful and extensive plain surrounded on all sides by rolling hills with mountains behind them, forming a bowl or cove some sixteen miles across. The plain was covered with grass, sage, and prickly pear. Although the mountains did not appear high, their peaks were snow-covered. Lewis realized that the expedition had been climbing all along, ever since leaving the Great Falls, the gradual rise of the land invisible to the eye. They were now high in the mountain range. He could taste the mountain air, drier and thinner. 337

That night Seaman had an unexpected session of grooming, with Lewis using a comb to work some of the snags and burrs from his coat. Passively resistant, the big dog tried to pull away until Lewis spoke to him sharply. Then he resigned himself to the tugging and pulling. Afterward, to his surprise, he felt a greater freedom of motion, an airiness as the wind ruffled his coat.

The next morning the Indian trail disappeared. Lewis decided to abandon the tributary stream he had followed from the Jefferson River and to head straight across the valley floor toward a pass now visible between two high cliffs to the west. Keeping McNeal and Seaman with him, he sent Drouillard out to his right, Shields to his left. If either man sighted the lost Indian track, he was to raise his hat on the muzzle of his rifle as a signal. No shooting. They must do nothing to alarm any Indians who might be in the vicinity.

They had advanced about five miles when Lewis felt his heart trip. Straight ahead of him—something moving!

With his spyglass he sighted on the distant object, about two miles away. The image leaped into the glass—an Indian on horseback, coming straight down the sloping plain toward him! And he was an Indian wearing garments unlike any Lewis had seen before. Armed only with a bow and a quiver of arrows, he rode an elegant horse with a rope bridle and no saddle. *Shoshoni!*

Blood racing, Meriwether Lewis advanced slowly, not altering his pace. The savage on horseback, clearly aware of the presence of strangers, continued his cautious approach, halting only when they were about a mile apart.

Alert to the newcomer, Seaman trotted forward, a warning growl in his throat. Lewis stopped him. "Stay, boy! Let's not worry him any more than he is already."

Lewis had rehearsed what he would do at such a moment. He took his blanket from his knapsack and unfolded it. Holding the blanket by two corners, he flapped it over his head and let it settle to the ground, as if spreading it before him in invitation. Three times he repeated this signal of friendship. Then, after commanding Seaman to stay with McNeal, he began to walk toward the solitary Shoshoni rider.

Far out on either side of him, however, Drouillard and Shields had either failed to observe this little drama or had ignored it. Continuing their own advance, both men had proceeded a little ahead of Lewis. He wanted to signal them to halt, but they were too far away to hear his shout, and he was afraid to scare off the Indian by firing his gun.

As Lewis and the Indian drew closer to each other, Lewis saw that the warrior was becoming uneasy, glancing first over his left shoulder toward Drouillard, then over his right shoulder at Shields. Lewis fumed silently. What was wrong with them? They were his most experienced men, that was why he had them along. They *knew* better! To the Shoshoni it must surely appear that he was in danger of riding into a trap. While he approached the man in the center, the two out on his flanks would get behind him.

In desperation Meriwether Lewis stopped, spread out his blanket, placed his gun and spyglass upon it. He also took from his pack some of his Indian gifts—a looking glass, an awl; beads, and other trinkets—and placed them on the blanket. "Stay here and watch," Lewis told McNeal. "Seaman, stay! I'll meet this gentleman alone."

Holding out his empty hands, Lewis began to walk toward the Indian. He had come within about two hundred yards when the rider wheeled his horse and began a nervous retreat. Drouillard and Shields, oblivious of the situation, were still advancing. In exasperation Lewis waved his arms. At last Drouillard saw his signal and halted.

Shields, head down, plodded doggedly forward.

Lewis called out to the Indian. *"Tab-ba-bone!"* he shouted. He pushed up the sleeve of his leather shirt to reveal the white of his arm, untouched by the sun. *"Tab-ba-bone!"*

He had drawn within one hundred yards when the Indian suddenly turned his horse and lashed him with a whip. The horse leaped across a narrow creek and galloped off, disappearing into the willow brush.

The four men camped that night near the head of the valley, Drouillard and Shields somewhat subdued from the sharp reprimand their captain had given them for their failure to exercise good sense. By frightening off the Shoshoni, they had endangered the entire expedition. Seaman also felt the bite of Lewis's mood when the comb was used more vigorously to free the last of his tangled mats. When the grooming ended, however, even Drouillard grunted approval. It was good for the Bear Dog to present such a proud appearance.

Everyone felt a meeting with the Shoshonis was near.

Trail

On the morning of August 12, 1805, Lewis had McNeal cut a pole and attach the flag to it. The banner would be another peaceful signal to any Indians they met.

The party walked along the base of the hills surrounding Shoshoni Cove in search of the Indian trail. After a short time they found a broad road that entered the cove from the northeast and led to the southwest. It brought them once more to the tributary stream of the Jefferson River which they had abandoned yesterday.

As they followed the Indian road with rising eagerness, the stream turned abruptly to the west. Ahead of them, plainly visible at last, was the way through the mountains.

By now the stream was little more than a trickle. Long-legged young Hugh McNeal, a Pennsylvanian by birth who had joined the army for adventure and found it in the Corps of Discovery, jumped down into the brush and planted one foot on either side of the rivulet. "Thank God!" he boasted. "I have lived to bestride the mighty Missouri!"

340   The others laughed at his extravagance. They scrambled up the gradual slope, shouting exuberantly at each other. Seaman bounded along with them, sharing their excitement. And at last, a half-mile short of the pass that separated the waters of the Missouri from those of the Columbia, east from west, Meriwether Lewis knelt beside a spring that gushed from the rock at the foot of a hill. The pure cold water was ice in his throat, the most delicious he had ever tasted. This, he thought, exulting, was the fountain of the mighty Missouri—the source he had come three thousand miles to find!

Meriwether Lewis rested briefly beside the spring. Then he hurried up the last gentle rise to the top of a ridge, the others following. There they stopped, speechless. Lewis stared off to the west. Here at last he stood on the backbone of the continent. The wind was strong in his face, and cold, a breath from the snowy peaks of the Rocky Mountains whose mighty shoulders unfolded before him, range upon range, greater than anything he had imagined, at once an exhilarating spectacle and a sobering challenge. Standing beside him, Seaman lifted his nose to the wind and the tantalizing mysteries it carried.

Lewis and his men stood a moment in silence, broken only by the strong breezes and the fluttering of the flag at the end of the pole in Hugh McNeal's hands.

Eagerness broke the spell. The group plunged down the trail, steeper on the western side of the mountain, much steeper, twisting downward through a heavy growth of pines. Less than a mile from the top Lewis broke away from the trail toward the green, leafy growth that marked the course of a stream. A moment later, crashing through the brush, Lewis dropped to his knees beside a pretty mountain stream that gathered speed and volume as it rushed down the hillside.

Seaman, in his customary way, thrust his face into the clear mountain stream to drink from the bottom, lifting his head after a moment with dripping jaws. Meriwether Lewis cupped the cold water in his palms and drank eagerly. Words formed that he would later write in his journal, seeking in quiet words to express a boundless joy: "Here I first tasted of the water of the great Columbia River."

The dream he had nurtured for a decade—a third of his lifetime—had come true. He had crossed the Continental Divide.

Beyond those mighty peaks to the west lay his final goal: the Pacific Ocean.

341

Part five

down

to the

sea

29

The means I had of communicating with these people was by way of Drewyer who understood perfectly the common language of jesticulation or signs. . . . it is true that this language is imperfect and liable to error but is much less so than would be expected. the strong parts of the ideas are seldom mistaken.
—MERIWETHER LEWIS, A u g u s t   1 4 ,   1 8 0 5

n the morning of August 13, 1805, Meriwether Lewis, three soldiers, and his dog Seaman came down the steep trail from what would come to be called Lemhi Pass to the broad river valley that was the homeland of the Shoshonis.

The first Indians Lewis sighted were two women and a man, with some dogs, about a mile distant. While Hugh McNeal held the flag high on its pole, Lewis made the sign of friendship with his blanket—to no avail. As soon as the Indians saw them, the women jumped up and fled. The man waited until the strangers were close enough for Lewis to shout to him before he retreated out of sight.

"Damn it!" Lewis swore. "They can't all run from us!"

Curious about the Indian dogs who lingered behind their masters, Seaman trotted eagerly toward them. They were a nondescript pack, all of them with their ribs showing, and the sight of the huge black dog advancing on them produced great excitement, causing them to yelp and mill about. But before Seaman or any of his companions could get close, the dogs ran off. When Seaman started to race after them, Meriwether Lewis whistled him back.

Within an hour the explorers came suddenly upon three Indian women digging roots in the grassy verge of a gully. The approach of the white men had been concealed from the natives by deep ravines. The two groups confronted each other unexpectedly at a distance of no more than thirty paces.

One of the Indians, a young woman, jumped to her feet and ran off as swiftly as a deer. The others, an old woman and a child, were slower to react. When they realized that they could not escape, they sat on the ground and bent their heads in resignation, as if presenting their vulnerable necks for the blow that was certain to follow. As Seaman trotted toward them, he heard the old woman murmur to the child in a low chant, sounds similar to those he had heard from Sacajawea.

Lewis called out to the Newfoundland. "Easy, boy, let's not frighten them."

Placing his rifle on the ground, Lewis walked up to the old woman. He seized her bony hand, lifted her gently to her feet, stripped back his sleeve to reveal the white skin of his arm and said, "*Tab-ba-bone!*"

Trembling, the woman stared first at his arm and then into his blue eyes, so different from her own. "*Tab-ba-bone?*" she repeated in a quavering voice. The word sounded very different on her dry lips than on his. Her puzzlement yielded to sudden understanding. She swung toward the child, who had momentarily forgotten her fear as she gaped at the Bear Dog standing amiably a few feet from her. "*Tab-ba-bone!*" the old woman cried, her voice now crackling with excitement.

At this moment the young woman who had run off reappeared on a rise about fifty yards away. Lewis turned quickly to Drouillard. "Have the old woman call the other one back. McNeal, let's have the blanket and some of those trinkets. And Seaman, sit! Don't move until I tell you!"

The old woman seemed to comprehend readily the gist of Drouillard's signs. She beckoned to the younger woman, who started forward slowly, poised to flee. By this time McNeal was laying out a display of beads, pewter mirrors, and other gifts on the blanket. The young woman's round face and small,

346

sturdy figure reminded Seaman so much of Sacajawea that he began to moan back in his throat and stamp his feet.

"Stay!" Lewis said firmly. And then, speaking to the child, he said encouragingly, "Go ahead, you can touch him. The Bear Dog will not harm you."

His tone and gestures gave meaning to incomprehensible words. The child took a tentative step closer to the dog and reached out. Her fingers grazed the top of Seaman's head. She jerked them back as if burned. Seaman's tongue lolled out of his mouth.

As soon as the women grasped the friendly intentions of the white strangers, their fear quickly evaporated. Soon they were exclaiming over their gifts, showing them to each other, and chattering animatedly. Meriwether Lewis daubed each of their cheeks with vermilion, which appeared to delight them almost as much as their presents. And the Shoshoni child found the courage to pet Seaman, her black eyes round with awe over the dignified obedience of the Bear Dog who sat at his master's command without moving.

The Indian women joined Seaman and his companions as they started along the trail, now too broad and plainly marked to miss. The road ran parallel to a stream off to the left, set in a pretty valley. The river interested Lewis almost as much as what lay ahead on the trail.

They had walked no more than two miles when Seaman's ear's pricked up and he trotted alertly ahead of the others. The sharp-eared Drouillard also heard something. He held up his hand in a signal to halt. "Horses!" he said. "Many horses come."

They appeared in a rush on the road ahead—at least sixty Shoshoni warriors on horseback, armed with bows and arrows except for a few with old trade muskets. They were visibly agitated and ready for battle. When they saw the strangers, they pulled up sharply.

Without hesitation Meriwether Lewis placed his rifle on the ground at his feet. He took the flag from McNeal and, selecting an impressive warrior at the head of the

347

band of Indians, advanced toward him at a measured pace, smiling and calling out, *"Tab-ba-bone!* And I hope that means something to you, you hawk-eyed Hannibal. I come in peace."

The chief glared down at Lewis and his men. He was relatively small in stature but had an imposing presence. His skin was dark, more like the Sioux than the lighter-skinned Mandans and Minitarees. His fierce expression was accentuated by his gaunt features. His black hair hung loose and was cropped short. Like all of the warriors ranged about him, he was dressed in a long, loose shirt ornamented with quills painted in different colors, worn over full antelope skin leggings. But his most singular garment was a kind of tippet draped over his shoulders, fashioned of a fur collar of otterskin from which hung innumerable tight rolls of white ermine—at least a hundred skins in every cape!

As Lewis and the Shoshoni confronted each other, the three Indian women rushed forward, jabbering excitedly and displaying their gifts. Lewis heard the old one say, *"Tab-ba-bone!"* as she stabbed a bony finger toward Lewis. He took this cue to display once more the remarkable whiteness of his skin under his shirt. This excited all of the Indians. The little girl, who had also been babbling for attention, rushed over to Seaman and threw her arms around the Newfoundland's neck. This seemed to excite the Shoshonis even more.

Abruptly the chief swung down from his horse. He stepped over to Meriwether Lewis, threw his left arm over Lewis's right shoulder, and pressed his cheek to Lewis's. As he did so, he cried out loudly, *"Ah-hi-e! Ah-hi-e!"* The enthusiastic embrace left paint and grease smeared over Lewis's cheek.

"What does he mean?" Lewis asked Drouillard, who was now suffering the same greeting.

"I t'ink it mean he very happy, he much pleased."

Other important warriors had dismounted, and they, too, pressed their painted cheeks to those of the white men, one after another, until Meriwether Lewis rolled a despairing eye at his companions and thought that he would soon become very tired of the Shoshoni national hug.

For the next thirty-six hours Meriwether Lewis and his party were treated with ceremonious courtesy by the Shoshonis at their village beside the Lemhi River. The chief, whose name was Cameahwait, had a lodge prepared for his guests. The Indians took off their moccasins, a sign of trust, as they sat in the council circle, and there were speeches on both sides, Drouillard translating by signs with surprising effectiveness. An elaborately formal pipe ceremony sealed their friendship. The Indians celebrated long into the night in the manner the men of the expedition had witnessed all across the Plains, with tireless music and dancing. Lewis begged off at midnight, exhausted by his march.

He went to his blanket hungry. He and his men had had the last of their meat the night before. The Shoshonis had nothing to offer but some cakes made of serviceberries, which Cameahwait generously shared.

The Snake Indians, Meriwether Lewis learned, lived a meager existence in the mountains, often going hungry, but here they were safe from their enemies, who had never followed them to their mountain home. When there were salmon in the river—surely, Lewis thought, that mean this stream did lead to the Columbia!—they had fish to eat. In the winter they went hungry. In the spring and at the end of summer they crossed the mountain and descended to the Missouri to hunt buffalo. Whenever possible they went with other Shoshoni bands or joined with friendly Flathead Indians, for the protection of numbers. Even so they ventured only as far into the Plains as necessary to find the buffalo herds, for always the Pahkees waited to attack them. Just this past spring Cameahwait's people had been attacked, their lodges destroyed and twenty warriors killed. It was in mourning for these losses that Cameahwait and most of the other warriors had cut their hair short.

The chief impressed Lewis. A Shoshoni did not become a chief by inheritance. All Shoshonis were equal, Cameahwait explained gravely, each warrior was his own master. A man was followed by others only when he won their confidence. He did not command; he led by his example and inspiration. Cameahwait, Lewis saw, was such a man. No man in a village of a hundred warriors commanded as much respect.

Poor the Snakes might be, but they had one thing Lewis prized—horses. Part of the herd, which he estimated at seven hundred horses, was on display the day after his arrival when the Indians staged an antelope hunt. Armed only with bows and arrows, they tried to run down an antelope by riding after it in relays until they wore the fleet animal down. Though this day's hunt was a total failure, Lewis had the opportunity to observe the Shoshoni's expert horsemanship and the quality of their mounts, many of them superb specimens.

Lewis lost no time telling Cameahwait of his goal of reaching the western ocean, and of his need for horses.

350   Cameahwait seemed responsive. He agreed to accompany Lewis back to the forks of the river beyond the mountain, and to bring horses to help carry the white men's baggage.

When the time came to leave, however, Lewis discovered that most of the chief's followers had turned reluctant. The same Indians who had danced and celebrated with his men two nights in a row with great merriment now regarded them with sullen suspicion.

"What's got into them?" Lewis demanded of Drouillard.

"Some of dem say, we are not what we pretend. Dat we speak with double tongue."

"But they were so damned pleased with us last night!"

"Dey don't like cross de mountain. Dey t'ink we might lead them to ambush."

"By the Lord! They think we're in league with the Pah-kees?"

"Dat is what dey t'ink."

Dismayed, Meriwether Lewis tried not to show it. Any such reaction would merely confirm the Indians' suspicion. He knew Cameahwait had been impressed with the white men's generosity that morning when Lewis had shared with him the last of his flour, with which Lewis made a kind of pudding with berries. He also thought the chief a brave and intelligent leader. If he was to have his horses, he thought, it would only be through winning Cameahwait over.

Facing the chief in front of his lodge, Lewis spoke carefully but vigorously. "I am sorry that you and your people have so little confidence in us. Among white men, it is considered disgraceful to lie even to an enemy or to attempt to trap him by falsehood. And we come not as enemies but friends." Cameahwait regarded him impassively, and Lewis asked Drouillard in an aside, "Do you think he understands that?"

"He understan'."

"Tell him if his people continue to think so meanly of us, no white men will come to trade with the Snakes, or to bring them guns and ammunition with which to kill the antelope and the buffalo and defend themselves against their enemies."

While Drouillard translated by means of a rapid sequence of gestures, Lewis studied the hostile faces surrounding him. It annoyed him that the Indians were so capricious, singing and dancing for their visitors one moment, suspecting them of skulduggery the next. Sometimes all it took was a single whisperer, one man afraid or suspicious, to infect a crowd. The disease was not unknown among whites, Lewis thought grudgingly.

When Drouillard stopped signing and glanced at him expectantly, Lewis faced Cameahwait, staring into the Shoshoni's black eyes without wavering. "I must go back over the mountain to meet my people as I have told you. There is a party of white men coming to the place where the two rivers meet. The Shoshoni woman I have spoken of is with them. Their boats are filled with many things, including gifts from the Great White Father for the Snakes. If there are among the Shoshonis any men who are not afraid to die, who are men and warriors, come with me, and you will see the truth of what I have said."

From the flash of anger in Cameahwait's eyes Meriwether Lewis knew that he had struck a nerve. He had challenged the bravery of the Snakes.

"Cameahwait will go with you—he is not afraid to die!"

When Lewis rode out beside the chief a short time later, the impulsive nature of the Shoshonis was soon verified. Only seven or eight warriors joined them as they set off. They had scarcely ridden a mile before another dozen or so joined them, and soon afterward what seemed like the entire Shoshoni village, men and women, were riding along behind, singing and chanting, all in good humor, their earlier moodiness as evanescent as the wind.

Two nights later, lying sleepless at camp in the lower part of Shoshoni Cove, within sight of the forks of the Jefferson River, Meriwether Lewis had reason to worry about the childlike capriciousness of the Indians. By then a large number of the natives who had followed him across the mountain pass had deserted. He listened to Cameahwait snoring beside him—or feigning sleep—and thought that the fate of the expedition now seemed to rest on the uncertain balance of Shoshoni whims.

Their first enthusiasm had begun to wane even as they crossed Lemhi Pass and started down the mountain. That first night everyone, white and red, went hungry. Sensing the unnatural quiet of the camp, Lewis had Drouillard remind the Indians of the presents and foodstuffs carried in the expedition's canoes. He also had Drouillard describe the giant black man who traveled with the whites, a man whose skin was neither red nor white but as black as night. This giant was enormously strong, Drouillard said, and he had curly hair unlike any the Indians had ever seen. Even the irrepressible good nature and remarkable intelligence of the Bear Dog, whose tricks they had seen and who listened just like a man when the white man spoke, did not intrigue the Shoshonis as much as the promise of meeting the black giant. Lewis was

convinced that only the possibility of seeing York kept many
of the Indians with him.

Their suspicion resurfaced the next morning when Lewis
sent Drouillard and Shields out to hunt. His request to the
chief to have his warriors stay behind for fear they might alarm
any game in the vicinity appeared to some of the red men to
be evidence of duplicity. The hunt might be a ruse, enabling
the advance spies to warn Pahkees waiting below so they could
prepare a trap. Under pretense of riding out on their own,
some of the warriors followed the white hunters on horseback.
When they all had disappeared, the brooding among the remaining Shoshonis became almost palpable.

One of the Indians shouted. The others instantly became
alarmed, lethargy falling away like a blanket shed. An Indian
rider raced toward them, whipping his horse, waving one arm
frantically above his head. But as he drew near a different
murmur of excitement began to spread among the Shoshonis.

Then Cameahwait was shouting at his white friend.
"What is it?" Lewis asked, forgetting that his words were
meaningless to the chief.

353

But the chief smiled broadly. *Your hunters!* With his hands
he pantomimed the actions of a man with a rifle. *White hunters
have killed a deer!*

There was a headlong rush down the mountain. The Indians rode at a wild gallop. When Lewis, riding double behind
a warrior, protested the pace, the Shoshoni leaped off the horse,
flung the rope bridle at Lewis and ran ahead on foot. Seaman
was so excited that he raced after the Indians and was a
quarter-mile ahead before he realized that Lewis had fallen
behind.

When the meat-starved Indians reached the fallen deer
they fell upon it in a frénzy, like a pack of animals, tearing off
chunks of raw flesh and pieces of intestine and stuffing the
bits into their mouths while the blood ran down their chins.
Sympathetic yet appalled by the sight, Lewis had Shields re-
serve a quarter of the deer and give the rest to the natives.

A short time later the scene was repeated when the band

came upon a second deer Drouillard had shot. Here, beside a creek, Lewis stopped to cook some of the meat for himself and his men after allotting most of it to the Shoshonis. The Indians devoured everything without cooking—down to the soft parts of the hoofs. Only when Drouillard arrived with a third deer he had slain and Lewis portioned it out in the same manner, only then did the ravenous hunger of the Indians begin to be satisfied.

For a short while the white men's generosity with meat, and proof that the hunters had not been sent out as a trick, quieted the Indians' fears. But when the party moved on across Shoshoni Cove and came within sight of the forks below, there was no sign of the boats. A murmuring began again.

Meriwether Lewis tried to hide his consternation. He had already warned Cameahwait that his fellow white chief might have been delayed coming up the river, but no such caution could prevent the restless unease that immediately gripped the Indians. When Cameahwait insisted on presenting Lewis and his companions each with a handsome tippet—the chief himself placed the cape around Lewis's shoulders—Lewis guessed that his purpose was more than sudden generosity. The tippet made the sun-dark white men in their skin garments look more than ever exactly like the warriors around them.

Realizing that some of the Indians were already slipping away and that he was in danger of losing them all, Lewis sought a way to defuse their suspicion. On impulse he held his rifle out to Cameahwait, and he placed his cocked hat on the chief's head. As the startled chief took the gun from him, Lewis said, while Drouillard hastily signed his words, "Take my rifle as proof that I have not deceived my friends, the Shoshonis. If you find any of your enemies hiding in those bushes down below, use the gun on me, for then I would have lied to you and you should defend yourself."

Lewis had his companions do the same. Now, his actions clearly said, not only were he and his men unarmed but no enemies could tell them from the Indians. Seeing that he had gained some credence with Cameahwait but that others re-

354

mained uneasy, Lewis decided to gamble on another strata-gem. He announced to Cameahwait that his friend with the boats had promised to send someone forward with a message he would leave at the forks, saying when he would be coming.

Lewis smiled to cover his concern as he explained to Drouillard. "We must stall them, or we'll lose them all. I left a note for Clark on a willow pole at the forks. Bring it back to me. I have to make them think it's a letter to me from Clark, and that he is to arrive soon at the forks."

At Lewis's suggestion an Indian rode with Drouillard down to the forks of the river, about two miles away. While they were gone, Lewis displayed a general cheerfulness that hid his concern as he counted the remaining members of the Shoshoni band. By the Lord, more than half of them were gone! How had they managed to melt away like that?

He worried about the note. A couple of weeks ago, at another fork of the Jefferson, Lewis had left another note for Clark on a willow spear. Unfortunately he had carelessly cho-sen a green shoot. A beaver had come along before Clark did. Finding the green pole tasty, he had chewed it off and carried it away, taking Lewis's note into the river with him. When Clark had arrived at the forks and found no note to guide him, he had turned up the wrong branch ...

What if this latest note had met some similar accident? What if Clark had been delayed far down the river? What if —God forbid—a band of Pahkees *did* by chance appear?

Soon, however, Drouillard and the Indian returned triumphantly, Drouillard brandishing the note retrieved from the forks. Meriwether Lewis made a show of reading it before he announced to Cameahwait, "It is as I hoped. My fellow chief is but a short distance down the river, and he will soon be here to join me with all of our goods."

The ruse calmed some of the Indians' fears. Lewis led them to the lower part of the cove and made camp. But with the coming of darkness all of the natives' fears revived. Most of them, refusing to sleep near the campfires, slipped off into the dark to hide among the bushes. Lewis realized there was

355

even a deliberate precaution behind Cameahwait's decision to sleep alongside Lewis's mosquito netting.

Lewis suffered through a long and sleepless night, uncertain what the dawn would bring. Beside him, Cameahwait grunted and snored. Nearby, Seaman snapped futilely at the whining mosquitoes that plagued him. Around them the cove was dark and still.

Where was William Clark?

Where were the boats?

30 every article about us appeared to excite astonishment in their minds; the appearance of the men, their arms, the canoes, our manner of working them, the black man York and the sagacity of my dog were equally objects of admiration.
     —MERIWETHER LEWIS, August 17, 1805

*O*n the morning of August 17, 1805, William Clark had the detachment up early. The men dragged themselves wearily from their blankets, splashing cold water from the river in their faces to shock themselves awake. All of them had sore feet and muscles that seemed more painful in the morning. Pryor was nursing a dislocated arm, Charbonneau a twisted ankle, Gass a strained back, Clark the draining tumor on his ankle. Yet each day they pushed themselves to the edge of exhaustion again, lifting and towing the canoes over rapids and shoals in the shallow, narrowing stream, spending most of the day in the icy water. At night even the clouds of mosquitoes could not keep them awake.

The previous day Clark had sent scouts up the river. They had reported a fork about four miles ahead by land, more than twice that distance along the twisting course of the Jefferson River. From the forks, they said, an Indian trail climbed toward the mountains to the west. Listening to the news, Sacajawea felt a stab of anticipation. *So near!* The thought whispered in her mind like a breeze in the tops of the tall pines. So near that the steps of her People were still imprinted in the dust of the trail.

While the detachment started upriver with the boats, Clark, Sacajawea and Charbonneau walked on shore. When Clark paused to check on the boats' progress, Sacajawea and her husband ranged ahead. The stocky interpreter was relieved not to have to work in the water hauling a canoe. He knew the principal reason Clark had him ashore was the presence of his squaw and their *bébé*, but that was all right. Walking was easier than dragging the boats, whatever the excuse.

Sacajawea scanned the terrain ahead, her eyes always searching. This land was familiar to her—the smell of it, the weight of the mountains, the very shape of the long grassy slopes, the sage brush as high as a man's head, and the leaning heads of the sunflowers along the riverbank. She had left it as a captive, a child tongue-tied with fear. She was returning as a woman, walking with her husband, carrying her first child on her back.

358   She glanced behind her at Clark's tall figure, now about a hundred hards away. He was hatless this morning, and his red hair burned in the sun like a flame. She thought of the incident a few days before when Clark had sternly reprimanded her husband . . .

She had quarreled with Charbonneau at supper. She had spoken defiantly to him, something an Indian woman never did. And he had struck her sharply.

Some of the men had jumped up, protesting. Captain Redhead immediately intervened. He grabbed Charbonneau by the shoulder and spun him around. He was so angry that his face was as red as his hair. "I will have none of that, Chabono, do y' hear? Ye should be ashamed to strike a woman, and ye'll not do it again!"

"*Ma femme*, she say—" ·

"I don't give a damn what she said! Strike her again, and ye'll answer to me!"

Before William Clark's wrath Charbonneau had turned

silent and surly. He hadn't anticipated the reaction, for he had done nothing more than any Indian warrior or any squaw man did when his woman gave him trouble, was disobedient, or spoke out of turn. He didn't think of himself as having done anything wrong, and here he was being glared at by his fellows as if he were some kind of pariah, and dressed down by Captain Clark in front of everyone. But Charbonneau was a prudent man. He knew better than to defy the redhead.

At the time Sacajawea had taken a sneaking pleasure in Captain Redhead's quick defense of her. Afterward she felt a sense of pride. His actions said that she was a person of worth who must not be struck like a stubborn animal.

In truth, she had been neither hurt nor surprised by Charbonneau's blow. Clark's response had surprised her more. A squaw who defied her husband expected to be punished for it. That was simply the way it was. In the white man's world, apparently, it was different. A white man—even a chief—did not strike his woman with his fist. She wondered how white men kept their wives from being disobedient . . .

Charbonneau had rarely punished her. Though often brusque and demanding, he was more tolerant than any Minitaree warrior of his station. An important man, an interpreter, who could also hunt and trap and do many other things, he treated her well. She knew that in his heart she had become his favorite wife, ahead even of Otter Woman. And he was very proud and gentle with Pomp, whom he called Jean Baptiste.

A blow was not such an important thing to an Indian woman. A warrior did not punish his children, especially a boy, because that might instill fear where one wanted only courage. But a squaw was another matter.

Something caught Sacajawea's eye, diverting her thoughts. "Husband!" she called out in Minitaree. "What do you see—there on the hill?"

"Eh? What's dat? I no see . . . by gar, *oui!* Somet'ing . . . someone come!"

Unable to contain her feelings, Sacajawea began to leap up and down, dancing with joy. Charbonneau gaped at her in astonishment. "They are my People!" she cried.

There were three or four riders in view, Indians on horseback. From their garments and adornments Sacajawea knew instantly that they were Shoshoni. The fur tippets worn by the men, the long shirts ornamented with quills and with the tail of the antelope left on, the moccasins of one rider covered with the skin of a polecat and the tail trailing at his heels—yes, yes, they were her People!

Hopping about with excitement, she whirled and waved to Clark, who quickened his pace when he saw her signal. She placed the fingers of her right hand in her mouth and sucked them, making the universal Indian sign that said, *These are my People! Among them was I suckled and given life!*

The Indian riders were now close enough to see that she was the Indian woman of whom they had heard, who traveled with the white men they had come to find. They began to sing enthusiastically. The sounds rang in Sacajawea's ear with a special magic, awakening the voices of her childhood. Tears blurred her eyes.

By the time William Clark reached her side, Sacajawea was blinking away her tears. She was determined to present a face of calm and serenity, its surface unmarred by choppy waves. But it was difficult, very difficult.

Suddenly she clapped her hands and laughed aloud with pleasure. She had recognized Drouillard on one of the horses. Without his skin cap, wearing a fine tippet and riding a Shoshoni horse, he looked exactly like an Indian.

Captain Redhead, more animated than she had ever seen him, began talking to Drouillard. Captain Lewis, she heard, was waiting not far ahead. He was encamped above the forks with a party of Shoshonis who had come over the mountain with him from their home on the river . . .

Everything followed very quickly. Clark alerted the men with the boats that Lewis had found the Shoshonis and was waiting for them with a party of Indians who had many horses.

Louis Charbonneau

Then Clark, Charbonneau, Sacajawea, and Pomp set off with the Shoshonis. Before she could catch her breath, it seemed, or quiet the rapid beating of her heart, she was riding double with a Snake warrior, wondering why he had cropped his hair short, which was usually a sign of mourning. Her thoughts were not only of the People but also of her family whom she had believed lost to her forever, her father, her sisters and brothers. Were any of them among the people waiting on the hill above the forks? Would they know her, a woman who had been to them only a child?

They turned up the slope near the forks of the river, climbing toward a broad meadow surrounded by mountains. She recognized Shoshoni Cove, for here her people had often camped when they came over the mountain to hunt. As the horse she rode drew near the camp, she saw Captain Lewis standing by a fire, a proud Shoshoni chief beside him. Other Indians were all about the camp, more than two dozen men and some squaws as well. All were watching her and Charbonneau and Captain Clark on their horses.

Sacajawea slipped from her mount as soon as the rider halted it. For a moment she stood uncertain. Then she began to walk toward the watching Indians, her heart pounding.

One of the Indians, a young woman like herself, broke away from the others. She ran toward Sacajawea. "Ah-hi-ee! My friend—it is you!"

Sacajawea cried out as she recognized Willow Child, with whom she had played in her village. They had been together in the river when the Minitarees attacked, and both had been kidnapped. After a few days they had become separated, taken off by their separate captors, and Sacajawea had never seen her friend again.

Now Willow Child's story emerged through shrieks and tears of joy, while Meriwether Lewis and William Clark looked on in amazement at the transformation in the impassive Indian woman who had traveled up the Missouri with them. Willow Child had escaped one night while her captor slept. She had followed the river back toward the place where the three rivers

met, subsisting on berries, hiding in the bushes when a band
of Pahkees passed by. Eventually she had come upon another
group of Shoshonis who were returning from a buffalo hunt.
With them she had crossed the mountains and found her own
people. And now her friend had also returned!

The Shoshoni chief welcomed William Clark with a
warm, cheek-to-cheek embrace (while Meriwether Lewis
grinned). Clark sat on a white robe and smoked with Cameahwait and two other chiefs, taking off his moccasins as the
Shoshonis did. When talk stumbled, Lewis looked around for
his interpreter, Charbonneau, and his wife, hoping that all the
feminine squealing was over—though he admitted to himself
that he had been moved when he was told the gist of Willow
Child's story and understood the reason for the tearful reunion.
Beckoning Charbonneau over to the little grove of willow
boughs that had been set up for a council, Lewis told him to
bring Sacajawea. Drouillard was still below with the boats.
Sacajawea and Charbonneau would have to interpret alone
until one of the Frenchmen arrived.

Sacajawea entered the council circle demurely, in a manner befitting a woman in such a situation. She sat with her
head bowed, not looking up. She was among her People now,
and never had she known a woman of the People to sit in a
council.

As Captain Lewis spoke, she listened closely. With Charbonneau's help she was able to translate Lewis's speech into
Shoshoni. The Indian words, so long unused, began to flow
more smoothly as she talked. She was grateful for the times
she had been able to talk to Otter Woman in their own tongue;
otherwise she might have forgotten. She said that the white
chiefs were grateful for the friendship of the Shoshonis, and
that they brought greetings and gifts from the Great Father of
the Seventeen Nations who lived in Washington.

The chief sitting opposite her—she had not yet dared to
look into his eyes—answered for his people, welcoming Chief
Redhead as he had earlier welcomed Chief Lewis. As Sacajawea listened, haltingly translating the Shoshoni words into

Minitaree for Charbonneau to reinterpret, she felt a trembling inside her that she did not at first comprehend. There was something familiar in the chief's voice ... something that teased her memory.

She tried to peer at Cameahwait without raising her head. She gasped aloud. Her heart began to race. And then, as disbelief gave way to full recognition, she felt tears gush like the waters from a hot spring, scalding her cheeks. She rose, trembling. On weak legs she walked the few steps toward the Shoshoni chief. Taking her blanket, she knelt before Cameahwait, placed the blanket over both of them, and threw her arms around his neck.

The white men looked upon this extraordinary scene with their mouths open. Cameahwait, at first taken by surprise, appeared to struggle to control his own emotions while he awkwardly returned the embrace and spoke quietly to the Indian woman.

After a few minutes Sacajawea was able to compose herself. She returned to her place in the council circle facing the Shoshoni chief. When she told Charbonneau what she had discovered, he relayed the information to Lewis and Clark, explaining the symbolic meaning of Sacajawea's gesture in placing her blanket over herself and the Shoshoni chief. By an almost unbelievable coincidence, not only had the expedition found Sacajawea's own band of Shoshonis, but the principal chief, Cameahwait, was her brother!

363

For Sacajawea the rest of that day was a blur. The brief morning council was followed by the arrival of the entire Corps of Discovery with the canoes at noon. For dinner the white men shared some of their flour and meat, after which they entertained the Shoshonis. The Indians marveled over the color and strength and agility of the giant black man, York, whom Sacajawea seldom thought of any more as black but only as her friend. They shouted with amazement and approval over the tricks performed by the Bear Dog who was also her friend.

And they stared in disbelief when Captain Lewis fired his air gun, the most incomprehensible marvel of all, true evidence of great medicine.

Late in the afternoon, beneath a canopy made from one of the boats' sails, while the shadows of the mountains grew long across the cove, the formal council was held. This time the translation was three-way—Sacajawea as the Shoshoni interpreter, Charbonneau communicating to her in Minitaree, Francois Labiche translating Charbonneau's French into English for the captains. To the participants the procedure did not seem too cumbersome. Indians at council were never in a hurry, and both Lewis and Clark had learned a similar patience.

Sitting at the center of the council, Sacajawea was able to speak with composure now. She told her People why the white men had come up the long river, of their need for the fine horses which the Snakes owned in abundance, of the future trade that would come to the Shoshonis because of their friendship with these first whites to reach their homeland, and of the goal the white men had to cross the great mountains and reach the giant lake at the edge of the world.

It was the most exciting day of her life.

Lewis and Clark decided that, while Lewis bartered for horses at Shoshoni Cove and prepared to transport the expedition's baggage over the mountain, Clark and eleven men would go ahead to the Shoshoni village. From there Clark would explore the river system for a passage to the Columbia River.

Sacajawea and Charbonneau accompanied Clark, along with Willow Child and most of the Shoshoni warriors—who would be preparing to leave shortly for their autumn buffalo hunt.

Thus Sacajawea returned to the valley where she had been born and to the village of her People beside the Lemhi River. The river, only ten paces across, was smaller than her memory of it. So was the village, which numbered about twenty-five lodges made of willow boughs. She learned that the skin lodges she remembered from years ago had been destroyed by the Pahkees during this past spring's buffalo hunt, in a raid in which twenty Shoshoni warriors had died.

All of the people of the village, women and children as well as warriors, surrounded her and Captain Clark and the rest of Clark's party. They stared in wonder especially at York, who had accompanied the group, but they also chattered excitedly about the Snake woman who accompanied the whites, a woman of their own village—for many of them remembered her.

The afternoon of her arrival at the village, Sacajawea functioned once again as an interpreter, along with Charbonneau and Labiche, as William Clark questioned Cameahwait and an old man of the village about a possible route to the Pacific Ocean. The news was not encouraging. The way to the south was impassable, said the old man, who was called Toby. It led across mountains and deserts where no man could survive. To the north there was a westward-flowing river forking with the Lemhi River, but it plunged into steep mountains where there was no trail to follow, the cliffs falling straight to the river, which became an endless rapids that no boat of any kind could pass.

Later that afternoon, determined to explore the rivers to the north for himself, William Clark and his men left the Shoshoni village, guided by Toby, who knew the rivers well. Charbonneau and Sacajawea stayed behind. They were to lead some of the Shoshonis back to Lewis's camp the next day, bringing a sufficient number of horses to carry all of the expedition's baggage across the mountain.

The entire village had seen that Sacajawea was now an important person among the white men, one who sat at their councils and spoke for them. That circumstance, coupled with the miracle of her return from the dead, made her a celebrity. The women and children crowded close around her that evening, eager to question her and to listen to her story.

There was sadness, too, in her homecoming. She learned

365

that all of the family she had left behind were dead except for Cameahwait and another brother, who was away from the village hunting. But her sister had had a boy, now motherless. To the approval of the entire village, Sacajawea promptly adopted the child as her own.

Charbonneau, with his strange manner of speech and his bushy beard, was a source of great curiosity to them. On the day following their arrival at the village, however, the interpreter's presence as Sacajawea's husband became more than a novelty.

She was kneeling in front of the lodge especially prepared for her, displaying her son on his white doeskin robe for the admiration of the village women. There was a commotion in the crowd, which parted to let a stocky warrior push through. He peered at Sacajawea, nodded, then glared at Charbonneau. His words were loud and bold. The crowd fell silent. Sacajawea climbed slowly to her feet.

"Eh? What is dis?" Charbonneau said. "Who is dis man? What he say?"

Sacajawea looked gravely at the Indian. Though he was grayer now, older, and—or so it seemed to her—smaller, less imposing, she had no trouble recognizing him. "I am betrothed to him," she said quietly. "He has come to claim me as his wife."

"What? You tell him—you are Charbonneau's woman!" But, in spite of his bluster, Charbonneau experienced a sinking feeling in his belly, a portent of trouble. He was a squaw man. Although he knew little of Shoshonis other than his two Snake wives, he knew Indian customs well.

Sacajawea explained the custom among her people. An infant girl was often pledged in marriage to a grown man, the union to take place when the girl became a woman old enough to bear children. "I was betrothed to this man as a child," she told her husband. "My father received two horses in exchange. According to the custom of my people, he has a right to demand that the bargain be kept."

Charbonneau began to shout angrily. Bristling at his tone,

the Indian warrior shouted back at him. The words of their quarrel were incomprehensible to the two men, only the anger requiring no translation. Sacajawea bowed her head. The man to whom she had once been betrothed already had two wives, but he was insisting stubbornly on his claim. Under Shoshoni law, she knew, that claim could not be denied.

Frightened by Charbonneau's yelling, Pomp began to cry. Meriwether Lewis, hearing the commotion from the nearby lodge prepared for him by Cameahwait, walked over to see what was going on. He frowned when he discovered Charbonneau stomping back and forth at the center of a crowd, pawing his beard and shouting angry threats.

Sacajawea picked up her baby and held him, rocking him back and forth as she murmured soothing reassurances.

Abruptly the Indian who claimed her as his next wife stopped talking. He stared at Pomp, who ceased crying as the turmoil around him quieted down. The warrior now wore a heavy scowl as he spoke to Sacajawea. She answered him in Shoshoni.

367

"What he say now?" Charbonneau demanded.

"What's this all about?" asked Meriwether Lewis. He was startled when the Indian woman turned toward him with a delighted smile.

Sacajawea said to her husband, "There is no more need for scolding words."

"Eh? By gar, Charbonneau not give you to dis man—"

"He does not want me now."

Becoming exasperated, Meriwether Lewis insisted on an explanation. When he learned the root of the quarrel, he was disturbed. In the midst of his attempts to barter for horses, he wanted no trouble with the Shoshonis, nor did he wish to be confronted with a Solomon-like dilemma.

"Is no matter," Sacajawea said happily in broken English.

Through Charbonneau, suddenly mollified, she explained. As soon as the man who claimed her had discovered that she had already had a child by another man, he had announced disdainfully that he no longer wanted her.

"He's renouncing his claim?" asked Lewis, relieved.

"He say I can go with the man who hides behind the bush growing on his face."

During the few days she spent in the village of her childhood, Sacajawea lay awake at night in her lodge, listening—over the snores of her husband—to the murmur of the river nearby, her mind filled with memories. And a strange feeling grew inside her . . . the feeling of being a stranger in the place that claimed her heart.

She had come home, but she was different. She was no longer the child of her memories. This was another sadness —the discovery that, although she had come home, it was home no longer.

When William Clark returned to the Shoshoni village on August 29, 1805, he found Lewis still engaged in negotiations to purchase more horses for the expedition. Clark had explored the rivers to the north, including a western branch the Indians called the River of No Returning. He had established to his satisfaction that there was no river route through the mountains. But, from his old Indian guide Toby, he had learned of the trail taken by the Nez Percés, a nation of Indians who lived west of the mountains on a tributary of the Columbia, whenever they came over the Bitterroot Mountains to the Missouri valley to hunt buffalo. This was a land route by way of a trail that was difficult, rocky and heavily timbered, with little or no game to be found along the way. Clark saw this route as the expedition's best choice, and Meriwether Lewis concurred.

That night, the eve of the expedition's departure, Sacajawea sat in the lodge of her brother. Cameahwait said, "We will go over the mountains at sunrise to hunt the buffalo. All of the village will go."

"The People are hungry. It is right that you go."

"And you, my sister?"

"I go with my husband. We go to find the great lake where other white men live, where the sea shells my brother wears in his hair are found."

Cameahwait nodded. He had known her answer before asking. "The bearded one, he is a good husband to you?"

"Yes. I am his Number One wife." The dimness of the lodge hid her smile. "He is not good steering a boat, but he is a good husband. And he is father to my son."

"Your choice is the same a warrior would make."

Or an important person of the tribe, Cameahwait thought. It was disconcerting at times to realize that his sister held important status among the white men. The two chiefs treated her with great respect, and it was evident that she traveled with them as an equal in station to any of the white soldiers. When the white chiefs counciled with the red men, Sacajawea and her husband sat in the council circle.

Cameahwait felt pride that his sister had returned to her village in this way. They were of one blood, one blanket. At the same time, it was . . . unsettling. Among her own people, a Shoshoni woman did not have such importance. She collected berries when they were ripe, dug roots from the meadow, attended to the horses, cooked, dressed skins, made garments for herself and her family, collected wood and built fires, tended the lodge, packed the baggage whenever the family moved to a new camp. 369

She did not sit in councils, or speak for the chiefs.

"It is good that you have come back to the land of your fathers."

Sacajawea bowed her head, tears in her eyes.

"But it is right that you do not stay."

She glanced up quickly. Blinking as she struggled to compose herself, she nodded. "It is true."

"You are different from Shoshoni woman. Living among the Minitarees and the white men has made you different."

"I am Shoshoni."

"Yes, but . . . you are more. You are not only of one place. You are of two places."

For a long time she was silent, gazing at her brother with love in her heart, and with sadness. "Yes," she whispered at last, "I am more."

She was of two places now. Of two people. Her heart was pulled in two directions, but there was no doubt in her mind, only sadness.

"I will see my brother again, and my sister's child, who is now my own son and who will sleep in the lodge of my brother."

Cameahwait nodded, seeing her tears. Such displays were unbecoming in a warrior. They were natural in a woman.

It was right that his sister felt sorrow. Parting was a little death.

When Cameahwait went down with the People to hunt the buffalo in the morning, her face would turn instead toward the setting sun, toward the place beyond the shining mountains where the white men lived on the shore of the bad-tasting water.

31

we travelled untill after dark in hopes to find water but could not find any. we found *Some Spots of Snow* so we *Camped* on the top of the *Mountain* and melted *Some Snow*. this *Snow* appears to lay all the year on this *Mount*. we drank a little portable *Soup* and lay down without any thing else to *Satisfy* our hunger.
—JOHN ORDWAY, *Sept. 15, 1805*

The pack horses led the way—in the end Meriwether Lewis had succeeded in purchasing twenty-eight to add to the two Shoshoni horses that William Clark had obtained from Cameahwait. Following the column, Seaman glanced back over his shoulder toward the Shoshoni village. The women and children congregated at the edge of the camp, watching him as they had throughout his brief visit. Some of the village dogs tagged along for a while before dropping off, one by one.

Just as the Shoshonis had initially been frightened of the white strangers, so the Indian dogs had been wary of the Bear Dog, who was nearly twice the size of the largest Shoshoni dog. But Seaman, as curious as his master, was soon going through a ceremonial sniffing of noses and a general head-to-toe examination with various dogs, all stiff-legged but with wagging tails. A few of the Indian dogs cringed and barked and slunk away, but the newcomer's amiable nature was soon apparent. Before long Seaman was romping along the riverbank in the midst of a pack, taking in the neighborhood smells, drinking deeply of the cold water of the Lemhi River.

Enjoying his brief stay in the village, Seaman had been
at his best when Sacajawea proudly showed him off. Then he
strutted along beside the Indian woman in obvious pleasure
at all the attention he was receiving. He also sat and lay down
at her command—simple tricks she had carefully rehearsed,
to Meriwether Lewis's amusement, during the journey up the
Missouri. The amazed reaction of the Shoshoni villagers was
reward enough for both Seaman and Sacajawea.

Now Seaman realized that another adventure was beginning, a different phase of his journey. After so many months
on the river, the Newfoundland relished the change to walking.
He had no trouble keeping up with the men and the pack
horses—or even with the captains, who were riding.

After following the Lemhi River past the fork where
Clark had explored the River of No Returning, the expedition
headed north, led by the old Indian guide Toby and four of
his sons. The trail climbed over stony hills, overgrown low-
lands, dams, deadfalls, places where the men had to hack a
way through the thickets, and one stretch so tedious the frustrated soldiers named it Dismal Swamp. Seaman picked his
way through the tangle more easily than the men or the
horses, and he even had time along the way to explore the
wooded hills.

As the trail climbed toward a mountain pass, the slopes
became as steep as the roofs of houses. The horses frequently
slipped and stumbled, in danger of falling. One was injured.
Several others were saved only by the frantic efforts of the men
to keep them from plunging down the hillside.

The weather turned cold and drizzly. Three of Toby's
sons, not liking the treacherous climb, turned back; the old
man and one son remained. During the fourth night, it
snowed. Game was scarce, and supper that night was a few
grains of parched corn. Seaman, puzzled but uncomplaining,
went hungry.

In the morning the ground was covered with snow. The
day's march was delayed while the baggage coverings thawed

372

out. When the expedition finally got under way, they climbed
to a dividing ridge. After following it a short distance, they
discovered a creek their guide remembered. Descending the
trail beside the creek to a small valley, they came upon the
camp of a band of Indians.

These natives were Flatheads, so-called not from any
physical deformity but from the gesture used to identify them
in the sign language of the Plains. The band, which numbered
about four hundred, including eighty warriors, was en route
over the mountains to join the Shoshonis in the autumn buffalo
hunt. To Meriwether Lewis's delight, they had a fine herd of
about five hundred horses. And they proved to be very friendly,
prepared to smoke with the whites—the first ever seen on this
creek, they said—and to trade and talk.

The latter proved difficult. The Flatheads had a peculiarly
lisping manner of speaking unlike any other Indian speech the
captains had heard. Over the next three days, besides buying
and trading horses, Lewis worked at recording a vocabulary
of this difficult language. He was more successful bartering
for horses, exchanging seven of his lame ones for good, purchasing thirteen more, three of them colts.

That first night camping next to the Flatheads, Seaman
relaxed, taking his cue from the friendly relations he observed
between his companions and the Indians. When the men took
to their blankets, Seaman dozed outside the captain's tent.
There were no animal noises to disturb the quiet of the wooded
mountainside or to alert the dog to danger.

He woke in thick darkness. Clouds shrouded the moun-
taintops. The fires had burned down to coals, casting little
light beyond the circle of each fire. Seaman listened to the
silence. Something had awakened him.

He rose quietly. Near one of the sleeping men, a shadow
moved, hugging the ground. Then, off to the right, another.
With a warning growl Seaman rushed forward.

A dog gave a frightened yip. Suddenly there were a half-
dozen scrawny dogs in flight, bounding over the men who

groped their way out of muddled sleep and reached for their guns. One dog dashed by the startled sentry. Seaman's deep bark was answered by a chorus of yelps.

One of the men started to swear. "Goddam them Indian dogs! They stole my moccasins!"

When the excitement was over and order was restored to the confused camp, it was discovered that a number of hungry dogs from the Flathead camp had sneaked among the sleeping soldiers, stolen four or five pairs of moccasins, and eaten them. Seaman had interrupted their meal.

Except for that brief moment of excitement, the stop among the Flatheads was uneventful. When the Corps of Discovery parted from the Indians after three days, pleased with the encounter, they had forty horses and three colts. Able to redistribute their baggage to make the loads lighter, they proceeded on down the mountain to the Bitterroot Valley, following a handsome stream they called Clark's River.

Three nights after parting from the Flathead Indians, the expedition camped by a large creek that spilled down a canyon from the west. The Lolo Trail that followed this creek, old Toby said, would lead them across the Bitterroots to a branch of the Columbia River. The explorers called the creek Traveler's Rest Creek and their camp Traveler's Rest. There they stopped to rest and hunt.

By this time some of the men claimed to be able to feel their backbones through their bellies, but on the first day at Traveler's Rest the hunters brought in five deer. For the first time in a week everyone's stomach was full. Seaman did not have to rely on a few scraps from Meriwether Lewis or York to keep his stomach from growling.

One of the hunters, John Colter, also brought in three Flatheads he had met in the canyon. By signs they indicated that their people lived on the far side of the mountain, on a river where salmon were caught. The news confirmed Old Toby's claims about this trail.

The old guide also said that Clark's River eventually turned westward and fell into the Columbia. However, much

374

closer to Traveler's Rest—in fact, just a few miles to the north—a fork of the river had its origin in the Rocky Mountains just a short distance to the east.

That first night at Traveler's Rest, the two commanders pressed Toby for details. "You say this branch of Clark's River heads near the Missouri?" Clark asked him.

Toby grinned, showing stumps of yellowed teeth, and nodded. The garrulous old Indian liked to show off his knowledge—sometimes, Clark thought, to the point of claiming more information than he actually possessed. Toby piled up some little mounds of dirt to indicate mountains. With a stick he drew a wavy line to show the course of the river flowing from this range of the Rocky Mountains into the Bitterroot valley. Through the usual relay of interpreters—Sacajawea, Charbonneau, and Labiche on this night—Toby's intelligence was spelled out. The eastern fork of Clark's River began near an easy pass across the Continental Divide. By following this branch, a traveler would require only four sleeps to reach the Missouri from Traveler's Rest. Such a trail would follow the Medicine River on the eastern flank of the mountains, and would thus intersect with the Missouri River near White Bear Island.

Lewis and Clark exchanged sober glances. Each man was thinking of the long weeks of struggle up the shrinking course of the Missouri and Jefferson Rivers. Fifty-two exhausting days, Clark calculated, for a journey that might be made in four!

After a long silence Meriwether Lewis said, "We didn't have horses for such a march. Not then."

"And we might not have them now, had we not gone the way we did."

What else could they say? Neither man believed in looking back in a negative way. What was done was done. Still, Toby's revelation was important. "This fork will be worth exploring on our return this way," Lewis said with his customary confidence.

Clark grinned at him. "With horses."

375

From Traveler's Rest there followed three days of hard climbing over rocky hills and through precipitous hollows. Sometimes the men of the Corps of Discovery chopped a path through dense forests of spruce, pine, and fir. At length, exhausted, they crossed the ridge and camped in a small glade beside a creek that flowed westward down the mountain.

Bellies were tight again. The hunters brought in little game—only one deer and a few pheasants, hardly enough to feed the party and their two Shoshoni guides even for a day.

The next day offered rain, hail, and snow, steep ascents and descents of the thickly timbered mountains, even a stretch of fallen timber almost impossible for the horses to cross. Toby led them down the canyon where the creek was joined by another branch and became a formidable mountain stream, eighty yards wide, stony and rapid. Here, opposite a small island, they camped.

376   That day the hunters had found nothing. After a brief discussion, the men voted, with their commanders' permission, to kill one of the three colts. They cooked and ate half of it. They named the south fork of the river Colt Killed Creek.

Seaman's portion of the meat was small. He wolfed it down in one gulp and glanced up expectantly at York, who shook his head in sympathy. When Seaman wandered around the camp, anticipating tidbits here and there from the men at supper, he was disappointed. The men were in much the same state as he was, still hungry after their meal, glowering at the cooks as if some mistake had been made.

But the soldiers knew better. Part of the colt had to be saved for the next day. They already knew it would be a bad one.

Old Toby had somehow taken them away from the main trail, which wound along the top of a ridge rather than down into the canyon. A short distance below Colt Killed Creek the bottom became impassable. In the morning they would have to climb back up the mountain to the spine of the ridge. Staring

Louis Charbonneau

up at it in the sudden gloom of the canyon at evening, they saw a mountain that appeared to go straight up.

The next day even Seaman found the climbing hard. His tongue was soon hanging out. But for the men the way was much more troublesome, and for the horses almost impossible. The trail switched back and forth, sometimes climbing over rocks and fallen trees, at others angling almost straight up. Much of the way resembled a ruined landscape, where the trees had burned and toppled in every direction. Horses kept slipping. Time and again one of them lost his footing, fell down the steep slope, and crashed against a tree or rock. The men struggled to get them back on their feet. None was so badly hurt that he could not walk. The column kept climbing.

Early in the afternoon the horse packing Lewis's portable field desk and small trunk lost his balance on a steep part of the trail. He toppled over in slow motion, struck the slope and tumbled down the mountain, neighing wildly in his terror.

Seaman pursued the falling horse down the steep slope, barking in alarm. Forty yards down from the trail the horse skidded off a rock and smashed against a tree. There was a crumpling sound. The horse lay still.

When Meriwether Lewis reached the horse, he expected to find him dead. To his amazement the horse rolled a wild eye at him. With the help of a half-dozen of the men, Lewis got the animal to his feet. The horse shook himself, rolled his eyes and snorted. He was relatively unhurt. The crumpling sound had been wood splintering as Lewis's desk was ruined.

It required the hard efforts of ten men, pushing and pulling, to haul the fallen horse forty yards back up the face of the mountain to the trail that John Collins dubbed "a sorry excuse for a road."

The men were all badly fatigued by now, hungry and sore, and their views of this route across the mountains were not charitable.

At the end of the long day they reached the top. Here on the ridge they stared at a snowbank three feet deep. They regarded it with mixed feelings. The mountaintop was cold,

the wind cut through their torn and patched leather garments. On the other hand, there was no water; they could melt the snow for cooking the rest of the colt and for drinking water.

Seaman tried to slake his thirst by thrusting his head into the snowbank, as he customarily did into water. He quickly gave that up. The cold snow got up his nose and made him sneeze, and it did little more than wet his tongue. He was grateful when Lewis melted some of the snow and offered it to him in a dish, along with a morsel of horsemeat. The piece of meat was so small that Seaman was not sure he had swallowed it when it went down.

Half a colt, and one pheasant killed that day, did little to ease the hunger of thirty-three grown men and a woman, all ravenous from their exertions of the day. All went to their blankets hungry and cold. Only Pomp, still nursing, seemed satisfied.

During the night it began to snow.

Seaman lay under the thick branch of a spruce. It kept most of the snow off him. In the morning, while he listened to his companions' heartfelt curses, he padded around the camp through snow that was four inches deep.

The fresh fall of snow hid the trail. When the column kept losing its way, Lewis put Seaman out in front to see if the Newfoundland could sniff out the track. Even the dog was defeated by the snow. It continued to fall during the rest of that day, gathering thick on the branches of the pines from which, wet and soggy in the warmer part of the day, it fell upon the men passing beneath.

The trail, when they found it, remained steep and arduous. Frequently the slopes were entirely covered with fallen timber, which the burdened horses climbed over with great difficulty. By evening, when the weary detachment stopped, the snow lay six to eight inches deep everywhere. The air was very cold.

That night and the following day the two remaining colts were sacrificed for food. After that there was nothing left in the expedition's larder except for some of Meriwether Lewis's dehydrated soup, carried all the way from Philadelphia for just such a crisis as this. The men tried it and found it wanting. No one liked the taste of it; as hungry as they were, some spat it out in the snow. George Shannon was glad to share the last of his soup with Seaman. This being all the Newfoundland was offered for supper that night, he was less particular than the men. He lapped up the soup gratefully.

Coming upon Seaman as he was finishing this meager meal, Meriwether Lewis crouched silently beside him. He took the dog's big head in his hands and held him affectionately. "I believe you're the only one who likes my soup," Lewis murmured. "Pray God it keeps you alive . . . and the rest of us as well."

That night, September 17, 1805, in the captains' tent Lewis conferred privately with William Clark on their desperate situation. "How much more of this can we endure?" Lewis wondered aloud. "The men are becoming weak."

"Old Toby claims it can't be far to the plains of the Columbia."

379

"He's led us astray once on this mountain; I'm not sure we can trust his knowledge." The weakened state of his detachment weighed on Lewis's mind, making him testy. "The men cannot last much longer. The horses are in an even worse state. We must find food, Clark, as soon as possible. You'll have to find it for us."

Clark looked at him dubiously. "I don't know if we should divide our force . . ."

"We have no choice. Take the hunters in the morning and go on ahead. You must find us some provisions or we'll starve on this mountain."

Clark left early in the morning. The expedition stumbled on. That night they camped on the side of a steep hill, ate the last few pieces of the last colt with a little bear's oil, forced down some of Lewis's unpalatable soup, and even nibbled on some candles. They lay listlessly on the frozen ground in their blankets, gaunt and thin, beset almost to a man by boils and dysentery, too enfeebled to complain. Instead they thought of

Captain Clark and the hunters somewhere ahead of them on the mountain, and they had visions of the great buffalo herds of the Plains, of elk and deer and antelope in endless numbers, of huge sides of meat seared and sizzling over their cooking fires . . .

As hungry as his companions, Seaman was also, like them, losing some of his strength. Until now he had found the crowded pine forests, the fields of fallen timber, and the constant climbing up and down the steep, narrow trail somewhat easier going than either the men or the larger, clumsier horses. But on this day the Newfoundland had slipped once on a patch of muddy slope and tumbled head over heels, flopping thirty yards down the mountain until he banged against a large fallen trunk.

He lay breathless against the tree, more stunned than hurt. As Meriwether Lewis and several of the men scrambled down the slope to his side, Seaman gazed up at them with an expression of apology, as if expecting a reprimand. Instead he saw only concern. Lewis probed the dog's thin body with his fingers, shocked at the bones standing out under the thick coat, which had concealed Seaman's emaciated condition. But Lewis found no broken bones or evidence of severe sprains. Seaman was able to walk, limping a little and favoring his right front leg, the shoulder of which had taken the brunt of his impact against the fallen tree.

He was helped back up the slope to the trail. Shaking off his limp, he ascended the mountain in the wake of the column. It moved slowly, stumbling and laboring.

The next morning the detachment struggled past another desolate stretch of fallen timber—an alien landscape, thought Lewis, as if all the trees had been felled by one sweep of a giant scythe.

Suddenly, up ahead, Nathaniel Pryor gave a feeble shout. Lewis hurried forward. His gaze followed the direction of Pryor's trembling finger as he pointed.

In the distance, beyond a screen of timber, far below the ridge where Lewis stood, a large plain opened out.

Louis Charbonneau

Around him some of the men began to shout and pummel each other. A few even danced a feeble jig. Meriwether Lewis turned to the Indian guide, who had stopped beside him. "Is that where the Pierced Nose Indians live?"

Old Toby nodded, and Lewis closed his eyes against a flood of inexpressible joy.

William Clark and the hunters, traveling unencumbered, had reached the prairie in only two days after leaving the main party. The Nez Percés Indians, after overcoming their initial fright, welcomed him with genuine friendliness. They supplied Clark and his men with dried salmon and a bread made of camas root—so generously, in fact, that the entire group became sick from overeating and the drastic change of diet.

On the morning of September 22, 1805, Meriwether Lewis led the expedition down the mountain trail to a small meadow. There Reuben Fields found them. Dispatched by Clark as soon as possible, Fields carried a bag of dried salmon and another of bread.

Although the main party of the Corps of Discovery were sick and debilitated, some worse off than others, the ordeal of the Lolo Trail was over. They stopped in the meadow to eat and to rest. With elated grins they insisted that dried salmon was the best fish they had ever tasted. Three men—and Sacajawea, who had survived the trial better than most—shared portions of their fish and bread with Seaman.

Meriwether Lewis sat by himself, his back propped against a fir tree at the edge of the meadow. He needed to be alone for a little while with the delicious feeling of redemption and satisfaction that engulfed him. There were perhaps only two men in the world with whom he might have shared this moment fully. One was William Clark, waiting down below.

The other was Thomas Jefferson.

The Corps of Discovery had survived its worst crisis. They had triumphed over the Rocky Mountains. Below them, now, the way to the Pacific Ocean was open.

32 Ocian in view! O! the joy.
—WILLIAM CLARK, November 7, 1805

*T*wisted Hair was a dignified, cheerful man of about forty-five. Long, iron-gray hair hung in two queues over his shoulders, framing handsome features. He sat facing William Clark in a lodge of one of the chiefs of the first Nez Percés village Clark had come to when he descended the Lolo Trail to the prairie. Nearby, Meriwether Lewis lay exhausted. Clark and Twisted Hair had found him earlier that evening at the village with the rest of the main party of the expedition.

Clark stoically drew a puff of the Indian's vile-tasting kinnikinnick, which they had been smoking in the native ritual of hospitality. Once the Nez Percés got over their caution on meeting a white man for the first time, they had been uniformly friendly. One of the chiefs of the prairie villages had directed Clark toward a greater chief living on an island in the Kooskooskee or Clearwater River. He was Twisted Hair, whose sincerity and good nature had confirmed Clark's opinion of the Nez Percés as "the friendliest and most accommodating Indians I have yet seen."

"Tell me about the river," Clark said, while Drouillard signed his words.

Twisted Hair nodded cheerfully. On a white elkskin he began to sketch with the charred tip of a stick, working in silence. After a moment he sat back to observe his drawing. Lips pursed, he added a few more scratches. After further study, the chief tapped a wriggly line on the map with the clean end of his drawing stick and spoke, using a combination of words and signs that Drouillard attempted to translate.

"Down this river to forks of river where Snake people fish"—the chief tapped a line showing the Kooskooskee falling into a larger river—"is two sleeps." The pointer moved on, past marks indicating barriers in the river, to its conjunction with another river entering from the northwest and flowing westward toward the ocean. "The Columbia River is here, five sleeps more." And down the Columbia, Twisted Hair went on to say, pointing to a drawing of water flowing over a precipice, were the falls, another five sleeps distant. This route—only twelve days to the falls by the chief's estimate—would take the white men to their brothers who lived on the Great Waters.

William Clark stared avidly at the detailed map. It rep- **383** resented all that he had hoped to hear. The expedition could now leave its horses behind and take to the river.

The men were still weak from near starvation on the Lolo Trail. Meriwether Lewis was too feeble even to stay on a gentle horse that Twisted Hair selected for him to ride down to the chief's camp. Some of the other men could do no more than lie beside the trail until they were carried down. Their condition was initially made worse by cramps and dysentery, reactions to the dramatic change from a diet of meat to one exclusively featuring roots and fish.

In the bottom opposite the forks of the Kooskooskee River, William Clark set up Canoe Camp. All the men straggled in. Hoping for the best, Clark dosed most of them with Dr. Rush's pills. Those who were strong enough to lift an ax began to fell trees for the boats the expedition would now require.

Over the next ten days, under Pat Gass's supervision, the

work proceeded slowly. With regular food and rest, the men's strength gradually returned—though some, including Lewis and George Drouillard, remained ill throughout this stay. To lessen the hard labor with axes for his weakened crew, Gass borrowed a method of the Indians, using fires to burn out the interiors of the boats.

By October 6, 1805, four large dugout canoes and one small one were finished. Lewis and Clark were anxious to get under way. There was frost in the mornings, the breath of winter on the wind. Lewis had all of the expedition's horses rounded up—thirty-eight were found. He cropped their manes, so they could be easily recognized, and branded each with an iron that, with his usual foresight, he had brought along for just such an eventuality. The horses were left in the care of the cooperative Twisted Hair and his son.

The crews were now strong enough, their captains judged, to handle the boats even in rough water. "We'll have to grow stronger on the move," Lewis said. "We can delay no longer."

384

Where they had crawled up the Missouri, sometimes a yard or even a foot at a time, now they hurtled down the white water. The first day they ran ten rapids, the second day fifteen more. Late that second afternoon Pat Gass's canoe hit a rock. A hole opened in her side. John Thompson, thrown out of the boat, hurt his shoulder on the rock. The dugout sank almost immediately, dumping her crew into the boiling river.

They clung to the boat in water that, even though it was only waist deep, was much too swift for them to attempt to swim or walk to shore. Their danger came not from the depth of the water but the possibility of being torn loose and swept out of control into the rock-strewn rapids. Some of those trapped in this unhappy situation, yelling for help, could not even swim.

The other boats put in to shore. One canoe was quickly unloaded. Seaman, beached along with Meriwether Lewis's crew, ran up and down the shoreline barking at the men in the water.

"Grab him!" Meriwether Lewis ordered. "Don't let him go in the river!" As powerful a swimmer as Seaman was, Lewis was not yet ready to allow him to challenge these rapids, particularly since the dog alone could do little to rescue a boatload of men. "Cruzatte, you'll have to get them ashore."

Cruzatte's one eye did not blink. He was the expedition's most expert waterman. In a crisis such as this, he was the first one the commanders turned to.

A crew of volunteers piled into the unloaded canoe. With Cruzatte guiding them, they worked the boat against the current until they were able to maneuver close enough to Pat Gass's stranded crew for the men in the water to grab the rescue boat. Quickly the frightened men were taken aboard. A cord was attached to the submerged dugout. With the men on shore hauling on the line, the damaged canoe was slowly dragged to safety.

Luckily the damage was repairable. The expedition lay over for a day to dry the goods that had been thrown into the river and to patch the split in the side of the canoe.

By then old Toby and his son, who had stayed with the expedition all the way from the Shoshoni village on the Lemhi River, had seen enough—not only of the rapids but also of the recklessness of these whites, who hurtled into the white water with crazy shouts and wolfish grins. As darkness fell that evening, one of the men reported seeing Toby and his son running along the riverbank well above the camp, heading home. They hadn't even waited to be paid for their services.

The expedition was not without guides, however. Two of the Nez Percés chiefs had come downriver to join them, with a promise to stay with the boats as far down as the falls of the Columbia River—which was as far as either chief had ever traveled.

The next day, running another bad rapid—so violent and studded with rocks that the canoes had to be taken down the

385

chute one at a time—one of the dugouts rode upon some rocks and stuck. It was wedged between two rocks for an hour before another rescue crew could work it free. The damage, which again proved minor, was quickly repaired. After a short delay the boat was back in the water.

That night the expedition and its small fleet reached the confluence of the Kooskooskee and Snake Rivers. They called the latter Lewis's River.

Their white water experience had just begun.

On October 12, 1805, two Flathead Indians familiar with Lewis's River agreed to act as pilots for the expedition, rowing a canoe of their own. At dusk the boats came to the top of a churning rapids. This, the native pilots said, was a bad place.

Meriwether Lewis and William Clark walked along the riverbank below their camp to survey the rapids. The terrain, while mostly level, was very rocky. The expedition had left the timbered Rocky Mountains and the fertile prairie of the Nez Percés to enter a barren, treeless plain, where even firewood of any kind was scarce. The October wind blew across this empty wilderness unhindered, cold enough to tighten the skin on the two men's faces as they walked in a companionable silence. Seaman ambled along at their heels or trotted ahead to examine a bush of interest.

386

"I put it at two miles," said Clark with his customary precision, when they came to the bottom of the rapids. "It's the worst we've seen."

"But not the worst to come, if the Indians are to be believed."

Which meant, thought Lewis, that this rapids had to be passed in the water. The men were gaining both skill and confidence in handling the canoes. It was essential to rely on the one while bolstering the other . . . without reckless risk of lives.

Lewis gazed out over the turbulent river. There were rocks in every direction, some of them huge, and white water was everywhere. A ceaseless roaring sounded the river's fury. Both Lewis and Clark had to shout to be heard.

"I might be reluctant to try it," said Lewis, "but for the lateness of the season. We can't take time to portage around every difficulty."

Clark nodded thoughtfully. Less impetuous than his friend, he was similarly reluctant to lose a single day now that they were on the Columbia River system. With winter coming, and unknown obstacles ahead, every delay was significant. "There's a channel on the left side here. You can see it between those tumbles of rocks."

"I'll go down first with Cruzatte."

Clark started to object and fell silent. He knew Lewis's mind. The violence of these rapids had many of the men shaking their heads and wondering. If the boats were to run them, one of the captains had to lead the way. And only one. In the event of a serious accident, both commanders could not be at risk.

The next morning was bright and clear and cold. The 387 crews of the boats gathered along the riverbank as Lewis checked the baggage aboard the first two canoes selected to challenge the rapids. The men who couldn't swim stood aside a little disconsolately. They were to make a portage around the rapids, carrying the rifles, instruments and other valuables that were not to be hazarded in the boats. At William Clark's firm order and over the Indian woman's protests, Sacajawea and her baby were also to make the portage. Charbonneau, of course, was among those who couldn't swim.

The crews climbed aboard and settled into their places, unsmiling. Meriwether Lewis glanced up at the bank. "Seaman!" he called out cheerfully. Seaman jumped down from the bank and clambered into the bow of the first canoe.

"All right, lads," Lewis shouted above the tumult of the river. "Let's go for a ride!"

William Clark grinned. He knew instantly that Lewis had called his dog aboard the first canoe for one reason only—to show that there was nothing to fear. It was just another ride.

The two canoes pushed out into the river, one following the other, and were immediately caught by the current and thrown downstream. Cruzatte steered the lead canoe toward the left bank. The men dug in their oars and the boat shot into the channel—into the heart of chaos.

There was no time for thinking, only acting. Foam boiled around them. Rocks appeared and flashed by, miraculously missed. The lead canoe dropped into a trough and shot forward with stomach-wrenching speed. The next moment it pitched up on a curling wave and raced past another rocky barrier.

Oars flailed. Hearts seemed to stop when wood grated against rock, then hammered wildly as another narrow chute appeared ahead. The canoe seemed to the men riding her like a needle driving through a hole in the madness all about them.

A mile down the rapids, half of the wild run still ahead, Meriwether Lewis glanced forward along the length of the dugout and felt his own heart stop.

Seaman was sitting up!

388 Like the men handling the canoes, Seaman had had to get over his initial clumsiness and insecurity in the long, narrow dugouts; unlike some of the crews, he was totally fearless in the water and a superb swimmer. Before the first day on the Kooskooskee ended, he was lifting his head joyously into the wind as his boat lurched through a tumultuous rapids. Now, in the most dangerous run the boats had yet tried, the Newfoundland was again sitting up, legs spread wide and feet braced against the sides of the dugout, mouth open, face lifted to the wind and the icy, stinging spray.

Lewis shouted. In the tumult his cry went unheard. Then Reuben Fields saw Lewis's urgent gestures. Near the bow and closest of the crew to the dog, Fields leaned forward far enough to shove Seaman in the back. Seaman sprawled in the bottom of the boat.

He needed no other command. He lay where he was, facing forward, still lifting his head as high as he could into the exhilarating breeze.

Louis Charbonneau

A moment later the canoe flashed through a slot between two shoulders of rock and sailed into swift but settled water.

Only seconds behind, the second canoe, with George Drouillard steering, emerged from the foaming rapids.

The next day, in another rapids, three canoes struck rocks. All three emerged from the impact with little damage; all the boats got past the rapids. The expedition stopped for dinner on the riverbank, some of them savoring leftover dog, others settling for dried fish. Two miles after they got under way again, they came to a short rapids opposite an island. Perhaps because their earlier successes had made them overconfident, or perhaps only by unlucky chance, Drouillard's canoe struck a rock and swung broadside against it.

The crew were thrown into the river. The contents of the boat began to spill out—clothing, shot pouches, bedding, gunpowder. The stern sank partially beneath the surface as the canoe remained hung up against the rock.

One by one the drenched men dragged themselves out of the powerful current onto the huge rock, where they clung desperately to the wet, slippery surface. Several of them had the presence of mind to hang onto their half-submerged dugout to keep it from being swept away and smashed. Only one man escaped their plight, a Nez Percés chief who, thrown out of the boat, was luckily pitched into shallow water near the shore. Showing an unflappability to match that of the men who had grabbed the sunken boat, the Indian began to retrieve articles that floated by him from the canoe's cargo.

The other canoes had shot downstream so fast that they could not immediately help the shipwrecked crew. As soon as they reached smooth water below the rapids, both Lewis and Clark—in separate boats—had their canoes put ashore. The crews of the other boats managed to grab many of the floating articles that had been dumped into the river.

One large canoe turned back, manned by Cruzatte and

Labiche, the two most experienced rivermen, and three volunteers. Taking advantage of quieter water next to the island,
Cruzatte maneuvered the dugout opposite the men marooned
on the rock. After several aborted tries, the rescue craft finally
bridged the gap between the island and the men.

The two crews now worked quickly to unload the remaining cargo from the half-sunken canoe. A line was secured
to the stricken boat, and the stranded men were taken off the
rock. Before they were safely deposited on the island, they had
been clinging to their rocky perch in the middle of the rapids
for an hour. They were wet, cold, exhausted—and grateful.

The Corps of Discovery came down the Kooskooskee and Lewis's rivers in a rush. In ten days, even with layovers for canoe
repairs, they traveled two hundred miles. After surviving a
dangerous narrows on the morning of October 16, 1805—a
stretch of one and a half miles in which the whole fury of
Lewis's River was wedged into a channel less than twenty-five
yards wide and "as fast as a millrace"—the expedition reached
the mighty Columbia River. That evening they halted on a
point just above the forks and made camp.

Word of a party of bearded men had traveled down the
white water even more swiftly than the expedition's canoes.
Throngs of Indians came down to the forks to circle the camp,
singing and dancing. They saw that what they had heard was
true. An Indian woman, carrying her baby, traveled with the
whites. All Indians knew that a woman accompanying a party
of men was a token of peace.

Three of the Frenchmen—Labiche, Cruzatte, and Lepage—
had been the first members of the expedition to eat dog. But,
by the time they reached the Columbia River, most of the men,
including Meriwether Lewis, had acquired a taste for it. While
they lay over at the point where Lewis's River flowed into the
Columbia, the hungry soldiers purchased forty dogs from the

Indians for a few trinkets. Long since weary of fish, and with most of their camas roots lost when one of the canoes overturned, the men craved the real staple of their diet over the entire journey—fresh meat.

Once you got over your prejudice, most of them said, dog meat was as good as any. In time Meriwether Lewis even came to compare it favorably with the best veal, and it was superior, he concluded, to horse meat in any form.

When Sacajawea was offered a portion of the meat, which her husband greedily devoured, the Indian woman shook her head firmly.

"Go on!" Charbonneau growled. "Is good meat—good for bébé. Make good milk."

Sacajawea's jaw set in a stubborn line. "Shoshoni no eat dog," she said. Not even, she might have added, when they were near starvation from the absence of game. However hungry she might be, she would never taste such meat. Besides, through most of her life, she had been accustomed to long periods of going hungry and other times when there was only fish to eat.

William Clark professed to dislike the taste.

"You're just being squeamish," Meriwether Lewis told him.

"It doesn't set well with me," Clark admitted. In truth, the mere idea of eating dog was unpalatable to the redhead. He could never accept it, any more than the Indian woman could.

One of the Frenchmen, Baptiste Lepage, chuckling and telling the other soldiers to watch, offered a portion of dog meat to Seaman. He tried to cover the taste and smell by grilling the meat in bear's oil, hoping thereby to trick the Newfoundland.

Seaman approached the tin plate hungrily. Abruptly he pulled back. His nose wrinkled. When Lepage pushed the plate toward him again, urging him on—"Eh, what's wrong, boy? You eat, is ver' good"—the rumble of a rare growl sounded in Seaman's throat.

Suddenly George Shannon confronted Lepage. He knocked the tin plate from the Frenchman's hand, spilling the scraps of meat on the ground. "You want that, *you* eat it!" Shannon said angrily. "Leave Seaman alone! You try to trick him like that again, you'll eat more than dirt!"

During the past two years Shannon had grown considerably. He was a strapping young man now, broad-shouldered and muscular, with strong, big-knuckled hands. He looked very determined.

Lepage stared at the youth briefly, a defiant glare in his eyes. Some of the watching soldiers began to laugh. Then the Frenchman shrugged. "Ah, is no more good joke," he muttered. "Dat Seaman, he no fool. He know what it be, *n'est-ce pas?*"

No one tried such a ruse on Seaman after that. But dog, whenever the men could acquire the animals from Indian villages they passed, remained a staple part of the expedition's diet until they returned to the Plains the following summer.

On October 22, 1805, the Corps of Discovery reached the falls of the Columbia. After landing above the "great pitch," where the river tumbled over a perpendicular drop of twenty feet, the two commanders walked down the riverbank to examine the falls and possible portage routes. Meanwhile the men unloaded the canoes, and, when their captains returned, the entire crew carried the baggage past the falls over a portage of about twelve hundred yards, a third of the way clambering over a rock formation and another two hundred yards slogging through loose sand. They formed a camp below the falls, where a great many Indians from lodges both above and below the foaming pitch came to view them.

The following day, Clark took most of the men across the river in the now empty canoes. With great difficulty they hauled the boats over a portage of 457 yards, arriving at a channel about a half-mile long. Here the boats were put into the water; the best swimmers and rivermen climbed aboard; and they rode the channel past churning whirlpools. At the bottom of the channel they let the boats down the river on ropes over a series of smaller drops. One canoe broke free of its elkskin line. It was retrieved by Indians where the river opened out below the falls.

At three in the afternoon everyone had landed safely at the camp below the falls. It was then, when the day's demanding work was behind them, that the men began to feel the fleas biting.

"Holy old jumped-up Judas!" John Collins yelled. "I'm bein' eaten alive!"

Soon all of the men were hopping about, slapping at fleas. It was no use. There were swarms of them.

Later they decided that a recently abandoned Indian camp at the head of the canoe portage above the falls was the source of the fleas. No matter. There were other hordes of the insects waiting in every Indian lodge below the falls.

For now all the men could think of was getting rid of the biting critters. Finally they had to strip naked and try to brush them off. But, when they put their leather garments back on, they were instantly attacked again. And at this stage of their odyssey no one had a change of clothing.

Two-and-a-half miles below the falls the Columbia was blocked by an enormous black rock on the north side, which choked off the river and compressed it into a short narrows through which the water tumbled with a deafening thunder. William Clark studied the chute, about forty-five yards wide, with Pierre Cruzatte.

After a moment Cruzatte nodded while scratching absently at a flea bite. "*Oui,* she is bad but . . . es possible, I t'ink."

"It can be done safely? The problem is, we can't portage over this rock. We have to ride it out . . . if we can do it without drowning every man."

Cruzatte scratched and grinned and said, "We find out, eh?"

They all climbed back in the dugouts, even Seaman, who

393

was in the first boat with Cruzatte, and they shot through the neck of the narrows into the torrent. From the vantage of the huge black rock a crowd of Indians watched, incredulous at the wild daring of these whites—even their Bear Dog, and the Indian woman with her child, rode with them, though their boats were almost lost from sight in the foam! In a few frenzied moments the boats hurtled through the short narrows into the open river below, and the roaring fury receded behind them.

Both Meriwether Lewis and William Clark inspected the long narrows below the falls the next morning. Again it appeared that a portage over the rocky banks was impracticable. "We'll have to run the boats through," Clark said, with a confidence bolstered by previous successes.

"It might be wise to send the most valuable articles below the narrows with some of the men who can't swim."

"Aye, that'd be the safer thing."

As an added precaution Clark placed men with ropes along the three-mile stretch of the long narrows. If there was an accident, and anyone was thrown into the river . . . well, he might have a chance of survival if a rope could be thrown to him in time.

Down the chute they came, past walls of hard black rock, the river boiling and swelling with frightening force. Through the turmoil Clark on shore could hear the men in the boats shouting their challenge at the river and fate. One boat got through the whole length of the narrows untouched, then another, and a third. The fourth canoe shipped water and wallowed dangerously. The men on the bank threw a line to it and pulled the boat safely to the shore before it could sink. The last boat ran the chute while taking in only a little water. And who could blame lanky Hugh McNeal for standing up in the last boat, shaking his fists and yelling in triumph, even if he made the canoe start to roll and someone had to grab McNeal before he pitched into the river, still yelling. By God, nothing could stop the Corps of Discovery now!

Louis Charbonneau

In the evening of October 30, 1805, they reached the Cascades of the Columbia and camped opposite a very large Indian village. For the third day in a row it had rained. Everyone was sodden and weary, but they had been through so much that they had a peculiar kind of confidence in themselves, impervious to logical argument. So they stared at the "Great Shute," as William Clark called it, in which the thundering current was only 150 yards across, studded with large and small rocks, and dropped a total of 60 feet over the course of the cascades, they grinned their reckless grins and wished they hadn't finished off the last of their whiskey on Independence Day, this rain and cold on the Columbia was whiskey weather for sure, and the river was easy after this last challenge, that's what the natives all said, and by the Lord (as Captain Lewis would say), wouldn't it be something if there were tall ships waiting in the harbor for them, where the Columbia hurried to the sea . . .

The portage was hard. They unloaded the canoes in the morning and took them down past the first rapids, part of the way by water, the rest by hauling them over rocks ten feet high. The distance was less than a thousand yards, but every step of it was over bad rocks and wet, slippery slopes. Their moccasins kept slipping. They cracked ankles and knees and elbows on the rocks. It took all day to get two canoes down past the first bad chute. By then the heady exhilaration of the morning had given way to grim determination.

Over two days they got the other boats down and carried all of their baggage around the portage. The best swimmers took the boats through the lower part of the cascades, down into the open where the river widened out and the current slowed. Here all of the men gazed around them with a kind of surprise to discover that they had entered a different world, leaving the rocky, barren hills behind for a land of green, forested hills, of mist and fog and relentless rain.

Even the Indians seemed different here. Most of them were short, with broad faces. Many wore familiar garments such as a sailor's cap or jacket, or they showed off kettles, muskets or pieces of brass, artifacts of the white man's world. The women and girls all had flat heads, a formation produced by tightly binding the head of an infant female with a board that pressed against the forehead, causing it to grow flattened and angled back and forcing the skull almost to a point at the top. Men, women, and children were dirty and poorly covered, and so light-fingered that thefts became a daily problem. They were unpredictable, often unfriendly, sometimes openly insolent. "They've seen too many white men," Pat Gass observed, "and don't care much for what they've seen."

"Then it's up to us," said Meriwether Lewis, who had overheard, "to show them better!"

But it was the weather that plagued the explorers most. It was relentlessly cold and wet, intolerable by day and worse at night. The high waves and violent winds made every yard of progress a bitter and uncertain gain. They could see little of the land about them. The shores were rocky and barren, the pine-covered hills a dense and sodden green, covered with shrubbery so thick the hunters frequently could not penetrate it. But the river, shrouded in mist, had widened out—a hopeful sign that they were nearing its mouth.

November 7, 1805, was a cloudy, foggy morning, the sky dripping as usual, the damp cold penetrating the men's worn and patched leather garments. Miserable, godforsaken weather in William Clark's view. The boats started out in the fog and rain. The men were unable to see where they were going. It was a slow, hard pull against the heavy pounding of the waves.

After about twelve miles the fog became so thick that attempting further progress was dangerous. The boats were forced ashore. Where they landed, the shoreline was formed by rocky, broken hills that rose steeply from the waterline. It offered little in the way of shelter from the rain or security from the high, crashing waves.

About noon, however, the fog began to lift. It was like a curtain rising. First the explorers saw a huge rock about a half

mile from shore, thrusting out of the river about twenty feet
into the air. A good landmark, Clark the mapmaker thought.
The thick fog had not only screened the river but had muffled
all sounds, diminishing them. As the curtain rose, the muffled
roaring they had heard all morning became the unleashed
thunder of huge waves rolling inland from the sea to smash
against the rocks.

The men began to shout and pound each other on the
back. Joy spread through the beleaguered camp on the rocky
shore, whose mood had been as soggy as the morning's
weather. There was no mistaking the size and majesty of these
waves. Some of the men clambered up the barren hillside for
a better view. Charbonneau was among them, and from a
precarious perch he shouted down to Sacajawea. *"La grand
mer! La grand mer!"* The Indian woman, still carrying her nine-
month-old in his cradleboard on her back, was reluctant to
climb the wet rock. She stood in awe of the waves breaking
against the rocks, shooting foam and spray high into the air.
Charbonneau laughed and pounded a meaty palm against the
rock, as if his sighting were his own singular achievement. *"La
grand mer!"*

Pierre Cruzatte tried an impromptu jig—sans fiddle—
and lost his footing on the wet rock. He went sprawling, slipping toward the water. An instant before he rolled off a ledge
into the turbulent surf, Pat Gass caught him by the leg and
hauled him back to safety. Gass, too, was grinning and shouting. Even George Drouillard's imperturbable calm yielded to
this moment. He climbed higher on the rock than any of the
others, high enough to feel the power of the wind and to gaze
far out across the bay over the mountainous waves, seeing a
far horizon even he had not imagined.

Watching the men cavort on their precarious tumble of
rocks beside the great ocean she had never dreamed of seeing
with her own eyes until these past few months, Sacajawea
smiled, and wondered if she had enough roots to add to the
pot for dinner. Some of the salmon they had got from Indians
farther up the river was spoiled.

William Clark sought out his friend and partner, and for a moment he stood silently beside Meriwether Lewis, the two men listening to the tumult of the waves and the exultant celebrations of their companions. "Near four thousand miles we've come to see this!" Clark shouted above the crash of a wave that drenched them in its spray. Lewis, cherishing a moment he had dreamed of for more than a decade, a third of his lifetime, grinned back at him, speechless, for once too full of emotion for words.

The bare sum of miles seemed inadequate to express the dimensions of the voyage that had brought them to this turbulent shore, or the distance they had come from what had so long been only a vision in an old man's mind in the White House.

Oh, the ocean! By the Lord, they had reached the Pacific at last!

398 Although they were close to the mouth of the Columbia River that morning, the Corps of Discovery was in fact still fifteen miles away from seeing the main body of the Pacific Ocean. And for the next week they were held back by a series of violent storms. When they crossed one bay the waves were so high and choppy that many of those in the boats—Sacajawea among them—were seasick. One night, camping on a narrow shelf between rocks and the river, sleepers were driven from their blankets when the tide rose so high it threatened to wash them off the shelf. Another night they made a platform of logs and raised it securely above the waves to protect themselves and their baggage. For four long days and nights, they were pinned down by storms so violent they could not get out to hunt. They dared not even try to turn back to a better situation further inland. Clark called their sorry situation Camp Distress. They could only wait it out.

Then, on November 15, the weather cleared a little. Taking advantage of a favorable tide, the boats of the Corps of

Discovery pushed into the river and fought their way around the last point.

Now the whole ocean opened out before them. From the maps Lewis and Clark had brought with them, the commanders knew they were looking at Haley's Bay, named after the captain of an American brig who had anchored here in 1792. And the prominent ridge at the far western point of the bay had been called Cape Disappointment by a British trader who, a quarter-century ago, had tried to cross the land bar from the ocean to the Columbia River and failed, driven back in disappointment by a raging storm. Until now such names had been simply scratchings on suspect maps. All that had changed.

Now the overwhelming reality stretched out beyond the limit of vision. The swift, free-running waves—like small mountains, Pat Gass wrote—raced toward them out of an endless ocean, teasing the mind's vision beyond the horizon toward the Far East and all its marvels.

"Go for the glory, Billy!" George Rogers Clark had urged his younger brother.

The glory was yet to come, but the men and one woman of the Corps of Discovery had reached their final goal.

Bonaparte—whose sale of a distant piece of uncharted land called Louisiana had helped to make the journey of the Corps of Discovery possible—had had himself crowned Napoleon I, first emperor of France. In August, 1805, while Meriwether Lewis was crossing the Lemhi Pass in search of the Shoshonis, Napoleon had stood on the French coast staring over the crashing waves toward England. Behind him were massed over 130,000 troops, an army fed and clothed in part by money Napoleon had received from the United States for Louisiana. Denied his ambitions in a New World, Bonaparte was prepared to conquer a smaller one, just a short distance away across the English Channel.

But the admiral at the head of Napoleon's fleet felt less confidence than his emperor about confronting Admiral Horatio Nelson and the British naval guns in the narrow channel. Instead, Pierre de Villeneuve prudently sailed toward Spain.

In rage and frustration, Napoleon returned to Paris. His anger—and his army—were quickly directed eastward, toward Austria and Russia.

Late in October, while the Corps of Discovery was rushing down the Columbia River toward the Cascades, Villeneuve, his courage bolstered by the support of the Spanish armada, met Nelson and the British fleet at Cape Trafalgar, near Gibraltar off the southwest coast of Spain. In a brilliantly engineered battle, Nelson routed the combined French and Spanish fleets, capturing twenty ships while losing none of his own. Though mortally wounded aboard his flagship *Victory*, Nelson had forever destroyed Napoleon's hopes of invading Britain.

But if he could not triumph at sea, Napoleon remained invincible on land. At a small town in Czechoslovakia named Austerlitz, on December 2, 1805 (while Meriwether Lewis was ascending a small stream south of the Columbia River in search of a site for winter camp), Napoleon's army met the forces of Austria and Russia in the field. For the emperor the battle was a tactical triumph, the most brilliant of his career. The Austrian army was crushed, the Russians driven into retreat.

Napoleon rode across the smoking battlefield before cheering troops. England was denied him—but the continent was his. Within a year all of Europe would sue for peace.

On the far rim of the continent Napoleon had already lost, the Corps of Discovery settled in for the winter.

400

33 "at day light this morning we we[re] awoke by the discharge of the fire arm of all our party & a Selute, Shouts and a Song which the whole party joined in under our windows, after which they retired to their rooms were chearfull all the morning."
—WILLIAM CLARK, December 25, 1805
CHRISTMAS DAY AT FORT CLATSOP

*A*t the mouth of the Columbia the men of the Corps of Discovery gazed eagerly out to sea, searching the horizon for the tall masts of sailing ships. Some Indians further up the Columbia had reported the presence of such ships, feeding among the soldiers a desire for contact, however fleeting, with their own civilization. But they saw only the huge waves rolling toward them out of the empty sea.

Thomas Jefferson had issued Meriwether Lewis a re-markable open letter of credit against the United States government, at the same time urging him, upon reaching the Pacific Ocean, to send two of his men and his vital reports of the expedition back by sea—and, if necessary to their safety, to ship the entire detachment back. Lewis had no such intention, but he had hoped to send his and William Clark's journals by sea, and to use his credit to buy beads and other trading goods acceptable to the Indians, the expedition's stock of such items being reduced to what could be wrapped in one hand-kerchief.

There was no sign of any vessel.

Two weeks after the expedition moved back upriver in

search of a winter campsite, the American brig *Lydia*, under the command of Captain Samuel Hill, entered the mouth of the Columbia and sailed about ten miles up the river. Captain Hill dropped anchor near a small Indian village. From the Indians of the village Hill and his crew heard news of a small expeditionary force of white soldiers, led by Captains Lewis and Clark, that had been in the vicinity within the past fortnight. The Indians could not—or would not—reveal the present whereabouts of the expedition.

The *Lydia* stood off the Pacific coast throughout that winter. It was never sighted by the Corps of Discovery.

From November 16 to November 25, 1805, the main party of the expedition camped at a point overlooking the bay and the ocean beyond it to the west. There was a Chinook village just below them and other Indian villages just to the north on the smaller rivers that fed into the bay.

402

Waking each morning in her wet blankets, Sacajawea was in awe of the huge waves that broke with such fury onto the sandy shore. Never had she imagined such a great body of water or such an endless roaring. But there was wonder, too, in the very fact of her presence here, camped on this distant shore among white men who were known to her and red men who were strangers. For that, too, was beyond the scope of any dream.

She explored the nearby hills for roots and other edible foods. Some of the Indians who came to see the white men brought wappato roots and boiled licorice, which she tasted and found good. These Indians appeared friendly, but they were thieves. In spite of the cold and rain they were half naked, and their women had little dignity.

One of the Chinook chiefs who visited the camp, whose name was Del-ash-el-wilt, was accompanied by his old wife and many young squaws, whom she called her daughters and nieces. They were laughing and flirtatious in their conduct with the young white soldiers. Some of the men gave them ribbons and other trinkets and sported with them. Although Sacajawea understood such conduct and considered it normal for the soldiers, she did not approve of the immodest approaches of the young women, who did not wait to be sought out but offered themselves wantonly in exchange for small gifts.

While parties of the men went out to explore the bay and have a closer view of the ocean, Sacajawea remained with Pomp at the camp. She was kept busy gathering roots and helping with each day's cooking. Between chores she played on the sand with her son. Now a sturdy nine months of age and learning to walk, he was quite unafraid of the crashing waves.

The neighboring Indians gathered about the camp in great numbers each day. One day an Indian came who wore a beautiful robe made of sea otter skins. Meriwether Lewis exclaimed over the beauty of the robe, but when he offered the Chinook a blanket for it, the Indian refused. His people prized these robes very highly, he said. He would not trade it for such a trifle.

William Clark, who had been to the ocean above Cape Disappointment with a party of the men, returned to camp during this parley. He declared that the otter robe was the handsomest he'd ever seen. By this time Lewis was so taken with the unusual garment that he was determined to find a way to buy it.

Sacajawea, sitting nearby on her own blanket, listened to the bartering. The Chinook brave was very stubborn. Lewis offered him a knife, buttons, a few yellow beads, even a uniform coat. At each offer the Indian shook his head. Nothing, it seemed, would sway him to part with his robe.

Suddenly he spotted a single blue bead in the small collection that Lewis had with which to trade. Pointing at the blue bead, he spoke with more enthusiasm. Charbonneau, who was struggling to interpret, turned to Lewis and said, "He want

ti-a-co-mo-shack, de blue bead. He say dey are chief beads."
The interpreter shrugged and pawed his beard. "No blue bead,
he no trade."

Lewis scowled in frustration. "Damn it all, I should've
brought more of the blue. It's the color all of these natives
favor." He sighed. "It's a handsome robe, Clark."

"Aye, it's that."

Clark turned to find Sacajawea standing at his side,
looking up at Meriwether Lewis. The Indian woman was
wearing her long deerskin dress, caught about the middle by
a full belt fashioned entirely of blue beads. Without a word
she released the belt and held it out to Lewis. "He will trade
for many bead the color of the sky," she said.

Lewis stared in surprise at the belt. He had forgotten it,
and even if it had occurred to him, he wouldn't have asked
the squaw to give it up. He suspected—accurately—that it was
her most prized possession.

Doubtfully Lewis shook his head. "I can't let you do that."

"Eh, why not?" asked Charbonneau. "Is good blue beads.
It mean no big thing to *ma femme.*" Seizing the belt from his
wife, he showed it to the Chinook brave, whose eyes widened
visibly at the sight of it. "Fine blue bead," Charbonneau
boasted. "*Ti-a-co-mo-shack.* You take, eh, for skin robe?"

"I don't wish to . . ." Lewis's protest faltered as the grinning Chinook swept the otter skin cloak from his shoulders,
his eyes gleaming at the belt of blue beads dangling from
Charbonneau's hand. Lewis glanced at Sacajawea, who
smiled in shy pleasure at being able to do something to please
one of the white chiefs so much. "Tell your femme I will give
her a blue uniform coat in exchange for it."

"*Oui, c'est bon!* I tell her."

So the hard bargain was struck. Meriwether Lewis was
so elated with his new prize that he failed to see the wistful
expression briefly visible in the Indian woman's dark eyes as
she watched the Chinook strut off with her precious belt of
blue, which had encircled her waist for so many seasons.

Louis Charbonneau

Much later Lewis thought in passing what little pain Charbonneau had appeared to suffer in the exchange.

GEORGE SHANNON'S JOURNAL

November 24, 1805
the Wind & rain being verry disagreeable on this point, our captains have decided we must move to a better location for our Winter Quarters. the captains gave us all a vote on where to locate, I voted for returning up the river to the Falls where there is more game to be found. All had a vote, including Capt. Clark's servant York and the Interpreter's wife Janey. She wished us to go across the river to the south shore where there are more wappato roots to be dug up. There is also said to be more Elk there. The majority voted to cross the river. Capt. Lewis wishes to be near the Ocean so that we can make Salt, which we are out of. We also hope that a ship from the U. States may put into the Bay and find us.

November 29, 1805
a cold rain today. Capt. Lewis & 5 Men set out in our Indian canoe to find a winter camp. These men were G. Drewyer, Reuben Fields, John Collins, Labiche and Myself. We found an old Indian lodge which gave us shelter from the rain. Our dog Seaman was with us, and he was bothered excessive by fleas which was in this lodge, he bit & scratched all night.

December 7, 1805
a verry bad storm last night ceased at Midnight. Capt. Lewis & 3 men went back to the main party after we found a tolerable good site for our fort, among many Pine trees and above the tide level. It is up a small river from the Columbia about 3 Miles and is from the Pacific Ocian 7 Miles. Today the whole Party arrived. Drewyer & myself had remained here to hunt Elk. The woods is very

thick and in places the brush is so thick it is impossible to walk through it, making hunting verry difficult.

December 13, 1805

Drewyer & myself returned to our new Fort today after being away hunting, it rained nearly every day. We left Dec. 8th in the company of Capt. Clark and 3 other men to blaze a road from our fort to the Ocean. It crossed some woods and hills and bogs. We came upon a band of Elk and shot one, which we had for Supper and used the Skin to shelter us against the rain that fell that night. The next day Capt. Clark and the rest of the men went on to the ocean. Drewyer and myself went after the Elk to hunt. We kill'd 18 Elk and left most of them to be brought in after butchering them, all but 2. Upon our return to the fort we found the rest of the Party has been busy clearing land and cutting down trees, and raised two lines of huts with a parade ground between them. Sgt. Gass says the wood here splits very well and will make fine roofs.

406

December 17, 1805

Verry bad storm yesterday and rained all night. We got all the Elk meat into our fort, which has a Smoke house on the same side as the Captains Qtrs., the Interpreter's room & the Guard House. On the other side are 3 large rooms for the Men, one for each Squad. We began daubing the cracks. wet & windy all day. Many of the men are sick with Colds, fever, &c. from being wet and cold. Most do not have any socks to wear with their mockersons, which are always wet. Sgt. Pryor put out his shoulder lifting, Wm. Werner sprained his knee.

December 23, 1805

it has rained or snowed, or sometimes frozen rain for a full week. the huts are all covered & we begin finishing them, making furniture, &c. 2 canoe loads of Clatsop Indians visit us today. They are our nearest Neighbors, and our captains decided to name our fort after these Indians. Fort Clatsop.

Louis Charbonneau

December 25, 1805

I am spending my 3rd Christmas with the Corps of Discovery and this one finds us in a poor state. Our meat in this damp spoils quickly, notwithstanding that we keep a Smoke going under it day & Night. Our feast for this occation consisted of spoiled Elk meat and spoiled pounded Salmon which we got above the Falls of the Columbia and a few roots. Our 2 Captains divided up the last of the tobacco amongst the men who use it, as a Christmas gift. The rest of us they gave a Silk handkerchief. I rec'd one of the Hankerchiefs to keep as a Remembrance. The rain and snow continues every day.

December 28, 1805

weather warm & rainy. Capt. Clark ordered Drewyer, Francis Labiche & myself out to hunt. Today some Indians visit and told us of a monstrous Whale beached not Far from us. The high winds and rain prevented anyone going to see it.

December 30, 1805

We returned to the Fort today after hunting Elk for 2 Days, we killed 4 Elk. The woods and prairies being verry wet makes it disagreeable to hunt. 6 Men were sent out to bring in the meat, which they did in time for our supper. This day saw some sunshine, the best we have had since our arrival here, it only rained 3 Times.

January 1, 1806

We fired our guns to signal in the New Year. The local Natives having proved troublesom Capt. Lewis ordered that the Fort be closed each night at Sunset, with all Indians having to leave before the gates are closed, and a Sentinel is to be posted at all times. The Indians are vexed at being required to leave, they visit us all day. Some of them are Thieves, and others act verry arrogant towards us. The women wear short petticoats made of grasses twisted like Ropes, which hang from the waist and is not a sufficient covering at all times. 2 Men are sick

with Venereals which they have caught from these Women, Capt. Lewis treats them with Mercury.

January 6, 1806

2 of our Men, Willard and Wiser, did not return from the Ocean where they had been sent with the salt makers. Capt. Lewis directed Sgt. Gass & myself to go to the seacoast to inquire after the missing men. We came to the Ocean and found them safe & well at the Salt camp. Joseph Fields, Wm. Bratton & George Gibson are the Salt Makers, which they do by building a fireplace and boiling 6 Kettles with ocean water all day. They make a gallon of Salt each day, verry white & strong.

January 7, 1806

I remained at the Salt Camp, which is comfortable, altho the wind blowing from the Ocean is sometimes violent, and when it rains the rain is driven as Sgt. Gass says, on the horizontal. A number of natives stay near the camp, they are friendly and cause no trouble. Capt. Clark arrived with a party at the Salt Camp. The Interpreter & his wife were with him & others. Capt. Clark hired an Indian guide to take him to see the Whale where it is beached, which is South of our camp.

January 9, 1806

I have been hunting with J. Fields & Gibson. Tonight Capt. Clark & his Party returned from seeing the Whale. The skeleton of this monster measured 105 ft. long. Capt. Clark traded with the Natives for some blubber and whale Oil. While he was smoking with the Indians, one of them tried to play a trick on Hugh McNeal, acting verry friendly and leading him away from the others on a pretense. One of the squaws who knew McNeal cried out to warn the party that this man was an Enemy & intended to kill McNeal for his blanket and what few articles he had. Capt. Clark at once sent Sgt. Pryor and & 4 Men after them, and they found McNeal before anything happen'd to him, the scoundrely Indian was from another band & ran off. This is a sign that not all of these Natives can be trusted. They are not as well disposed to us as the Indians of the Plains, nor do they possess the same noble Virtues.

January 15, 1806
Rained verry hard today. Our cabins are snug & warm, but we are afflicted with fleas in our bedding which we try to kill each day from the blankets or we get no sleep from them. Our dog is sore afflicted with them. I have never been in a place which is so wet or has so many fleas.

Seaman's Pacific winter began in the exhilarating tumult of the ocean at Cape Disappointment, where he stood beside Meriwether Lewis as the huge waves crashed against the rocky shore. Though he could not comprehend what this scene meant to Lewis, he felt Lewis's euphoria. He ran along the wet sand, chasing a retreating wave, and when a new wave rumbled toward him, he threw back his own thunderous bark, reveling in the pure joy of the moment.

During the next few months he knew little of such joy and excitement. Most of the time he chafed in confinement at Fort Clatsop. He had felt free and at home in the High Plains, where he had come into his own; here he felt out of his element. Though he could tolerate the penetrating chill, the weather was no more to his liking than it was to the men. He was wet all the time. One storm succeeded another, day after day, and it seemed impossible ever to get dry. The dense coat that effectively kept out water for the swimmer was, once the New-foundland was thoroughly soaked to the skin, very slow to dry out. Even on those rare days when there was a glimpse of sunshine in the morning, by afternoon there would be showers, by nightfall the cannon boom of another arriving storm.

There were fireplaces in each of the sleeping rooms. At first they lacked chimneys, and, when Seaman lay near the fire to warm his waterlogged coat, the smoke from the fireplace

would sting his eyes and clog his throat, forcing him out of the hut—usually into another downpour. When the chimneys were finished and the huts made warm and relatively smoke-free, the heat would activate the swarms of fleas the men had brought to the fort in their clothes and bedding—and Seaman in his coat. And every visiting Indian brought new hordes of the insects.

They drove Seaman wild, never gave him any rest. The men, however plagued by fleas they might be, could gain some temporary relief by stripping down, brushing their clothes, killing the fleas caught in their blankets. For Seaman there was no respite. His thick coat, sodden from the rain, provided refuge for his tormentors. Wet and miserable, he bit and clawed and howled in his misery. With his biting and scratching, and the constant dampness, he developed sores on his back and haunches, and some of his hair fell out. Meriwether Lewis treated the sores with a herbal ointment he concocted. Seaman promptly tried to lick off the ointment, making his condition worse.

410

The soldiers at the fort were generally too sick themselves, or too cold and wet, to offer more than passing sympathy to their dog. And the hunters, with whom Seaman was always particularly friendly, were away from the fort for days at a time; finding enough fresh meat for the entire detachment was a never-ending chore.

Like his dog, Meriwether Lewis spent most of that winter at the fort. William Clark was more often afield, visiting one of the Clatsop villages, trekking to the salt-making camp at the ocean, or marching on down the seashore to view an enormous beached whale. Lewis oversaw the day-to-day operations at the fort, brought his journals up to date, directed the hunters in their tireless quest for food, and tried to combat the sinking morale of the men, who were always at their best when they were proceeding on, peering ahead to see what was over the next hill or around the next bend in the river.

Lewis was also kept busy doctoring his charges for assorted pains, pulled muscles, colds, flu, and rheumatism, gen-

Louis Charbonneau

erally treating them by bathing their feet in hot water and giving doses of laudanum and niter. The venereal diseases McNeal and Goodrich had caught from Chinook women proved more troublesome; so did two cases of serious illness from the salt camp. There, after weeks of damp cold at the beach, William Bratton had been crippled by back pains, and George Gibson was so ill that he had to be carried back to the fort when the salt camp was shut down late in February.

Indian visitors were a daily part of the scene at Fort Clatsop. Their comings and goings provided some of the few highlights of those dreary winter days for Seaman. Like the Indians of the Plains, these coastal Indians took a special interest in the Bear Dog. One old Chinook chief claimed to have seen such a dog on one of the white men's trading ships that came to the mouth of the Columbia. For most of the natives, however, the Newfoundland was unlike any dog they had ever seen, and they were amazed at his size and strength and intelligence.

Although the Indians who came to the fort were always friendly with Seaman—sometimes excessively so—he had mixed feelings about them. Because Lewis and Clark treated the visitors as friends, Seaman felt obliged to do the same. But he was not as demonstratively friendly with them as he was with his soldier companions. There was a slyness in some of the red men, a way of staring at him when they thought the white men were not watching, that awakened Seaman's distrust and made him uneasy with their smiling attentions.

Yet nothing happened to justify this unease. The dreary days slid by into March, which brought three more weeks of rain, hail, sleet, and snow, almost without interruption. But now there was a difference the dog could sense. Something was happening. The desultory activities of the previous months gave way to more energetic preparations. Seaman watched the familiar Missouri River ritual of baggage being packed, of canoes being caulked and repaired. He caught the impatience of the men who were weary of this wet and miserable seacoast, weary of tanning and sewing hides, weary of making 338 pairs of elkskin moccasins to keep them supplied for the return trip,

weary of staring at the same log walls and listening to the monotonous music of the rain. They always felt better when they were on the move. They were also anxious to get back to the rich menu of the Plains.

Responding to the change he felt in the men, Seaman's own excitement and anticipation grew day by day. He, too, was eager to put the smoky confines of the fort behind him, to escape the fleas and the dampness and the inactivity.

When the canoes were put into the river on the morning of March 23, 1806, the baggage placed aboard them, Seaman ran back and forth along the bank, whining in excitement.

But that morning only brought more wind and rain. The start was delayed until one o'clock in the afternoon, when the winds died and the skies cleared to a leaden gray. Meriwether Lewis ceremoniously turned Fort Clatsop over to Chief Comowool of the Clatsop Nation. The Corps of Discovery climbed into their canoes—three large boats and two smaller ones—and pushed off. Few of them looked back. Fort Clatsop had sheltered them through this unkind winter. Now they were glad to put it behind them.

When they reached the mouth of Fort River, the multiple channels of the lower Columbia basin initially confused them. But soon they were into the main stream, turning their boats inland, paddling against the current.

In the bow of the first canoe Seaman gazed forward eagerly, his nose lifted to the wind. Behind him and in the other boats, there were grins on the young, weather-seasoned faces of the men.

They were heading home.

Part six

encounters

34. All the Indians from the Rocky Mountains to the Falls of the Columbia are an honest, ingenuous and well-disposed people. But from the Falls to the seacoast, they are a rascally, thieving, set.

—PATRICK GASS, M a y 7 , 1 8 0 6

*O*n the evening of April 11, 1806, Seaman was kidnapped.

The Corps of Discovery had come to the bottom of the Cascades of the Columbia late in the day on April 9. They stopped to make camp near an Indian village just below the first rapids.

Already, on the way up the river, there had been some minor problems with the river Indians. As the expedition had learned last fall, these natives were less friendly than those of the Plains, more prone to stealing and acts of hostility. A sentinel detected one old Indian creeping into the camp on his belly during the night. Immediately he raised the alarm. The Indian, whose small band of six were camped a hundred yards below the expedition's fires, fled in fear. The others also retreated into the heavily wooded hills.

The next day almost the entire party of the expedition, save for a few who were sick or lame, worked at drawing the canoes past the worst part of the rock-strewn lower rapids, drawing the boats up on a strong elkskin rope—the only rope they had left that wasn't rotten from the dampness. That eve-

ning they camped at the bottom of the portage around the Cascades. Large numbers of Indians, mostly Wah-clel-lahs from villages below the falls with some Cla-clel-lahs from above, flocked around them all night.

Early in the evening John Colter, returning from a visit to a native lodge, held his hand behind his back as he approached William Clark near the captains' mess fire. With a grin Colter held out a pipe-tomahawk. Clark gasped. "Where did ye find that?"

The tomahawk had been stolen on November 4, while the expedition was on its way downriver. The moment he saw it in the Indian lodge, Colter said, he had recognized it as Clark's prize pipe-tomahawk. He had immediately grabbed it with a shout. "I know that pipe—that's our'n!"

The Indians in the lodge—there were three men and as many women with their children—had protested.

"God damn you! You stole this from the Captain!"

The Indians, becoming angry and defensive, had denied the charge. "Hell, Cap'n, they says they bought it fair and square from a member of another village. But when they tried to take it back, I wasn't having none of it. I hung onto it, and here you are!"

On questioning him, Clark learned that Colter had indeed threatened one of the Indians with his gun. They had all then become silent and sullen, but they had made no further move as Colter left the lodge with the retrieved prize.

"Well, I am glad to have it back. My brother George gave that to me. I'd given it up as lost for sure."

Meriwether Lewis put the entire camp on guard that night. Rain filled the darkness with its endless dripping, a reminder of the months at Fort Clatsop—but a reminder, too, that not far beyond these rapids the land became open, treeless, and dry. They were moving out of rainy country.

There was no more trouble during the night. In the morning the canoes were unloaded. William Clark took all of the ablebodied men with him to haul the canoes over the long portage—2,800 yards over a narrow, rocky, and slippery trail.

418

Louis Charbonneau

Hard coming down, Clark remembered; harder by far going up. The rain, which had let up briefly at dawn, started to fall steadily again, adding to the difficulty of the portage. The men had the canoes in the water much of the way on ropes, hauling them past the rocks.

One Indian, watching the men laboring on the towline, singled out two soldiers who were separated a little from the rest and threw stones at them. The men dropped the line and turned angrily, searching for the culprit, but the native ran off as soon as he was seen.

Five men plus Sacajawea and Pomp remained with Meriwether Lewis and Seaman at the lower camp to guard the baggage unloaded from the canoes. Three of the men had various foot or leg ailments; William Bratton was still so crippled by his neck and back pain that he could not even walk, much less drag a canoe; and Charbonneau was assigned to cook.

During the day Lewis was preoccupied both with getting the baggage ready for portage and with the Indians who crowded about the camp all day. Nowhere among these river tribes were the decorated shirts of the Sioux, the wondrously painted buffalo robes of the Mandans, the quill-worked shirts of the Shoshonis, or the decorated elkskin robes of the Nez Percés. The Wah-clel-lahs and Clah-clel-lahs, two bands of the Shahana Nation, were like poor cousins, Lewis thought— dressed in tatters, indifferently housed, flea-ridden, dirty, and ill-mannered. He was determined to deal with them in a fair-minded fashion, but they made it difficult.

Warning his collection of invalids to keep a vigilant watch against pilfering and leaving Seaman with them as a guard, Lewis left camp at midday and walked downriver to inspect some Shahana burial grounds. He made notes on the manner in which these Indians buried their dead, sometimes stacking the bodies several layers deep in the crowded sepulchers. Returning to camp, he added lengthy entries to his journal on the habits, dress, and customs of these river tribes.

In the evening the rain let up for a time. Pat Gass arrived

down the portage trail ahead of the other men to report to Lewis on the day's activity. Four canoes had been dragged up to the top of the portage. All were a little damaged but could be repaired. "The men's all wore out, Cap'n. I doubt they could pull a peapod over them rapids this night. Cap'n Clark says to take the last boat up in the mornin', when all hands is fresh."

Lewis nodded agreement. William Clark would not have given such an order without thoughtful consideration. The baggage, in any event, would have to wait for morning. The last canoe could be taken up at the same time.

"You had no more trouble with the natives?" Lewis felt renewed annoyance when he recalled the insolence of the morning's stone-thrower.

"Not while we was on the boats. There was some bit of commotion just now, comin' down. Private Shields stayed behind to buy a dog for supper from that village above the falls. He was bringin' it down when some of the savages, seein' he was alone on the road, tried to steal the dog from him. They shoved him off the road and grabbed the rope he had the dog on." Gass grinned at the recollection. "Ol' John, he pulled out that big knife o' his—he had no gun with him—and he was ready to gut them Indians if he got the chance. I do believe they seen the fire in his eyes, Cap'n. They let go his dog and skedaddled."

William Clark had arrived with most of the men while Sergeant Gass was making his report. He grunted in a manner that expressed his displeasure with the Indians' attitude and actions. "The beggars were fortunate to run when they did," Clark said. "As soon as the rest of us saw Shields was in trouble, we were ready to take any action necessary to defend him. Some of these Wah-clel-lahs are out-and-out scoundrels! They'd steal the moccasins off our feet if they could."

Pat Gass grinned. "Not like lettin' their dogs chew 'em, eh, Cap'n? Like those Flathead dogs?"

Clark glowered at the reminder. After a moment his expression eased off into a smile. The redhead's anger seldom lasted long. "If these locals could train their dogs as thieves, I'm sure they would."

As Lewis conferred with Clark about the day's progress, the other men were trudging wearily into camp. Smoke from the cooking fires drifted upward, the smell of burning wood and sizzling meat mingling with the damp smell of the pines. The expedition had nearly reached the edge of the timbered hills. Not far above the Cascades the open plain waited, barren and treeless for hundreds of miles. This was the last they would see of what they had come to think of as the rain forests of the lower Columbia.

As if to emphasize the thought, the rain began again, and the cooks scrambled to protect their fires. The soldiers, thoroughly soaked after hauling the canoes all day in the rain, merely hunched their shoulders and sought what shelter they could find.

An Indian approached Meriwether Lewis out of the rain. He didn't look like a Wah-clel-lah, being taller and thinner. He wore only a plain elkskin robe and a pelt over his loins, skimpy covering that might be seen anywhere on the Columbia from here on down to the Pacific. He mumbled something that Lewis did not understand. Then Lewis was startled to recognize some words in Clatsop, a smattering of which he had managed to pick up during the winter months among the coastal Indians. "What was that? What did you say about the Bear Dog? Something has happened to him?"

Lewis glanced around the camp. Seaman was nowhere to be seen.

"These bad Indians," the native said again in Clatsop. "They steal Bear Dog." He pointed inland, in the general direction of one of the Wah-clel-lah villages. "They go to houses, take dog." His glance flickered toward the cooking fires. "Wah-clel-lah eat dog."

Lewis did not have to ask for volunteers. Gibson, Pryor, and Collins had their guns already in their hands and were on their feet; others were ready to join them. "Three men

should be enough and can move fast. After them quickly, Sergeant Pryor! I'll be right behind you. Fire your weapons if you need help. And if those Indians won't let Seaman go, if they give you the least trouble or resistance, you are to fire on them!"

"Yes, sir!"

Seaman had prowled the lower camp restlessly all day. For the first few hours he was able to catch glimpses of the men hauling the canoes up the river on towlines, struggling along the bank with painful slowness. The morning was nearly gone before a shelf of rock and a curtain of rain combined to hide the men from Seaman's view.

When Meriwether Lewis went off downriver on his own —he felt Seaman's visibility at camp might prove more daunting to would-be thieves than the presence of a few sore-backed, sore-footed soldiers—Seaman took cover under a tall pine against the recurrent showers and scratched disconsolately at a new batch of fleas.

One of the Indians who had been hanging about the camp settled on his haunches nearby. He grinned at Seaman, revealing yellow teeth. A squat, broad-faced man with the sore, red-rimmed eyes seen on many of the river Indians, he wore a torn blue shirt and smelled strongly of fish.

Seaman did not warm to the Indian. He was acutely sensitive to both fear and hostility in humans, and many of these river Indians who had been in and out of the expedition's camps carried the odor of antagonism. Seaman wasn't sure about this one. The rain seemed to drown all smells other than the heavy scent of pine.

The Newfoundland was aware that both Lewis and Clark had been unfailingly hospitable toward the red men. Seaman could do no less. He would tolerate the stranger as long as he did not appear threatening to the camp or its people.

When Sacajawea came by and spoke to Seaman, the man in the blue shirt was very attentive. He watched as Seaman jumped to his feet, wagging enthusiastically, and followed the

Indian woman. But Sacajawea was preoccupied with helping Charbonneau prepare that evening's supper; she had located some roots and dug them up. Again Seaman was ignored.

He stopped beside William Bratton, who was still so crippled that he would have to be carried to the top of the portage. Bratton tried to prop himself up on an elbow. "What are you doin' here, lad? Why aren't you out chasin' down a deer for our supper?"

He fell back, gasping. The damp chill of the day made every movement more painful, forcing him to abandon the halfhearted effort to be cheerful.

When Meriwether Lewis returned from his visit to the Indian burial ground, the man in the blue shirt left the camp. For some time Seaman did not see him. Late in the afternoon, when some of the soldiers were beginning to filter down the portage trail, there was a commotion in camp. Many Indians were clustered about Lewis, demanding his attention, including a chief of the Clah-clel-lahs visiting from a village above the Cascades. And the squat Indian in the blue shirt suddenly appeared at Seaman's side.

423

"Dog come," he whispered.

Unexpectedly he slipped an elkskin rope around Seaman's neck.

Seaman felt the loop of the rope tighten. He glanced around the camp; no one was paying attention. The Indian tugged on the rope. Seaman was reluctant to accompany the stranger, but the circumstances spoke of no danger. This man was welcome in the camp. Seaman had even heard Meriwether Lewis speak to him cheerfully.

Seaman yielded to the pressure around his neck. He followed the Indian to the edge of the camp. As soon as the pair were screened by a stand of pines, two other red men appeared from among the trees. Over his shoulder Seaman had a glimpse of some of his soldier companions straggling down the trail from the top of the Cascades, too far away to notice what was happening at the edge of the woods.

The three Indians spoke urgently. Then they began to trot

away from the camp along a worn trail that climbed away from the river. Seaman loped along with them. To the south, ahead of them, the smoke from many lodges drifted above the trees to smudge the skyline.

Though puzzled by what was happening, Seaman was not yet truly suspicious. The Indians acted friendly. Clearly excited, they laughed and pummeled him playfully. They were not running so fast that he could not keep up without difficulty. The man in the blue shirt was loudly boasting of his prowess, recounting the cunning with which he had infiltrated the white men's camp to deceive and outwit them. Now look—what a prize he had captured!

The Indians had run nearly two miles from the river, maintaining a steady pace, when they heard a shout far behind them. The runners broke stride. One of them, peering back along their trail, called out sharply to the others. All three men began to jabber at once.

Seaman glanced over his shoulder. Coming over the brow of a rise, silhouetted against a stand of pine trees, were the familiar, buckskin-clad figures of three of the soldiers. One of them shouted again.

Seaman tried to turn back.

The rope around his neck tightened cruelly into a noose. The Indian holding the rope spoke angrily to his companions. He tried to run, dragging Seaman forcefully after him. Still unsure of the situation, Seaman let himself be pulled a few more steps, offering only mild resistance. But his friends were coming, calling out. Seaman's reluctance to leave them sharpened.

He looked back again. The pursuing soldiers were closer. The thief's two cohorts were becoming very agitated as they stared back at the advancing white men.

Then Seaman saw another familiar figure top the rise, recognizable even at some distance. The sturdy bowed legs broke into a run. Meriwether Lewis was coming after his dog.

Seaman balked. As he dug in, for a few seconds, the Indian in the blue shirt jerked frantically on the rope. His gaze rolled toward the advancing soldiers. Seaman caught the spurt of a new scent, sharp and unpleasant, detectible through the odors of dirt and sweat and fish: the smell of fear.

The Indian dropped the rope and ran.

One of the soldiers—Seaman recognized Pryor now, then Gibson and Collins behind him—shouted angrily, holding up his rifle and brandishing it. "You thievin' bastards! Come back, and I'll put a bullet in you!"

The invitation wasn't appealing to the panicked thieves. For all their small stature and short legs, they ran with surprising speed. The three soldiers pounded up to Seaman and stopped, panting from their run. They were caught between grins for their rescued dog and glares after the retreating red men. Collins was still growling aloud about rascals and no-accounts and teaching them a lesson. "We oughta kill a few," he snarled. "Then maybe they'd learn a lesson!"

Meriwether Lewis came up in time to hear Collins' threat. For once he said nothing to temper the soldier's wrath. The cold anger in Lewis's sharp blue eyes was, if anything, more dangerous than Collins's bluster. He stared after the Indians for long moment. "Let's get back to camp, then," he said. "Keep a sharp eye out."

Lewis picked up the rope that was still attached to Seaman's neck, slipped it over the Newfoundland's head, and threw it to the ground. "By the Lord, you're too amiable for your own good," he told his dog. His hand scrubbed Seaman's skull affectionately. "If they hadn't let you go, I'd have killed a few myself!"

425

A week after Seaman was kidnapped, the Corps of Discovery passed the first rapids below the falls of the Columbia. The daily struggle with the river had made up Meriwether Lewis's mind. He sent William Clark across the river to the Skillute village to buy horses. The Indians were covetous, the bargaining hard, the expedition's store of trading items almost gone. But Clark was determined and inventive—he even obtained

some horses for improvised medical treatment of a chief's wife. By the time the canoes and baggage had been transported above the falls, Clark had done well enough to commit the expedition to leaving the river.

Four men continued up the Columbia in two small canoes. The rest struck overland with nine pack horses to carry most of their baggage and a tenth for Bratton to ride. Crossing the plain toward Lewis's River, they had the good fortune to meet a band of Walla Walla Indians led by a friendly chief named Yellept, on whom they had bestowed a medal the previous fall. These were a different people from the often corrupt and hostile tribes who lived lower down the river. Yellept invited the white men to visit his village. He even brought them firewood—a priceless gift in this treeless plain.

The Corps of Discovery began to relax its truculent guard. Once again they were among friends.

Ahead, the snow-clad peaks of the Rockies were visible, thrusting upward against a clear blue sky.

426

The child was crying.

At first only mildly disturbing, the plaintive wail became as grating as the rasp of a saw biting through a stubborn knot. Even through the dreary months of rain and cold at Fort Clatsop, which had seen at least half the men of the expedition hacking and coughing with colds or limp in their blankets with the flu, little Pomp had remained a healthy, good-natured child. Now he was ill.

At first Lewis and Clark, the boy's self-appointed physicians, had put his complaint down to teething. But for several days he had also had violent diarrhea. And now, as the Corps of Discovery returned to the Kooskooskee and the lands of the Nez Percés, the lax had suddenly stopped and Pomp had developed a high fever.

In a corner of the captains' tent, by this time a tattered patchwork of assorted skins, Sacajawea sat on her haunches, crooning softly in Shoshoni to the restless boy.

Louis Charbonneau

"The jaw is much more swollen than it was yesterday," said Meriwether Lewis, wondering if the Indian woman's chant was a lullaby or a prayer to her gods.

"Aye," said the troubled Clark. "And I don't much like that swelling on the back of his neck."

York, awake like the others who shared the tent with Charbonneau, Sacajawea, and the baby, was hovering again, Lewis noted. York showed as much fondness for Pomp as did William Clark. "Stir up the fire," Lewis told him quietly. "We'll need more of the poultice, as hot as he can bear."

Sacajawea, who had heard the exchange, watched the black man as he left the tent. She trusted the two captains and York as well. Lewis's knowledge and skill in the properties of herbs and natural medicines exceeded that of any Indian medicine man she had known. And Clark—who had learned much from his partner over the past two years—had been so successful treating the parade of Indian patients along the Columbia and here on the Kooskooskee that his prowess had eclipsed even that of his partner. Lewis's treatment for Pomp was cream of tartar and flour of sulphur, which Sacajawea spooned down the child's swollen throat, supplemented with hot poultices of boiled onions applied to the swelling.

When York brought the hot poultice, Sacajawea took it from him wordlessly and applied it to Pomp's neck and to the swelling below his ear.

The searing heat brought a piteous cry.

427

On the morning of May 24, Pomp's raging fever had broken. Sacajawea fed him another dose of cream of tartar and continued to apply the onion poultices. That she had hardly slept through the night did not trouble her. Nor did her husband's absence that day. Charbonneau was not much use in such matters, sleeping through most of the turmoil—he had demonstrated an ability to snore through any thunderstorm—and grumbling when he did awaken. But Sacajawea knew with a certain wifely pride that her man had proved himself useful

to the captains in other ways. This morning he was off to one of the Indian villages to trade for roots and bread, staples the expedition badly needed, with hunting in the neighborhood so poor. Charbonneau might not speak the languages of these natives, but he understood Indians better than most white men. He knew how to communicate with them, whether through signs or simple understanding of how their minds worked. He was, she thought, a man of value. It did not occur to her, gathering fennel and onions from the prairie, that she might also be considered an important part of the expedition.

The medical practitioners were busy that morning. In addition to Pomp, there were other patients, including an old Indian chief carried to the camp from some distance away by his relatives. Examining him, Lewis raised an eyebrow at his partner. The old man was unable to use his arms or legs, or even to sit up. "We'll do what we can," Lewis murmured, "but I hold little hope, not knowing the cause of his condition."

He gave the chief laudanum for his pain, ointment for his limbs. In his heart Lewis knew they were palliatives only, not remedies, but the Indians seemed pleased, the old man grateful.

Lewis's medical skill had also been tested over the past few months by the case of William Bratton, crippled since his return from the salt camp in February. Though Bratton now ate heartily, he still could not sit up without severe pain, and he could barely hobble when he tried to walk.

It was John Shields who suggested the sweat hole for Bratton. "I seen it done," Shields explained. "You dig a hole deep enough for a man to sit in it. You build a fire down there, make it hot as Hades. Then you take the fire out and put the man in there with a jug of water to make vapor, cover up the hole and let him bake."

Meriwether Lewis listened with rising interest. He knew well the efficacy of steam baths in helping rheumatic afflictions like Bratton's. The sweat hole Shields described ought to work as well or better.

That morning the men dug a hole four feet deep and about three feet in diameter and built a roaring fire in the bottom to heat the walls. After Lewis judged the hole hot enough, the fire was removed, boards were put on the bottom to protect Bratton's feet, and a wooden bench was fixed for him to sit on. Then, stripped naked, the somewhat apprehensive Bratton was lowered slowly into the hole. Lewis gave him a kettle filled with water to sprinkle against the sides and bottom of the pit to create as much steam as he could stand. A covering of blankets over a frame of willow hoops muffled Bratton's yelps as the hot steam rose around him.

After about twenty minutes Bratton was lifted out of the hole, dunked twice in cold water, and returned to the private hell. Meriwether Lewis passed strong horse mint tea down to him—the only large mint he had been able to find in the area—and Bratton gulped copious amounts of the tea as sweat poured off him.

After an hour the treatment was stopped for the day. Wrapped in a blanket, Bratton collapsed on the ground.

His physicians could only wait and wonder.

429

On May 24, William Bratton was walking about the camp, for the first time in months declaring himself free of pain. The paralyzed Indian chief and his followers were so impressed that they begged to have him given the same cure. Though skeptical, Lewis began a course of sweat treatments for the old man while continuing Bratton's treatments over the next several days. Although the chief couldn't even sit up in the hole the first time, a younger man went down with him on the next attempt and held him up.

Over the next few days there was steady progress on all fronts. Pomp's fever left him. The swelling on his neck began to subside. Lewis discontinued the poultices and prescribed a salve made of pine resin, beeswax, and bear's oil mixed. For his part Bratton was so improved that he walked around the camp with ease. And even the old Indian began to gain some mobility in his arms and legs, to the point that, for the first time in a year, he was able to wash his face by himself.

By the first week of June Lewis was able to write in his journal, "Our invalids are all on the recovery."

Word of the white chief's powerful medicine spread among the villages along the rivers, tales that would be repeated often by the Indian campfires, so that even children and grandchildren would tell them, and they would become legend.

During this same period preparations went on for the homeward journey and its first challenge—the formidable Lolo Trail. All of the expedition's horses left in charge of Twisted Hair the previous autumn were gradually rounded up, save two that, the captains were told, had been taken by Toby and his son after they left the expedition on Lewis's River to return to their native Shoshoni village in the mountains. Those that had gone wild were reintroduced to the saddle.

A store of food for the trail was also gathered for the march, each man trading what little he had—an awl, a knitting needle, a bit of vermillion, skeins of thread or a yard of ribbon—for roots and bread from the Indians to supplement a scarcity of meat. Lewis and Clark even sacrificed the brass buttons from their uniform coats.

At last the preparations were complete. Everyone was anxious, thinking of home, friends, familiar faces.

At eleven in the morning on June 10, 1806, they set out.

Sacajawea, riding her own horse proudly, carried herson, now sixteen months old. Sometimes she let Pomp ride, seated before her and held snugly in place between her legs, gurgling happily. There was little evidence of the lump below his ear, nothing at all of his distress. Looking forward toward the head of the column, where she could see Captain Lewis and Captain Redhead on their horses, she felt the never-ending wonder that had brought her to travel with such great chiefs, and to see her firstborn spared by the power of their big medicine.

450

35

the indian whoman who has been of great service to me as a pilot through this country recommends a gap in the mountains more south which I shall cross.

—WILLIAM CLARK, July 13, 1806

*O*n June 15, 1806, the Corps of Discovery left the camas prairie of the Nez Percés—in full bloom with blue flowers at this time of year—and started back up the Lolo Trail. When they reached the ridge, they found it snowbound, the drifts twelve to fifteen feet deep. Though the snow was firm enough to support even the horses fairly well, it hid the trail completely, and there was no forage. Recognizing the imprudence of plunging ahead blindly without a native guide, the two commanders reluctantly accepted the necessity of turning back. Everyone was disappointed. As both captains noted in their journals, it was the first time on the entire journey that the party had been compelled to retreat.

Not until the last week of June did they set out again, this time with five Nez Percé guides and sixty-six horses. For the next five nights, lying on the frozen ground, their faces stiff with cold, they were reminded of the ordeal of this trail on the outbound journey, when their bellies were shriveled with hunger and the way ahead was fearfully uncertain.

They arrived safely at their old Traveler's Rest camp a little before sunset on the evening of June 30, 1806. There

they stayed over for a few days to rest, divide their baggage, council with their Indian friends, and prepare for their next adventure.

For the first time the expedition was splitting up. Like the branches of a river forking, two groups would go their separate ways in smaller and more vulnerable numbers.

Lewis and Clark had discussed and decided on the separation during the winter at Fort Clatsop, with a view toward exploring two important rivers and at the same time determining the best and shortest way over the Divide. Lewis with a small group would proceed north and then east from Traveler's Rest by what they now knew from the Indians was the most direct route to the Great Falls of the Missouri, much shorter than the loop they had taken on the outward journey. He would leave some of his men at White Bear Island to prepare for the portage around the falls, while Lewis and a few volunteers ascended Maria's River to determine whether that river or any of its branches lay as far north as the fiftieth latitude. Clark, meanwhile, would take a new trail across the Bitterroot range to the southeast—also recommended by the Indians—back to the head of Jefferson's River, where the canoes and caches had been left when the expedition met the Shoshonis. At Three Forks Clark's party would again subdivide, Sergeant Ordway leading nine men with the canoes down the Missouri to join Lewis's party for the portage, while Clark led the rest on horseback over the mountains to the Yellowstone River. The meticulous planning also called for Sergeant Pryor and a few men to take the horses overland to the Mandans. Clark, with Charbonneau, Sacajawea and Pomp, and the remains of his party, would descend the Yellowstone by boat. Lewis and his men, after completing their own exploration, would rendezvous with Clark at or near the junction of the Yellowstone and the Missouri.

On the evening of July 2, 1806, Clark and Lewis examined a map on which Clark had sketched the routes each man would take. Clark pointed at the line he had drawn for his own party. "The Flatheads told us they travel this way to hunt the buffalo in the Plains, and that it's an easier trail than the one we followed from the Shoshoni village. We'll come down from the pass to Wisdom River right here and follow it south. At Shoshoni Cove we'll dig up our caches, float the canoes we sank in the Jefferson, and start down to Three Forks." His finger stabbed the location on his map. "Ordway and his men will continue down the Missouri with the boats to join ye. If our information is accurate, my party will have a short ride over the mountains to the Yellowstone."

Meriwether Lewis studied the pattern of lines. His friend was a superb mapmaker, Lewis thought, admiring the detail even of those rivers and mountains Clark knew only from hearsay. "We may risk some added danger by traveling in such small forces," Lewis said thoughtfully, "but we'll be well-armed, our reputation for friendliness must be known to almost all the Indians by this time, and we'll be moving quickly. I believe the information to be gained is well worth the risk."

Clark regarded his partner with an affection momentarily clouded by worry. "The most serious risk will be yours, Lewis. The Blackfeet have a fearsome reputation—our guides are scared to go near 'em. And ye'll be striking directly into the heart of their territory."

Lewis shrugged off the warning. Clark's map was sketchiest where it speculated on the area north of the Missouri River bounded by the Rocky Mountains on the west and Maria's River to the east. Blackfoot territory. Often banding together with the Gros Ventres of Fort de Prairie, a nomadic Plains tribe linked by name to the Minitarees in the vicinity of the Mandans, the warlike Blackfeet suffered no one to invade what they regarded as their ancestral lands. "We must know how far north Maria's River goes. If possible, I'll follow it to its source and take observations. In the President's view of the French treaty, knowing the northernmost extent of the drainage of the Missouri and its tributaries is of absolute importance."

Clark voiced no objection. He had already expressed his concern over Lewis's plan, but he could not marshal arguments

convincing enough to defeat it. What Lewis said was undeniable. Accurately determining the full extent of the territory the United States had purchased was a crucial goal of the expedition. Now that they had mapped a way across the continent to the Pacific Ocean, they could hardly pass so near the northernmost boundary of the Missouri's watershed without making an effort to resolve that vital question.

"Ye must be careful, my friend."

Lewis smiled. "I shall be as judicious as if you were at my side. A measure of support that I shall sorely miss."

They were silent then, staring down at Clark's map. With one of his sudden dark premonitions, Meriwether Lewis wondered when they would see each other again.

The Nez Percé guides accompanied Meriwether Lewis and his party along Clark's River until they came to the eastern branch. There the Indians—fearful of encountering their mortal enemies, the Blackfeet—turned back after an emotional parting. In that exchange, carrying out a Nez Percé tradition, Lewis gave his name to one of the Indians; Lewis became White Bearskin Folded.

Included in Lewis's party were nine men—Reuben and Joseph Fields, George Drouillard, Patrick Gass, Hugh Mc-Neal, Silas Goodrich, John Thompson, William Werner, and Robert Frazier.

And Seaman.

The Newfoundland rejoiced in his return to the Plains. He trotted easily alongside the horses as Lewis and his party crossed an extensive plain, climbed up through timbered hills, and entered the craggy mountains. At one point, while crossing a high table whose terrain was broken by a great number of small hillocks and sinkholes—Lewis called it the "Prairie of Knobs"—Lewis took note of a delightful creek meandering across the prairie. By now virtually everyone with the expedition had had a river named after him—or her. Lewis named this clear, sparkling stream Seaman's Creek.

Louis Charbonneau

The explorers came across pony tracks and other sign, the fresh trail of a Blackfoot hunting party. Lewis put his men on their guard both day and night.

The way was easy. Two days past Seaman's Creek, they crossed the Continental Divide. Lewis's Nez Percé guides had advised him against one mountain pass, warning that the eastern slope was steep and cut by deep ravines. Lewis followed their suggested route toward another crossing a short distance to the north. There he crossed the dividing ridge almost without noticing the passage, the rise was so gradual and easy, and the descent down the eastern flank of the mountains was equally gentle. The timbered slopes soon gave way to the familiar rolling prairie of the Missouri Plains, treeless except along the river bottoms.

During those days on the trail, keeping up with the horses while traveling thirty miles and more each day, Seaman regained the best state of health and vigor he had enjoyed since the previous summer. The last of his fleas had been killed during three nights of freezing cold on the Lolo Trail. His coat recaptured its thick, glossy black. With a return to the rich diet of the Plains, he began to flesh out. His muscles were strengthened and hardened by the daily activity. His stamina increased, and he learned to pace himself, adjusting to the speed of his companions.

Only the heat of midday bothered him, draining away some of his energy. During the hottest hours he rested whenever the opportunity offered itself—when the party stopped for dinner, or when Meriwether Lewis paused along the trail to inspect a plant or to make notes of a stream or another landmark. And Seaman made the most of the cooler hours of morning and late afternoon, when he often ranged ahead of the riders or caught up readily if he had fallen behind.

As they came past naked buttes and long sweeps of grassland to the Medicine River bottom, everything was as Seaman remembered it—the grass fresh and green from recent rains, cottonwoods tall in the river bottom, the prairie alive with game of every description. There were large herds of elk, vast assemblages of wolves skulking around the camps at night, and buffalo without number. When the riders came in sight of the Missouri, Meriwether Lewis's breath caught at the number of buffalo in view. He estimated the shaggy herd at 10,000 within a two-mile circle on either side of the river. They were also uncommonly noisy. The travelers had arrived at the breeding time of the buffalo, and the bulls were in a constant uproar. Their bellowing continued all night, a restless turmoil that kept Seaman awake and on guard much of the night.

Lewis and his party arrived at the Missouri River, opposite their old camp by White Bear Island, on July 11, 1806, eight days after leaving Traveler's Rest. Lewis had the hunters shoot eleven buffalo, both for the meat they would need in the days ahead and for their hides. With the latter they set to work at once to make two boats, a round bullboat and a canoe, to transport themselves and their baggage across the river to the site of their old camp.

William Clark and his party crossed the Bitterroots following the Indian trail recommended by the Flatheads. As promised, the route proved to be both shorter and easier than the arduous trail taken the previous summer from the Shoshoni village. It brought the travelers to a level plain through which there ran a tributary of the Wisdom River. Here, however, the highly visible Indian track scattered in so many directions that it no longer offered a path to follow.

Sacajawea spoke up volubly. Since the Indian woman was seldom so talkative, Clark called Charbonneau over to translate. Sacajawea said that she remembered this prairie clearly. As a child she had accompanied her People here many times; with the women she had gathered the camas roots that grew plentifully in this soil.

"Ask her if she knows the way back to Shoshoni Cove," Clark said, "where we sank our canoes in the Jefferson."

Charbonneau posed the question to the squaw. Sacajawea nodded vigorously. She pointed southeast. "Soon we come to a high meadow, very long, surrounded by mountains. There is a gap in these mountains. When we come to this pass, we will see the high point of another mountain where the snow never melts. It is in the direction of our canoes."

The Indian woman's certainty convinced Clark. He led his group along the route she had indicated. In a short time they passed through a gap in the hills to a broad and very long valley ringed by high mountains. Exactly as she described it, Clark thought. He searched for the high, snow-covered peak Sacajawea had mentioned and quickly identified it to the southeast, framed by the notch of another pass, like a target caught in the sights of a rifle. There! Right on the button!

Covering 164 miles in only five days, Clark's expedition reached the forks of the Jefferson on July 8, 1806. The men who had been deprived of tobacco since a few twists were portioned out last Christmas day scarcely gave themselves time to unsaddle their horses before racing off to the caches buried the previous summer, where they eagerly began to dig.

Everything in the caches was found damp but intact— including, praise be, the store of tobacco. Only one of the canoes was damaged, although that one beyond repair. Clark had it cut up to make paddles and firewood. He parceled out generous portions of tobacco to each user, including himself.

457

The next day the canoes were repaired and the baggage packed ready for the boats. Wasting no time, Clark had his people in the canoes on the morning of July 10, except for Sergeant Pryor and a few men assigned to bring the horses downriver.

The entire party rendezvoused at Three Forks on July 13, 1806, while Meriwether Lewis was setting up his camp opposite White Bear Island. Here, where the Missouri began its long passage across the continent, the detachment was to separate once more into two units. After dining just below the forks, Sergeant John Ordway and nine men set off in the loaded canoes down the Missouri River. The river was high this year, the current swift. It would not be like poling upriver.

Late in the afternoon William Clark led his group eastward along the banks of the Gallatin River, the easternmost of the three streams that joined to form the Missouri. After advancing four miles, they camped beside the Gallatin. With Clark were Sergeant Pryor and seven soldiers—John Shields, George Shannon, William Bratton, Francois Labiche, Richard Windsor, Hugh Hall, and George Gibson—plus the interpreter Charbonneau, York, Sacajawea, and Pomp. They had forty-nine horses and one colt, both to ride and to carry their baggage.

For the second time in a week, Sacajawea remembered the way through the mountains. There was an old buffalo road, she informed Clark, southeast of the direction Clark had been inclined to follow. This trail crossed the mountains and was easy for horses. It was the road the People followed.

Two days later, on July 15, after a remarkably easy climb along the trail the Indian woman had recommended, Clark and his party crossed the dividing ridge on their way to the Yellowstone.

438

That same day, while Clark camped on a newly found river, Meriwether Lewis was pacing along the bank of an old one, the Missouri, at his camp opposite White Bear Island. Nearby some of his men were sorting out the goods they had dug up from the caches, which unfortunately had been inundated when the river rose higher than anticipated. The vitally important wagon wheels had been found intact, but many of the skins, robes, and medicines were either badly damaged or destroyed.

But Lewis's mind was not on the disappointment of the caches. He was nervous, pausing every few minutes to stare across the river in the direction of the Medicine River and its course to the west. Within his view a pack of wolves were scattered about the carcass of a buffalo. Lewis counted twenty-seven of them, all indolently aware of the white men's camp —and of the Bear Dog who patroled the camp's perimeter.

Counting wolves was a way of distracting himself.

Louis Charbonneau

George Drouillard had now been missing for three days.

On the morning of the twelfth, Lewis had discovered ten of his horses missing. He had immediately sent two men, Gass and Werner, to round up the horses. At noon Werner returned with three of them; Gass reported back at midafternoon, having found none of the seven horses still absent. Fearing them stolen by Indians, Lewis then sent Drouillard and Joseph Fields out to search for them. Only Fields returned at dark, unsuccessful.

Three days, Lewis thought.

Of all the men of the Corps of Discovery—brash young Shannon, steady John Ordway, reliable John Shields, soldierly Pat Gass, and all the others—Drouillard stood out. Hunter, trapper, riverman, scout, stalker, speaker of signs, this half-Shawnee, half-French woodsman was the best of all.

If he had had any mishap with his horse . . . if he had encountered a white bear while alone and on foot in the plains . . . if he had been surprised by a hostile band of Blackfeet . . . his chances of survival would have been small.

Behind Lewis a plaintive yip drew his glance toward Seaman. He was in time to see his dog clashing his jaws in futile combat with a cloud of mosquitoes. Lewis hurried to get under his netting as the cloud descended upon him, darting and whining. So thick were the mosquitoes that they even got into the men's throats until they choked on them. The summer had been much wetter this year than last, the grass was higher, there were more stagnant pools about for the insects to breed in, and the result was an almost intolerable infestation of mosquitoes. Lewis could not even write in his journal without taking refuge under his netting. At night Seaman sometimes howled with the torment. The men had built smoky fires in the hope of driving the clouds of insects off, but the only real relief came on those evenings when a brisk, cool breeze arose and carried the mosquitoes away.

Three days. What could have happened to him?

I'll take a couple of the men and go in search of him. But might that endanger the others? If, in fact, there are Blackfeet in the vicinity?

As always, the welfare of those he had been given to command was foremost in Lewis's calculations. He thought little about being in danger himself, but he was determined that Charles Floyd would be the only man in his charge who would not return safely to the United States.

The risk was a reasonable one. Ordway would be arriving soon downriver. Lewis would put the camp on its guard, leave Seaman to give any needed alarm. The dog was already nervous and exceptionally alert over the presence about the camp of wolves, white bears, and roaring buffalo bulls in heat. As soon as McNeal returned from the portage camp, then Lewis would take two men, Gass and one of the Fields, and—

"Captain Lewis!"

Lewis whirled as Werner called out. His gaze darted across the river, and his heart leaped. A dusty, buckskin-clad figure on horseback, lean and slump-shouldered in weariness, rode slowly down the slope toward the river bottom, scattering a family of wolves in his path. Drouillard!

440   He had come back empty-handed. Damn the horses! Lewis thought. Drouillard is back safe!

As it happened, it was not Drouillard who encountered a grizzly that day, but Hugh McNeal. Earlier in the day he had been sent below the Great Falls to inspect the caches dug near the old portage camp. He never got that far. Traveling slowly and sightseeing on the way, he did not arrive at Willow Run until late in the afternoon. He was tired enough to let his attention wander. As he rode slowly up to the creek, a white bear suddenly reared up from the concealment of the willow brush— only ten feet away!

McNeal's horse panicked. He bucked and leaped aside in a twisting turn. Caught by surprise, McNeal was thrown to the ground. He landed almost at the grizzly's feet.

The young soldier had his rifle in his hand. With an intimidating roar, the bear rose aggressively to his full height.

Having no chance to fire his weapon, no time to run, Hugh McNeal was plunged into fear as if into an icy pond. He couldn't breathe.

Acting without thinking, McNeal swung his long rifle by the barrel, using it like a club. He smashed the stock across the white bear's head. So forceful was the blow—and so hard that massive skull—the gun broke at the breach. The trigger guard cut the bear's nose.

Stunned, the bear sank slowly to the ground. He began to paw at his head with his feet, more befuddled than hurt but feeling the sting of the blow.

McNeal didn't wait to see how long it would take the bear to recover. He ran to the nearest willow, a sturdy tree taller than most of those along the creek. He climbed as fast as he could. His moccasined feet slipped on the bark. In his frenzy he cracked an elbow on one branch. Behind him came another angry roar. McNeal seized a high branch and hauled himself up just as the tree shuddered from a mighty swipe of the grizzly's paw. McNeal heard the long talons rake and tear at the bark.

441

Shivering, he scurried higher. He couldn't remember: Did grizzlies climb trees?

For three hours the white bear waited, prowling about the base of the willow where Hugh McNeal clung to his precarious perch. His arms and legs ached from the strain. Darkness stole across the prairie to pool in the creek bottom at Willow Run. In the gathering gloom the grizzly at last abandoned his prey. He lumbered off to the south, following the direction of the creek.

McNeal waited for several minutes. He stared after the bear, straining to hear any sound of him.

In the fading light of evening, from his lofty perch McNeal spotted his horse grazing in the plain more than a mile away. His heart pounding, he crept down from the tree and ran across the open prairie, frequently glancing back over his shoulder. His horse, hearing him approach, lifted his head and snuffled

nervously, as if prepared to run. McNeal clucked at him sooth-ingly. "Easy, laddie, it's just me, yer old friend. Don't go run-nin' off on me now. That's it, that's a good laddie . . ."

He swung into the saddle. Relief was so strong that for an instant he felt dizzy. Shaking off the momentary weakness, he reined his horse around and headed west toward camp.

Only then did he begin to chuckle over his escapade, delighted with his escape, delighted with his broken rifle, de-lighted to be *alive*! Now, by God, Hugh McNeal had his own white bear story to tell!

442

36 the Minnetares of Fort de Prairie and the blackfoot indians rove this quarter of the country and as they are a vicious lawless and reather an abandoned set of wretches I wish to avoid an interview with them if possible.
—MERIWETHER LEWIS, J u l y 1 7, 1 8 0 6

A fter making sketches of the falls of the Missouri on the morning of July 17, 1806, Meriwether Lewis struck over-land across the plain to the northeast, hoping to intersect Maria's River at or above the point to which he had ascended that river in June of 1805. With him were three men—Reuben and Joseph Fields and George Drouillard—and Seaman.

The party was smaller than Lewis had originally planned, so reduced that William Clark would have been alarmed had he known. The loss of seven horses had forced Lewis to alter his plans. At least four of the remaining ten horses were needed to help haul the wagons and baggage over the difficult portage route past the falls. Lewis decided the other six horses, allow-ing for loss or injury to any of them, would only support four men in the Plains. The men left behind could help with the portage.

Lewis and his companions camped the first night on the Rose River, a tributary of Maria's River that ran almost due east from the Rocky Mountains. Near the river they came upon the bloody trail of a wounded buffalo, first evidence that there were Blackfoot hunters in the area.

Lewis shared the watch that night with the soldiers. Seaman, always more wary in a new situation, was awake much of the night, observing each changing of the watch, suspicious of any activity in the darkness around the camp.

The next night, July 18, after passing immense herds of buffalo on the way, the four riders reached Maria's River somewhat above the place where Lewis had been a year ago. The river valley cut deeply into the level plain, creating hills and bluffs that rose up to two hundred feet above the water on either side. To Lewis's eyes it was a pretty stream, like the laughing-eyed cousin for whom he had named it. It was perhaps 130 yards across, its bottom lush with grass and brush and cottonwoods.

For the next four days the small party followed the northwest course of Maria's River. On the twenty-first, they came to a fork in the stream. The larger branch bore to the southwest. The other, the northern branch, intrigued Lewis more. How far north did it go? As far as north latitude 50 degrees? If so, the President would be elated. Such a discovery would extend the northern boundary of Louisiana.

The next day was a letdown. By nightfall Lewis knew that the branch of Maria's River he had followed, narrower and gentler as he ascended it, had climbed as far north as it would go, nowhere near the fiftieth parallel. Where it took a sharp bend to the west, Lewis ascended a rise south of the river. The mass of the Rockies dominated the western horizon. There, almost due west of the low hill on which Lewis stood, Maria's River had its source.

He had reached the northernmost point of the Missouri's watershed.

The four men made camp in the river bottom by a small grove of cottonwoods. For several days they had been picking up additional signs of Indians in the area. Lewis and his men were watchful and nervous. They were now deep into Blackfoot country. Sensing their jumpiness, Seaman became even more restlessly alert.

On the first day Drouillard, sent upstream to observe

where the river entered the mountains, found an Indian camp of eleven tipis abandoned within the last ten days. Tracks were all around them.

They remained three days in the river bottom. Each day was cloudy and rainy, frustrating Meriwether Lewis's attempts to take precise celestial observations. With the men becoming daily more nervous of the Blackfeet, Lewis reluctantly made his decision on the evening of July 26, 1806. In the morning he would break camp. Even though he had been unable to obtain the data he needed to establish the longitude of this location, he was unwilling to risk his men a day longer.

He named the site Camp Disappointment.

William Clark had arrived at the Yellowstone River on the fifteenth. He followed it down onto the plain and encamped in a wooded bottom on July 19—the same day Lewis and his men reached Maria's River and Sergeant Ordway with his party of nine landed at the White Bear Island camp after coming down the Missouri.

Clark and his party stayed there four days. Clark put his men to work making two canoes and the necessary oars and poles for the trip downriver. He had devised a unique design. From the longest trees his men could discover, he would make two dugouts, each twenty-eight feet long and up to two feet wide. These he would lash together, connecting them by means of a platform strong enough to hold much of the cargo. The boats would descend the river in tandem.

On the night of the twentieth, twenty-four horses disappeared. Clark sent Charbonneau, Shannon, and Bratton out to look for them. They found nothing. Pryor and Charbonneau were also baffled the following day; the plain was so dry and hard that tracks were almost impossible to detect. Finally the best of the trackers available, Francois Labiche, came upon some horse tracks on July 23, confirming Clark's suspicion that Indians had driven off the horses.

Early on July 24, 1806, Clark conferred with Sergeant

445

Pryor. He handed Pryor a letter that Clark had been working on during the layover. "It is addressed to Mr. Hugh Heney," Clark pointed out. "Ye'll remember him, I'm sure."

"Aye, Captain." A free trader associated with the Northwest Company, Heney had arrived at the Mandans in December of the winter the Corps of Discovery spent there. He had been the friendliest and best-liked of the traders, Pryor remembered.

"Ye're to deliver it to him personally. If he's not at the Mandans, ye'll no doubt find him at the Northwest post on the Assiniboine. Ye have twenty-six horses left. Leave about half of them at the Mandans in charge of their Grand Chief, Black Cat. Take the others with you to the Assiniboine."

In his letter to Heney, Clark discussed the desire of the United States government to establish friendly relations with the Sioux, and he sought to engage the trader as an emissary to the various Sioux tribes. He also suggested that, as American trading posts were established along the Missouri, Lewis and Clark would recommend Heney for the post of Indian agent. Pryor was authorized to give Heney three of his horses as part of his engagement; the others could be traded at the Canadian outpost for merchandise the expedition would need upon its arrival at the Mandans.

The canoes were completed. Pryor set off across the plain on the south side of the river, heading east, taking Richard Windsor, George Shannon, and Hugh Hall with him. Clark had all of his baggage placed aboard the two canoes and the connecting platform. This unique arrangement provided ample room for all of the cargo and the eight adults (and one child) who were to travel down the Yellowstone. In one of the boats were Shields, Bratton, Gibson, and Labiche; in the other Clark, York, Charbonneau, Sacajawea, and Pomp.

The Yellowstone River, although crowded with many islands, was very navigable. It was about two hundred yards at this point, bold, rapid, and deep. On that first day Clark and his party sped downriver sixty-nine miles.

446

Louis Charbonneau

Progress was equally rapid the next day. Late in the afternoon, having come nearly fifty miles since setting out at sunrise—in spite of delaying once to hunt and a second time to wait out a heavy fall of rain—the boats landed on the starboard side of the river, where Clark's attention was caught by a huge rock formation in the wide part of the bottom. Intrigued by the remarkable rock, Clark walked around its base, measuring it at 400 paces. The rock, on three sides almost perfectly perpendicular, rose a full 200 feet above the river.

"This I must explore!" Clark declared.

With several others he began to climb the one side of the formation that appeared to promise access to the top. It was a slow, hard climb. Sacajawea, with Pomp riding as usual in his cradleboard between her shoulders—though at seventeen months of age he was a considerable burden—followed Clark up the steep slope. Charbonneau, who started out with them, decided about halfway up that he was not really that much interested in gaining the top. His buckskins were black with sweat and beads of it ran down his cheeks into his beard. His woman could go, he didn't care. What was it, eh? Just a rock!

The climbers emerged onto the top, which was slightly dome-shaped, capped by about five feet of soil with a covering of short grass. At this height above the river bottom, the wind blew steadily off the Plains. The view was spectacular in every direction—over rivers and prairies, hills and bluffs, all the way to the distant, snow-covered peaks of the Shining Mountains.

For several minutes Clark delighted in this expansive view. He was hardly aware of the others who had climbed with him until a gurgling sound caught his ear.

Little Pomp's round, dark-skinned face was lifted to the wind, his black eyes sparkling, a smile of delight on his lips. Something tugged at William Clark's heart. In the past year he had become very fond of this sturdy, uncomplaining boy who had survived every obstacle from sickness and storms to boiling rapids and winter snows. Clark, who would have protested vigorously the suggestion that he was uncommonly sentimental, was in fact easily moved by simple demonstrations of affection and such common joys as a woman's smile or a child's laughter.

On the way down Clark paused at a place on the rock where Indians had engraved the figures of animals and other signs. Near these marks Clark made his own, using his knife to carve his name and the date: *Wm Clark July 25, 1806.*

He descended thoughtfully to the river bottom. There was still an hour or more of light remaining. He got everyone back into the boats and traveled downriver another twelve miles before another hard shower, accompanied by gusting winds, forced him to halt for the night.

After supper he produced his journal to record the day's events. Sacajawea was sitting nearby, murmuring softly to Pomp, who appeared to be asleep. Clark coughed. "I have decided," he said, pausing at what he perceived to be a pompous tone. He smiled at the Indian woman. "I shall call that magnificent rock Pompy's Tower."

An expression of childish delight lit Sacajawea's usually impassive face.

448

That same evening Sergeant Nathaniel Pryor and his three soldiers slept on the plain. On the morning of July 26, Pryor woke early, glared around the camp and roared, "On your feet, you men! Look alive! Windsor, damn it, where the hell are the horses?"

Richard Windsor had had the last watch. He looked bleary-eyed, confused, and worried. "I d'int hear nothin', Sarjint. They musta wandered off . . ."

"You bloody well better hope to hell they wandered off!"

There was no sign of the horses. Some of them had been caught on the far side of a dry creek bed the evening before when a sudden rain squall caused a flash flood, filling the creek to its banks in seconds. But the horses had been able to cross the creek as the floodwaters receded. This morning, in any event, the creek was down to a muddy trickle.

Louis Charbonneau

One hundred yards from camp Pryor stopped, his morning gruffness turning to anger and dismay. He stared down at the tracks of moccasined feet in the muddy plain.

Following the tracks, Pryor and his soldiers soon discovered where the Indians had rounded up the horses during the night and driven them off. "Goddam thieves!" Pryor muttered. "What are we doin', providin' horses for the whole Indian Nation? They can't have got far," he added grimly. "Let's get after 'em. Make sure you got your shot pouches."

On foot the four men followed the trail of the stolen horses. After five miles the Indians had disbursed into two groups. Pryor chose to follow the larger band, reasoning that it was more likely to include the stolen animals.

Five miles farther into the empty prairie Pryor stopped at the crest of a rise. He could see storm clouds over the mountains to the southwest. The day was warm and muggy. A heat haze shimmered over the prairie. Large herds of buffalo drifted slowly toward the southeast.

The Indians and the horses were gone.

449

After retracing their steps to their night camp, Pryor and his men packed up their gear, loaded it on their backs and trudged off toward the northeast—the shortest line, Pryor decided, back to the Yellowstone River.

They reached the river late that afternoon, descending to a wide bottom in which there rose a distinctive hill or mound thrusting two hundred feet into the air. Pryor had no way of knowing that William Clark had named it Pompy's Tower.

Near the base of the rock George Shannon shot a large bull buffalo. A short while later he killed another. The weary explorers butchered the meat, put the best cuts over a fire to cook, and set the hides aside. Gathering some stout willow branches under Pryor's direction, they began to make the wooden frames for two round, Mandan-style bullboats. One thing Pryor was certain of: they sure as hell weren't going to walk all the way to Fort Mandan.

They worked until after dark. By then they were able to stretch the wet buffalo skins over their basinlike boat frames. The hides would dry and tighten overnight.

In the middle of the night Nathaniel Pryor was awakened from exhausted sleep by a sharp stab of pain. He cried out. A snarl answered him.

Rolling frantically away from the terrifying sound, Pryor glimpsed the gleaming yellow eyes and bared teeth of a wolf. "Jesus Christ!" he yelled. "The son of a bitch bit me!"

He reached for his gun. The wolf, seeing another motion to his right, turned and attacked Richard Windsor, who was still lying on the ground. Windsor tried to protect his face with flailing arms.

George Shannon was the first to grab his rifle. It was already loaded; in the Plains he never went to sleep without the loaded gun at his side. He brought it swiftly to his shoulder, aimed in the dim glow from the campfire, and fired.

The wolf screamed once, leaped into the air, and fell on his side.

450

There was a long silence. The four men circled the dead wolf and stared at each other. As the initial shock wore off, Nathaniel Pryor was just beginning to feel severe pain where he had been bitten on the hand. "We had our goddam horses stole," he muttered. "We walked twenty miles across this goddam desert. And now I get bit on the goddam hand!" He glared at the others, who prudently held their breath and said nothing. "First light, soldiers, we get into these goddam Indian boats and get the hell out of here!"

On the morning of July 26, 1806, while Sergeant Pryor and his men were doggedly walking across the prairie in pursuit of their stolen horses and William Clark was descending the Yellowstone at a rate of seventy miles a day, Meriwether Lewis and his party rode south across the open plain from Camp Disappointment. The prairie was interrupted by swells and gentle rises and occasional flat-topped buttes. Moving south from their camp, before long the riders came upon the twisting course of the southern branch of Maria's River. It had a narrow bottom bordered by steep cliffs.

Deer were often found in the river bottoms. Drouillard descended to hunt for their supper while Lewis and the Fields brothers rode across the highland south of the bluffs. Seaman tagged along behind them, his tail drooping. The day was warm, the air heavy.

Topping a rise, Lewis saw a wide cleft in the prairie that dropped sharply away toward the river, which was visible as a shining white ribbon about 150 feet below the highland. A few minutes earlier he had had a glimpse of Drouillard picking his way along the south bank of the stream. Lewis could not see him now.

What he did see brought a jolt of excitement. A band of Indians was clustered on a ridge overlooking the canyon of the river. A short distance below the ridge were at least thirty horses, half of them bearing Indian saddles.

For several moments the Indians were unaware of being watched. It was clear to Lewis that they were following Drouillard's progress in the river bottom below.

Seaman growled. "Quiet, boy," Lewis murmured.

One of the Indians turned his head. At his shout the others whirled about. Watching them through his spyglass, Meriwether Lewis was able to read their agitation on discovering him. In an instant they ran down the slope to their horses, gathered them up, and drove them toward the ridge.

Lewis made a quick decision. From the number of Indian horses saddled, he guessed that he and his men were badly outnumbered. Their own horses were indifferent, not to be relied on to outrun pursuit. Moreover, Lewis would not abandon Drouillard, alone at the bottom of the canyon.

"Let's go to meet them, lads. Keep your wits about you."

Leading the way, he rode toward the Indians. When he was about a quarter mile off, one of the warriors jumped on his horse and rode straight toward Lewis. At a distance of about a hundred yards he stopped abruptly. Lewis instantly

451

dismounted and held out his hand in a signal of friendship, beckoning the Indian toward him. Either the friendly gesture was misunderstood or deliberately ignored—the Indian wheeled his horse and galloped back to his companions.

All of the red men then mounted and rode toward the advancing party of whites. Lewis counted eight warriors. He wondered if there were others out of sight to account for the number of horses saddled.

"We may have trouble with these gentlemen," said Lewis calmly to the Fields brothers. "They're either Gros Ventres of Fort de Prairie or Blackfeet, and from what I've heard of both it doesn't matter much which they are. If they think they have us sufficiently outnumbered, they'll attack. If so, they'll have to kill me to lay their hands on my gun, my horse, or my baggage. I trust you will make the same resolution!"

"Aye, sir," Joseph Fields said truculently. "We'll fight to the death if needs be." His brother murmured assent.

They were all nervous, but from what he had seen, Lewis guessed that the red men were equally apprehensive.

When the two groups had come within one hundred paces, all of the Indians halted except one. He advanced steadily.

"Wait here," said Lewis.

He rode out alone to meet the leader of the Indians.

The two men stared at each other as they halted. The warrior was a very muscular man with a fiercely scowling expression. When Lewis offered his hand in friendship, however, the Indian immediately clasped it. Relieved, Lewis rode past him to the lineup of warriors and greeted each one in turn. While the Indian leader did the same with Reuben and Joseph Fields, all of the savages displayed a general attitude of cordiality. Several of them pointed at the huge Bear Dog and spoke animatedly among themselves.

Everyone then dismounted. By signs the Indians expressed a desire to smoke. Lewis replied that his pipe of peace, which he wished to smoke with his new Indian friends, was in the hands of the man down by the river. He indicated that one of the red men should accompany Reuben Fields in search of Drouillard so that they might all smoke together.

After Fields and the redskin rode off toward the river, Lewis tried to question the Indians by signs, seeking to identify the tribe and any chiefs among them. His first guess was that they were Minitarees of Fort de Prairie; in fact, they were Blackfeet. They indicated that three of their number were chiefs. Though he was skeptical, as a further demonstration of his friendly intentions Lewis presented one of the supposed chiefs with a medal, another with a flag and the third with a handkerchief.

By now Lewis was convinced that there were no more than eight warriors in the band, and that they had been as alarmed by the accidental encounter as were Lewis and his men. He suggested that, as the sun would soon be setting, they should all ride down to the river bottom together where they might smoke and council at their ease.

As they rode toward the canyon, the Indians remained bunched together. Joseph Fields watched them suspiciously. Seaman trotted alongside his companions, curious about the strangers but taking his cue from Meriwether Lewis, who presented an appearance of cool self-assurance. The slightest suggestion of fear, Lewis knew, would only encourage any latent treachery in the Blackfeet.

Drouillard and Reuben Fields met them en route. With Drouillard present, Lewis felt his small party more ready to meet any duplicity. In addition, he could now turn the main part of communication over to the leathery *metis*, who was far more skilled than Lewis in the language of signs.

They descended a very steep bluff to a small, narrow bottom about a half mile long. Above and below this shelf the river washed steep bluffs on both sides. Near a group of three tall cottonwoods the Indians formed a semicircular lodge of buffalo skins, the shelter open across the front, and invited Lewis and his men to join them.

As they smoked throughout the evening, Meriwether Lewis quizzed the Blackfeet. He learned that this small band

belonged to a much larger hunting party camping near the mountains to the west and that not far away another band of Blackfeet was on its way to the mouth of Maria's River.

Although he was careful not to show it, this news alarmed Lewis on behalf of the other members of the expedition who should now be at the forks. With a bold indication of confidence he suggested that the Indians should send one of their number to their chiefs, inviting them and all of their warriors to a general council of peace at the conjunction of the Missouri and Maria's rivers. The Blackfeet did not immediately respond. "Let's let them sleep on it," Lewis told Drouillard.

Lewis and Drouillard were to share part of the Indian lodge while the Fields brothers slept near the fire outside. While the others bedded down, Lewis took the first watch. He stayed awake, Seaman watchful at his side, until nearly midnight. Then he woke Reuben Fields. "The Indians are all asleep," Lewis told Fields in a low voice. "But keep a close watch. If any of them leave camp, wake us all at once."

454

"Yes sir. D'you think they might have a try at stealin' our horses?"

"I would be surprised by nothing."

Meriwether Lewis lay down near the opening at the front of the lodge, intending to sleep only lightly.

The next thing he knew it was first light, and he heard George Drouillard shout, "Damn you! Let go my gun!"

37 The Fieldes told me that three of the indians whom they pursued swam the river one of them on my horse and that two others ascended the hill and escaped from them with a part of their horses, two I had pursued into the nitch one lay dead near the camp and the eighth we could not account for . . .
—MERIWETHER LEWIS, July 27, 1806

T

he night was cloudy, the darkness thick along the river bottom. Seaman watched Lewis and his friends smoke and talk with the Blackfeet long into the night. At first puzzled, for he had sensed hostility in the Indians at the initial contact, Seaman gradually relaxed his vigilance when he perceived that Lewis and the soldiers appeared to be at ease.

At last the ceremonial pipes were put aside. The Indians took to their robes within the wings of their shelter, a simple structure of buffalo hides spread over a pole frame. Seaman stayed awake with Meriwether Lewis through the first watch. After Reuben Fields took Lewis's place, Seaman lay near the front of the lodge. The camp remained quiet and peaceful. Dozing lightly, the Newfoundland was frequently awake, listening to the trickle of the stream over its gravel bed, watching the huddled shapes of the strangers where they lay, hearing Joseph Fields snore in his sleep. Seaman was not the only one awake in that bottom. There was an occasional whisper of sound from the brush, and, when the wind quickened, he caught the scents of wolf and fox. Once a series of barks

snapped Seaman's head up. The small wolf of the Plains barked remarkably like a dog.

In the darkest hour of the night, when only Joseph Fields—taking the last sentinel duty after relieving his brother—appeared to be awake, one of the Indians rose silently from the ground at the back of the lodge. Although the man made no more noise than a cloud floating across the face of the moon, Seaman lifted his head. He watched the Blackfoot slip under one of the skins that formed the back wall of the shelter, moving so quietly that Fields did not even turn his head.

Seaman waited. He was curious but not alarmed. Had not these Indians, like so many others of the mountains and the Plains, been accepted by his companions as their friends?

After a while, when nothing happened, the Newfoundland rested his head between his front paws and listened to the reassuring sounds of Lewis, Drouillard, and Reuben Fields breathing deeply as they slept.

Seaman dozed.

A low yipping woke him. It came from the brush beyond the three cottonwoods under which the Blackfeet had raised their lodge. After a moment the shrill cry was repeated, this time more clearly.

Seaman rose to his feet. Joseph Fields, half asleep, caught the movement out of the corner of his eye. The sentry relaxed when he saw Seaman moving quietly toward the edge of the clearing. The dog often played sentinel, Fields thought drowsily, at times to the great advantage of the expedition.

Repeated high-pitched yelps drew Seaman away from the encampment. The sounds seemed to drift off as soon as he approached their source. Without realizing it, he was drawn some distance along the river bottom. He was unaware of the passage of time. The sky gradually turned from black to gray to a luminous silver. Morning light began to filter down into the canyon, throwing the steep cliffs into sharper relief.

Pausing to listen for the elusive yipping, Seaman was aware of the coming of dawn. Pockets of the river bottom filled

Louis Charbonneau

with light like pools of water. From farther up the river a flight of ducks burst upward and flapped directly over his head, climbing swiftly toward the rim of the high cliffs that now crowded close to the river on either side.

"Sea . . . man," a voice whispered. It was strangely guttural, mouthing the two syllables with difficulty.

Seaman had not heard the tantalizing yips for several minutes, and the unexpected whisper raised his hackles as he spun around.

A Blackfoot Indian grinned at him.

Slowly the stiff hairs subsided on the back of Seaman's neck. The incipient growl died in his throat. Once again he was deceived by the apparent friendliness of the Indian, reinforced by Meriwether Lewis's acceptance of the natives' hospitality.

"Sea—man," the Blackfoot repeated, this time with more confidence.

His smile was ingratiating, a gratuitous display of gleaming white teeth. Seaman eyed him cautiously, though as yet he had no reason for suspicion. He did not connect this excessively friendly stranger with the yipping sounds that had drawn him away from the camp, but something about the man awakened the memory of another Indian who had tried to lure him away from his companions, another stranger who had carried about him the sweaty smell of treachery.

As the Blackfoot reached a hand out as if to pet him, Seaman backed off a step. Then the man struck swiftly. He had one hand behind his naked back, hidden by the fringe of his leather leggings. His arm unfolded. He was holding a long stick at the end of which dangled a noose of leather. With a flick of his wrist, he dropped the twisted leather loop over Seaman's head.

At that same moment the morning stillness of the canyon erupted in angry shouts. Seaman knew at once that he had been betrayed. As the noose dropped over his head, he leaped back. The sudden movement only tightened the coil of leather around his neck. The more he danced and pulled at the end

of the line, the tighter the noose became, choking off all air to his lungs. Dimly he heard a shot rattle along the river bottom, followed by another. Black spots flickered before his eyes, and though it was now dawn, the blackness of night crept from the corners of his brain and washed over him.

In the confusion of waking, Meriwether Lewis thought, I never should have slept. He yelled at Drouillard, "What's the matter?" In the same instant he wondered, Where is Seaman? Why didn't he warn us?

Drouillard couldn't answer him. He was too busy scuffling with one of the Blackfeet at the front of the lodge. Beyond them, in the open, both Reuben and Joseph Fields were shouting angrily. Seeing Drouillard in a fight with the Indian for the possession of his gun and shot pouch, Lewis reached behind him for his own rifle. *Gone!*

He scrambled to his feet. Drouillard, he knew, could take care of himself—he already had his hands on his rifle and was contesting with the Indian for it. The brothers Fields were chasing another Indian who had made off with their two rifles. By the Lord! They deceived us well!

Then Lewis saw another Blackfoot running away, Lewis's Harpers Ferry rifle in his hand. Drawing his pistol, Lewis set off in grim pursuit. It was early to be up and running—he hadn't had time to get his wits about him—but the blackguard wasn't going to get away with his gun!

"Put down that gun!" Lewis shouted in his best parade-ground bellow of command. "Or by God I'll shoot!"

Lewis was only twenty yards behind the Indian, close enough for his harsh warning to take effect. The Blackfoot halted. He turned around slowly. At that moment Reuben and Joseph Fields reappeared. Both men now carried their rifles, evidence that they had overtaken the thief who had carried off their weapons. As the Indian placed Lewis's rifle on the ground, Reuben Fields approached the thief aggressively. "Lemme shoot him, Cap'n! Just give me the word!"

"No! He can't harm us now."

The Blackfoot retreated cautiously, his gaze shifting back and forth between Lewis and Reuben. Lewis stepped forward quickly to retrieve his rifle. About this time Drouillard arrived on the scene. Lewis saw that he had also recovered both his rifle and his pouch. There was a seething anger in Drouillard's eyes that Lewis had never seen before.

"Can I kill that son of a bitch, *Capitaine?*" Drouillard asked, almost echoing Reuben Fields's plea.

"No," said Lewis. "He doesn't appear to wish to kill us now."

Allowing the Indian to retreat, Meriwether Lewis tried to discover what had happened in the encounters the others had had. Before he could say anything, Joseph Fields shouted, "They're after the horses!"

It was quickly obvious what the Blackfeet were up to. Two of them, including the one who had taken Lewis's rifle, were now trying to drive off several of the horses. Others were gathering up the rest of the horses, both their own and those the white men had brought with them. "Fire on them if need be!" Meriwether Lewis commanded. "Don't let them steal our horses!"

Lewis broke into a run in pursuit of the first pair of Indians. He was so close on their heels that they ran past a dozen of their own horses in their hurry. They had several animals before them, herding them into one of the steep canyons that cut into the bluff and offered the only means of escape to the highland above. Several times Lewis yelled at them to stop. They paid no need. And at last, out of breath, his chest heaving, Lewis came to a stop on rubbery legs. He couldn't run any farther. Instead he raised his rifle to his shoulder. "Halt! I'll shoot if you don't release my horse!"

Did the Blackfeet understand his words? Lewis wondered. No matter, they know my meaning.

One of the red men jumped behind a rock. He yelled at his companion. The second warrior, who was carrying a rifle of his own, spun around and aimed the weapon at Lewis.

From a distance of thirty paces Meriwether Lewis shot him in the belly. The Indian dropped to his knees as if his legs had been kicked from under him. He toppled forward. Propping himself up on his right elbow, he fired his gun an instant before he rolled out of sight behind another rock.

Hatless, Lewis felt the wind of the ball's passage over his head.

He reached for his shot pouch to reload.

He didn't have it.

Realizing that either his pouch had been stolen or he had left it on the ground where he slept, Lewis coolly appraised his situation. He faced two men who were now behind cover, at least one of them armed. One was wounded, but Lewis did not know how badly. To attack them both with only the one charge in his pistol, and no chance to reload, would be more than reckless.

He turned back toward the camp. On the way he met Drouillard, rushing to his aid after hearing shots. "I shot one of them," Lewis confirmed. "The horses they had ran up the canyon. We'd better get back and try to catch as many as we can. Are any of our people hurt?"

"*Non, Capitaine,* but Reuben, he stick his knife in one Blackfoot when he catch him. Dat one, by gar, he is dead."

Back at camp Lewis and Drouillard began to round up some of the Indian horses and collect their baggage. Reuben and Joseph Fields soon returned, leading four of their own horses. "Two of ours are gone," snapped Lewis. "Very well, we'll replace them with some of the Indians' horses. We must be off quickly!"

"*Capitaine* . . ."

Lewis turned toward Drouillard. "What is it?"

"Seaman," said the hunter. "Our dog, he is gone."

Lewis's shocked understanding was accompanied by a stab of remorse. In the furious moments of action since his sudden awakening, he had had only a fleeting thought of his dog, peevishly wondering why Seaman hadn't given the alarm. Now, at Drouillard's words, he felt the chilling touch of fear.

Louis Charbonneau

"Has anyone seen him?"

Both Reuben and Joseph Fields shook their heads. Drouillard said, "They have trick him. Else he warn us . . ."

Lewis began to shake with rage. Damn them! And damn his own carelessness in letting himself sleep so soundly!

"We get him back," said Drouillard softly, but with such cold determination that Lewis was jolted out of his own blind anger.

"It's too late," he said.

The others stared at him.

"They said their main party is not far away. Some of them must already be riding for help. If we're to save our scalps, and those of our friends, we've no time to lose."

As usual it was the others Lewis was thinking of—the men he had led into this predicament and those who were now waiting for them at the mouth of Maria's River, vulnerable to an attack they would never expect.

"We must ride at once," said Lewis. The decision, his tone said, was final. "Saddle the horses and put on our packs—quickly, now!"

As they hurriedly prepared to leave the river bottom, in an angry gesture Meriwether Lewis gathered up some abandoned quivers of arrows, bows, and two shields. He threw them into the campfire. For a few seconds he watched them burn.

The Indians had fled so hastily they had left most of their baggage behind. Spotting the flag he had so generously given one "chief," Lewis reclaimed it. His glance caught the medal that was still around the neck of the Indian Reuben Fields had stabbed to death. Lewis's mouth tightened. Let him keep it. It will remind the others who and what we are.

As they mounted their horses, a thought struck him. "Can you account for all of the Indians? There were eight of them, but . . ."

The others counted quickly. There were the two Meriwether Lewis had pursued toward the canyon. The Fields brothers had chased the main group of Blackfeet. Three, they

said, had crossed the river with some of the horses. Two others had ascended to the plains by means of another canyon.

"That's only seven," said Lewis slowly.

"*Oui*," George Drouillard answered him. "There was one other . . ."

"The eighth man," said Lewis, and a pall of sadness came over him like a cloud, bringing the darkness of melancholy. "He is the one who took my dog."

There was no question of pursuing the thief. Lewis knew that he had to save his men, if he could, his expedition, with all that it meant to his President and his country—and, finally, himself.

He could wait no longer.

"Let's ride, then," Meriwether Lewis said in a tone of bitter acceptance. "Ride like you never rode before!"

Seaman woke to pain and indignity. He was being dragged through the underbrush by his two hind legs, upside down with his head lolling and his tongue protruding from slack jaws.

Consciousness flooded his brain. The noose around his neck had been loosened so that he was no longer choking. His first instinct was to thrash violently to free himself. Something stopped him. He did not reason out the necessity to keep his captor from knowing that he was awake, recovering swiftly, nor did he directly connect his plight to the memory of games and tricks Meriwether Lewis had taught him. But he remained limp, as if he were playing dead.

There was a shout nearby, someone splashing in the river. The Blackfoot who was dragging Seaman dropped his burden on the sand of the riverbank. The gurgling rush of the water over its bed of gravel was so near that Seaman could smell and feel it. He lay motionless where he had been dumped.

The Indian had been joined by another. The two men were arguing, their voices raised with an edge of panic. One of them shouted in anger.

Seaman opened his eyes. Neither of the Blackfeet was looking at him. One stood knee-deep in the river, gesticulating toward the night camp, then pointing across the way where another Indian was herding several horses. The man on shore hung back. The Bear Dog was his prize of battle.

Seaman came to his feet in a rush. He staggered once. The Indian who claimed him lunged for the end of the leather loop around the dog's neck. For the first time in his life, Seaman's teeth slashed at a man. They ripped across the Indian's arm, leaving a bright ribbon of red behind.

"Aiyee!"

The Blackfoot's cry of pain shivered in Seaman's ears, but he was already running. While he rested, the strength had rapidly returned to his legs. He raced downriver, veering into the edge of the stream at one point where the walls of rock closed in, then gaining the shore again as the bottom widened out.

Ahead of him three cottonwoods stood tall against the cliffs. Just beyond them, its half-conical shape distinctive, was the lodge the Indians had raised the night before.

463

With a joyous, triumphant bark of greeting, Seaman ran toward the clearing, where smoke still curled from the campfire.

The camp was abandoned. The men, their horses, their baggage, all were gone. Seaman gave one last thundering bark, as if to call them back. The bark echoed down the river canyon, dying away to a deep, pervasive silence.

He was alone in the wilderness.

38

Ruben Fields chased an Indian who ... was running of[f] with R. Fields and his brothers Jo Fields Guns Reuben overhalled him [and] caught hold of the 2 guns had his knife drawn & as he Snatched away the guns perced his knife in to the Indians heart he drew but one breath the wind of his breath followed the knife & he fell dead.

—JOHN ORDWAY, July 28, 1806

After pawing the loosened leather loop from around his neck, for a few vital seconds Seaman prowled about the encampment, peering inside the empty lodge, skirting the body of the dead Indian who lay not far away, sniffing at the confused melee of horse tracks, noting the absence of any of the men's effects. The signs conveyed only a blunt, simple message: Meriwether Lewis and the other three men were gone.

The tracks of eight or nine horses led up one of the ravines that gave access to the highland. When Seaman emerged from the cut, he saw only the empty prairie rolling away from him and some low, sloping hills with smoothly muscled flanks. The horse tracks were clearly visible, leading away from the river toward the south.

He heard a shout. Glancing back down the ravine, he saw the half-naked figures of several of the Indians running about the deserted camp. One of them started up the incline toward the top of the bluffs where Seaman stood.

For a long moment the Bear Dog stared down the slope at his enemy. Then he turned and, without a backward glance, set off at a steady, ground-covering trot.

Meriwether Lewis and his three companions crossed a creek at twelve miles, having reached it at a relentless gallop. Climbing up the south bank of the creek, Lewis paused for the first time to stare back across the plain.

No pursuit. Would a small band of poorly armed Indians—he believed they had only one gun left among them, having lost one that Lewis carried off after the battle—attempt to follow and engage four white men who could oppose them with rifles? They were warriors, he thought, not fools. One of them might be following as a scout; if so, he would be difficult to spot. Otherwise the Indians' first act almost certainly would have been to dispatch their best riders to report to their two main hunting parties in the vicinity.

One of those bands, Lewis remembered, was said to be near the "broken mountains" on their way toward Maria's River.

He exchanged a wordless glance with his men. Not one of them was afraid of a fight, but none was so foolish as to be eager to confront a sizable Blackfoot war party in the open plain. With a brief nod Lewis set off again, urging his horse to a run.

The day turned warm, but there was no rain. Pools of water lay in the prairie from previous rains, and it was not punishingly hot—in short, an excellent day for hard riding.

By late morning Lewis's horse was laboring. Lewis stopped just long enough to switch his saddle to one of the Indian horses, a superior animal to the one he had been riding. He recommended that his men do the same. The Indian horses, having run all morning without a burden on their backs, were still fresh and strong. Only Joseph Fields had trouble with his Indian mount, but Fields was stubborn. Once he was securely in the saddle, his horse settled down.

The riders continued to push on at a fast pace. At three o'clock Lewis saw ahead of them the bluffs and treetops marking the passage of Rose River across the prairie. The discovery

465

gave him considerable satisfaction. It told him their course was true. It also said, by his estimate, that they had come more than sixty miles from their night camp in a single hard ride.

They ate dried meat from the provisions in their packs. For an hour and a half they rested in the river bottom, more for the benefit of their horses than for themselves. They were, however, exhausted and sore from eight hours in the saddle —not handsomely crafted English riding saddles, Lewis thought ruefully, but improvised coverings of buffalo hide and a little grass padding, hardly more than a leather apron to which stirrups were attached.

At the end of their rest the four men tried riding along the river bottom, but the twisting course of the stream caused them to have to cross and recross it several times to avoid a longer, more circuitous journey. Meriwether Lewis soon decided to abandon the river and to strike out again across the open plain.

Climbing to the prairie on the south side of the river, they rode on in a generally southeast direction as fast as Lewis dared to push their horses. The plain was now covered with great herds of elk and buffalo, the latter so thick the riders sometimes had to swing in wide circles around them.

They continued until dark, covering another seventeen miles southeast of Rose River, before Lewis called a halt for supper. Drouillard shot a buffalo cow, from which they cooked only a small portion of meat, leaving the rest.

This time they rested for two hours. A moon appeared in that quarter of the sky not covered by dark, lowering storm clouds. The moonlight touched the prairie with silver, penciling in a scene that would have appeared tranquil and lovely had it not been for the incessant roaring of the buffalo bulls and the men's knowledge that danger might strike at them any time from the darkness.

For Meriwether Lewis the night held another disturbing mystery. What had happened to Seaman? Had the treacherous Indians deceived his dog by some ruse, taking advantage of his good nature, like those wretched thieves on the Columbia? Or had he suffered a fate more unthinkable?

If he were still alive, Seaman was now eighty miles behind them, abandoned in their hasty flight from the scene of the conflict. Lewis did not question his decision not to take time to search for his dog. But the knowledge that he had done what he had to do, not only for himself but for all the men under his command who might now be in danger, did not lessen his anguish when he thought of that loyal Newfoundland, his stalwart companion from the very beginning of his long journey. Lewis could not think of him now, left to his fate, without pain and regret.

When the four men set off once more, riding in darkness, Lewis was content to proceed at a leisurely pace. He wanted to put as much distance between himself and the Indians as possible on this first day, but he was convinced that, even if the Blackfeet had picked up their trail, they would never be able to catch up. The only worry now was that one of the war parties might already be on its way to Maria's . . .

467

They rode another twenty miles that night. When they finally fell off their horses at two in the morning, by Meriwether Lewis's estimate they had ridden one hundred miles in the day. They were asleep almost as soon as they lay down.

Save Lewis himself. Taking the first watch, he stared brooding into the darkness, still thinking of his dog. After an hour Drouillard relieved him. Then only that prince of hunters and woodsmen was awake, quietly watching and listening. He, too, thought of the Bear Dog, and wondered.

When Seaman had first come to the High Plains two summers ago, it was like opening a door and feeling a fresh, invigorating breeze. He had stepped through that doorway into what seemed to be a remembered landscape. He had immediately felt at home. The natives of the Plains who had seen him had stared as if at a ghost, a creature of their own mythology.

The dogs like him who had roamed these hills and prairies centuries ago had bequeathed him a legacy of strength and courage, determination and intelligence. But he had developed other qualities as well; perhaps dominant among these was devoted loyalty. His primary attachment was not to this free, windswept land but to the men with whom he had crossed the Plains. Especially the intense, thoughtful, sometimes moody Meriwether Lewis.

Nearly four years old in this summer of 1806, Seaman had reached full maturity. In the three years of his journey from Philadelphia to the rim of the continent and halfway back, he had grown in size, strength, and intelligence. The mental agility that Meriwether Lewis had delighted in exhibiting for the Indians had matured. It was much more than a talent for performing tricks. Like those who had traveled so far with him, Seaman was uncommonly resilient, alert, adaptable to changing situations and unexpected adversity.

Now, alone, he confronted a challenge beyond anything he had experienced. After the vexing months of indolence at Fort Clatsop, the spring and summer months on the trail—ascending the Columbia, crossing the Lolo Pass, coming over the Continental Divide from Traveler's Rest, and exploring Maria's River with Meriwether Lewis and the other men—had prepared Seaman for what he now faced. He would have to travel even farther and faster, going night and day. The cloudy weather would help. Although the midday heat was enervating, it did not devastate him as it had the young dog who ventured onto the Plains two years ago. Seaman had learned to live with the land, its heat and its cold, its winds and its silences—and with those who lived upon the land.

He had also learned the duplicity of some red men; he would not trust readily or be easily tricked again. But some of the animals of these Plains, who relied upon ferocity rather than deception, presented a more immediate obstacle to the dog's survival. Not the herd animals, the deer and elk and buffalo, but their predators. The white bears. And the wolf packs.

Seaman had observed them often. He knew their cunning and savagery. He would have to match it with greater cunning—and, if necessary, with a ferocity to equal theirs.

The prairie was as level as a table. South of the stream where the morning's conflict had erupted, it was bare even of stones and prickly pear, which made running much easier for Seaman. Nor did he encounter enemies of any kind that morning. There was only the prairie itself, seemingly endless, and the horse tracks cut into soil still soft from recent rains.

The black dog paced himself, knowing instinctively that he might have a long way to go. The trail he followed appeared to grow fainter as the hours went by, as if he were moving backward in time. The horses, goaded by their riders, were galloping faster than Seaman could. Their wide-spaced hoof-prints told their own story: the horses ran as the antelope or the deer fled from the hunter—in fear.

This day was warm but not hot, the sun frequently hidden behind gray clouds. Shallow pools caught in the depressions of the plain slaked Seaman's thirst.

When the sun was at its highest, he rested beside a shallow creek where he found brush to shade him. He stayed there for nearly two hours. Sometimes he glanced back along his own trail, but he saw no Indians in pursuit. Most of the time he gazed steadily toward the southeast.

Then he was on his feet again, trotting with the same steady purpose, his eyes on the horizon in the direction the horses had taken.

He came upon a huge buffalo herd in his path, stretching as far as he could see in either direction. He wove among the shaggy animals, who paid him little attention. But Seaman remembered that others generally followed the herds. The wolves would not be indifferent.

The sun dipped lower, dropping into the arms of the distant, snow-covered peaks. A breeze picked up, cooler, reviving the Newfoundland's flagging energy. The cooling wind enabled him to keep going.

There was a bright full moon in that part of the sky not

covered by clouds; by its light he was still able to follow the trail of hoofs. Long after dark he smelled water even before he heard the rushing of a stream. He approached the bluff cautiously. At the edge of a mud bank he peered down at the slow movement of the Rose River. Its surface gleamed white in the moonlight. The horse tracks were plain in the river bottom.

Seaman started down the bank. He halted, his muscles taut, nose quivering. His muzzle lifted. A strong, earthy smell filled his nostrils.

The white bear.

He hesitated. He could not see the bear, but he knew it was there.

So were the tracks he followed.

He descended to the river bottom with every sense alive. Along the bank there was thick brush and a few scattered cottonwoods. The bear smell was pervasive, heavier because of the dampness by the river.

And suddenly, as he weaved past some willow thickets, the white bears were in front of him—not one but two. One was a large female, the other a young male scarcely half her size. Belligerently, as soon as she saw the intruder, the mother started toward Seaman with a growl of warning. Seaman trotted straight toward her.

The grizzly attacked. Like all of these huge animals, she moved with surprising speed. But, when she was in full charge, she had too much momentum to change course quickly. At the last moment, just before the bear reached him, Seaman veered sharply to his left, evading a lethal swipe from a paw, and ducked past her.

Now the smaller bear was directly in his path. Seaman didn't hesitate. He ran straight for the river and leaped from the bank.

The water was murky and very cold. Although Seaman swam powerfully and the current was torpid, he was carried some distance downstream before he reached the far bank. By then he was far away from the angry white bears he had disturbed. They made no attempt to follow him across the river.

Concealed in the brush above the south bank, Seaman rested. His muscles ached. He licked quietly at some cuts on his feet. Since morning he had traveled—according to Meriwether Lewis's calculation of the distance from the fight site to Rose River—about sixty-three miles.

In his mind there was no thought of stopping.

39 But if a superior force ... should be arrayed against your further passage, and inflexibly determined to arrest it, you must decline its further pursuit, and return. In the loss of yourselves, we should lose also the information you will have acquired.
—JEFFERSON'S INSTRUCTIONS TO LEWIS,
June 20, 1803

*M*eriwether Lewis woke at daybreak from a sound sleep. He stared up at a leaden sky. His first thought was, We will see more rain today.

He sat up suddenly, memory of the previous day jolting him wide awake. He roused the others. Like them, he groaned with each movement. He was scarcely able to stand, his whole body was so stiff and sore from yesterday's punishing ride. While the men complained in the manner of soldiers first awakened, Lewis calmly reminded them of their situation. "We have Blackfeet behind us, and perhaps ahead as well. We have good reason to know their hostility toward us. We must be in the saddle as quickly as we can."

He allowed the men a few minutes to chew some of the buffalo meat cooked the night before. As they were loading their packs and saddling their horses, Reuben Fields suggested, "We can ride straight for Grog Spring and cross the Missouri there and come down the river on the south side. Keep the river between us and them savages."

"It be safest way," George Drouillard agreed.

"For us, perhaps," said Lewis. "But what of our main

party? They should be at Maria's River waiting for us, or on the way there." He shook his head. "If what we've learned of the Indians is true, one of their large hunting parties is already moving toward Maria's point. We must get there by the shortest possible route. To cross the Missouri and go down the far side would take us all day." He paused, searching the sober faces before him. He saw the answer he had hoped to find. They were ready to do whatever was asked of them. "We will have to risk our lives if necessary. We're the only ones who have news of those treacherous gentlemen we smoked the peace pipe with night before last. We owe it to our fellow soldiers to warn them. Their lives depend on us. Once we are all joined and prepared to meet an attack together, I doubt even the Blackfeet will find such a fight a pleasing prospect." Catching the reins of his horse, he stepped into the saddle. "If we're attacked in the plains on our way to the point, let us tie our bridles together and stand and defend ourselves as one man . . . or sell our lives as dearly as we can!"

This speech, so long and serious and honorable, such a mix of grace and inflexible determination, might have sounded pompous from another man; from their captain, these men knew, it was simple truth.

The morning remained cloudy and cool, the threat of a storm heavy in the air. The clouds were tumbling very fast before strong winds. In spite of his encouraging words, Lewis had found the prospect of climbing back on his horse intolerable. Though much of his stiffness left him as he rode along, he felt every step in his bones.

The riders continued to head east on a route that would bring them closer to the bluffs of the Missouri River below the Great Falls. They had been riding about twelve miles, and were not far from the river, when Drouillard halted, his left hand up in a signal to stop.

"What is it?" asked Joseph Fields.

"I heard it, too," Meriwether Lewis said. "Sounded like a gunshot. From the river, d'you think?"

"Maybe it be one of our hunters, eh?"

473

When there was no repetition of the sound, the brief mood of elation faded. They resumed their ride parallel to the bluffs above the Missouri's north bank. After another hour, having traveled an additional eight miles, all of them heard very distinctly the echoing crash of several rifle shots. This time there was no question of imagining them. The sounds came from the river on their right.

The four men exchanged quick glances. No one needed to comment. Without a word they urged their horses into a gallop in the direction of the river. When they reached the top of the bluffs they stared down into the canyon. The thunder of the falls some distance upriver was very loud, but they hardly heard it. All their attention was riveted on one thing: the white pirogue coming toward them around a bend—and five small canoes bobbing behind it!

Reuben and Joseph Fields began to shout, not thinking that they could not be heard from the top of the bluffs a hundred feet above the noisy river. Then Lewis fired his gun in the air. He had the inexpressible satisfaction of seeing faces in the canoes lift toward him. Some of the men in the boats pointed toward the bluffs.

Joyously Lewis and his companions picked a way down the bluffs to the river bottom. They heard the swivel gun in the bow of the pirogue fired in salute and the rattle of small arms fire to welcome them. Scarcely had they arrived beside the river, when the boats turned in toward the bank. A sea of grins, Lewis thought, to match his own—Ordway, Colter, Whitehouse, Cruzatte, and a dozen more—all safe, by the Lord! All once more reunited!

Cautiously, Seaman crept from the brush and climbed the low south bank of Rose River. The morning was overcast; a cool breeze stirred the grasses into a ragged dance. Nearby, a buffalo bull bellowed as if in pain. A huge herd sprawled across the prairie as far as Seaman could see.

The white bears were gone.

Louis Charbonneau

There were no horse tracks visible in the undulating plain. Perplexed, Seaman trotted along the riverbank. Within a mile he came upon deep hoofprints gouged into the bank where horses had climbed from the bottom. The tracks led south and then east, where the sun was only a promise behind lowering clouds.

Seaman had been trotting along at a steady, ground-covering pace when he heard the snarling of wolves. He saw them almost immediately—a pack of about a dozen swarming around the carcass of a dead buffalo, fighting among each other over shreds of meat. Several of the wolves, sensing the Bear Dog's presence, veered toward him. The lure of the carcass pulled them back.

Seaman gave the pack no temptation to abandon their easy meal for one more difficult. He swung east, circling around them. When he was a quarter-mile downwind, he turned south again, drawn by the smell of a recently abandoned campfire. Seaman knew at once that Lewis and his friends had stopped here during the night. He was able to link their presence to the slaughtered buffalo on which the wolves now fed.

475

From their night camp the riders' trail was easy to follow. After a while Seaman heard a familiar grumbling that gave voice to the trembling of the earth beneath his feet. He remembered the mighty falls; he thought he smelled the muddy river. In spite of fatigue, he quickened his pace.

Then he heard the wolves behind him, talking to each other. Over his shoulder he caught a glimpse of the pack. They were strung out across the prairie in his wake, racing in pursuit.

One of the wolves ran at him.

Seaman understood at once. More than once while on the Plains with Meriwether Lewis or George Drouillard, he had observed the wolves chase down a deer in relays, using one of the pack at a time to pursue the frightened prey, running it in a circle until that wolf tired and another took his place. Seaman had watched the Shoshoni hunters try to use the same maneuver to exhaust and finally catch an antelope.

The Bear Dog knew that he could outrun one or two of the wolves, not all of them. Just as he could defeat one or two in a fight, not all.

He ran on. There was a tight hard knot in his chest that would become worse. His legs were tired, and once he stumbled. The blood drummed in his ears.

The lead wolf, the one who had first taken up the chase, was very close to him now. Seaman could hear its labored panting. If it got ahead of him and forced him to turn into the deadly circle . . .

Seaman dug in his paws and pivoted. The wolf, surprised, was almost on top of him. It tried to swerve away. Seaman attacked in that moment of surprise. His teeth slashed across the wolf's left shoulder, laying it open.

The wolf staggered, howling in pain. Seaman hurled himself at the smaller animal, using superior weight and strength to drive him to the ground. He struck instantly for the fallen wolf's vulnerable throat.

476   Then Seaman was up and running. Blood flecked his teeth and dripped from his mouth.

The rest of the wolf pack reached their fallen leader a moment after Seaman ran off. A few of them continued to pursue the Bear Dog. Others hesitated. Then one of them fell upon the dying wolf. In seconds all of the pack converged in a snarling, killing frenzy.

Seaman ran on, alone.

Proceeding rapidly down the Missouri River in the canoes, Meriwether Lewis learned from Sergeant Ordway of his arrival at White Bear Island on the nineteenth, of the difficulties met on the portage, and of the party's general success in bringing everything down safely from the upper camp to Portage Creek. "We brought the canoes down on our wagons like we done before," Ordway said, "only this time we had the horses to pull, which made it easy 'cept when they bogged down in the mud." Only one man had been injured, Ordway said. Peter

Wiser had cut his leg so badly with his knife that he was incapacitated for work.

"I'll look at his leg as soon as we stop," Lewis promised.

The caches at Portage Creek had been opened and most of the goods buried in them recovered. The white pirogue had been found in good condition. Ordway and his group had left the creek in the boats the previous day, proceeding down the river until they spotted Lewis on the ridge that morning.

With Lewis and his men safely aboard, the boats now dropped down the river to a landing opposite the principal cache. After cautiously scouting the plains above the river, they opened the cache. It had caved in. Many of the articles buried in it were damaged or destroyed—in particular, to Lewis's dismay, two large white bear skins of his own and the furs and animal skins collected by many of the soldiers. Some stores of gunpowder, corn, flour, pork, and salt had suffered little damage; the parched meal was spoiled.

Lewis had the reclaimed goods hurriedly packed and loaded aboard the canoes. The party then set off for the mouth of Maria's River. They approached the point cautiously. Alerted by their captain to the potential danger of a Blackfoot attack, every man watched the bluffs and the bottoms for a flicker of color or movement.

As soon as they landed, Meriwether Lewis sent several men out to reconnoiter the adjacent country and report back any indication of activity. They found only immense herds of buffalo and elk near the forks.

While the scouts were searching for the Blackfeet, other men quickly dug up the small caches near the point. Most of the articles were found in good order. To Drouillard's disappointment, three of his prize steel traps were missing.

While everyone was thus occupied, Pat Gass and Alexander Willard arrived overland on horseback. They had crossed the river to the north side two nights before to ride down, packing the meat the party expected to need while waiting for Lewis at Maria's River. There followed several more minutes of exuberant congratulations over the successful reunion.

477

Trail

In the midst of this celebration, the rain that had been threatening since dawn swept down the Missouri toward the forks. Lightning streaked across the sky, and thunder boomed overhead like crashing cannon. Hail added the rattle of smaller arms to the din.

The forks offered little cover from the storm. In the deluge Lewis and several men rowed over to the island in the point, where he hoped to launch the red pirogue. They pulled away the brush under which the boat had been concealed. Lewis stared at it in disappointment. The body of the red boat had rotted beyond repair.

Lewis had the men pull the nails and ironworks from the ruined pirogue. They might be useful later. Through the steady downpour he gazed for the last time around the point.

So far we've been fortunate, he thought. Perhaps the Indians had been overly cautious, or were waiting to attack in full force. No matter. When they reached the forks, they would find no one.

Seaman followed the horse tracks across the prairie. Although it was only the middle of the day, it became very dark. Strong winds buffeted him. Suddenly there was a brilliant flash of light. Thunder rumbled across the heavens, and the entire sky seemed to split open with a tremendous crash. Rain poured down upon the dog as if the thunder had indeed opened a rent in the sky. In a few seconds, in spite of his dense coat, Seaman was soaked to the skin.

The tracks he followed filled with water and mud. In a half-hour the entire plain was awash. He plodded on, slower now, head and neck bent against the downpour.

The trail disappeared in the deluge.

Through that afternoon Seaman blindly trotted eastward, the direction in which the last visible tracks had pointed. The storm passed on, leaving the prairie a lake of mud. The soupy surface made each step heavier, sapping the dog's energy.

Late in the day the familiar rush of the rapids drew him

to the bluffs overlooking the Missouri River. Gazing down from the heights, Seaman knew that he had been here before, with Meriwether Lewis.

His heart hammered. There were horses in the river bottom!

Seaman had to travel some distance along the bluffs before he found a path down to the bottom. There he came upon some of the horses Lewis and his friends had been riding. Turned loose when their riders took to the canoes, the horses grazed along a stretch of the bottom where the grass was lush in comparison to the plains above.

The storm had not washed out all of the signs that revealed where the canoes had put ashore and Lewis had greeted his men, shaking each by the hand. Here the saddles had been stripped from the horses, the baggage transferred to the boats.

The saddles had been left on the riverbank.

Seaman stared at the tumbling current of the Missouri. He was drenched, weary, footsore, and hungry. In two days he had trekked over a hundred miles across the prairie to this bank of the Missouri. Now those he followed had vanished down the river.

479

He slept that night under the shelter of a cottonwood near the riverbank. After dark another storm came, the rain so heavy that it threatened to pound him into the sandy bottom. Exhausted, he slept through the storm.

Twenty-five miles away, Meriwether Lewis and the members of the expedition who were now with him camped below the mouth of Maria's River. Having no shelter from the storm, most of them—including Lewis—lay in water all night.

Though Lewis could now look ahead to rejoining William Clark at the mouth of the Yellowstone and reuniting the Corps of Discovery, he could not forget that one of its most loyal members had been left behind. Through that miserable night it was little consolation that he and his men had escaped unharmed.

In his heart he knew that Seaman was lost forever.

40 Early in a cloudy morning we commenced our voyage from the mouth of Maria's river; and the current of the Missouri being very swift, we went down rapidly.
—PATRICK GASS, J u l y 2 9, 1 8 0 6

For three days it rained almost without letup. The air was cold. To Seaman the rain was both curse and blessing. It made his progress slower and harder across the plains and in the river bottoms. The mud clogged his feet. He was miserably wet all the time, for he was almost always in the open, exposed to the incessant downpour. But the coolness was invigorating; hot weather would have sapped the dog's waning strength. And the storms also drove the wolves to seek escape from the battering rains. Seaman did not encounter another of the hungry, roving packs.

From Maria's River Seaman traveled over 150 miles across the plains in four days. Most of the time the craggy bluffs and river hills forced him some distance north of the Missouri. At night, and sometimes during the daytime when a stream or canyon offered easy access, he descended to the river bottom to search for any sign of his friends' passage. He failed to find the camp near Slaughter River where Lewis and his party had stayed on the twenty-ninth, or the camp on an island where the boats had put ashore on the thirtieth.

On the fourth day, August 1, 1806, the rain ceased in the

early afternoon. The Newfoundland welcomed the chance for
his coat to dry out, though it took the rest of the day. That
night he rested longer than usual. He was very hungry. Two
days earlier he had gorged himself on the carcass of a buffalo
drowned at a river crossing. He had not eaten since.

Although the air was cool and dry on August 2, Seaman
labored. The lack of food and the daily toil across the prairie
had weakened him. His muscles were sore, his eyes bloodshot,
the pads of his webbed feet cut and swollen. At dusk, when
he came down from the hills toward the river, he limped
badly.

He followed a stream that fell into the Missouri River.
Finding no camp at the forks, he plodded slowly along the
north bank of the river, his head drooping to the sandy bottom.
The cliffs loomed dark above him. Except for the timeless
music of the river, there was only an awesome silence all
around.

A smoky smell brought his head up. The scent was damp
and stale. In spite of his weariness his steps quickened. He
came to the place where Meriwether Lewis and his companions had stopped on the night of July 31—two nights ago. The
steady rainfall of that night and the following day had failed
to erase all evidence of the men's presence here on the riverbank for one reason only—they had taken shelter in some
abandoned Indian lodges.

Cautiously Seaman entered the largest of the skin tipis.
It was empty, but he found Lewis's smell almost at once, along
with other familiar odors.

After a while he lay down. He rested his head where
Meriwether Lewis had slept.

He was lying there, drained of all feeling, when he heard
the sound of rifle shots racketing across the prairie.

Seaman hobbled out of the lodge. Sounds on the Plains
carried great distances. Though Seaman did not know it, the
hunters were twenty miles away.

Limping on bleeding feet, he started downriver in the
gathering darkness.

On the morning of August 3, 1806, William Clark guided his twin canoes ashore on the wooded point at the conjunction of the Yellowstone and Missouri rivers, where the expedition had camped on April 26, 1805, while proceeding upriver.

There was no sign of Meriwether Lewis and the main body of the expedition. With the prospect of a fair day ahead, Clark formed his camp to wait for his partner. He had his men begin to unload the canoes and the platform that joined them. After so much recent rain everything was thoroughly wet. This was his first opportunity to dry out clothes and skins. Most of the meat, he soon discovered, was spoiled from the warm dampness. He had it thrown into the river. His hunters went out into the plains to find game.

Except for trees in the river bottoms, the prairies here at the forks rose in a long, smooth, open expanse. The upper part of the Yellowstone, by contrast, had been bordered by rolling hills covered with pine trees. Gradually, as Clark had descended the river with his party, the pines had thinned out, the hills had flattened, until now there was neither tree nor hill, only the endless prairie.

That day the hunters had poor luck. There was surprisingly little game in the vicinity. The great buffalo herds had apparently moved to the south and east.

What *was* present in the point were untold numbers of mosquitoes. Millions of them, Clark thought, slapping futilely as he tried to bring his account of the Yellowstone River journey up to date: 837 miles since he had descended the mountain to this river, he wrote; all but two hundred of that distance covered by his party in two canoes lashed together. Almost all of it uneventful. Even the series of rapids in the area of the burnt hills—he had given them the names Bear, Buffalo, and Wolf rapids—had presented no serious obstacle. Clark had found a deep channel on the left side of the river, where the boats had paddled past the rapids without incident.

Clark slapped at another mosquito and swore. He had

hoped to meet Lewis in the point. How long could he and his people endure these infernal hordes of insects? Worse than he had encountered on all the long journey! And he at least had his mosquito bier to sleep under. The rest of his party were defenseless. Even their surviving blankets were riddled with holes large enough to admit a platoon of mosquitoes.

It was not until the second afternoon on the point that Clark discovered how badly Pomp was bitten. The child was crying—an occurrence so rare in the normal course of events that Clark immediately paused where Sacajawea was crooning in an attempt to soothe the boy. "What is the trouble with him?" Clark asked, concerned. "Is he . . . by God in heaven!"

The child's face was swollen and blotchy from innumerable mosquito bites. One of his eyes was almost completely closed. His upper lip was puffed up out of shape. The Indian woman herself was scarcely less afflicted, though she would never, thought Clark, utter a murmur of complaint.

So bothersome were the relentless clouds of whining mosquitoes that no one in the party slept much that night. Clark concluded that there would be no relief as long as they stayed in this point. And with hunting poor in the vicinity and the time of Lewis's arrival uncertain, he decided to move on.

483

In the morning the canoes were loaded. Clark wrote a note to Lewis, telling him of his plan to move downriver to a better location to camp and hunt. He attached the note to a pole at the point where his friend could not miss seeing it.

As his boats pushed out into the familiar muddy river, enjoying the luxury of paddling with its powerful current rather than against it, William Clark peered back up the river canyon to the west. His own journey of the past month had met no serious hazard or incident. But what of Lewis and his men?

Why hadn't Lewis arrived at the point?

On the morning William Clark arrived at the mouth of the Yellowstone, three hundred miles up the Missouri River Meriwether Lewis was preparing to break camp.

Lewis and his men had proceeded swiftly down the Missouri from Maria's River, averaging seventy miles a day and quickly outdistancing their Newfoundland. Had they continued at the same pace, they would have left Seaman so far behind he would have been irretrievably lost. But on August 1, when the rain let up, Lewis decided to lay over for a couple of days to dry out clothes and waterlogged cargo, with special attention to the skins of some bighorn sheep he had shot as trophies.

That day and the next, he sent his hunters out onto the Plains, where he had spotted large herds of deer. The Fields brothers, Colter, and Collins all stayed out through the night of August 2. The reports of their rifles could be heard even at dusk. By then, the weather having been fair and warm during his layover, Meriwether Lewis had succeeded in getting everything dried out sufficiently. He was prepared to set out at sunrise, intending to pick up his hunters on his way downriver.

Lewis was awake at dawn on August 3. George Drouillard was already up, boiling water for some of Lewis's herb tea. The hunter seemed restless, almost ill at ease. Lewis thought, Something is bothering him.

The other men crawled out of their blankets, groaning and shivering. The air in the river bottom that morning was very cool. The men slapped their arms and peered at the sky to see if there would be sunshine or rain this day. Sunny, looked like. None of those big thunderheads piling up like mountains in the sky.

Meriwether Lewis heard a kind of sigh. He glanced curiously at Drouillard. The lean woodsman's whole attitude had changed from moments earlier. A thin smile touched his lips, relieving the sharpness of his features. "*Capitaine,*" Drouillard said softly. "Look . . . across de river!"

Lewis stared. The morning sunlight danced off the waves, and for a moment what he saw was unreal, like a mirage . . . an image of his dog floating in the air above the rushing current. Then, across the wide river, came a resounding bark.

Louis Charbonneau

Lewis's shocked disbelief yielded to a bounding joy. The vision was real! It couldn't be, but by the Lord it was! Seaman!

He began to shout. Others took up his cry, and soon the men were hopping up and down as if to a soundless fiddle, dancing on the riverbank.

GEORGE SHANNON'S JOURNAL

August 6, 1806

a verry Stormy day, with Thunder, hail & rain. the Winds being so violent forced us in our skin boats to lay by for two hours in the middle of the day, all our goods wet through. the Yellowstone River is much wider now, with more sand bars, but we proceeded on in the P.M. and arrived at dark at the Missouri R. Here we discover'd a Letter from Capt. Clark to Capt. Lewis, which Sgt. Pryor took down, as we believe Capt. Lewis has already passed down before us. We are all well but verry anxious to rejoin the members of the Permanint Pty. We have made very good progress in our skin boats, which took in hardly any water anywhere on the river, notwithstanding the rapidity of the current. Tomorrow we will proceed down the Missouri R. in the expectation of meeting our friends. Mosquitoes verry troublesome tonight in the point. Some showers late.

August 8, 1806

Having discovered the camps where the Permanint Pty. has been only a short distance before us, we paddled rapidly down. This morning, knowing our friends were near us, we set off verry early, the night being Cool & Clear continued into the day. at 8 A.M. we caught up to Capt. Clark & his Party where they were staying over to hunt. All are well and greeted us warmly. This morning we set off in such a hurry that Sgt. Pryor forgot his saddlebags at our camp. Capt. Clark sent him back with Wm. Bratton to retrieve it. We are to delay & wait for their return. Gibson and Shields downriver to hunt. All are

in high spirits at our rejoining the Party, they were concerned about our Fate. Capt. Clark was much disturbed to learn that we took down his note to Capt. Lewis which he left at the forks of the Yellowstone, for Cap. Lewis is now without guidance as to our whereabouts. Capt. Clark also exceedingly regrets the loss of the horses which was intended to be delivered to the Assiniboine Post, but is cheered by our good Fortune in following him down the Yellowstone R. in our skin boats. Clear & Cool this eve. Sgt. Pryor ret'd after dark with Bratton & his saddlebags.

August 11, 1806

We are proceeding on. Cloudy & cool last Night with some Rain. We set out early, the day cleared becoming Fair & Sunny, we landed on a sand bar for breakfast and delayed 2 Hrs. to dry our Meat in the sun. After setting out again, at 12 o'Clock we saw a canoe on the bank and met 2 White men from Illinois. We stopped & Cap. Clark talked with them. They said they left Illinois in the Summer of 1804. They said they knew of our Expedition but that it was generally believed that we had all Perished in the Wilderness. These Men spent last winter among the Tetons of the Burnt Wood. The savages, who were verry troublesome to our Party when we met them, robbed the 2 Men and wounded one of them in the leg. They are Jos. Dickson & Forest Hancock. Dickson is the one who was wounded and still limps from it, he has no love for the Tetons. These men are hunters & trappers who are going to catch beaver. Capt. Clark advised them on the best places to hunt. After we left them we proceeded on & camped on a point opp. a Creek. We expect to lay over tomorrow to wait for Capt. Lewis. All are concerned about him and the rest of our Party. It being 6 Weeks since we parted at Traveler's Rest. All are anxious to return to our Country.

486

41

With rispect to the exertions and services rendered by this estimable man Capt. Wm. Clark on this expedicion I cannot say too much, if sir, any credit be due to the success of the arduous enterprize in which we have been engaged he is equally with myself entitled to the consideration of yourself and that of our common country.

—MERIWETHER LEWIS TO THOMAS JEFFERSON,

September 23, 1806

"*Damn* you! You have shot me!"

The pain was a fire in Meriwether Lewis's hip, hot as a branding iron. The impact of the ball had knocked him onto his side. When he first tried to rise, anger flooding his brain, he couldn't move. The terror of paralysis weakened his loins.

His teeth clenched in stubborn determination, he pushed the panic aside. "Cruzatte!" he yelled. "Damn you, answer me!"

Silence.

Following Clark down the Missouri River past its junction with the Yellowstone—he had found only a scrap of Clark's note where Nathaniel Pryor had torn it from a pole on the point, but ample evidence of Clark's passage—Lewis had kept his hunters busy at every opportunity, not knowing how much hunting Clark's party had been able to do. Shortly after noon on August 11, opposite some burned hills, Lewis had spotted a large herd of elk grazing on a sand bar thickly covered with willow brush. He beached the pirogue on the shore of the bar. Not wanting Seaman to frighten the game, Lewis ordered him

to stay in the boat. Lewis went into the brush with Pierre Cruzatte after the elk.

With his first shot Meriwether Lewis killed one elk. Cruzatte wounded one, a large female that stumbled off into the brush. Not wanting to lose the animal, Lewis sent the Frenchman off to the left in pursuit while he circled to the right. The willows were so thickly overgrown that for several minutes he could not see the wounded animal. When he saw her, twenty yards ahead, Lewis raised his gun to fire.

In the instant before he squeezed the trigger, there was the crash of another rifle shot. The ball slammed into Lewis's left thigh just below the hip joint, spun him around and dropped him to the ground.

"Cruzatte!" he shouted again. "Peter, where the hell are you?"

When he had first felt the terrible pain of the bullet striking, Lewis had supposed that Cruzatte, whose one-eyed vision was poor at the best of times, had mistaken him in his brown leather clothes for the elk. Now he began to question that quick judgment. What if it wasn't Cruzatte who shot him?

Another possibility undercut his anger. Were there Indians hiding in the brush? That would explain the bullet that had struck him down—and Cruzatte's silence as well. If so, how many were there?

The men in the boat! He had to get back as quickly as possible!

Grabbing a stout willow branch, Lewis dragged himself to his feet. He hobbled off through the dense brush, which whipped and cut his face. In spite of the fire in his thigh and buttocks, he tried to run. He could feel the blood filling the seat of his deerskin pants—there must be a quart of it, he thought. As he stumbled on, he kept yelling Cruzatte's name. "Cruzatte! Get back to the boat! Indians!" he called out his warning. "Hear me, Peter? Back to the boat!"

He ran more than a hundred yards before he caught sight of the pirogue. The soldiers rose in consternation as they saw their captain staggering toward them, wobbling on his feet, waving his rifle and shouting. "Indians! I've been shot—I hope not mortally. Every man to arms—we must save Cruzatte!"

Reacting instantly, the men grabbed their guns. Seaman barked excitedly, leaving the pirogue in his eagerness to join the hunt, but Lewis ordered him back. When Lewis wheeled around, he swung too quickly and nearly fell. His sun-dark face went pale with pain. "Follow me!" he cried hoarsely to the men.

He tried to lead the way back through the tangle of willows to the place where he had been shot. After a hundred yards the pain and stiffness in his hip and thigh were so severe that he could scarcely walk. He was holding the others back, he admitted reluctantly to himself—endangering them and the Frenchman.

"I can't go on," Lewis gasped. "You must go without me. Sergeant Gass, find Peter. Save him if you can. If you're over-powered, retreat in order to the boat. Keep up your fire, and they will not overrun you."

Grim-faced, the young soldiers quickly disappeared into the brush. Lewis set his teeth and started back toward the pirogue. His head was swimming. For the last few yards he had to drag himself over the sand. Smelling blood and sensing that his master was hurt, Seaman came out to meet him, his protective instinct overriding obedience to the earlier command. Lewis located his air gun and crawled behind the pirogue. He had his loaded pistol and rifle as well as the air gun. Seaman lay near him, whining anxiously.

The minutes ticked by. Sweat ran down Lewis's forehead into his eyes. Whenever he moved, the pain of his wound was blinding. He thought he could feel the lead ball in his pants, which were soaked through with blood. *That means it passed through without hitting bone. I am not crippled.*

After what seemed a very long time—it was twenty minutes—Lewis saw movement at the edge of the brush. He rested his rifle over the gunwale of the pirogue and aimed. He brushed the sweat from his eyes.

489

One by one, leatherclad figures emerged from the willows. Lewis squinted when the figures blurred. The image cleared.

Firmly in the grasp of Sergeant Gass and protesting volubly, Pierre Cruzatte stumbled into view.

There were no Indians.

The Frenchman, obviously very distressed on discovering what he had done, came toward Meriwether Lewis on shaking legs. "*Merci! Merci, mon Capitaine!* I do not know 'ow it 'appen! I swear—I shoot at de elk secon' time. I chase her. I never hear you, *Capitaine*, I swear!"

Lewis stared at him. He was reluctant to censure a man who had served him so well. Cruzatte, he guessed, had been so alarmed by his mistake that he had been afraid to come to his aid. "It was an accident," he said shortly. "What's done is done." He turned to Patrick Gass. "Help me out of these clothes, Sergeant. I must see how bad the wound is and attend to it."

As he had suspected, the bullet had passed through his left thigh. Narrowly missing bone, it had continued on across his left buttock, gouging a deep and nasty-looking flesh wound that bled profusely. Lewis dressed it as well as he could, packed tents of patent lint into the bullet holes and suffered himself to be lowered into the bottom of the pirogue.

He raised himself up on an elbow. "Send some men back for those elk, Sergeant. We may need the meat."

He fell back, his head spinning. He was hardly aware of the soldiers returning or of Seaman lying near him. The pirogue was loaded, other canoes arrived, and the boats pushed off into the river.

The following day, August 12, 1806, at one o'clock, Meriwether Lewis lifted his head when he heard one of the men in the boat shouting. With a feeling of relief and satisfaction that not even his pain and stiffness could dim, Lewis saw William Clark hurrying toward the riverbank. Behind him the smoke of a campfire curled upward against the endless sky.

Lewis fell back. He had won through, after all.

That night, having proceeded down the river to a point a little below Charbonneau's Creek, the Corps of Discovery made camp. For the first time in a month and a half the entire party was reunited. Everyone was in camp, joined by the two trappers from Illinois, who had decided to return to the Mandan villages with the expedition.

Meriwether Lewis was carried from the pirogue and laid on a tattered blanket near the campfire. William Clark washed and dressed his wounds, thinking back to the anguish he had experienced that afternoon when he saw Lewis lying in the white pirogue, unable to rise. The wound was ugly, and Lewis was obviously in extreme pain. Examining the path of the bullet for the second time, however, Clark was sanguine in his appraisal. "I believe ye'll soon be on your feet again, Lewis. It's a bad flesh wound, no more. It could have been much worse."

"I doubt it could feel worse."

The air was cold, a brisk wind blowing in from the southwest with a promise of rain. Listening to the talk of the men, the sounds of laughter, Cruzatte plucking at his fiddle as he tested out some new gut strings, Clark sensed the mood of the party, a pervasive feeling of pride and confidence in themselves. They had done what they set out to do. Everyone felt it. When they passed Charbonneau's Creek a year ago and the beaver dam just beyond it, where Baptiste Lepage had once set traps with some Indians, the explorers were venturing beyond the highest point on the Missouri ever reached by anyone other than the red men of the Plains. Now they had been to the fount of the great muddy river. They had crossed the Rocky Mountains. They had reached the Pacific Ocean, and returned. The vast western wilderness was no longer a mystery to them. When they camped here the first time, like prisoners

491

of the Dark Ages they had huddled close around their camp-fire, a tiny circle of light and warmth surrounded by an endless night. Now the West was a landscape of the mind. Even its dangers were beginning to be minimized in their conversation. Well, they have earned their sense of accomplishment, Clark thought, every man of them—and one Indian woman.

"Tell me again, Mr. Dickson," said Lewis, "of the state of things among the natives."

"I fear your message of peace has been too quickly forgotten," said Joseph Dickson, one of the Illinois hunters. "The Mandans and the Minitarees are at war with the Arikaras. The Assiniboines are at war with the Mandans as well, and they attack white parties whenever they can find them. We heard that one of the Hudson's Bay traders was killed by them earlier this summer. They're a bad lot, the Assiniboines."

Lewis frowned. "Perhaps it's as well that Sergeant Pryor didn't get that far with his horses. He might have come under attack."

492 "It's clear we will have to council with Black Cat and that Minitaree fellow, One-Eye, when we reach the Mandans," William Clark said. "I expected more of their promises."

"You will have to speak for both of us." Lewis winced as he moved. Then he smiled, sloughing off the momentary moroseness. "You'll have to do the writing for both of us as well, my friend—it's difficult for me in this position. I believe I'll just enjoy the life of an indolent sailor for the rest of our journey."

Clark laughed. "I can't see ye bein' indolent for as much as a fortnight. Ye'll be up and about before then, collectin' more plant specimens for Mr. Jefferson."

Lewis's smile became pensive. "The President . . . I cannot express with what pleasure I look forward to our meeting once again."

Lewis knew, as did his friend Clark, that their fame was now assured. The Corps of Discovery had achieved nearly all that Thomas Jefferson had envisioned, in some parts even more than he had dreamed. The oceans had been joined by human ingenuity, effort, and courage. The entire western half of the continent had been opened to the American imagination.

Clark turned toward the captains' ragged tent just as Sacajawea emerged after nursing Pomp. Nineteen months old, Clark mused. The Indian custom was to provide children with mother's milk much longer than he believed was true in his own society.

She saw his tall form silhouetted against the campfire and smiled shyly, deference little diminished after the better part of two years since she had first come down the river from Metaharta to the white men's camp below the Mandan villages. Pomp squealed with delight at sight of Clark and babbled, "Cappy Wed!" The soldiers had slyly tried to teach him to say "Captain Red."

"Ho!" Clark exclaimed. "What a talker ye are, to go with your dancing feet."

He took the boy from his mother and held him up above his head, Pomp laughing in total trust. Clark swooped him down and swung him around to more shrieks of laughter. Then his own grin slowly sobered as he held the child before him and studied the dark-skinned features, the black intelligent eyes. He was thinking suddenly of their impending parting.

"He speak many word," Sacajawea said proudly. "White men's word and Indian word."

"He's a bright lad." Clark hesitated, cleared his throat. "Ye've given some thought to what I said? You and Charbonneau?"

"Eh? What is dis?" Charbonneau asked, appearing out of the shadows. "What have we say?"

Clark turned toward the stocky Frenchman, who had to peer up at the much taller redhead. "I was asking your *femme*, Janey, if ye've decided on my offer. He's a good, bright boy, your Baptiste. He deserves to have a good education. If ye'll

493

bring him to St. Louis and leave him with me, I'll see that he gets it. Ye know my fondness for him. I'd raise him as my own child."

Charbonneau and Sacajawea exchanged glances. There was an awkward silence. Sacajawea felt the pride that she had known ever since Captain Redhead spoke of this offer. She thought how fine it would be for her firstborn to have this teaching among the white people. She knew now that her world and her son's world had changed forever. There would be many whites who would come up the river and cross the shining mountains, just as she had done. It would be good for her son to speak as an equal among the whites, to know their ways as well as the ways of Indians. But not yet . . .

She shook her head, a tiny gesture, and as if to give it meaning reached out to take her son from Clark's big hands. She carried him easily, though he was heavy.

"It is not yet," Charbonneau said, not meeting Clark's eyes. "It is good, what you say. My Baptiste, he fine boy, need good school. But he no weaned. He stay wit' his mama long time yet. *Ma femme*, she no want him go away now, he too young, *comprenez*?"

Clark nodded slowly. The night darkness away from the fire put his eyes in shadow, and Sacajawea could not see his reaction. Yet she felt his disappointment keenly.

After a moment he spoke again to Charbonneau. "We've been a long time together. I'd like to help ye if I can. If ye decide to leave the Minitaree village and come to live among white people, I'll see ye have a piece of land to farm, and some horses, cows, whatever ye need to make a good living. Ye'd have security, Charbono, for yourself and your wife and children. And if it's trading with the Indians ye still want to do, I can help ye there as well. We might even work something out together on a small scale."

Charbonneau scowled, embarrassed and pleased by Clark's generous gesture. He pawed his stubby fingers through the graying beard. "I'm a squaw man," he said at last. "In the city Charbonneau is nothing. Here . . ." His gaze peered at the

494

shine of the river under the stars, the blackness of the wooded bottom, the long reach of the plains rising away from the Missouri to the south. "By 'm by, one day, I might visit Montreal, see *mes amis* . . . but just visit, you understan'? Den I come back." He nodded, convincing himself as he talked. "Dis place, she be better for me. I no go back."

"Ye mean to stay among the Indians?"

The Frenchman nodded.

William Clark looked down at the child in Sacajawea's arms. He felt a welling of deep affection that carried with it the knowledge of impending separation. He blinked moist eyes. *At the Mandans*, he thought. *There I may lose my little dancing boy.*

"When he old enough," Sacajawea said softly, as if she had read his thoughts, "we come."

The camp became quiet. Seaman lay relaxed, toasting his back in the heat of the fire, drowsily content. No scent of danger caused his nose to quiver, the hairs to rise on the back of his neck, the ears to prick. The wilderness had become his familiar. It would continue to beguile and excite him; its hazards were no less real for being known. But he had met every challenge it could offer him—undaunted.

The Bear Dog rose, as if such thoughts had teased him. He made a casual, unhurried prowl of the camp, circling behind the soldiers lying on the ground, Cruzatte still picking at his fiddle, Pat Gass bent over his journal, eyes inches from the page as he wrote laboriously by firelight. From the captains' tent came the sleepy voice of little Baptiste, with its exaggerated swings from muffled laughter to contented gurgles. Seaman paused near Drouillard, who stood watchful on a bluff overlooking the river. The woodsman nodded at him, as if the two shared a secret understanding.

Then, as if satisfied, Seaman strolled back to the fire. He hardly limped at all anymore. He accepted a pat on the flank from one of the men, a chuckle, a soft whistle from George

Shannon (no longer a boy), gestures of affection and camaraderie from others as he passed.

The men felt more relaxed. Seaman's nightly circuit of their camps had been a familiar routine since their first night on an island near the mouth of the Missouri. It reassured them that no danger threatened. All was well.

Meriwether Lewis turned a little toward the fire. The slightest movement was agony, but he knew that this would pass. William Clark was right; he had been fortunate.

In two days, he thought, the Mandans. Before the snows of winter, home.

A gust of wind blew sparks toward him. They died quickly on the sandy shelf. The wind blew free and cold across the open plain, carrying whispers of dreams, triumphs and tragedies yet unknown.

Seaman, dreaming by the fire, growled low in his throat, and gave short, smothered barks, his legs and feet twitching. In his dream, the chase was on.

496

It is with pleasure that I announce to you the safe arrival of myself and party at 12 OClk. today at this place with our papers and baggage. In obedience to your orders we have penitrated the Continent of North America to the Pacific Ocean, and sufficiently explored the interior of the country to affirm with confidence that we have discovered the most practicable rout which dose exist across the continent by means of the navigable branches of the Missouri and Columbia Rivers . . .

—MERIWETHER LEWIS
TO THOMAS JEFFERSON AT ST. LOUIS,
September 23, 1806

epilogue

fter reaching St. Louis and the official end of their journey on September 23, 1806, the soldiers of the Lewis and Clark expedition were discharged from their duties. The two commanders, feted at length in St. Louis, left in late October, Lewis escorting the Mandan chief She-he-ke to Washington. Word of their triumphant return preceded them. A letter from Clark to his brother George, printed in the Frankfort, Kentucky, *Palladium* on October 9, caused a sensation. It was soon reprinted in newspapers all across the East.

While William Clark was reunited with his numerous family in Louisville, Meriwether Lewis went on to Washington to report in person to his commander-in-chief. He arrived there with She-he-ke, or Big White, on December 28, 1806, to the cheers of the capital's populace. Some believe that Clark delayed his own journey to Washington in order to give his friend Lewis his well-earned moment of glory alone.

While Congress debated a suitable reward for the members of the expedition, Meriwether Lewis strongly recommended that Corporal Warfington, who had brought the keelboat *Discovery* back to St. Louis from the Mandans and had served so well up to that time, share in the rewards equally with those who had gone on to the Pacific—and that Private Newman, discharged for his insubordination to Lewis but who earned his captain's respect by his later conduct at Fort Mandan, also receive his full share. Though Secretary of War Henry Dearborn had recommended that Lewis receive a larger reward than his partner, Lewis insisted that Clark share equally with him, with no distinction of rank. On March 3, 1807, Congress passed a bill authorizing Thomas Jefferson to reward the soldiers of the party—Warfington and Newman included—with 320 acres of land each and double pay for the time served with the expedition. The two leaders of the expedition also received double pay and 1,600 acres of government land each—the equal sharing Meriwether Lewis had always sought.

William Clark lived a long and distinguished life after the expedition. In its immediate aftermath he was named a brigadier general of the Louisiana Militia, while Meriwether Lewis was appointed governor of the territory. A little over a year later, on January 5, 1808, Clark married the young Julia (Judith) Hancock after whom he had named Judith's River. Theirs was a happy union that produced five children. Unhappily, she died in 1820. A year later Clark married a widow, Mrs. Harriet Kennerly Radford, a childhood friend of Julia's. They had two children and, by all accounts, an equally happy life together until her death in 1831.

In 1813 Clark was named both governor of what had become Missouri Territory and Superintendent of Indian Affairs. He was reappointed successively until 1820, when Missouri became a state. In 1822 Clark was appointed Superintendent of Indian Affairs at St. Louis, an office he held for the rest of his life and in which he became perhaps the best friend the Indians had. For a quarter-century he was involved in virtually every important Indian Council. He is credited, according to historian John Bakeless, with some thirty Indian treaties. He intervened in many tribal disputes, tried to keep peace, fought for justice for the Indians against white exploitation, and was the "Chief Redhead" to whom all of the leading chiefs turned in friendship, trust, and even awe.

In his late years in St. Louis, white-haired now, tall and erect as always, he entertained distinguished visitors from the East and West with a genial hospitality. One of his sons, who had graduated from West Point and enjoyed a distinguished army career of his own, retired from the service and settled nearby. William Clark moved in with him. On September 1, 1838, at the age of sixty-eight, he died peacefully in the home of his firstborn son, Meriwether Lewis Clark.

Meriwether Lewis, unlike his friend Clark, proved unlucky both in love and in public service. Though his name was linked with various "fair ones" (in his words), none of these relationships was successful. And when he assumed the governor's office in Louisiana Territory in 1807, he encountered a tangle of political rivalries and jealousies worse than anything he had met in the wilderness.

499

In the wake of Aaron Burr's treasonous schemes against the government—aborted by Jefferson's proclamation accusing him in the same week Lewis and Clark triumphantly returned to St. Louis in September, 1806—Governor Lewis was compelled to remove many Burrists from office in Louisiana, and in so doing he made numerous enemies. One of the most implacable was the secretary of Louisiana, Frederick Bates. The two men did not get along, and some of those Lewis had removed from office encouraged the breach between them. Envious and resentful of Lewis's fame, Bates did everything he could to belittle his reputation and undermine his efforts as governor.

In addition to difficulties in office and the growing threat of war with Britain and the danger it posed to the Louisiana Territory, Lewis was besieged by financial setbacks and illness. And his benefactor in Washington, Thomas Jefferson, had

retired to Monticello, after finishing his second term. James Madison was now President.

Everything came together in 1809. After the Mandan chief She-he-ke had been attacked by Arikaras while trying to return to the Mandans in 1807 (in a fight in which George Shannon lost his leg), he remained on the hands of Lewis and Clark at St. Louis for the next two years. Finally, Lewis authorized Manuel Lisa's Missouri Fur Company to form a force of 125 well-armed men, led by Pierre Chouteau (Lewis's old St. Louis friend), to escort the chief, his wife and child, and René Jessaume and his family back to the Mandan villages. The sum authorized was $7,000 (inflation was already evident), later augmented by another $500 to provide Chouteau and his party with tobacco and powder as Indian presents.

The Secretary of War in Washington refused to honor the final $500 draft. Other bills Lewis had sent to Washington were also returned. He was suddenly in severe financial trouble. His debtors began clamoring for payment. With the help of Bates and other enemies, rumors spread of Lewis's profligacy, illness, and an increasing drinking habit.

Finally he determined he would go to Washington to appeal his case and clear his name. He left St. Louis by boat on September 4, 1809, intending to travel by ship out of New Orleans. A week later, en route, he made out his will as a precaution before a dangerous journey. By then he had learned that British warships hovered off the coast and he would have to journey overland rather than risk interception by the British ships. He wrote his mother that he hoped to see her soon, as he was coming to Washington.

Lewis started out. He carried with him both the papers he needed to defend himself and his journals of the Voyage of Discovery to the Pacific. He stopped at Chickasaw Bluffs for two weeks, staying at Fort Pickering, an army post he had once commanded. On his arrival there, he was seriously ill and, according to the commanding officer at the fort, Captain Gilbert Russell, in an intemperate state in which Russell feared his might take his life.

Louis Charbonneau

After two weeks of rest and treatment, Lewis seemed himself again, though weakened by the bloodletting that was part of his treatment. He set off for Washington by way of Nashville, following the old network of Indian trails called the Natchez Trace. He was accompanied by a Chickasaw Indian agent, Major Alexander Neeley, and two servants.

After about ten days on the trail, a journey made more arduous by excessively hot weather, Lewis came in the late afternoon of October 10, 1809, to Grinder's Stand, a group of crude log cabins in the forest within the jurisdiction of Tennessee and about seventy miles short of Nashville. Major Neeley had stayed behind at their morning camp to search for lost horses. Lewis was accompanied that night only by the two servants. He was in a depressed mood, muttering about the lies that had been told against him and attempts to ruin him.

What happened that night is still a subject of conjecture and debate. After a light supper and a little drink, Lewis retired to a cabin alone, the two servants staying in the stables to watch the horses. According to Mrs. Grinder's later testimony, her husband was away. She stayed with her children in the main house.

Some time during the night, shots were fired. After a long delay Meriwether Lewis staggered up to the house and asked for water. Alone and frightened by the shots, the woman refused to answer. After going away, Lewis returned a second time with the same request. Again his plea went unanswered.

On the morning of October 11, 1809, the government post-rider came to Grinder's Stand on his way to Nashville. He found Meriwether Lewis's body lying off the road more than a hundred yards from his cabin. He had been shot twice, once in the head and a second time in the chest. He had either taken his own life in a deranged moment of extreme depression or—not an uncommon occurrence on the Natchez Trace—he had been brutally attacked, robbed, and murdered.

One of the most magnificent personal odysseys in American history had come to a sudden, violent, and tragic end.

Most of the volunteers for the expedition were professional soldiers, and many returned to army service; others disappeared into the obscurity of civilian life. There were some exceptions.

George Drouillard, so valued by Lewis as "our principal dependence as a woodsman and guide," ascended the Missouri once more in 1807 with Manuel Lisa's fur-trapping expedition. Ordered by Lisa to pursue and bring back a deserter "dead or alive"—orders Lewis had once given him—Drouillard shot the deserter, Antoine Bissonnette, at the end of a chase. A year later, back in St. Louis, Drouillard was tried for murder and found not guilty. In 1810, while with another Manuel Lisa expedition up in the vicinity of Three Forks, Drouillard was caught alone by hostile Blackfeet, surrounded, and killed after a long fight.

Feisty John Collins also was lured back to the High Plains and was killed while with the William Ashley trading expedition in a fight with the Arikaras on June 2, 1823.

John Colter, one of the original nine Kentuckians and perhaps Lewis's first recruit in the fall of 1803, requested discharge at Fort Mandan when the expedition returned there in August, 1806. The captains agreed, with the proviso that no other member of the party ask for the same early discharge; the others all assented. Colter then ascended the Yellowstone as a guide with the two Illinois trappers, Hancock and Dickson. Returning to St. Louis the following summer, he met the Manuel Lisa trapping party on its way toward the Yellowstone. Colter agreed to turn around once more and join them. He became an emissary for Lisa's party with the Crow Indians.

Two years later, along with John Potts, another member of the Corps of Discovery, Colter signed on with the trapper Andrew Henry to return to the upper Missouri. The party was attacked by Blackfeet; Potts was killed and Colter captured. Stripped and turned loose unarmed to be hunted down by Blackfoot warriors, Colter eluded them, hid under a tangle of logs in a river while the Indians searched for him, and, re-markably, made his way—naked and on foot, for seven days —across the Plains to Fort Manuel. He is credited with being the first white man to discover the geysers in what is now Yellowstone National Park. When he tried to describe what he had seen, skeptical listeners referred to his fanciful tale as "Colter's Hell." He died, still a young man, in 1813.

John Newman settled in St. Louis and married. He later became a trader himself, traveling up the Missouri in the 1830s. In the spring of 1838, he was killed by a Sioux war party not far from the Missouri.

George Shannon, the youngest member of the expedi-tion, was among those who, along with Nathaniel Pryor, tried to return the Mandan Chief She-he-ke to his home in 1807 after the chief returned from his visit to Washington and Monticello. The party was stopped by Arikaras, no longer friendly; Shannon was shot in the leg, which had to be am-putated. He later assisted Nicholas Biddle in editing the first published edition of the Lewis and Clark journals. William Clark invited Shannon to join him in the fur business, but the young man chose instead to study law. He became a prac-ticing lawyer in Kentucky, was twice elected to the Kentucky House of Representatives, and, after moving to Missouri, be-came a judge. He died suddenly, in 1836, while in court in Palmyra, Missouri.

John Shields, that invaluable gunsmith, blacksmith, and all-around repairman, did some trapping for his kinsman, Daniel Boone, after the expedition. Like many others of the Corps of Discovery, however, he was short-lived, dying in 1809 in Indiana.

One of those who had a long life was Alexander Willard. He fought in the War of 1812 and later settled in Wisconsin. In 1852, forty-six years after returning from the Pacific with the expedition, he set off with his family in a covered wagon for California. He died there in 1865, at the age of eighty-seven.

Pat Gass, who published his own journal of the expedition

503

(made pretty, unfortunately, by an English teacher who helped prepare the rough journal for publication), stayed in the army, fought in the War of 1812, and lost an eye in the Battle of Lundy's Lane. He was discharged and pensioned in 1815. In 1831, at the age of sixty, he married twenty-year-old Maria Hamilton; they had six children. When he died in April, 1870, just short of his ninety-ninth birthday, he was the last surviving soldier of the Lewis and Clark expedition.

York, William Clark's lifelong companion, was freed by Clark after the expedition and given a wagon and six horses. He went into the wagon business in Kentucky and Tennessee. According to Clark's statement to the writer Washington Irving in 1832, York died of cholera in Tennessee.

Toussaint Charbonneau was discharged from the Corps of Discovery at the Mandans in August, 1806. For his services as an interpreter, and "the price of a horse and Lodge purchased of him for public Service," he was paid the sum of $500.33⅓. He wanted to accompany some of the Minitaree chiefs to Washington as their interpreter, but the chiefs refused to go. After turning down Clark's offer to buy him a farm in Illinois, Charbonneau stayed with his wife and family among the Indians, living the only life he really knew, serving occasionally as an official interpreter. There is a record of his arrival in St. Louis in 1839, a white-haired old man of eighty, seeking some past-due pay from the government—which the Superintendent of Indian Affairs at the time paid him. Charbonneau then turned back up the Missouri and vanished into the wilderness, a squaw man to the end.

Jean Baptiste Charbonneau, or Pomp, was brought to St. Louis by his father and mother two years after their return from the Pacific. True to his word, Clark undertook Pomp's education. When the boy was in his late teens, he met Prince Wilhelm Paul of Württemberg, who was on a hunting trip in the West. Impressed by the young man, the prince took Baptiste

with him to Europe to further his education. Baptiste did not
return until 1829, when he was twenty-five. He became a well-
known guide and interpreter for western adventurers, traveled
with such famous mountain men as Kit Carson, and joined
the Gold Rush to California. He is said to have died of pneumonia en route to the gold fields of Montana in 1866.

Sacajawea brought her child to St. Louis with her husband in 1808 and spent some time in that city—her first in-
timate experience of the way the white man lived in his villages.
But as neither she nor Charbonneau were happy with city life,
they soon returned to the wilderness.

In 1811 Charbonneau traveled up the Missouri in a keelboat to Fort Manuel, which the trader Manuel Lisa had established on the Yellowstone. With him was his wife. A clerk
of the Missouri Fur Company, John Luttig, who kept a journal
of this period, wrote on December 20, 1812, that the Snake
woman wife of the interpreter Charbonneau died on that date
of a fever. He added, "She was good and the best woman in
the fort, aged about 25 years; she left a fine infant girl." Many
historians believe that the wife was Sacajawea and that the
infant girl Lizette was their second child. In notations in some
account books he kept in 1825–26, William Clark listed what
he knew at that time of the fates of the members of the expedition. Opposite Sacajawea's name, he wrote simply,
"Dead."

Others say that it was Otter Woman—who was also
Shoshoni and of about the right age—who died in 1812. There
is at least oral testimony that, after a bitter quarrel in the year
1822, Sacajawea left Charbonneau and went south to live
among the Comanches. Eventually, homesick for her own people and the children she had not seen for many years, she
returned to the upper Missouri. She found her People, led by
Chief Washakie, living at Fort Bridger, Wyoming. Sacajawea
spent the rest of her long life among the Shoshonis on the
Wind River Reservation. Indian legend has it that in her last
years a warrior pitched his tent nearby who called himself

505

Baptiste. She was found wrapped in her blanket on the morning of April 9, 1884, dead at the age of ninety-six. The man who lived nearby and spoke many languages died a year later.

If this story is true, they were the last of that band of explorers who could still remember the bitter cold of a Mandan winter, the melting tenderness of Charbonneau's *boudin blanc*, the thunder of the Great Falls of the Missouri, the magical parting of the Gates of the Mountains, the hunger of the Lolo Trail, the first salt taste of the western ocean.

No one knows the fate of Seaman, Meriwether Lewis's dog. The last known reference to the noble Newfoundland was in Meriwether Lewis's journal entry at the White Bear Island camp on July 15, 1806, just prior to the departure for Maria's River. "The musquitoes continue to infest us," Lewis noted, and then added, "my dog even howls with the torture he experiences from them."

It is only speculation, but it seems unlikely that Seaman could have met any serious accident in the last weeks of the expedition without any of the journalists mentioning it. The inescapable conclusion is that he returned with Meriwether Lewis to civilization and ultimately joined his master in the governor's house in St. Louis.

As a personal note, I like to think that, if Seaman had been with Meriwether Lewis on his last journey up the Natchez Trace, no matter what happened that night at Grinder's Stand, whether Lewis battled demons within or without, he would not have fought alone. His story would have had a different end.

about the author

LOUIS CHARBONNEAU grew up in Detroit, Michigan, and served with the U.S. Air Force in England during World War II. He considers himself a professional writer who has often done other things to make a living. He's been an English teacher, advertising copywriter, newspaperman, columnist, and book editor. He's written children's fiction, radio and TV dramas, short stories, and, especially, science fiction, western, suspense, and historical novels. Trail *is the outgrowth of a lifetime interest in both western history and dogs (he has bred, trained, and exhibited champions in several breeds). He lives in Lomita, California, with his wife Diane, three dogs, and a number of cats.*

BOOK MARK

*The text of this book was composed in
the typeface Linotype Walbaum
with extracts in Nicolas Cochin and
display typography in Lord Swash and Plymouth
by Crane Typesetting Service, Inc.,
West Barnstable, Massachusetts*

*This book was printed
by Berryville Graphics,
Berryville, Virginia*

Frontis Map by Compass Projections

Calligraphy by Luc Raphael Bessiere

BOOK DESIGN AND ORNAMENTATION BY
CAROL MALCOLM
AND
RAZZLE DAZZLE